Praise for *Laurie Lee: The Well-Loved Stranger*

'When Laurie Lee died in 1997, the sense of loss was widespread. Millions of people had read him, seen and heard him on TV, and studied him with pleasure at school … Yet even among those who loved him, no one really knew him. Even to himself he was always something of a stranger … His life makes a captivating story, and Valerie Grove tells it wonderfully … Few literary biographies will give more pleasure.'

– Michael Duffy, *Times Educational Supplement*

'Laurie Lee's virtues far outweighed his faults, and it is Grove's obvious affection for her subject that makes her book so tender and graceful … a touching elegy to another age.'

– Craig Brown, *Mail on Sunday*

'To know Laurie was to love him, and this shines through Grove's pages … Her book comes as close to knowing the well-loved stranger as we are likely to get.'

– Sean Day-Lewis, *Literary Review*

'Wholly admirable … Valerie Grove enlightens rather than disillusions us.'

– David Hughes, *The Independent*

'Lee devoted himse   world …
A brisk, v

– Hilary S

THE LIFE AND LOVES OF

Laurie Lee

VALERIE GROVE

The Robson Press

This new edition published in Great Britain in 2014 by
The Robson Press (an imprint of Biteback Publishing Ltd)
Westminster Tower
3 Albert Embankment
London SE1 7SP
Copyright © Valerie Grove 2014

Valerie Grove has asserted her right under the Copyright, Designs and Patents Act
1988 to be identified as the author of this work.

All rights reserved. No part of this publication may be reproduced, stored in a
retrieval system or transmitted, in any form or by any means, without the publisher's
prior permission in writing.

This book is sold subject to the condition that it shall not, by way of trade or
otherwise, be lent, resold, hired out or otherwise circulated without the publisher's
prior consent in any form of binding or cover other than that in which it is published
and without a similar condition, including this condition, being imposed on the
subsequent purchaser.

Every reasonable effort has been made to trace copyright holders of material reproduced in this book, but if any have been inadvertently overlooked the publishers
would be glad to hear from them.

The publisher would like to thank the following for granting permission to use
copyright material:

Pam Matthews for the letters of Tom Matthews; Peter L. Potts for the letters of
Molly Smart; Rachel Mooring Aldridge for the letters of Wilma Gregory; Lady
Selina Hastings and Roland Philipps for the letters of Rosamond Lehmann; Miles
Huddleston and Charles Osborne for the letters of John Lehmann; Jill Balcon for
the letters of C. Day-Lewis; Betty Farmer (née Smart), Celia Goodman, Georgina
Hammick; Val Hennessy, Emma Smith, Julian Bream and Brian Patten for their own
diaries and letters; and U. A. Fanthorpe for the poem 'Dear Mr Lee', from
A Wandering Brief, Peterloo Poets, 1987.

Unless otherwise stated, all photographs are from the Laurie Lee Collection.

ISBN 978-1-84954-687-4

A CIP catalogue record for this book is available from the British Library.

Set in Bulmer by Soapbox
Printed and bound in Great Britain by
CPI Group (UK) Ltd, Croydon CR0 4YY

MIX
Paper from
responsible sources
FSC
www.fsc.org   FSC® C020471

Contents

Preface

A NOTE ABOUT names: Laurie made the rules about people's names. He was always Laurie (Lol to intimates), never Laurence. His wife was baptised Katherine Francesca, after Tolstoy's Katerina, and as a girl she was Kathy. Laurie's first reference to her was as 'Kati' (in *A Rose for Winter*) but he then decided that the letter C was softer and more feminine, and renamed her Cathy. (She said that his changing her name 'tells you everything you need to know about our marriage'.) After Laurie's death she reclaimed Kathy, with a K. So I refer to her as Kathy – except when quoting from LL's diaries, notebooks and letters in which she is 'Cathy' or 'C'.

Jessy was baptised Jesse – not Jessica – but Laurie decided later that Jessy was nicer, so Jessy she is in this book.

Acknowledgements

KATHY LEE'S WARM hospitality was beyond the call of any dutiful keeper of her husband's flame. And I could not have written this book without the co-operation of Laurie's closest blood relations: his daughters Jessy Lee and Yasmin David, and his brother Jack. My original editor was Annie Lee, Jack Lee's daughter-in-law, whose familiarity with the story made working on the text a pleasure. I thank the trustees of the estate of Laurie Lee for permission to use Laurie's papers. And I am grateful to Pat Kavanagh, Laurie's literary agent as well as my own, for proposing to Laurie in 1996 that I might write about him.

The letters of Wilma Gregory lent to me by her niece Rachel M. Aldridge were absolutely vital, revealing episodes otherwise unknown and unrecorded. So were those of the Smart sisters, Betty and Molly. Roy and Mary Campbell's daughter Anna Campbell Lyle, Kathleen Epstein's daughter Kitty (the Hon. Mrs Wynne Godley), and Anne Dunn Moynihan, former wife of Michael Wishart, were all helpful about the Garman family background, as was John Byrne, literary executor of Michael Wishart. Mavis Nicholson's two televised interviews with Laurie evoked him at his best. And I am thankful that John King, whose BBC films of *As I Walked Out One Midsummer Morning* and *A Rose for Winter* are masterpieces, was still able to talk to me about Laurie with great perception, six months before he died.

It was significant that so many people had preserved their letters or their family's letters from Laurie. Since I completed my research in 1999, many of the following (as well as some of those mentioned above) have died, but I remain indebted to all of them: Laurie's

sister-in-law Nora Lee; Lt-Col. Val ffrench Blake MC, D S O ; Clare
Francis; Christopher Fry; John Fuller; Celia Goodman; Georgina
Hammick; Lady Selina Hastings; Val Hennessy; Elizabeth Jane
Howard; P. J. Kavanagh; Pam Matthews; Emma, Lady Monson;
Alan Ross; John Ward and Antonia Young. I thank Emma Smith
for lending me her wonderful Indian diary of 1946, Brian Patten
for sending extracts from his diary, and the Devas family for letting
me see their precious Holiday Books, with drawings by Laurie.
Without Dr Barry McLoughlin's Russian-speaking expertise and
trips to Moscow to furnish me with documentary evidence I could
not have broached the Spanish Civil War episode, and without
Richard Rogers of Buenos Aires, and his surprise visit to Slad in
the summer of 1998, we might never have identified 'Sufi' and her
Spanish phrases. Michael and Helga Still's Castillo San Rafael, in
the almost unaltered hills above Almuñécar, provided the perfect
base from which to experience the Spain that Laurie loved. Nina
Drummond was an excellent sleuth in Colindale archives.

The following people were also helpful: HRH The Prince of
Wales; Dannie Abse; Bill Alexander; Jill Balcon (Mrs C. Day-Lewis);
the Revd David Barlow; Virginia Barrington; Adrian Bate; Barney
Bates; Anne Olivier Bell; Rt Hon. David Blunkett MP; Michael
Bott; Lord Bragg; Julian Bream; Paul Burroughs; Judy Campbell;
Mavis Cheek; Douglas Chisholm; John Clive; Christopher Cook;
Johnny Coppin; Simon Courtauld; Sean Day-Lewis; André
Deutsch; Prosper Devas; Bob Doyle, Jr; Michael Eaude; Viscount
and Viscountess Esher; the late U. A. Fanthorpe; William Feaver;
Mary Fedden (Mrs Julian Trevelyan); Jim Fern; Jock Gallagher;
Stephen Gardiner; David and Judy Gascoyne; Roberta Green; Jill,
Duchess of Hamilton; Jeremy Hayes; Daphne Hardy Henrion; Jill
Hepple; Susan Hill; Jeff Hoare; Jennifer Hovmand; Christopher
Howse; Dr Jim Hoyland; Lord Hutchinson of Lullington; Martin
Jarvis; Rebecca John; Anne Kidman; Pam Kirby; Bobby Kok; Chris
Eldon Lee; Lynda Lee-Potter; Jeremy Lewis; Bob Light; Charles
Light; Roger McGough; Douglas Matthews; Iain Morley; Sir John

Mortimer; Andrew Motion; Clare Moynihan; John Moynihan; Rosaleen Mulji; Michelle Newell; Philip Oakes; Mary Omond; Katie Paltenghi; David Parker; Jill Paul; Alan F. R. Payne; Henry Porter; George Pownall; David Queensberry; Paul Robinson; Jeremy Robson; Kay Rogers; Diana Roper; Jim Rose and Mrs Pam Rose; Richard Ryan; Jeremy Sandford; Vernon Scannell; Kate Searle; Anne Sebba; Laurence Seidler; Anthea Sharp; Monica Sims; Adam Sisman; the late Natasha Spender; Sir Roy Strong; John Summers; Malcolm Tarling; David Tarratt; Joy Thacker; Gwyneth Thomas; Revd C. E. Leighton Thomson; Helen Thornton; Joanna Trollope; Rosemary Trollope; Alan and Joan Tucker; Lady Tucker; Claudia Wolfers Vasquez; Ted Walker; Johnny Wallace; Michael Watkins; Brian Wharton; Edward Williams; Professor Peter Wilson; Joan Winterkorn; Anne Wintle.

And I send undying gratitude to Mr Neville Smart, my old English master, who started it all with Micky Thumps, and encouraged me to write about Laurie, whom he considered 'a man in a million'.

1

Annie Light of Sheepscombe

PROLOGUE

To be in love, of course, is to take on the penthouse of living, that topmost toppling tower, perpetually lit by the privileged radiance of wellbeing which sets one apart from the nether world. Born, we are mortal, dehydrated, ordinary: love is the oil that pumps one up, dilates the eyes, puts a glow on the skin, lifts us free from the weight of time, and helps us see in some other that particular kind of beauty which is the crown of our narcissism.

... At best, love is simply the slipping of a hand in another's, of knowing you are where you belong at last, and of exchanging through the eyes that all-consuming regard which ignores everybody else on earth.

LAURIE LEE'S WORDS on love were written later in life, emotion recollected in tranquillity. But no account of his most deeply heartfelt love is to be found in his published work. He wrote about this crucial episode only in his diaries, straight from the heart. He confided the agony and the ecstasy of his passionate wartime affair with Lorna Wishart, née Garman, the great beauty who was his muse, the inspiration of his poems and guardian of his literary ambitions. Laurie's life was changed forever by Lorna, and she broke his heart.

But she was not alone in taking Laurie under her wing. From boyhood, he had always made women want to advise and soothe him, because they loved and believed in him: his mother and sisters, his girlfriends and lovers, his wife and daughters, and many indispensable women friends.

When Laurie Lee's friends gathered at St James's, Piccadilly, in October 1997 for a service of thanksgiving, not one female voice was heard. The congregation heard Laurie's voice, on tape, and listened to him playing 'Andalucía' by Granados on his violin. Words and poems of praise were spoken, by twelve good men. Laurie was a pub man and a club man, so the impression he gave was of a man who enjoyed men's company. But without his women, the boy who left school at fifteen undecided whether to paint or write could never have become the Laurie Lee of legend.

Not that Laurie ever quite acknowledged this. He claimed to love women, but he never paid tribute to their influence on him as mentors; only as cosseting, embracing, accommodating creatures. He liked women, but in their place.

The one woman he did honestly acknowledge in print, and immortalise in *Cider with Rosie*, was his mother, Annie Emily Light…

• •

The Bloom of Candles, Laurie Lee's second slim volume of poems, was dedicated to 'Annie Light of Sheepscombe'. He should have put 'Annie Light of Quedgeley', she reproached him. 'I *wish* you had said Quedgeley. That's where my love of beauty & of books & of solitude in my own little wood was born, and where my beloved old schoolmaster Mr Beacon encouraged me.' As a girl Annie got top marks for composition and music. But her schooldays were cut short. As the eldest child and the only girl, she was needed at home to help bring up her five brothers, Charlie, Sid, Tom, Ray and Fred.

Quedgeley, now a suburb of Gloucester, was a village in 1879 when Annie was born. Her mother (née Emma Morse) was from a yeoman farming family. Annie's father, John Light, had been coachman at Berkeley Castle. The Light family view is that their grandfather John had an air about him, and 'could have dined with the kings of England'. Moustachioed, dandyish in checked waistcoat and buttonhole, John Light is pictured in 1902 at the coronation celebrations in Sheepscombe, cutting a dash.

Laurie did investigate his family history. An exercise book labelled 'Roots' listed all the local seventeenth-century Lights and Morses – yeomen, butchers, gentlemen – who might have been his antecedents. 'But whatever the illicit grandeur of her forebears,' as he wrote, 'Mother was born to quite ordinary poverty.'[1] Two of her brothers went off to fight in the Boer War; all five were cavalrymen in the Great War. Laurie saw the returning uncles as 'bards and oracles … the horsemen and brawlers of another age, whose lives spoke of campaigns on desert marshes, of Kruger's cannon and Flanders mud'. Three came back eventually to Gloucestershire.

When the brothers left home in their teens, Annie went into service in stately homes, which gave her a lasting respect for the gentry (she would curtsey, Laurie said, to the squire's governess) and a refined taste for the accoutrements of the Quality: good china and porcelain, feather beds and linen sheets, silver cutlery, old paintings, inlaid walnut furniture, tapestry hangings, leather-bound books. Among prim housemaids and imperious butlers and cooks – about whom she would write satirical verses – the scatty Annie 'was something beyond their ken', Laurie wrote. She was pretty, however, and often told her boys that she had once entranced a whole regiment of soldiers when dressed in her Sunday best on a street corner in Aldershot.

Then her father left Berkeley Castle and took a pub, the Plough at Sheepscombe, and when her mother died, at fifty, Annie came home to help her father behind the bar: 'a lonely young woman, mysteriously detached, graceful in face and figure' but also volatile, witty and adept at handling drunken customers. More durably than anyone else Laurie wrote about, it is Annie, with her warmth, optimism and courage, who lingers in most readers' minds.

She obviously liked children, or she would not have answered the advertisement placed in the local paper by a widower, Reg Lee, manager of the Co-op grocery in Stroud, seeking a housekeeper for himself and his family of four children. Annie was just thirty, short and shapely with a bright, intelligent face, when she arrived on the doorstep of his redbrick terraced house in Stroud. Reginald Joseph Lee was six feet tall, precise in manner and immaculate in dress. Annie fell in love at first sight. A few months earlier, the same local paper had reported the death in childbirth on 15 April 1910 of Reg's wife, the beautiful Catherine Maude Critchley, under the headline 'Sad death at the Uplands'. Mrs Lee, wife of the 'well known and greatly respected' Mr R. J. Lee, former organist at Holy Trinity Church and conductor of the Stroud Co-operative Glee Society, had died giving birth to twins, her sixth and seventh children.

Such was the lot of the Edwardian bride. Catherine Lee had produced Arthur Reginald in 1901, Marjorie Winifred in 1903, Dorothy Clair (one of twins, the other being stillborn) in 1904, Phyllis Maude in 1906, Harold Mortimer in 1908. The newborn twins died on 24 June 1910, six weeks after their mother.

The bereaved Reg stayed a while at Burleigh House, Brimscombe, with the children's grandmother Critchley. The eldest boy, Reg junior, remained with his grandmother, to be taken into her family business, Critchley Bros, making knitting needles and safety pins in the Chalford Valley.[2] So there remained four children – Marjorie, Dorothy (Doth), Phyllis and three-year-old Harold – to be taken on by Annie.

Reg married Annie a year later, on 11 May 1911, and they lost no time in starting a new family. In 1912 a daughter, Frances, was born. Jack (Wilfred Jack Raymond) followed in January 1913; Laurie (Laurence Edward Alan) in June 1914; and Tony (Anthony Lisle) in January 1916. Laurie was baptised at, and named after, Stroud's parish church, St Laurence.

Laurie's birthplace was in Slad Road, Uplands, Stroud – at 2 Glenview Terrace. Here Reg installed Annie and the brood in the crowded house where the sisters created a vortex of fun and laughter – and screams, when Jack tumbled down the steps on one occasion, fracturing his leg. When Laurie was born, Jack had scarlet fever; and Laurie was sickly from birth. He wrote of lying seriously ill for many months, still and silent, staring at the ceiling 'for a year' he claimed, 'in a motionless swoon' – and was being laid out as dead until Annie, arriving home, revived him. 'I must tell you if I never have,' wrote Annie to Laurie, in 1947, 'that your Dad helped me to nurse you very patiently when you were ill & through that careful nursing you are alive today.' Laurie could recall, from those infant days, the prismatic light from a spinning glass ball that hung over his pram.

After the outbreak of war, Reg left to join the Royal West Kent Regiment. He would be back, Annie thought, when hostilities were over. In 1917 Reg arranged for his family (minus the daughter Frances who had died in infancy) to move to a cheaper cottage in the village of Slad, two miles east of Stroud in a winding valley, then 'a place of long steamy silences, punctuated by horses' hooves and mowing machines, sleepy pigeons and mooning cows'. This was the move with which *Cider with Rosie* so memorably opens. Laurie was just three. 'I love you for that story,' wrote Annie. 'You brought back so many things to my memory so vividly. How when you first got out of West's cart & was placed at the top of the bank and the grass was so long & high, how frightened you were & how you cried…'

The oak-beamed three-storeyed cottage, 'with rooks in the chimneys, frogs in the cellar, mushrooms on the ceiling, and all for three and sixpence a week',[3] still stands, in its half acre, down a steep bank in the centre of Slad. It was a T-shaped farmhouse of Cotswold stone, known as Bank Cottages (now 'Rosebank'). The Lees were in the downstroke of the T, and two old ladies Mrs Waldron and Mrs Tyrrell – later Granny Wallon and Granny Trill in *Cider with Rosie* – shared the crosspiece, one living above the other in perpetual enmity. The windows, deeply recessed in thick walls with upright mullions, were screened by beech and yew trees. Only shafts of sunlight lit the dim interior. By night there were shadowy pools of lamp and candlelight. Somehow Annie found room for all seven children and herself to sleep, including the baby Tony in a cot, and the eldest Harold in a camp bed under a bookcase. Laurie and Jack shared the attic with the three older half-sisters.

'Yes, when we went to that house in June 1917,' Annie recalled, 'I had so many happy brave young people to help me and it was *beautiful* weather – hot, sunny & dry & the flowers in the garden were blooming, oh it was lovely, syringa, lilac, roses & pansies & in a few days your Daddy (as he was then) came & hung up the pictures.' But Reg, recalled to his regiment in Kent, never again returned to his family. When the war ended he joined the Civil Service, and would visit Slad only once or twice a year. He sent her £1 a week ('Dear Nance – Herewith the usual – Yours, Reg'). In Jack's view his fastidious father took his chance to escape from the messy household he had left behind. Besides, he became involved with his landlady, Mrs Reynolds, known as Topsy, in the southern suburbs of London.

So Annie was the pivot and focus of the boys' lives: scatty, garrulous, emotional. 'She was too honest, too natural for this frightened man,' wrote Laurie, 'too remote from his tidy laws. She was after all, a country girl: disordered, hysterical, loving. She was muddled and mischievous as a jackdaw. She made her nest of rags and jewels ... and couldn't have kept a neat house for her life.'[4]

Everyone who knew Annie mentioned her collection of mismatched china pieces, and the wild flowers in vases which filled her kitchen. Picking flowers for Annie was something all the village children did. She couldn't sew or cook: her porridge was lumpy and her lentil soup was 'like eating hot, rusty buttons', Laurie said. But what she lacked in housewifery she made up for in artistry. She taught them to appreciate books. She made Laurie an observer of skies and spring leaves, and a lover of music and rhymes, stories and songs. From Annie came the creativity of Laurie and Jack.

She was known for her curiosity and neighbourliness, her obsessive letter-writing on tiny scraps of paper (she would spend hours in Stroud post office, which had a table and chairs for this purpose), her enthusiasm for picnics and her hopelessness with money. Every six months a cheque for 'the Critchley money' – dividends from the first wife's family business – would arrive and save them from desperate straits. Laurie and Jack grew up with a horror of debt, having so often had to walk to Mr Dover's to pay the rent, promising, 'We'll send the rest in a fortnight's time.' They also became fiercely punctual because of 'the misery I endured when she sent me to hold the bus while she found her corsets', Laurie said. Helen Thornton, daughter of the Slad vicar Cyril Broadley Hodson, remembered:

> Everyone on the bus looked out for Mrs Lee, scrambling up the steep grass bank with the hook of her umbrella held aloft, so it would be seen before her head emerged, in a long black coat with a fitted waist, and black hat. She was known and loved by all – driver and passengers alike.

Helen's mother, the vicar's wife (who was incidentally Great-aunt Muriel to Joanna Trollope), befriended Annie. Both loved reading. 'Mother would find Mrs Lee spreading newspapers over the wet kitchen floor, and as she couldn't resist reading them, I think my mother sometimes had to finish the floor for her.'

But in the evenings, the boys would collect firewood and they would crowd round the fire, while Annie read or sang in the glow from the paraffin lamp. The death of her only daughter Frances, at four, made her sentimental about little girls; brothers and sons being 'her lifetime's lot'. Once the three helpful stepdaughters had gone (they all married in 1927), her shrieking increased; Laurie's teenage diary is peppered with references to 'Mother's tongue'.

Diana Roper, Marjorie's daughter, remembered visiting Annie's cottage as a child:

> We'd arrive from Stroud on the bus, down the bank through the overgrown garden, and there'd be a squawk: 'I'm not expecting you!' but she was always welcoming, in a navy or black soft

dress with a white fichu or piece of lace, a silver chain, a scarf, a cameo. She smelled of Eau de Cologne. The house was filled with the scent of flowers and greenery.

Inside was a clutter of tables littered with books, vases, candles. She surrounded herself with things: piano, harmonium, piles of newspapers. 'She always had something of interest – a newspaper cutting, a picture for her scrapbook, a piece of old netting so that I could dress as a bride.' She gave Diana a Royal Academy catalogue of Dutch paintings with a note: 'Study them all dear, specially Vermeer and Jacob Maris.'

Marjorie, Dorothy and Phyllis were comfort-givers and figures of fascination. Having inherited the beauty of their mother, Catherine Critchley, they would sail past the infant Laurie 'like galleons in their busy dresses ... How magnificent they appeared, those towering girls, with their flying hair and billowing blouses ... At any moment one was ... swung up high like a wriggling fish to be hooked and held in their lacy linen.'

The ending of the war seemed to Laurie inexplicable: 'Oh the end of the war and the world! ... and Mother had disappeared,' he wrote of his infant panic. When Laurie's account was published in *Orion* magazine in 1947, twelve years before it became the first chapter of *Cider with Rosie*, Annie read the article with maternal pride, but was stung by the reference to her absence, which might sound like negligence. She sat down and wrote Laurie her own account of why she had been away in London on that day in 1918 – ten closely written pages in which every moment of her absence was remembered in minutest detail. Her letter is worth quoting as it gives both the flavour of her personality, and her narrative skill:

As fortune would have it, in November 1918 I had a telegram from Auntie Hilda at Sittingbourne in Kent saying Uncle Fred my youngest brother was very ill in a hospital there & asking me to go to see him. Your Dad said Yes, of course Nance you must go, & travel up with me tomorrow, which I said I'd do, tho' I felt a compunction about leaving you children alone. So I went with Dad and he left me somewhere on the journey & I went on alone, but was met by Hilda at the station, we went straight to the hospital, and I saw poor old Fred, but by that time he was on the mend, I *was* glad to see him & he was delighted to see me.

I heard from your father, we had letters on Sundays then, to meet him by the Fountains at Trafal. Square midday on Monday. There were rumours in the hospital of what was going to take place on the Monday ... I arrived at Victoria Station exactly at 11 o'clock & my dear old Uncle Tom was outside the barrier waving his hat on his stick & three officers were on the platform walking along arm in arm & singing, and Uncle was beaming & he said, 'It's over Annie, it's over! The war's over my girl come along' so he took me under his wing and *what* we saw when we got away from the station takes some describing. He took me to his home at Covent Garden, where was my dear Auntie Nell & Cousin Bess & we went to meet your Father at Trafalgar Square. It was lovely. My Uncle said 'Look! the fountains have not played during the war': but there they were playing once more. We went about seeing crowds and crowds of cheering people & in a minute or two your Dad came up to me. There were men selling flags & I bought one a French one, oh I hope it is not destroyed, as I am not sure myself where I put it ... Your Dad took us to the Stoll Theatre in the evening & we heard speeches & wonderful music & patriotic songs, one being 'Land of Hope & Glory' another the Marseillaise, Dad, Bess & myself joining in – oh my heart the Tears start at the memory of it all. But I felt I *must* tell you *why* I was not at Slad with all you dear children. I wanted to be, but I was involved with them, Uncle, Aunt, Bess, travelling back to Stroud next day Nov 12th. I had sent a wire to Marjorie to ask her to meet me, with Eyers Waggonette. I said, 'Order Eyers.' Well, you *all* came to meet me, & I had a lot to tell you, and how glad I was to see all you dear little ones again & Marjorie had been so good. And Dorothy too. I often thought

how cruel it was of me to leave you all – but I went to see poor
Uncle Fred, that is how it all came about. So dear Laurie forget
that bit. I would *never* have left you all otherwise, then I should
have seen the happenings in Slad. Never say or think bad of me
Laurie. I tried to be good, but there I'll say no more. God bless
you Ever Your Loving Mother.

Jack and Laurie grew up despising Reg, for deserting their mother,
leaving her with two broods of his children. His photograph – 'trim,
haughty, with a badged cap and a spiked moustache: I confused him
with the Kaiser,' Laurie said – remained over the piano. 'She waited
for thirty years,' Laurie wrote, of Annie's desertion by Reg. 'I don't
think she ever knew what made him desert her.' But she certainly
knew about Mrs Reynolds, 'Auntie Topsy', since Reg eventually
brought her to Stroud with him when he visited his son Harold
during the Blitz.

'When I think Laurie of his cruel mean ways & how cruelly he
treated you boys & neglected you all again & again, I could wring his
neck. Yes I could...' wrote Annie in 1945. 'I cannot think how he can
have the cheek & the impertinence to bring "Tots" or "Toots" to Stroud
– dear Laurie enough of this.' But when Reg died she was all forgiveness.
'I grieve about him passing on before I ever could be reconciled to him,
or to hear him speak kindly to me, for I always loved him.'

Annie usually preferred to remember the happy days. It was she
who recalled all the details of life in Slad, the folk tales, the neighbours, the children's songs, the way to make plum blackberry wine
– and furnished Laurie with these details when he needed them. Her
letters to him in the 1940s often contained oddments: 'Mother sent
me an assortment of cuttings – Borotra's secret of youth, a picture of
Painswick, and a 10-year-old article on Lloyd George.' Annie had
all the maternal virtues in abundance, but also the maternal deficiencies: she was increasingly needy and clinging, indulgent and
sometimes self-deluding.

When *Cider with Rosie* came out in 1959, every critic singled her out as the dominant portrait. 'Laurie Lee's mother will be remembered long after Whistler's mother has sunk into oblivion,' wrote one.

> It is to Mrs Lee – haphazard, lackadaisical, fanatically unselfish, tender, extravagant, with her love of finery, her unmade beds, her litters of unfinished scrapbooks … her remarkable dignity, her pity for the persecuted, her awe of the gentry … that this book belongs, rather than to the Rosie of the title.[5]

One critic 'would willingly have swapped both my mother and my life for his mother and his life. He became a poet. How could he help it with a mother like that?'[6] All agreed that Laurie had been 'splendidly and richly mothered'.[7]

Laurie wrote to a friend in 1959:

> I wish more people had known her, and I wish for her own modest sake that she had known how many 'figures' she had admired at her village distance – Harold Nicolson, V. Sackville-West, Cynthia Asquith, Priestley etc. – picked her out in their reviews of the book for a particularly affectionate mention. This would have knocked her sideways.[8]

Annie lived just long enough to see her two elder sons distinguish themselves: Jack as a film director, Laurie as a writer, 'my Poet son'. When Laurie sent her *The Bloom of Candles*, dedicating it to her, 'like a dear blind idiot' she wrote, thanking him:

> It was sweet of you & a tribute of love to your silly old mother who never could see an inch beyond her nose, or it would have been different for all of you – in fact there'd never have been a you or any of you – but there you are in the world, and though to me it does not seem true that you and your brothers have accomplished what you have, I'm thrilled and proud of you, bless you! You were such a dear little boy, loving & dreamy.

2

A Steep Cotswold Valley
1918–1931

SLAD, OR THE Slad, originally the Slade, meaning stream, is an odd village, never picturesque in the postcard sense. The eponymous stream once divided the Domesday villages of Bisley and Painswick. Slad is half-hidden from view on the road from Birdlip to Stroud, which runs straight through the middle of it. But it sits in a green valley 'more exotically lush than is decent to the general herbaceous smugness of the English countryside'[9] in Laurie's words; and the Cotswold motorist is diverted there by the signpost 'Scenic Route'.

Laurie often said he had never wanted to romanticise rural life. 'I was poor,' he said. 'Everybody was poor. It wasn't all rising fields of poppies and blue skies. A large part of it was lashing rain; chaps walking round dressed in bits of soaking sacking, and children dying of quite ordinary diseases like whooping cough.'[10] He did not name Slad in his book, but its identity was soon known. The stories he told – the murder of the braggart from New Zealand, the escape of Jones's goat, 'huge and hairy as a Shetland horse', the Browns' sad ending in the workhouse – were village legends. The schooldays he described were every village child's. They all went hay-making in summer and carol-singing in the snow; played hop-scotch and tag, bowled hoops and whipped tops. They played quite safely in the middle of the road; they could see a horse and cart coming a mile away. 'When we were kids,' says a note in one of Laurie's notebooks, 'we used to light fires in the open and bake sparrows in coffee tins after first stuffing them with shredded coconut. They tasted chiefly of burnt feathers and coffee dust.'

There had once been prosperous cloth mills in the valley, until steam-driven machinery relocated the woollen business to the coal seams of the north. The 1880s had brought unemployment, poverty, migration. Slad's last mill, in the corner of the village called the Vatch, employed 600 men, women and children until the 1890s when its chimney stack fell. What remains is a scattering of houses and farms on the valley's slopes. There was no road through the valley until 1801. When Laurie was born, Lewis Eyers kept horses in stables next to the Woolpack inn, and his cart could take you to Stroud, two miles along the road. The first weekly bus arrived in 1924; soon there was Thorpe's daily motor-bus. There was no gas or electricity, no drains or piped water; every cottage had a well.

There was a church and a chapel, a post office, two pubs – the Star and the Woolpack – and the Hut for penny dances, whist drives and mothers' meetings, dominoes, darts, cards, billiards, and the Slad Players' performances of comic songs and sketches. Slad's one substantial house, the originally Jacobean Steanbridge House, was occupied by a benevolent squire, Samuel Gilbert Jones, who opened his garden for Sunday School treats, and his ponds for skating and fishing. A village woman acted as midwife, another would lay out the dead; there was a grave-digger, a pig-sticker and a dry-stone waller. Families often intermarried. Villagers bottled fruit, kept pigs and hens, trapped pigeons, collected kindling, fermented flowery wines, and bartered home-grown vegetables, eggs, rabbits and game. There was a heroic village cricket team. Life was intensely communal, with choir-outings, concerts and harvest festivals. Once a year the entire village went by charabanc to spend the day on the tidal muds of the Severn. Otherwise they just amused themselves. Laurie's diary often records that he and Jack 'hovered' or 'lurked'.

Laurie always said he was lucky to land here at the age of three, in a village community with a way of life still dominated by the horse, in a valley where life was a glass-bottomed boat, you could see through to all the details of life, animals, neighbours, and nothing was concealed, nothing got between us and the history of our neighbours, both tragic and comic, and we only had each other for entertainment.[11]

Laurie said he was born with a careworn face and developed into a tubby, square child with little red eyes, who stared and sniffed and was covered in warts and whose teacher called him Fat-and-Lazy. In fact the photographs show an average-sized, wart-free small boy who looks, like most small boys, adorable. But he suffered from the chronic ill-health that was to dog him all his life.

Framed in Laurie's study is his first letter written to his mother at the age of ten in 1924, when she must have been away:

Dear Mother: How are you going on. The ride to Weston yesterday was lovely. When we got towards Bristol, we saw two 'Bristol fighting Aeroplanes'. We had a lovely day there, except in sometimes the wind brought spray up from the sea. I bought some rock for the girls and daddy, and I got some for you when you came back. My legs pained ever-so when I came home. We saw the docks at Bristol three times. I went in Bristol Cathedral. While I am allright I think we shall have to stope here, or it will be too late for post.

From your loveing son, Laurie
XXXXXXXXXXXXXXXX.

A year later, Laurie was winning a prize in a Bird and Tree competition[12] with an essay on 'The Dabchick', alias the grebe. He described how he watched a pair of grebe building a nest of reeds and 'in a few days five white egges were layed'. Slad School's headmistress, Miss P. M. Wardley, encouraged pupils to observe wildlife and enter this contest each year. Laurie said, of Slad School: 'We learnt nothing abstract or tenuous there – just simple patterns of facts and letters, portable tricks of calculation, no more than was necessary to measure a shed, or read a swine-disease warning.' But that basic grounding enabled Laurie at eleven to write clear, well-punctuated script. The three Lee boys spoke well too. Annie did not allow dialect or slang. They sang in the choir and acted in plays at the church hall, where the vicar's daughter, Helen Thornton, remembered them in a sophisticated whodunnit, in raincoats and trilby hats.

When Laurie was thought lost in Spain during the Civil War in 1938, Jack sent him a letter reminiscing about their childhood haunts:

> Do you remember how we used to float logs down 'Joey' stream as far as the 'whirlypool' and how we stopped up the drain by trying to float Harold's boat through it? And those walks over to Painswick Beacon to lie on our stomachs and, shading our eyes from the afternoon sun, look out across the Glo'ster plain to that lovely line of the Malverns? ... Sunny days those were. Strange and sad to think that those simple irresponsible joys (I deliberately forget the unhappy days) will never occur for us again.

At twelve, Laurie went to the Central Boys' School in Stroud. Jack had gone the year before, but found it uncongenial, and Annie, who thought he was the bright one, accorded Jack the common privilege of the eldest son and sent him instead to the Marling School, a traditional grammar school on the Cainscross Road with a Latin motto over the front door. It was founded by the Marling family, owners of Vatch Mill. 'Jack was at Grammar School, and his grammar was excellent,' as Laurie drily wrote. Jack believed that this educational divide started a lifelong rift between the two brothers, hitherto so close, who had always done everything together.

Jack was in the sixth form when a local factory near Nailsworth, which made 'Erinoid' plastics from dried milk, asked the school to recommend a smart young man. He was chosen, in March 1930, to enter a career in factory management, cycling three miles home at three in the morning after the night shift.

Laurie's notebook for 1928, when he was fourteen, the year at which his most famous memoir ends, is the commonplace book of a schoolboy who might easily have become an artist or a musician instead of a writer. It contains drawings and caricatures, and poems by Keats and Tennyson. There are pages headed 'Books in my possession' and 'Books I have read'. He had long outgrown Annie's collection of Penny Readers, and the days when, lent a book by a neighbour, he was astonished at the idea that he might read it: 'I used it as a tunnel for my clockwork train.'[13] Now he was reading almost exclusively Edgar Wallace. He lists fifteen pages of Wallace titles – *Sanders of the River*, *Barbara on Her Own*, *The Four Just Men*, *The Man Who Knew* etc. A list of Wallace's 'Criminal Books' enumerates the murders in each. He practises Wallace's signature. He lists his sets of cigarette cards. There are two short stories of his own, one about life in the trenches, one an account of helping a neighbour, Mrs Robinson, to fetch water from the spring as she is 'having a stockbroker to tea'.

Another list is significant: 'Concert and Dance Appointments'. Laurie at fourteen was in demand to play his fiddle at dances: twenty-two engagements between the autumn of 1928 and January 1930, mostly in Slad Hut, the recreation hall given to the village by the Misses Bagnall, who lived at the Old House with their donkey. Laurie's trio, with Harold Iles on piano and Les Workman on drums, earned five shillings a night with free lemonade and buns. So the boy Laurie Lee was not quite the 'turnip-faced grinning oaf' he later alleged, but musical and artistic, good-natured, and very keen on keeping lists.

Laurie left the Central School at fifteen when – he claimed – Miss French said, 'Off you go and I'm glad to get rid of you.' But she taught him English, his best subject. Forty years later Laurie presented Miss French with a copy of *Cider with Rosie* at the Linden School, Gloucester, when she retired as head. She later wrote in the school magazine: 'Our Speech Day this year, was quite an event, as we were honoured by the presence there, of Mr Laurie Lee, the

Gloucestershire author and poet, who, incidentally, was an old pupil of mine.' Laurie annotated this comma-crazed sentence in the margin: 'My English mistress – hence my trouble with punctuation.'

Laurie's life from fourteen to eighteen was dominated by his violin, known as Fritz, 'after our old friend Kreisler', and his bicycle called Oscar. His boyhood diary is full of rain-soaked cycle rides, often with a puncture 'as wide as the mouth of a frog'. He had been taught the violin by a music teacher named Travis Cole who would cycle round the villages, selling lessons for sixpence. Jack remembered Cole's starting refrain – 'Up bow!' – and 'Don't give your bow a penn'orth – give it the whole shilling's worth.' Laurie practised every night.

> My three lovely half-sisters were very tolerant, but sometimes I used to hear a voice downstairs saying 'Oh Mum does 'e 'ave to, 'e's been on all night' and it was time to wrap it up in my silk scarf and put it away. But they wouldn't dream of knocking on the door … Those dear girls would never question my liberties.[14]

Two weeks before his sixteenth birthday, Laurie started work. 'A pretty eventful year on the whole,' noted Laurie of 1930, promising that if he continued the 1931 diary past March (last year's record) he would treat himself to a bottle of Moët & Chandon at 17s 6d. A nephew and niece had been born; he had been to Worcester at Easter ('bit of a washout') and had visited Uncle Ray near Malvern. He had ordered a new nib for his Conway Stewart fountain pen, and *Melody Maker* monthly from Smith's. 'But the greatest event happened in June, the 12th to be exact – I started work. Messrs Randall & Payne, Chartered Accountants, 4 Rowcroft, Stroud is the firm that has been fortunate in securing my services.'

At the back of the diary Laurie noted: 'I have met the following through the office's medium: In order of importance they are:

Walter Richards Payne FCA – the Guv'nor.

Mrs Payne – his wife.

George Percival Leslie Hudson – junior partner.'

The list continued through articled clerks down to caretaker.

Laurie was the office boy at 10s a week. He would arrive on his bike, violin slung over his back. Sometimes he was towed uphill by the bus on the ride home, and he was constantly lashed by rain. He had to run errands, organise the post, make tea and write up the ledgers in a neat, cursive hand. The first Thursday each month was 'postal orders, Directors' Receipt book, green envelopes and gas company cheques'.

His immediate boss in the mahoganied, gas-lit office was irascible Teddy White, ex-Army Pay Corps, who terrorised the staff. Intolerant of anyone with artistic pretensions, White gave Laurie a hard time, I was told by Alan Payne, son of the chairman. Laurie's poems on scraps of paper infuriated the obsessively tidy White.

Sometimes he would be sent out to get a signature.

> Mr Payne having an attack of liver did not come to the office at all this afternoon. I had to go up to his house at 5 o'clock with some letters. I was shewn in by Cook, and after picking my way through divers leopard skins lying about the floor I knocked at Mr Payne's room. He was sitting in front of a roaring fire in the comfortable drawing room. It has pictures, prints, & china plates hanging on the walls & it is sparsely but tastefully furnished. Myriads of small dogs were rushing about the room. If this is the way Chartered Accountants do themselves I shall have to see about it.

'Mr Payne is a gentleman,' he noted Pooterishly. 'I saw him in Gloucester and he put himself out to wave to me.' But after a few months there Laurie considered himself 'not a very good business person because I think of too many damn things at once'. If the books did not balance, he had to stay behind and chase up the missing money: 'one of Fate's buffets'.

'How does anything exciting happen in a blasted office?' Laurie asked himself. Miss Lewis prattled of an aunt who read fortunes in tea-leaves. Colleagues argued about the merits of chapel-going. One of the clerks suggested that they design an office crest: 'Mr Hudson proposed three pencils rampant on a field of blue ink.' There was excitement on 23 October, however. 'Mrs P. R. Goddard, wife of the fellow who won the £1,000 Crossword Puzzle in *The People*, came into the office and brought his cheque. I had the job of cashing it.'

After work he could double his salary by teaching the fiddle to villagers. He had three students: Mrs Twining, Mrs Munby and Kenny Oakey, a young lad with a good ear. And he was always prac-tising for the next concert or church bazaar with Harold and Les. 'Out all evening to play dance music. Started off with "William Tell" and we did let it rip. Our best tune is "You will remember Vienna".' Afterwards he would roll home with the moon, Oscar and Fritz. He also bought a ukulele, 'as much in need of a second instrument as a good dinner is in need of a second vegetable'. On the crystal wireless set he listened to Henry Hall and the Savoy Orpheans, Jack Payne and other big bands, and Albert Sandler's classical concerts (Laurie wrote for his autograph). He discovered Schubert and Beethoven. A Wagner prom cast him into a blank depression, but *Der Rosenkavalier* from Covent Garden impressed him, though he could not understand a word. 'After tea wrote a little, read a little, drew a little. Listening as I write to a beautiful selection of Mendelssohn.' He saw and enjoyed his first Gilbert & Sullivan, *The Pirates of Penzance*. He and Jack went into Stroud to buy an HMV gramophone: 'Mother signed on the dotted line and the thing was ours. There were a couple of records thrown in which I chose with great felicity: Dances from Henry VIII by German, and Haydn's Serenade played by Albert Sandler.'

The eighteenth of November 1931 was an auspicious date. He went to the White Horse Inn at Painswick to audition, and was engaged by Arthur Swain and his Blue Rhythms, for two dances. Laurie analysed his fellow musicians: Arthur the pianist 'a good fellow, not overloaded with intellect, but musical ability brilliant', Alvin the tenor sax 'superior to the others where the grey matter is concerned', Ernie on trumpet 'quite a stout fellow but will never suffer from brainstorms', and Tony on the banjo 'the blight, the prize wart of the show. Excessively presumptuous.'

Like any teenage boy Laurie was not disposed to lyricise the colourful qualities of his mother. ('I gave her a lot of silence in my teens ... didn't talk to her enough, or listen when the others had gone away in her life,' he later said.[15]) 'Mother has been talking at full speed for the last hour. It does get on your bally nerves.' Annie would shriek and scream whenever torrential rain swept down the bank. It is a very sheer drop, at the mercy of floods, and Jack remembered quaking with fear as water, leaves and twigs hurtled down. But in the garden Annie could 'order the earth to bloom with a royal wave of her hand while we boys did the heavy digging', Laurie recalled.[16]

    There was in the tiny cottage, even with only four occupants after Harold had gone and the sisters all married, considerable commotion. 'The house was most uncomfortable. What with the weather, the muddle, my stiff neck & mother's tongue it was hell!' They had a dog called Rover that kept running away; the water did not always boil for the tin bath. 'House and mother in a state of chaos. She was getting ready to go to London, and she had about four hours work and about thirty minutes to do it in. I tried to help but things got worse so I oiled out. Mother invariably breaks things when she's flustered.' 'Had a hell of a row with J[ack] this morning & let him have a few home truths. He is a damn prig at times & thinks he's so superior with his big talk.'

    At weekends Annie and her boys would visit the sisters, aunts and cousins for tea or Sunday dinner: 'about half a hundredweight of potatoes ... marrowfat peas, and some slices of ham cut thick. I have never been so fat in my life.' When they visited Uncle Charlie, the forester, they admired his tree nursery where hundreds of tiny beech, ash and larch trees were planted in close rows 'like radishes' in 1930–31. Today, Uncle Charlie's giant beech trees overhang the winding road from Bull's Cross into Slad.

Laurie was receptive to the natural scene, the call of the cuckoo and the state of the moon, a lifelong fascination and an inspiration to purple his prose. 'The sun shines shame-facedly from an imperial sky mottled with small fleecy clouds … But it deserves some homage, for like the hand of an invisible artist, it touches the trees with a riot of burning copper…' 'Cycled back over Horsepools & strove to appreciate the serene majesty of the plain. It is peerless just now. Ridges of trees veering away to the blue distance and the coppery Malverns.' He adopted the descriptive style of whichever author he had borrowed from the public library. He had yet to discover Dickens, Lawrence and Joyce. He found Priestley's *The Good Companions* engrossing; it is touching to read Laurie's analysis of Priestley's skill in conjuring up a smoky industrial town when, twenty-five years later, Priestley was the critic loudest in praise of *Cider with Rosie*. But mostly Laurie loved Jeffery Farnol, Sax Rohmer and Warwick Deeping. 'Deeping is a master of similes,' he discovered, and promptly began peppering his prose with similes. 'I woke up feeling as sleepy as a library lizard this morning' … 'I'm as miserable as Inge the Dean, but so is the weather' … 'found that the bike tyre I had mended so judiciously yesterday was as flat as a biscuit' … 'The depression increases as I feel as misplaced as a stick of garlic in a cherry trifle.'

Under the influence *of All Quiet on the Western Front*, he tries writing in the historic present. 'This morning I go for a walk up Scrubs way … This afternoon a man comes up from the Infirmary to tell Mother that Grandfather is very ill. Jack sets off to Woodchester to tell Uncle Tom, while I cycle up to Uncle Sid's. Cycle down the Painswick Rd to the bowl of the valley where I explore a ruined manor…'

(His grandfather Light dies the next day.)

When the cinema arrived in Stroud and Gloucester, Laurie went every week. He saw Douglas Fairbanks Jr in *The Dawn Patrol*, Jack

Buchanan and Jeanette MacDonald in *Monte Carlo* and Rudy Vallée in *The Vagabond Lover*. His favourite film actress was Madeleine Carroll, 'my idea of the perfect Jeffery Farnol heroine'.

He wrote letters to a girl called Pat Robinson, a friend of his sisters, who became a kind of mentor. She lived with her elderly mother in Birmingham and sent him *The Hunchback of Notre Dame* for his seventeenth birthday in June, a month of rain: 'Bengal climate: sodden grass, mud, dripping trees, and June the month of roses and sweet-smelling hay is turned to a month of November-like gales, of postponed cricket matches and washed out fêtes.'

As Laurie later said, the village was small, in half a mile of valley, but the details of its life seemed enormous. In April 1931 the first telephone was installed in the Slad post office, and soon Laurie recorded: 'This lunchtime I did something that I have never done before. I had vocal intercourse with an inhabitant of Slad, without being at Slad. In short, I rang Mrs Oakey.' On 26 April, 'We filled in the Census form tonight. An historical event.' In May a new vicar, the Revd Cyril Hodson, arrived. On Election Day, 31 October, when the National Government was formed, 'Mother polled for Perkins (Con) whose majority was 16,500.'

They watched Farmer Webb catching rabbits with a ferret; were awakened at 4 a.m. by the bloodcurdling howls of foxes from the garden; went to a rummage sale and got 'a Slazenger tennis racquet, a good pair of skates, an operatic record and a couple of tennis presses for one and sixpence'. They played whist and quoits for penny stakes. One night a policeman stopped him for not having his bicycle lamp on: 'First time in my life I got to grips with the law.' On summer evenings Laurie and Jack would play strenuous tennis 'with Eileen and other gentry'. They cycled to fairgrounds and air shows. If it rained Laurie painted 'a fair lady from a Farnol novel' or 'a portrait of Jack which I shall call Adonis reclining'. On the day of the Whitsun treat, Laurie had tea with the vicar and considered himself a 'social success'. Mostly they just loitered with other boys at Bulls Cross, a mile up the road, and 'spouted rot'.

Life seemed crowded with noteworthy incident. On 26 May Laurie saw his first elephant, from a local circus. 'It was a flabby worn-out looking thing rather like a perishing bicycle tyre – but it was an elephant.' On 19 September he saw giraffes, gorillas, lions and bears, on the chara outing to Bristol Zoo. On Derby Day, 3 June, in the office sweepstake Laurie won six shillings, having drawn the favourite, Cameronica.

He purchased, as he put it, a new suit of clothes.

> The waistcoat is a glorious thing, double-breasted with lapels. The trousers are long and baggy. The coat has one button and is also very natty. Each day I feel conscious of the saw that Hepworths publish in its truth – 'Clothes make the man.' J and I went to church this morning, rather staggered Lionel Ballinger with our sartorial glory.

And then there were girls: 'the maiden situation'.

> The Clarks lass is a nice girl although a trifle fast which of course to the uncynical is no handicap. The one in Woolworths merits closer attention by the connoisseur but is a trifle childish. The two Aldridges from the typewriting school are in every way eligible but unresponsive. And there are a few miscellaneous ones hanging about who would go like fire at a little attention – such fields to conquer.

He was half envious of Jack who was bold enough to take girls to the pictures: 'An awfully prosaic idea of love-making don't you think so brother Farnol? But still under the influence of a glance of coquetry or at the sight of red lips and a trim waist we all do it.' Jack would 'make love' – flirting and lovemaking meant the same thing in those days – to the Hogg sisters, who could throw seductive over-the-shoulder glances like Pola Negri, and would call at the Lee cottage on the slightest pretext. ('A fine thing, a sofa,' Laurie discovered.)

Girls would inquire for him at the office, but he was indifferent; then on 31 March an invitation came from a girl named Peggy for Easter weekend, and Laurie danced a jig. But Laurie and Peggy merely played ping-pong. 'I may as well hermetise,' he concluded.

Jeffery Farnol romances taught Laurie about the joys of 'yearning', and also the indulgence of over-writing. 'As I strode along between the dark hedgerows feeling the gritty road crunch beneath my feet … a great longing seized me to attain "the Ideal" – and then an owl hooted and this mournful sound seemed to accentuate the seeming hopelessness of my yearning.'

That summer Laurie first found the Whiteway Colony, two miles from Slad, between Sheepscombe and Miserden. A girl named Margery, from the typing school above his office, took him there. The colony had been founded by the Tolstoyan Anarchists, a group of liberal-minded schoolteachers, clerks and shop assistants who bicycled out from Croydon on a hot summer's day in 1898, inspired by Leo Tolstoy's Utopian ideals. In Gloucestershire they could buy land at £7 an acre. They ceremonially burnt the title deeds and built wooden houses, each in one acre with no fences.

The colonists rejected marriage, grew fruit and vegetables, threw pots, knitted and wove, organised camps, buried their own dead, and ran a school which 'encouraged initiative and natural abilities'. Women wore white smock dresses, men sandals, shorts, beards. In 1901 one of the colonists, a young baker named Sudbury Protheroe, appeared at Stroud court charged with indecency, having been out on the highway in his shorts when he unluckily met the disapproving vicar of Bisley, the Revd Herbert Edgecumbe Hadow. The Whiteway Colony was much visited by left-wing intelligentsia, including Malcolm Muggeridge. Descendants of the original colonists still flourish, in the much-improved wooden houses.

At Whiteway Laurie was invited to vegetarian suppers and watched the colonists doing folk dancing in the colonnaded village hall, a former sanatorium. It was also the venue for Esperanto classes, play-readings, lectures, and meetings of the Peace Pledge Union:

during the Spanish Civil War, Whiteway accommodated a dozen Republican refugees. Laurie joined the Whiteway Club and went to their gramophone recitals to hear Richard Tauber or Paul Robeson, and played at their Saturday dances, for which he designed posters after the style of Picasso. Whiteway gave him his first smattering of politicisation. It was there that he met the composer Benjamin Frankel, and the mysterious 'Cleo' who was to feature in *As I Walked Out One Midsummer Morning*.

Laurie was not the untravelled youth he later made out. (In a 1992 radio interview he claimed he'd never even been to Tetbury, eight miles away, until he was nineteen.) In fact he cycled long distances – Birmingham had 'the biggest Woolworths I've ever seen' – and motored with an uncle and aunt in a car named 'Matilda' to Stratford, Warwick and Leamington Spa. On 23 August he set off to cycle to Oxford, a colleague having bet him a shilling that he couldn't get there in under 3 and a quarter hours. He reached sister Dorothy's in time for dinner. Jude-like, he went to the Cathedral service the next day, visited Worcester College and Magdalen Tower, sketched New College and St John's, went to the Radcliffe Camera, and to the Electra cinema to see *Min and Bill*.

The day after his seventeenth birthday ('Meagre post') he reported: 'Self clearly at a dead end. The range of hills, low, breathing mystery; the rolling plain, stretching away to the blue haze in the Midlands, emitting Romance & a poignant suggestion of what might have been.'

But Boxing Day 1931 'will go down in my history as a day of varied experiences. Of sport, rustic boredom, middle-class bliss, domestic complications and moreover an idyll.' He had watched Earl Bathurst's hounds meet, seen Cirencester beat North Cerney 2–1 at football, walked on the 'blasted heath', and after some discord at home, spent the evening with Hilda Simpson and her family. 'It was about 11 o'clock that the idyll was enacted. It was an experience that I shall never forget.' (This was probably Laurie's first kiss.) 'This week has made history but such history that I can keep to myself.'

Two items in his 1931 diary are worth remarking. 'There was a fire along London Road yesterday,' Laurie noted, 'and the owner came in to claim today as expected for their monthly fire. The insurance money will carry them on for a bit I suppose & then the can of petrol will be brought out again.' (This is the origin of the 'piano factory fire' in *Cider with Rosie* that caused Laurie to be sued for libel thirty years later.) And on 15 April he reported on 'the Spain trouble'. 'King Alfonso abdicated & left Spain in a warship for an unknown destination ... Learnt that Alfonso has gone to France & there's a hell of a row in Madrid, but more scrapping is going on at Barcelona.' These were the earliest rumblings of the unrest that developed into the Spanish Civil War.

One other event from Laurie's childhood, recorded in *Cider with Rosie*, cannot be overlooked. He was knocked down by a bicycle, one dark night in 1924, which may have been what triggered his epilepsy. Of all his childhood ailments, the two-day concussion after the accident had the deepest impact. 'That blow in the night,' he writes, 'scarred me, I think, for ever – put a stain of darkness upon my brow and opened a sinister door in my brain, a door through which I am regularly visited by messengers whose words just escape me, by glimpses of worlds I can never quite grasp, by grief, exultation, and panic...' At that time, epilepsy was untreatable and regarded as a mental illness, carrying a stigma of enduring shame for those afflicted by it. Epilepsy is common, mysterious and, even today, frightening. Though Laurie's was manageable, much of his secretive behaviour could be explained by his anxiety about imminent oblivion and loss of control, which he feared more than anything.

Laurie's affliction – Julius Caesar's 'falling sickness' – was shared with many writers of genius: Byron, Dr Johnson, Flaubert, Dostoevsky (who described the 'state of startling illumination and euphoria' before an attack) and Edward Lear, who kept his 'terrible demon' a secret except from his diaries. Edward VIII's and George VI's youngest brother John was an epileptic, kept away from his family and out of public view. Those close to Laurie knew about his epilepsy, but throughout his life he strove to keep it a secret from the world at large.

On 11 June 1931, 'I've learnt more in this one year of the things that matter,' he noted, 'than I did in five years of school life.'

3

'The well-loved stranger'
1932–1934

'I DID PRETTY well,' Laurie said, looking back fifty years. 'I had a golden blond, vulnerable, idealistic face. Women cosseted me. I had an open face which said "love me" and I was enveloped by love.'[17] Like many men at that time (and indeed since), he found female intellect unnerving. Yet the girls who were drawn to him were intelligent, well-read, and keen to encourage a poetic youth.

At seventeen Laurie was considered good-looking in a vaguely artistic way: less exquisite than Rupert Brooke, but of that fair type, with a heavy lock of hair falling over the forehead and a wide, full-lipped, sensual mouth. He also had effortless charm. His brother Jack found him a hard act to compete with.

> He could paint, he could write, he was a musician and a damn good one. And I was none of these things. He was a poet. It gives you a romantic aura, doesn't it. It was very tough for me, plodding away at my factory. Laurie lived on a wave of effervescence.

With Laurie, girls felt free to talk about the moon rising from behind a hill, or the scent of rain-washed lilac. 'It's beautifully easy to write to you!' wrote one, waxing lyrical about a springtime walk through the Golden Valley, with its mist of bluebells, and banks bright with primroses. Laurie matched in kind their pantheistic outpourings. 'You who can see beauty & put down what you feel about it, should offer praise to Heaven for those gifts,' they told him.

This chorus of encouragement came from two bright sisters, Molly and Betty Smart. They were cousins of Arthur Swain, the jazz pianist whose band Laurie had joined in 1931. They lived in a semi-detached villa named Annesbrook in suburban Gloucester. Theirs was a happy, cultivated family; their mother, known as 'Lady', was invincibly cheerful; their father was an avid reader and an excellent musician. Molly, black-haired and green-eyed, and five years older than Laurie, wrote: 'I think you & I are going to be very firm friends – fellow conspirators.' It was a kind of threat. She taught in the village school at Hillesley, and wrote poetry herself. She sent him her verses for his critical comments, addressing him as 'Laurielee' because 'your names together make music & separately they don't. I love musical names, don't you?'

But the irrepressible Betty, at sixteen, was the first to fall in love with Laurie. She wrote, during a Latin lesson at her school, Ribston Hall in Gloucester, thanking him for sending Jeffery Farnol's novel *Peregrine's Progress*, a romantic saga which he had found entrancing, and which modern youth would find unreadable. It tells of a well-born boy of nineteen, wandering the countryside learning the tinker's trade and falling in love with Diana, a wild gypsy maiden.

Betty saw Laurie as a perfect Peregrine, the Farnol hero, 'oblivious of the world and its narrow-minded conventions, finding his poetry in the stars, his philosophy of life in the great tall trees ... D'you know what Peregrine means? Wanderer! Isn't it great. Cheer-ho, Betty.'

Laurie and Betty's first encounter had been at the White Horse pub in Painswick, run by the Smart girls' aunt Georgie, mother of Arthur Swain. 'Three things I noticed before tea,' Betty later wrote. 'You could talk English without murdering the grammar; you loved your music; and you were saying to yourself "Hmmm – an empty-headed little ass. Thinks of nothing but boys & dress & amusements." This made me horribly self-conscious, and I became gayer & more empty-headed.'

Their friendship flourished through reading Farnol, or *1066 And All That*, aloud on Sunday walks; and through going to village hops.

'Was your last dance a success, with lots of pretty girls bringing you sausage rolls?' Betty would ask. 'Molly and I are going to a leap year dance on the 29th. The ladies choose their partners, and everyone wears a mask until midnight. Doesn't it sound thrilling? Lady Molly hopes your elder brother will be present.' Jack and Laurie made a non-aggression pact over girls, so Jack steered clear of Betty though she was the prettier sister. Betty would report to Laurie about the 'topping floor and the marvellous band', and the fact that 'half the fellows were squiffy'. Later she reported that their mother had over-heard this conversation.

'1st fair damsel: Who's that young fellow playin' the fiddle?
2nd fair damsel: That be Laurie Lee.
1st fair damsel: Laurie Lee, eh. What do a do?
2nd fair damsel: 'E don't do nothin'. 'E be on the dowel.'

Betty soon progressed to invoking D. H. Lawrence, 'who seems to know women uncommonly well'. After seeing Laurie, Betty would lie awake, dreaming, like the heroine of *The Virgin and the Gypsy*, 'and it seems to her that all her form is outlined as with molten metal. I have often felt the same way.'

Meanwhile Molly was sending frank criticisms of Laurie's poems: one 'hackneyed', one with scansion askew, one crude. But she also told him: 'Don't *ever* stop writing Laurie ... Your lightness of touch is remarkable. I envy your colour of phrase (and I'm too conceited to envy most people).' Laurie promptly destroyed the offending poems, eliciting paroxysms of grief from Molly. 'Why oh why did you burn your poems? How can you be a fellow conspirator if you burn the evidence of your crimes?' Betty, she reported, was 'very put out' at his sending his poems to Molly. 'She said you are *her* friend, before you are mine, and stalked out of the room waving a toothbrush and towel threateningly.' Then, Betty told Laurie, 'Molly has of course written a poem about your poem'. She had too.

His poem was 'I dreamed of you' and fifty years later Laurie could still quote it verbatim. 'I dreamed of you one April night ... when the moon in silv'ry splendour bright ... hung poised in a realm of clouds…' He told an interviewer that he had written it pushing a bike up Painswick Hill, and had never written it down.[18] But he did: and he also kept Molly's poem 'Reaction', subtitled 'On "I dreamed of you"'. ('How can I write/When through my dazzled mind/Your magic phrases dance?')

Molly was curious to know if the 'delightfully Farnolish nymph of the woods' in Laurie's poems really existed: if he'd lost his heart at seventeen, she warned, he would regret it, as she had done the same. 'It isn't pleasant to go through life without a heart.' (Molly had just ended her romance with Martin Matthias, a classics undergraduate at Balliol. She had written a poem called 'Departure' about that.) In 1933 both Molly and Laurie had poems published in the *Gloucester Citizen*: Laurie's 'Jazz', and Molly's 'Haresfield'. 'Isn't it topping?' wrote Betty. 'Please address my sister as THE Miss Smart (famous 20th-century poet). I just love the people I love to be appreciated by others. Isn't life glorious? Least, it is for me.'

Clearly, Betty was a Pollyanna, but as Molly described her in 'Betty: A Sketch' (girlish laughter in her soft brown eyes, etc.), she was also wise beyond her years, kind to tramps, and 'seemed to find goodness in everything'. (She was still finding goodness in everything to the end of her days.) Laurie renamed Betty 'Helen'; and she took to calling Laurie 'Euryalus' after the warrior of Virgil's *Aeneid*. Laurie looked him up and discovered he was beheaded. ('Silly boy, it was his *life* that mattered, & anyway, he was brave.') Seeking other mythological models, Betty reinvented Laurie as a verray parfit Arthurian knight, saving damsels, and told their story as an idyll.

> One day, she was introduced to a young musician, whose mouth proclaimed him a poet, an idealist or a cynic. He turned out to be all three … The young musician was searching for a peerless creature, a Diana … On a cold evening, with a half-mad moon racing the stars, the young musician took his lady in his arms and told her that he loved her. The whole world was theirs. It

was truly a night of magic. They loved – it was enough. Their
love grew & autumn glowed with the beauty of it.

Betty never forgot that night, 10 October 1933, when Laurie kissed
her and said, 'God knows I love you, Helen.' ('Bless his heart, it was a
fantasy,' she recalled. 'But a fantasy we wove together.') At sixteen she
had their life together mapped out. They would be marvellously happy.

> O Laurie, a little cottage and a wireless and a grammy and books
> and each other. Let's go scrounging round lots of funny little
> shops & plan & pretend & dream. And let's go to the Cathedral.
> We've got to go on being companions ... and Laurie, when you
> realise that I'm an ordinary mortal after all, be generous, for
> always I will be, as you have named me, Helen, your Diana.

She conjured up scenes of domestic bliss in their cottage with
blue and white china and an inglenook. She would darn his socks
and bustle about, while he would dig the garden – 'lavender and
rosemarie, hollyhocks & lilies-of-the-valley & violets & roses,
delphiniums & sweet peas, & clumps of lupins' and write poetry. A
blue-eyed baby boy named Keith Allen would

> warm his little pink toes on the fender, gravely watching the
> flames, as he listens to your tale ... I want Keith Allen to see the
> loveliness all around him ... Should I send him to an elementary
> school? I want him to meet every class of boy & girl, but he shall
> never go to Oxford, even if I have sacks of money.

Laurie was not yet repelled by these sentimental fantasies. He
suggested 'low oak beams and fire dogs'. 'I should like them too,'
Betty responded at once, 'and infinitely comfortable chairs with lots
of cushions and wide arms. Long windows that stand open all day. I
want trees outside, and laughter and peace within. I want cool green
dresses for myself and huge ridiculous hats.'

Probably contemplating future domesticity from his office in Stroud, Laurie confided to Betty his black moods, the weary dissatisfaction of working at a futile job, his desire to escape. She wrote consolingly to 'My very own dear darling'. These moods would pass, she said, if he overcame his cynicism. His life was not futile. The people around him had dreams too. She loved the Slad valley as he did: why leave it?

For all her dreaminess, Betty was a girl of some insight and sensibility. She admired Laurie's scorn for convention, his determination to 'go for it', and his ability to 'take a whack and get up again'. She knew that 'first love is often not last love' and that both were really 'in love with love'. Poets were fickle and sought the ideal woman.

Beloved, you told me you would always love me, but you won't … Things I do and say will begin to irritate you beyond measure. But for my part Laurie I do love you, and on Friday I was aching for you to come and fold your arms round me and kiss me and kiss me and not stop.

And when Laurie accused her of preferring his letters to him, she said it was true: he, like her, was typically English, less self-conscious on paper. When they met, she would adopt a pose of casual flippancy, while Laurie affected a morose reserve.

Meanwhile Laurie was being advised by his older penfriend Pat, now an ambitious secretary in Birmingham. She encouraged Laurie in self-improvement – why not enter the poetry competitions in the *Birmingham Post*? Her mother had won half a guinea for an essay. Pat shared Laurie's appreciation of Rupert Brooke and John Drinkwater, and advised him to read Somerset Maugham and the plays of John Van Druten. Her drama group were doing Shaw's *You Never Can Tell*; would he get it from the library and give his opinion?

'And now about your verse: please don't be hurt, but your short poem brought to mind Herrick's "Whenas in silks my Julia goes". I don't like "sea" being made to rhyme with "worthily". The ending "ly" should always have the short vowel sound.' But when Laurie did have a poem published in the *Birmingham Post*, and an essay on platonic friendships, Pat (his platonic friend) was 'most awfully pleased and proud'.

Laurie plainly allowed Pat, who was involved in a lesbian relationship with a girl named Phyl, to be a mentor. He requested guidance from her about his 'Helen'. Pat understood because she loved her Phyl as he loved his Helen who sounded 'a delightfully winsome little creature – almost faunlike'. She marvelled that having played cricket with the boy Laurie, and nursed him through 'the Edgar Wallace stage', she should now be his confidante. But she warned him sternly against going too far. Just because he read books he must not consider himself a man of the world. And although 'kind and sensitive almost to a fault' he must not 'live in a world of dreams & lovely thoughts'.

> My dear, I wonder how old this girl is. And I wonder how much you know of all the dangers and responsibilities … This is your first experience of love: don't risk sullying its beauty. Did you hear about my cousin Eric, who was rushed off to a registry office? He was weak; you are not. Waiting is hard, but you must. Do you realise how advanced you are for your years?

Laurie invited her to Slad for a weekend. Pat's mother thought this 'improper', so Annie wrote too. That weekend, they talked until Laurie fell asleep in Pat's arms. He confided that Betty's father had discouraged her from seeing him. Laurie had had a seizure one day in the Smarts' sitting room while playing Handel's 'Largo'; he suddenly went rigid and fell on the floor. Afterwards Betty's father asked her not to see Laurie again, arguing that there was no future for them, and that he was only thinking of her happiness. But Betty was defiant. They plotted a holiday together in a caravan at the seaside. 'Doesn't it sound too utterly delicious? Waking in the morning & dashing down to a deserted beach in a bathing costume?' But the Smart parents vetoed it. Betty wrote:

When I said that it was a damned shame that we couldn't go
away with you, mother replied, 'Betty, we want none of that
language in this house if you please.' I retired crestfallen. Later
however, Mother was carrying a pile of plates from the dining
room to the scullery, and managed to drop one, and a well-
seasoned 'Bugger!' rent the air.

In June, the month of his nineteenth birthday (1933), Laurie and
his brother Tony did go away with the sisters (with Pat and Phyl
too), to camp at Stratford. They saw *Richard II*. They borrowed a
punt from the managing director of the Daimler factory, who took a
liking to them. They played Debussy's *L'Apres-Midi d'un Faune* on
a wind-up gramophone. There was a thunderstorm, and a rainbow,
and dozens of nightingales descended on the Avon and sang. Molly's
poem about Laurie at Stratford began:

So I have left you there
(O Beautiful and young)
Among the willows and the dragonflies.
Your gold hair flung
From off your brow. And where
The slowly reddening sunset lies
Upon the stream, I'll find
Your soft desirous mouth...

Molly later confessed that she had fallen hopelessly in love with
Laurie on 'that mad magic night'.

Remember how wet the grass was under our tennis shoes – and
how shy the nightingales were at first? And how heavy the night
air was with the scent of syringa – and how a fish made a sudden
splash in the silence – remember? Whatever happens Laurie,
whether we grow old and lose our sense of beauty – we shall
have this to remember, and there's no one else I could have

shared that night with as I shared it with you. I was so utterly
grateful to you for not attempting to kiss me – any other man
would have – bless you for that Laurie dear.

Laurie could flirt with Molly because he had suggested a breathing
space with Betty; and anyway he had now met a more exotically
pretty girl who was far more exotic than the Smarts, with dark
curly hair and a charming smile. Sophia Rogers, known as 'Sufi',
had moved to Slad from Buenos Aires with her English father and
Spanish mother. In one respect, Sufi influenced Laurie's life most
of all, because (as he said later in life) the reason he went to Spain
was that 'a girl in Slad from Buenos Aires taught me a few words of
Spanish'.[19] This sounded most unlikely, but in fact that is exactly
what happened.

Ethel Rogers, landlady of the Fortune's Well guest-house at
Sheepscombe, had a brother named Alfred, who had gone out to
Argentina as an accountant with the railway company Ferrocarril
Central Cordoba. In Buenos Aires Alfred met a Spanish girl,
Serafina, and married her in Montevideo. They had five sons and one
daughter, Sufi. In 1933, Alfred retired and brought his Argentine
family to settle near their Sheepscombe relations, in a new bungalow
named Overdale, just below Bulls Cross in Slad.

Richard, Sufi's youngest brother, remembered that his father had
met Laurie in the Woolpack where they discussed poetry. Laurie
began visiting their bungalow and would go out walking with Sufi
– but the Rogers parents insisted that Richard, aged eleven, should
chaperone them. 'Laurie was a joyful person,' Richard recalled. 'A
nice chap, and very handsome. Sufi tried to teach him how to speak
some words in Spanish…'

Laurie said, fifty years later, in an interview:[20] 'If only I'd known
at eighteen that those strange, complicated, romantical, remote,
mysterious creatures who dominated my waking and my sleeping
were quite simple and uncomplex after all. Girls! … they sustained
me in a state of anguish and torment.' But his naivety had been

fruitful: the unattainability of girls was the source of all his juvenilia. 'And who knows, without such practice I might not have got into Pseuds' Corner in *Private Eye*.'

Betty found the two-month separation unbearable. She wrote in July to say what 'awful mutts' they had been: they could conquer any obstacle. Her parents had been married twenty-five years, and each would be lost without the other. 'There's romance in their lives, which we with our rather scornful idealistic view failed to see.'

On the second anniversary of their meeting, Laurie wrote to Betty, now studying for her School Certificate, and she replied with renewed conviction:

> You are in your nineteenth, I in my seventeenth year. We are going to come through this with our chins decidedly up. I am convinced that there never was such a love as ours, and never will be. I'm exactly the sort of woman to make you happy. In fact I'm *the* woman. The world is before us, demanding to be explored. My youth is dedicated like a poem to you, full of vigour and beauty and great thoughts and tears and ringing laughter and music. I'm full to my finger-tips with life ... and tonight my warrior Euryalus, I love you.

Molly was meanwhile lending Laurie records, recommending books, discussing Burne-Jones, whose paintings of beautiful pre-Raphaelite faces Laurie thought 'repetitive'. 'Doesn't the same thing apply to every artist?' argued Molly. 'Your D. H. Lawrence (egoist that he is) tells his own story over and over again – a different name but always it's the same character.'

Early in 1934 Molly the aspiring writer went to train as a nurse in Birmingham. She found it sickening to be surrounded by malformed, broken bodies, and gangrenous limb stumps rotting from venereal disease. She longed to lean against the wet bark of trees again. The flowers in the wards, 'great stiff daffodils', could not compare with the wild ones in Newent woods. She was a lark shut up in a cage. By April she had decided to fail her exams, though guilty about the fees her parents had paid, and dreaded going home as the prodigal daughter. But she must leave this sordid life or go stark mad. At the same time she was encouraging Laurie to get away himself.

'Laurie Lee, *why* don't you clear out of Stroud? You're simply wasting your time, and you'll never be content there. Even if you don't find happiness you'll at least be living.'

In May 1934, Laurie had decided he would go to London. Pat wrote approvingly: 'And so Piping Peter is going to town?' He would be broadened by seeing life outside his native village, and might do great things. 'Goodbye my dear. Our friendship is one of the love-liest things in my life. Through you, and in stumblingly trying to help you, I have found such happiness...'

Laurie left behind other broken hearts. One Rita Louise, whom he had invited to go with him, wrote: 'Laurie dear, This must be the end. I have no regrets, no reproaches, and last weekend will always be wonderful to me. But I can't break away ... Do understand.' (She wrote again, wanting to come and collect her copy of *Ulysses*. Laurie's farewell letter had 'made it almost worthwhile saying goodbye'.)

In the office of Randall & Payne, young Alan Payne, knowing how unhappy Laurie was, felt no surprise when his father got Laurie's resignation note explaining that 'I am not suited to office work.'

Laurie promised Betty he would see her on his return, but she replied firmly: 'When you come back, I shall not be here.' She saw him as Frances Cornford saw Rupert Brooke, as a young Apollo golden-haired, standing on the verge of strife. 'You,' Betty wrote, 'whose weapons are your pen, your pencil & the way one lock of your hair falls over your eyes ... I'm glad I met you Laurie.'

As Laurie said later, moving from one's birthplace is a basic instinct. Men have a yearning to wander. But in his case he had to escape from the small tight valley closing in around him, 'the cottage walls narrowing like the arms of an iron maiden, the local girls whis-pering, "Marry, and settle down."'[21]

4

Laurie Walks Out
1934–1935

SO LAURIE WALKED out one morning in June 1934, just before his twentieth birthday, wearing thick boots, and carrying a small tent, a tin of treacle biscuits, and his violin in a blanket. Annie waved him off from the steep cottage bank with a 'gnarled red hand'. He describes her as old and stooping; she was in fact in her mid-fifties.

He was not yet bound for Spain, merely London. Why did he walk? He could have cycled. The train would have cost 4s 6d. But walking out was the poetic route to the gypsy life, the W. H. Davies mode, the romantic troubadour's way. Laurie Lee had unwittingly begun creating his legend.

He headed towards Wiltshire, slept under the stars, and woke in the rain to find two cows breathing over him. ('The lowing herd winds softly o'er the Lee' as a friend wrote, years later when he published this tale.) He almost turned back, but could not face his brothers' gloating. Within a day he passed through Malmesbury and Chippenham; soon he was in Salisbury, and, taking a detour, in order to see the sea, in a week he was at Southampton.

Sleeping in a doss-house run by 'an old hag with a tooth like a tin-opener', he began busking, learning to leave just two pennies in his hat. Slow melodies ('Loch Lomond', 'The Rose of Tralee', 'Ave Maria') were the most lucrative; women were more responsive. He moved along the coastline of Hampshire and Sussex, finding the real sea a disappointment, not what Hardy and Farnol had led him to expect: a shabby shoreline suburbia of new bungalows. At Bognor

Regis he camped out on the sands with 'a fluid young girl of sixteen, who hugged me steadily throughout one long hot day with only a gymslip on her sea-wet body'.[22]

That is all he writes about 'Mollie' – but he kept her seven-page letter, written a few days later and addressed simply from 'The Beach', received by Laurie at Chanctonbury in West Sussex.

> Dear Laurie, You are right, it was a dream. You said midsummer madness: we were both rather in the clouds. I shall always remember how we talked about anything and everything with such ease! But afterwards I think I was a spectator, watching two strangers playing a part. Perhaps you felt that too.

This Mollie, like the Molly he'd left behind, also shared his favourite authors and books and interests, in a strange 'mingling of sympathies'. Both were furious about the hideous housing developments along the coast, and the muddle of politics and injustice. And though sharing his rosy halo of youth and beauty, she felt maternal towards him, and hoped they would be friends for ever. She asked about Chanctonbury Ring, the Iron Age hill fort on the South Downs, regarded as an iconic site:

> Didn't you find Romans in every tree and short, dark Britons in every bush? I can't tell you how I envy you, the magic in the loveliness & the loneliness means more to me than anything, and I can find it so rarely. Yet there are you, saturated in it day and night, getting more experience, excitement of new places, and thrills of fresh beauty ... Laurie, you can't think how lucky you are. And your love of music is another blessing I envy with all my heart.
>
> Laurie, we may never see each other again ... but you have courage and a strong sense of true values. I would like to keep your friendship if you think mine worthwhile. Write to me if you care to, mon ami, when you reach London tell me

how you get on. Good luck & good hunting! Yours for auld
lang syne, Mollie.

Evidently Laurie would have no trouble in finding romantic Mollies
and Betties, wherever he went. Something in him made girls respond
in this way. On he tramped. The pearl-chokered ladies of Worthing
in their bath-chairs gave him, for one hour's fiddling, 38 shillings:
'more than a farm-labourer earned in a week'.

On the Sussex Downs, living on dates and biscuits (an affectation,
he later admits; he saw himself as T. E. Lawrence 'in a desert sand-
storm blowing out of the wadis of Godalming'), he met Alf, a veteran
tramp in a deerstalker hat. The highways thronged with vagrants
then: there were nearly two million unemployed in Britain. At night
they brewed tea in billy-cans by grassy roadsides and Alf taught him
about wearing layers of clothes, and how to flannel housewives and
dodge police.

Via Ascot (in Ascot week), Windsor and Stoke Poges, he arrived
at Beaconsfield, and beheld London. 'Cleo, my girlfriend, was somewhere out there; hoarding my letters (I hoped) and waiting.' Laurie
wrote that he had met sixteen-year-old Cleo, 'the beautiful daughter
of a Communist agitator', earlier that spring at the Whiteway Colony,
where she lived with her family in a caravan. This was certainly true,
but Cleo's real name was Julie Marshall. The Marshalls had previously lived in America, until her father was deported for political
activities and sought refuge at Whiteway. 'Cleo' had 'a husky, nutty,
Anglo-American accent, huge brown eyes flecked like crumbled
honey, a smooth leggy figure, lithe as an Indian pony'. They had
'pretended to be in love'.

But before Laurie found his way to Cleo's Putney address, he
went to 3 Greville Place, St John's Wood. This was where the musician Ben Frankel, another new friend he had made at Whiteway,
lived. Fifty years later, when Laurie met John Clive, who was about
to become his tenant in Slad, he noticed Clive's London address in
Greville Place and said: 'Does it have a studio in the garden?' Yes,

said Clive, the studio is still there. 'That's the first place I stayed, when I arrived in London,' said Laurie. 'It belonged to a famous conductor and composer.'

But sooner or later Laurie was with Cleo's bohemian family, who were living in a half-demolished house on Putney Heath. Her father arranged a job for him on a local building site. So Laurie moved into digs above a café in the Lower Richmond Road and quickly made friends, including a black American sailor from Missouri, an extra-vagant greeter ('Gouge mah eyes, shuh good to see you'), and Philip O'Connor,[23] a curly-haired aspiring poet whose verses were 'rhapsodic eruptions of surrealist fantasy'. (O'Connor later briefly resurfaced in Laurie's diary in 1958, when they met by chance in Soho.)

Pat wrote asking for news in her matronly way. 'As you know, I've never been to London, & never had any desire to visit it. I imagine it to be a cruel, relentless beast, & I shall feel very much more at ease when you are home again.' She feared he was keeping hectic hours and late nights, and would catch his annual bout of 'flu in the town air. If only she could hold his head soothingly against her breast, in the kitchen at Slad! Again she urged him to resist sexual indulgence: 'Discipline of the body is essential to a happy & successful life. Think of Keats' "Beauty is truth, truth beauty. That is all ye know on earth, & all ye need to know."' She added: 'For heaven's sake don't think I'm preaching.'

By day Laurie was pushing cement in a wheelbarrow, building a 'squat, unbeautiful, pretentious' block of flats on Putney Heath. His labouring comrades were diminutive Cockneys, old lags, con-men, drifters, the lowest of the building-site hierarchy; they pilfered, gambled, and rolled cigarettes. 'London then seemed almost nineteenth century, dusty, down-at-heel, secure. Wages were low but life was cheap and easy. A tot of whisky for 6d, a 9d seat in the cinema, cigarettes 20 for 11d – as a builder's labourer earning £2 5s a week I lived the life of Reilly.'[24] In the evenings he played snooker, went to Queen's Hall concerts and the Ballet Russe, and listened to jazz. He met 'stern young students and workers who held gatherings in cold back rooms. Popular Front posters hung on the walls, and there were experiments in sex, responsible, clinical and pure.'

He paints a picture of himself as a solitary, luxuriating in rootless melancholy, wandering on Putney Heath, or through the City and down the Strand. 'I walked the streets of Soho, bought foreign newspapers which I couldn't read, studied art-books at Zwemmers, smoked black Mexican cigars, and played the newfangled pin-tables in the amusement arcades.'

Pat had been camping and having 'top-hole picnics' with the Smart sisters, but advised him to 'cut right away from both girls'. However, he did write to Molly, and she replied ('Surely you know I've been *aching* to write to you for months?') from the Smarts' 'vulgar' new bungalow called Capri in Wellspring Road, Wotton. Betty, captain of her school, about to read English at Exeter University, was still 'a bubbling fountain ... the spirit of joyousness'. 'Adolescence gleams from her; her eyes sparkle and her cheeks glow.' So Betty's heart was not broken. Molly herself was fending off an amorous Cambridge undergraduate, but she assured Laurie she would not get engaged, as her brother Roy had recently: marriage ought to be abolished, and if she were ever caught in that web of convention she would suffocate. Was Laurie homesick, with an ache in his heart for Slad?

Apparently not. In October Laurie's first poem in a national paper was published by the *Sunday Referee*, whose 'Poet's Corner' in that year also featured Dylan Thomas and David Gascoyne. Laurie's poem won him £1. It was called 'Life', and was about grass growing and being cut down and growing again. It began:

> A shower of seed falls in the earth;
> and there, unnoticed by the sky, is birth.

'This poem,' said Victor B. Neuberg, editor of 'Poet's Corner', 'is sensitive to the edge of eeriness.'

'My dear, How proud I am!' wrote Pat. 'When you publish your first book of poems let me be first to share your joy.' She urged him to 'turn an honest half-guinea' by entering further contests. The *Weekly Post* wanted 300 words on the most interesting person you have ever met. Or why not take up calligraphy for commercial gain? A boy she knew got £5 a week for italic writing on Christmas cards. She sent Laurie a broad-nibbed calligraphic pen.

On the back of this letter, Laurie practised his italic script with Pat's pen. What he wrote, over and over, was the name of Sufi Rogers. Soon Sufi herself was writing to Laurie from Slad in her own copperplate hand, and her charmingly fractured English. She had run into Laurie's mother in Stroud, and Annie showed her Laurie's poem in the *Sunday Referee*. Sufi told him she was taking cookery classes and would bake some cakes for him 'when you visit us at Xmas time. My mother remember you very much, and she said, you are a very nice big friend. I have my own becylce [*sic*] and it helps me to go to the Country dances at Whiteway every Saturday and Wednesday night…'

The '*Lección en castellano*' she appended to her letter gave Laurie the following phrases: *No vale la pena* (it's not worth the effort), *No vale un comino* (it's not worth a cumin-seed), *Carajo* (prick: 'especial word') *No tiene inteligencia* (s/he has no intelligence), and *Bebí venga aquí* (Come here baby). (Richard Rogers, her youngest brother, was always called Bebí.)

> *Asomate a la ventana*
> *paloma del alma mía*
> *lavate la cara con agua fría*
> *cachándote una pulmonía* – Lord Byron
> (Lean out of your window, dove of my soul/wash your face in
>   cold water and catch pneumonia.)

But Laurie was not yet fixed on Spain: he told Molly he might go to Italy. 'Oh yes, let's go to Italy quickly, before our hearts are cold and old. Sun on stones, and blue-blue sea,' Molly responded. 'Oh Laurielee, all the stored-up laughter in me bubbles and winks at the thought of Italy ... I know how you felt about Heine's Travels; I've just been reading Munthe's novel San Michele, and now I shall not rest till I've seen Capri.'

Molly affected jealousy over Laurie's published poem. 'Damnable that I've been striving all my life to reach a spot, and in seven lines you land there – Grrrcha! And actually I'm a much nicer person than you are!' She sent some of her latest efforts. 'Truthful opinions please.' One of them was 'A Sonnet for Laurie', beginning:

> Surely this stretch of earth will know you tread
> Your own loved ways again; will feel your feet
> Move soft amid her last-year's leaves that spread
> Brown-gold profusion through your woods...

Yes, it would. Laurie went home at Christmas, and joined Sufi's family at their bungalow deep in snow. Sufi's brother Richard, who drew a good pencil sketch of Laurie that week, said Laurie talked then about going to Spain, mystifying Sufi's parents: why should he want to travel through an impoverished and disturbed country, playing his fiddle?

Laurie and Molly duly had their reunion at Edge church. He gave her a volume of Oscar Wilde, and their friendship altered from that day. With Betty away, Molly felt free to offer Laurie a physical relationship (without any fussing about love) and thereafter she signed her letters exotically 'Mariquita', Spanish for 'Ladybird', an improvement on humdrum Molly. Her letter after their meeting was rapturous: the thought of the strong smooth hardness of his body against the 'petal-pale softness' of hers set a mad orchestra ringing in her brain. She wanted to lift her face to the moon 'and shout with a mirth deeper than laughter'. His touching her lips 'sent flame after flame of moonfire through me'. 'Desire is a flame that runs through one's body in a shower of stars.' And so she began to bombard Laurie with seductive and exclamatory letters about her 'soul-shaking' desire. The consummation must wait (for Betty's sake), but until they met again he must dream of her and 'oh! write soon! Soon! Querido mío! Mariquita.'

Ever since Laurie had gone to London, Jack too had been restless. He would walk to the top of Swift's Hill, and wonder what to do with his life. His younger brother seemed to have all the talents; he must find a different one. At the factory he had risen to assistant manager, and bought his first car, a 1928 Singer, for £22. The previous year he had been given a camera for his twenty-first birthday by a girlfriend (annoyingly, Laurie proved to be a natural photographer too) and it sowed in Jack the idea of being a film director. He wrote to several directors for advice, and one, Paul Rotha, responded. Jack went to London to see him, and Rotha advised him to apply to the Regent Street Polytechnic (now the University of Westminster). They would take him for £25 a term. He promptly sold his car, got on his bike, and began to save up the fees.

That January he saw his brother off at Stroud Station. Laurie moved into new digs, rent 25s a week, at 1 Werter Road, a small Victorian terraced house on the corner of Putney High Street. The landlady was a blonde Cockney, Mrs O'Neill ('Mrs Flynn' in *As I Walked Out*), with a meek spinster sister known as Wid, whom Laurie called 'Beth'. Mrs O'Neill was a chain-smoking Mrs Malaprop, sweeping floors in a dressing gown each morning, transformed into a Gloria Swanson at night, while Wid hovered anxiously in the background and cooked large suppers for Laurie. As always, Laurie was cosseted: the two women would bring him Guinness, and nurse him when ill. Werter Road suited him, and became his recurrent London base for the next eight years. (And when Jack eventually came to London, he too lodged at Werter Road.) Meanwhile Molly and Pat cosseted Laurie's intellect, advising him what to read and what to see – Gielgud's *Hamlet*, and Diana Wynyard in *Sweet Aloes*: 'Opening at Wyndhams on the 31st – go see.'

In May 1935, there was a dispute over non-union labour at the building site, and all work stopped for two weeks. A towering labourer with big fists and a square, bitter face ('prototype of the worker-hero in Soviet posters') emerged to address the men and called the comrades out on strike. This was Fred Copeman, who had already been jailed after the naval mutiny of Invergordon, Scapa Flow.[25] The next time Laurie would see him was during the Spanish Civil War, when Copeman was Commander of the British Battalion of the International Brigade at Albacete, and according to Laurie, recognised him: 'Oh, it's you – the poet from the buildings. Never thought *you'd* make it.'

The strike ended and the building work was finished at the beginning of June 1935. Laurie was feeling 'beefily strong' and fit. He was free to explore the world; frontiers were still wide open. 'There were rumours from China and Abyssinia, but I for one didn't heed them.' He considered France, Italy, Greece – all merely 'names with vaguely operatic flavours'. He knew no languages, except the Argentine-Spanish phrases taught to him by Sufi. Spain it would be. He saw himself 'brown as an apostle, walking the white dust roads through the orange groves'.[26] Or perhaps he just wanted to be able to swank to girlfriends, as he admitted sixty years later.

Anyway, it was a brilliant career move. His wanderings in Spain, and his chance encounter with the Spanish Civil War, were two episodes he was able to draw on for the rest of his life.

Molly, alarmed at Laurie's imminent departure, announced that she was coming to London. She had dreamed of Laurie pointing to the horizon crying, 'Look – the island of Crete … We will find it together, you and I, Mariquita!' So she had taken the post of nursery governess to a handicapped child in a family named Whitelaw in Sutton, Surrey. She would come to him after tea on Thursday. 'Be gentle Laurie – hold me softly against the strong throb of your heart – and kiss me till I am content. Then play to me – will you?' They met several times, and for the last time on a hot summer day. They leaned on a gate in a Surrey lane under chestnut trees. Laurie said, 'God, I wish I didn't love [England] so much!' Then he took her back to his Putney room and played Debussy on his violin. More rapturous yearnings ensued.

> Oh Laurie – Laurilee – the relentless beat of your heart! It beats
> into my brain, into my virgin womb, making life leap within me.
> All my life now, there will be the eternal thrust and throb of your
> heart. So look back and remember a green Surrey lane in June
> and a woman who loved you...

'For the first time in my life,' as Laurie wrote much later in *As I Walked Out*, 'I was learning how much easier it was to leave than to stay behind and love.' On 1 July 1935, describing himself as an 'art student', grey-eyed and five foot nine, he was issued with his first passport.

A week earlier, on his twenty-first birthday, he had gone to see his father in suburban Morden. It was a dispiriting encounter.

> He handed me £8 and said, 'You were due for £10, but you
> borrowed £2 when you were fourteen, so I've knocked that
> off.' He told me the greatest composer in the world was Eric
> Coates.[27] I was a musical snob at the time and thought 'He can't
> be my father.'[28]

Warningly, Mariquita sent a sonnet called 'Haunted!' which ended with a threat that she would appear in his dreams everywhere, haunting him. Undeterred, Laurie bought a £4 one-way boat ticket to Vigo.

Mariquita persisted:

> You will come back, you with your fair Saxon beauty. You are
> part and being of this England – and soon you will be surfeited
> with sun, and slim brown bodies sunning swiftly to decay – and
> you will long to slake your thirst in green Surrey lanes, and on
> the hills of Gloucestershire. You will long for the coolth of apple
> bloom against your lips – and voilà! you will be home. But come
> quickly, my dear, and don't forget or regret Mariquita. Good
> night and Good luck, querido.

No wonder Laurie was gripped by wanderlust.

5

'Un vaso de agua'
1935–1936

IN JULY 1935, with knapsack, blanket and fiddle, Laurie boarded a Royal Mail Line ship from Tilbury for the two-day crossing to Vigo. He originally had a more ambitious aim, to go from Spain through France to Italy and Greece. And if he had not known, thanks to Sufi, how to say 'Déme un vaso de agua, por favor' ('Give me a glass of water, please') he might have headed directly for the Balkans. He knew nothing of Spain, but was untroubled by his ignorance. It was 'the most vivid time of my life, the most free, sunlit. I remember thinking, I can go where I wish, I'm so packed with time and freedom.' His first thought, stepping ashore, was how foreign it all was. The bricks and tiles were foreign. The donkeys brayed in a foreign language. But 'I felt it was for this I had come: to ... look out on a world for which I had no words; to start at the beginning, speechless and without plan, in a place that still held no memories for me.'[29]

When he awoke after a restless night on a green Galician hillside, he heard the shouts of women washing clothes in a stream, thumping them against the rocks, and singing: almost Moorish, open-air voices that carried from hill to hill.[30] He set out aimlessly in a south-easterly direction, towards Zamora. Everything was new and strange. He discovered the blistering intensity of the Spanish sun in summer, the hallucination-inducing thirst. 'Spain is no Arcadia,' as he said in his first radio broadcast about it, in 1946. 'It is harsh, raw, bare, savage, and almost entirely devoid of prettiness.'

Nobody could describe Laurie's adventure more memorably and evocatively than he did. Nor can every detail of his vagrant life be verified after eighty-five years. His diaries, with their graphic observations, their aural snapshots of peasant dialogue, which enabled him to write *As I Walked Out One Midsummer Morning* in 1968, were stolen from a BBC car in Segovia in 1969 – a cause of much later wretchedness. Did Laurie take the route he described, skirting the mountains of Leon and walking the valley of the Douro? Probably. His passport was stamped at La Linea on 22 September, so he reached Gibraltar after ten weeks of following a zig-zag route. A later diary mentions setting off from Toledo for Madrid, not vice versa, as in his book. John King,[31] who later retraced the journey with Laurie, by air and car, found the distances so vast that he suspected that Laurie might perhaps have hitch-hiked rather more than the two short car rides he admits to, into Valladolid and Madrid. (And so what? King shrugged.) But the weeks Laurie spent in Toledo, and in Almuñécar, where he spent two-thirds of his Spanish year, are heavily corroborated.

Annie was wretched with anxiety, she recalled later,

> wondering if you had enough to eat, and where you were, and where you slept. And I used to think perhaps the Spaniards were cruel and might kill you, & Jack & I were alone in the old home, for Tony was on his job travelling. That was when I started getting grey hairs. Those were cruel days to me.

It is as true today as in 1935 that you can travel miles over parts of Spain without coming across a village. Even from an exhilarating high-speed AVE train, there are vast, gaping vistas of plains, hills, and acres of olive groves. Even if Laurie's loping stride was covering twenty miles a day he would spend whole days in monotonous solitude. He was wearied by the bare, mile-high plain of Castilla, with boulders 'as big as churches' and air 'thin and clear as prayer'. His first night in a posada (a muleteers' hostel), sharing a noisy supper with carters and drovers, was the first of many such stops at ancient oak doors: 'Gorged with stew and warmed to idiocy by wine, I was a stranger but felt at home.'

It is easy to see why Laurie felt at home. The villagers who so hospitably welcomed 'el rubio', the blond young traveller, were just like the folks back in Slad, only shorter, darker, and poorer still. 'In a strange way I found it very like Gloucestershire. People seemed to be living the same kind of lives, sharing each other's dreams and passions and gossip, knifings in the back, and so on, but anyway living a coloured, red-blooded life in which they were all involved.' The farmers, the old crones, the children, reminded him of his villagers, 'the carters, innkeepers, the dust-covered farm-boys, grandmothers and girls'.

As he said in a broadcast he made in 1992:

> Here was I, a young boy, golden-haired and beautiful, appearing from nowhere and bringing music which meant happiness. The whole look on their faces changed. I couldn't go wrong.
>
> I was just a ragged minstrel, and they received me with medieval courtesy, gave me hospitality and asked me almost Homeric questions: what's it like in your town? what's the price of bread in your city? are you married? There was gossip, wine, and a kind of pride in hospitality and generosity which one can't experience again. The corruption of tourism has destroyed that.
>
> They lived hard and semi-starved lives, but if I unrolled my blanket ... and they saw my violin, their faces would soften and crease, there'd be a cry of ¡Música! ¡Música! They liked Schubert, strangely enough, but I'd play paso dobles and even the old ladies would dance a few creaky steps around the patio. The violin was a passport of friendship wherever I went, and I got to learn some of their old songs which made my life more intimately shared with them.[32]

The peasants taught him Spanish words and treated him like a child, miming offers of purple wine and stews of kid and beans at trestle tables, surrounded by woodsmoke, donkeys, dogs and pigs. Often he woke up lying on a rock in the bare mesa 'with a circle of cloaked figures quietly watching me, like a ring of crows'. He was the stranger within their gates. 'They asked for news from the outside world. They had this inquisitiveness. Now,' he said forty years later, 'the children rushing out to greet the stranger have been replaced by hundreds of Fiats, and the country is poisoned by TV soap operas, and will never recover.' But the romantic affection for the old Spain that began in 1935 intensified throughout his life, and resonates in every loaded phrase of *As I Walked Out One Midsummer Morning*.

In Zamora he met young itinerant German musicians from Hamburg: Artur the violinist, Rudi the accordionist and Heinrich the flautist. This prompted him to try living by his violin. He parted from the Germans after a drunken night at a village dance, and turned towards Valladolid because its name seemed so pleasing. In a village en route he collapsed with a fever in a blur of sunstroke. He was rescued – 'the first mouthful of mineral water burst in my throat like frosted stars' – and given a lift into Valladolid. In this baleful city of 'rancid shadows and scabby dogs, sweating pavements and offal-filled gutters', he acquired for half a peseta an elaborately worded licence to play his fiddle: it looked like a Royal Charter. As in Sussex, women were more generous than men.

Thereafter he played in markets, inns, cafés and the occasional brothel. From Segovia, where he slept beneath the Roman aqueduct, he crossed the Sierra de Guadarrama and only then, he said, did he feel 'really involved in Spain'. There is no doubt, said Laurie's Spain-dwelling fellow poet Ted Walker, that Laurie truly 'understood' Spain. 'He got the people, the topography, the richness, the attitude to life. If there's an afterlife I'd like to be part of a tertulia comprising Richard Ford, George Borrow, Gerald Brenan, Jan Morris, George Orwell and Laurie Lee.'

In August Laurie discovered Madrid, much smaller than Madrid today, and clamorous with tram-bells. The streets and bars he described are still there. In the Calle Echegaray, you can find the tapas bars he described: 'voluptuously' furnished, with varnished bullfight posters, and wine in stone jars, and prawns and pajaritos in little saucers. 'Stepping in from the torrid street, you met a band of cool air like fruit-peel pressed to your brow and entered a cloistered grotto laden with the tang of shellfish, wet tiles, and wine-soaked wood.' In Madrid he says he encountered 'a ripe young widow'. He also found a letter at the post office (filed under E for Esquire) from Molly Smart, alias Mariquita. She had received his letter, urging her to leave her job and join him. But from a thousand miles away, she sang her siren song about 'the grey Cotswold stone walls, the silver pillars of the beech trees, the low friendly soft drawls of Gloucestershire people…' She would share his gypsy life, were she not 'a soul in comfortable captivity': and besides, he must remember 'vers l'oubli' from Ford Madox Ford. One day he would come back 'and complete what was started on a hot July day on a Surrey hill'. 'When you return you will still be Laurie of the sensual mouth and your surprisingly white body will be tanned to corn gold.'

In Toledo, Spain's ancient imperial capital, forty miles south of Madrid, Laurie collapsed with a fever. Once recovered, he headed for the town's central square, the Plaza de Zocodover. He was playing his fiddle when he spotted a family group at a café table: the father a big, expansive figure in a hat, his wife demure in white. They were the poet Roy Campbell, his wife Mary, and their younger daughter Anna. It was Laurie's first meeting with a poet, and a blessed encounter. Campbell walked tall and talked tall, as Laurie later wrote.[33] He was the antithesis of the conventional image of the poet: physically exuberant, garrulous, one who held tables in thrall with his luminous eyes and his fantastical tales; but also deeply sensitive and wildly generous. More importantly, Mary Campbell was one of the Garman girls. Laurie could never have imagined then what a central place the Garman family would soon occupy in his life.

Mary was the eldest of the seven Garman sisters, daughters of the late Dr Walter Chancellor Garman of Wednesbury, Staffordshire. Dr Garman, whose profile was darkly aquiline, like a handsome Spanish don, had ruled his family – two sons as well as seven daughters – with an autocratic, even tyrannical, hand. Their mother was Irish, the illegitimate child of Lord Grey (and half gypsy, some said). The nine 'somewhat bizarre' children[34] – Mary, Sylvia, Douglas, Kathleen, Rosalind, Helen, Mavin, Ruth and Lorna – grew up in an Elizabethan manor house, Oakeswell Hall, with a retinue of maids, gardeners, nanny and governess – until suddenly impoverished by their father's death in 1923.

In 1920, Mary and her sister Kathleen had run away from the melancholy Midlands to London. Two strikingly beautiful girls, not yet twenty, with dark hair, large slanting green eyes and wide mouths, they were instantly noticed. The sculptor Jacob Epstein gazed upon them across the Harlequin restaurant in Beak Street, Soho, sent over a note, asked Kathleen to sit for him, and fell for her forthwith. The morning after their first night together, he modelled her head, and she remained his muse for ever more – becoming (as his mistress) mother to three of his children, and eventually Lady Epstein. (In 1922, Epstein's first wife, Margaret, called one day to confront Kathleen, and shot her in the shoulder; Kathleen staggered out into the arms of her brother Douglas, who happened to be walking by.)

Mary, who studied at the Slade, had a similar effect on the young South African poet Roy Campbell. In 1921, aged nineteen, Campbell was living near the sisters in Bloomsbury. One day Mary introduced herself to him in Charlotte Street. She was said to be a man-hater: but this 'only made it more of a challenge, more exciting', he wrote, 'and more of a responsibility to capture her for myself for ever. None of my very best horses were ever easy to break in.'[35] Campbell too fell in love instantly, a 'Dantesque sensation'. He went back to Regent Square with her and stayed three days and nights. They married at Oakeswell soon after, to the dismay of the cook: 'And I always thought Miss Mary would marry a gentleman with a park!'[36]

They spent their first married Christmas with Augustus John (who called Mary 'Little Lord Fondle-roy') in Dorset, and had uproarious evenings with the gypsies and with Francis Macnamara (father of Dylan Thomas's wife Caitlin, and of Nicolette, who will enter this story later). The Campbells went to live first in South Africa, then in Sussex, where Vita Sackville-West fell in love with Mary in the Weald village post office.[37] In 1928 Roy and Mary took their daughters Teresa and Anna to Martigues, called 'the Venice of Provence' because of its five canals. The Campbells arrived with £10. Vita sometimes sent them money, but Roy's aversion to all things Bloomsbury was fuelled by Vita's obsession with his wife.

In Martigues, the Campbells met a big, blond handsome half-Norwegian fisherman, Marius Jean-Baptiste Polge, known as 'Grandpère'. When Mary's younger sister Helen came out for a summer holiday in Martigues, she fell in love with Marius, married him, and had a daughter, Katherine Francesca – who would eventually become Laurie Lee's wife. So Roy Campbell's life and Laurie's were to be linked for ever, via the Garman girls.

Roy and Mary had one day decided to leave Martigues, 'fold our tents like Arabs, and as silently steal away', to Spain, where Roy could indulge in bullfighting, calling himself 'Ignacio Roig'. Arriving in Toledo in 1935, they rented a house under the cathedral wall. Mary, a recent and passionate Catholic convert (she was a Carmelite tertiary and had abandoned make-up, cigarettes, trousers, and wine except at meals), went daily to mass. But before supper they would always go to the Plaza de Zocodover. So here they were, in the hour of the paseo, when 'Laurie Lee made his debut in Toledan society'.

Anna Campbell, aged nine at the time, recalled the encounter in her memoir, *Poetic Justice*: 'At that hour the whole square came to life. The girls in their best dresses strolled back and forth, receiving compliments from the youths: "Adiós guapísima", and so on.' Laurie startled everyone by striking up sentimental Schubert songs. Soon the general chatter drowned the sound of his violin, but the Campbells could still see him sawing away, and felt rather sorry for the lad with sunburnt skin. Mary asked him in French whether he was German, and he replied in Spanish that he was English. Roy bade him sit down, and soon invited him back home, to dine in a central open courtyard, after which Anna 'danced like a firefly'[38] and Laurie and Roy sat up talking till dawn, Roy reading his poems 'The Sisters' and 'Horses on the Camargue'. 'Nothing could have suited me better at that hour, and at that place and time of my life. I was young, full of wine, and in love with poetry.'

Laurie stayed for a week, exploring Toledo, seeing El Grecos, sleeping on a mattress among sheaves of Roy's unfinished poems, listening to Roy in the evenings, singing and talking. (Roy was 'drinking like a madman' at that period – four litres of wine a day.[39]) 'He'd sailed whalers, swum Hellesponts, broken horses on the Camargue, fought bulls, and caught sharks bare-handed,' Laurie heard. He had quieter daytime discussions with Mary, who reproved Laurie for his atheism: 'I wanted the excitement of doubt, the satisfaction of mortality,' he wrote, 'the freedom to make love here and now on earth. Beautiful Mary would have none of it.'

(Ten months later the Campbells had to flee from Toledo when the city was temporarily taken by the Republicans; Roy, also a Catholic convert, took the side of Franco, whom he eulogised in his poem 'Flowering Rifle'.)

Having left the Campbells, Laurie crossed the Tagus and went on south, accompanied for a few days by a tramp – to Ciudad Real, Valdepeñas, Bailén, Córdoba, and followed the River Guadalquivir to Seville: 'Ever since childhood I'd imagined myself walking down a white dusty road through groves of orange trees to a city called Seville.' There he met a sailor who gave a dark hint of coming trouble. 'If you want to see blood, stick around – you're going to see plenty.' On to Jerez, to Cádiz of the tall narrow lanes, to windblasted Tarifa, and to raffish Algeciras, where he stayed two weeks for threepence a night, and which he later always pronounced his favourite hideout. On 22 September 1935 he reached Gibraltar, which, as he reminisced in a BBC film in 1962, 'crouched like a dog on the glassy sea … and after 500 miles of Spanish thirst I could almost hear the rattle of tea-cups'. He walked into Gibraltar, too broke to be persona grata, and was allowed to spend two nights in the police cells in Irish Town. After two days of English tea he was escorted back to the frontier, to carry on walking the coast road east from San Roque to Malaga.

The Costa del Sol is now an unbroken string of high-rise hotels, restaurants, discos, supermarkets – a byword in tourism for how not to develop a Mediterranean coast, almost obliterating any view of the sea. But in 1935 it was a primitive, winding road dotted with fishing villages: Estepona, San Pedro de Alcántara, Marbella, Fuengirola. 'At the time one could have bought the whole coast for a shilling.' He was in Almuñécar by the end of October 1935. And there, for the most part, he stayed.

Almuñécar (where the classical guitarist Segovia once lived) sits on the southern coast of Andalucía, subsisting since Phoenician times on its salted fish. What Laurie saw was 'a tumbling little village on an outcrop of rock in the midst of a pebbly delta, backed by a bandsaw of mountains'. It had been a Moorish stronghold, an Arab market town, and the main port of the kingdom of Granada. It fell to the Castilians in 1489 and a battered cross stands on an offshore rock celebrating the spot where the defeated caliphs sailed away when driven from Spain. But all past glories had faded by the time Laurie arrived. It was a town without distinction. He describes it as 'grey, almost gloomily Welsh. The streets were steep, roughly paved … and the square was like a cobbled farmyard. Part of the castle was a cemetery, part of the town hall a jail.'

It was a poor place, 'infected with fatalism, a kind of subdued and deliberate apathy'. Its matriarchal women and small bony menfolk had only two kinds of livelihood: the sugar canes ('rustling dryly in the wind') and meagre fishing. But a Swiss named Theodor Weiss Christien ('Herr Brandt' in Laurie's book) had built a hotel on the grey strip of sand that passed for a beach – in the hope of attracting tourists, but about thirty years too soon. Herr Weiss kept the

Hotel Mediterráneo open while the other hotel, the Palace, closed for winter, by offering thés-dansants, buffet suppers and musical concerts. He employed Laurie as odd-job man and as violinist in the saloon at night. So Laurie decided to hole up here for the winter.

He shared a room in the attic with a Jewish boy named Jacobo Meyer. Jacobo was interpreter, tout, boot-boy and gigolo, knew everyone, and played a nimble accordion, so he and Laurie became the hotel band. Laurie sent his mother a typed programme, today very faded: 'Programa del concierto de violin (Don Lawrence Lee) y piano (Don Jacobo Meyer) esta noche a las 10 en el Hotel Mediterráneo.' They played twenty pieces, including Schubert's Military March and several Spanish dances, serenades, paso dobles and tangos. The tune most requested was one called 'Río Rita'.

Laurie said years later that he befriended fishermen, waiters and

> some rather grand girls, fiercely chaperoned, who came down from Granada. One, Consuelo, wrote me a little poem. She wasn't allowed to speak to me because of her strict Catholic parents but her friend would pass me notes. The poem went to the tune of La Cucaracha. 'Tall compared to a poor stunted fisherman/Blond and handsome and slim/Is a boy who has arrived/to play the violin/in the Hotel Mediterráneo/He is called Lorenzo...' I'd never had a poem written for me [not strictly true] and I've adored her for ever. Her voluptuous face and huge dark eyes still haunt me. Consuelo is still one of my favourite names.[40]

One night in November, Laurie's violin playing was heard by the only guests in the hotel, a young English couple on their honeymoon. The bride had tonsillitis and kept to her room, but heard the strains of the music while her husband sat downstairs. Twenty years later in London, Laurie met the couple again: they were the architect Lionel Brett, later Viscount Esher, Rector of the Royal College of Art, and his wife Christian, famous beauty and a distinguished painter herself. The two had met when Lionel was still at Eton, and they were passionate travellers. After their wedding in October 1935 they made for southern Spain, where few tourists ventured. They travelled from Barcelona on buses full of chickens, aiming for Gibraltar, hoping to find a British hotel. The bride's new hide luggage took a battering as they rattled down the mountain roads into Almuñécar, which seemed a depressed and poverty-stricken place. Three decades later, when *As I Walked Out* had been published, the Bretts (not yet Lord and Lady Esher) realised that Laurie, whom they often saw at London literary and artistic gatherings, was the same boy who had played the violin in their honeymoon hotel.

There was brief euphoria in Almuñécar after the Socialist victory in the general election of February 1936, when censorship was lifted and a breath of freedom wafted through the Hotel Mediterráneo: the young fishermen and labourers came to dance, expressing their new liberty in blithe confidence that they were the masters now. Today, there is a small obelisk-shaped monument to Laurie Lee on the site of the hotel (demolished in 1980) and the township of Almuñécar has published a pamphlet[41] verifying Laurie's account of the town, quoting two ancient townsmen who recalled Laurie and all the characters he mentions: Manolo the waiter, Felipe the chef, 'Gambas' the crippled porter, and El Gato (Francisco Gutierrez Sáez, alias Frasco El Gato), a farm labourer who joined the anarchist group FAI. They thought they had been victorious in the election, as Laurie says; but 'the news was not victory for anyone, but a declaration of war'.

That spring, Sufi Rogers was also in Spain with her family, visiting her mother's native village in Asturias. Sufi tried to contact Laurie without success. When the Civil War broke out, the Rogers family had to escape on horseback through woods and byways to the Galician seaport of La Coruña, where street fighting was in progress: they waved their British passports and thankfully boarded a Royal Mail ship back home to England, and the Cotswolds.

But Laurie was departing for Algeciras, whence he sailed – with a friend[42] – for Morocco. His passport shows that he was in Morocco from 11 to 14 March 1936: it was because of this passport stamp that he was detained and questioned in Albacete during the Civil War, since Franco had used Morocco as his rebel base that spring. 'I'd been in the very nest of intrigue, but knew nothing about it ... We'd spent most of our time in the rooms of small hotels, behind shutters, smoking hash.'

At the end of April, Molly, full of come-hither desire for sun-browned Laurie, gave up her job at Sutton and decided she wanted after all to go abroad. Receiving Laurie's letter had made her throw off her clothes and gaze into her mirror.

> My eyes are alive Laurie, wary, a little mocking – and my shoulders are most vividly alive – you brushed them into awareness with your lips, so that the bloom of them is peach-smooth to kiss; my breasts are such small eager pulsing things, I think your hands were made to hold them amigo ... and my heart is beating a mad tattoo of desire!

She could hardly have made her meaning more clear. They must soon fulfil the promise they had made at Richmond. 'I think I want a child of yours more than I've ever wanted anything in my life before. Come to me soon Laurie querido ... Mariquita.'

No hope of that. Laurie had just formed a friendship with a female of a very different (and much more useful) kind. Wilma Gregory, a spirited Englishwoman aged forty-nine, had bought a house next to Almuñécar's church in Puerto de Granada (now the site of the town's Cultural Centre). Wilma was left-wing, literary, well-connected – she dined with the Laskis, knew the Roosevelts and had worked for Rebecca West – and her distinctive personality and determined temperament fixed itself on the young poet. Another lucky encounter for Laurie.

Wilma (née Meikle) was born in 1886, youngest of six sisters. With a scholarship to Somerville, Oxford, she fell in with Fabians, found herself 'quite good at public speaking', and went down without taking her degree to join the suffragists. In 1914 she offered her services to her heroine, Rebecca West, then living with H. G. Wells in Norfolk. In 1916 Wilma Meikle published a book, *Towards a Sane Feminism*, which Rebecca reviewed with unusual respect as 'one of the few feminist books that have a style': 'neither shrill nor frenzied, but musical as a little river of wit leaping from rock to rock of solid argument'.[43] By the time Rebecca had her baby Anthony (by Wells), Wilma – who had never done housework in her life – was installed as housekeeper-companion. Wells found Wilma intensely irritating and she got in the way of their lovemaking. 'You see ... we haven't much more than ten or twelve years more of love and naked-ness and all those dear things ... Clear Wilma out,' Wells wrote to Rebecca in 1916. 'She is an unreal, discontented person ... I shall be glad when she is married and off the menu.'[44]

Release came in September 1917 when Wilma married Theodore Gregory (né Guggenheim), a lecturer at the London School of Economics. The couple had little in common and it was a 'dreadful' marriage in Rebecca West's view. 'I was constantly bewildered, and felt more and more lonely,' Wilma recalled later to her sister. 'Well, in some ways I have always been lonely ... but marriage I found the loneliest state of all.' In 1930 Theo Gregory became a professor in Manchester, and the couple separated. So Wilma went travelling, accepting reluctantly an allowance from her husband but frequently cabling her sisters to send £10.

She lived in Madrid and in France and then, in 1936, arrived in Almuñécar, which she described to her sister as 'inconvenient for all forms of civilisation', but not without charm, 'once one has accus-tomed oneself to the surrounding filth'. Her flat was overrun with black beetles but it had wonderful views from the roof terrace, with a date palm silhouetted against the night sky.

> One has to put up with a picnic life ... One can buy nothing civil-ised in the village and Granada is 94k away, Malaga 84 by extremely slow bus on dangerous roads which stops at all the villages to

deliver the mails. But I find the village life rather fascinating and enjoy being on friendly terms with the peasants and fishermen.

It was a Communist region, living under Communistic regulations, but she employed a daily cleaning girl, and herself became medicine-woman to the village children, dispensing aspirin and disinfectants, 'my ignorance of medical matters being profound'. In a letter she claimed, 'I am the entire British colony of Almuñécar in my own person.'

Wilma was regarded by her family as difficult and prickly. But her letters reflect a woman of spirit and sometimes of pellucid if loquacious wisdom. She said she had a French cast of mind: she liked nothing better than argument, and logical discussion of abstract concepts. She also liked to take charge. And when she met Laurie, an aimless young wanderer with poetic and musical skills, she made 'the English boy poet' her protégé and nurtured him with leech-like devotion. 'I found him living as a vagrant,' she wrote, 'quite penniless & practically uneducated, with these really remarkable gifts for poetry & art & music, handicapped by frequent though slight attacks of epilepsy or "le petit mal".'

In May, as Laurie relates, tension in the village increased. His expedition into the hills, to take a mysterious message to a farmer about seed-potatoes (code for hand-grenades) is a tale rich in *ambiente*: he waded across a river on horseback which was 'like sitting on a cupboard' and found the farmer's wife ('squatting by the stove and tossing scraps of food to the pig') serving up a pot of migas stew: 'a thick porridge of maize sprinkled with dried sardines, tasting of sackcloth'. In June, his diary records how he left Almuñécar with his fiddle and busked his way in Granada, Almería, Luja and Murcia. The earliest account Laurie wrote about this was a 1941 piece for John Lehmann's *Penguin New Writing*.[45] He describes a night of playing his fiddle with frenzied and wine-soaked passion ('I am possessed by insane happiness') in a candlelit cellar full of clapping, stomping vineyard workers who sing wild laments of desolation and death.

till the cocks carve sharp
gold scars in the morning
and carry the stirring sun
and the early dust in my ears.

The citizens of Almuñécar confirm that the day after their unsuc-
cessful attempt to take Altofaro, a grand piano was burnt (as Laurie
later described), in the Plaza Mayor. Laurie describes seeing the
body of a young Falangist boy shot dead: his name was Julio Mateos.
The Communists took over sugar production at the La Fabriquilla
sugar refinery, and most of the holy images were taken from the
church to the beach of San Cristobal and tossed onto a great pyre.
'Everyone seems to be waiting for something… We live on rumours,'
wrote Laurie in his diary.

In England, Wilma's sisters wrote anxious letters to the Foreign
Office, with immediate results. On 7 August, W. H. Montague-
Pollock wrote from the FO: 'I am directed by Mr Secretary Eden
to inform you that Mrs Gregory was evacuated to Gibraltar on the
1st August.' Laurie's diary describes the excitement of the arrival
of a British destroyer in the bay, of meeting three naval officers
in Herr Weiss's hotel, and being told to pack up within ninety
minutes. The entire town gathered on the beach as Wilma and
Laurie boarded a small boat, then a launch, which stopped alongside HMS *Blanche*. 'The officers are charming,' wrote Laurie, 'but
do a considerable amount of drinking. I played to 'em a bit on deck.'
The warship delivered Laurie and Wilma to Gibraltar, whence they
sailed to Marseilles by P&O. They disembarked at Marseilles on 7
August, took a train to Paris, and on 9 August 1936 embarked at
Dieppe for England.

6

A Hovel with Acreage
1936–1937

LAURIE AND WILMA arrived home in August to an England 'snoozing under old newspapers and knotted handkerchiefs'. They were met at Victoria Station by Jack and his girlfriend Phyllis Hawke, from Stroud, and Laurie returned to Slad to receive 'the traditional cosseting of the prodigal'. But the homecoming soon palled.

Leaving Almuñécar had been a betrayal, he often said. He had stumbled on the war, by happening to be there: he had not chosen it as a cause. But he felt guilty about having abandoned Spain, 'already sealed off by the hypocrisies of non-intervention', and wanted to return to the friends he had made in those noisy cellars filled with music and political passion who now faced, he realised, a catastrophe. 'I might have given up the idea if I hadn't suddenly fallen in love,' he wrote, 'but the result of that experience, which went deeper than anything I'd known before, only made my situation all the more intolerable.'

This was the version of events he wrote thirty years later in the epilogue to *As I Walked Out One Midsummer Morning* – thus casually eliding the summers of 1936 and 1937 into one. In fact it was not until August 1937 that he met the woman with whom he fell so deeply in love and who made things 'intolerable'. A year passed before the *coup de foudre* struck – a year which he never later mentioned at all. He had no job and no wish to go home to Slad. So Wilma carried out the plan she had outlined in Spain. She found a place for them in Padworth, a hamlet twelve miles from Reading comprising a few knots of cottages, a great house, a small church and a rectory.[46] The legal description of Rosemary Cottage was 'hovel with acreage'. It was tiny, primitive and remote. No path led there; they had to wade across a swampy common, and beyond it lay nothing but woodland.

On Wilma's allowance from her husband, she would keep Laurie and enrol him in the art department of Reading University as a half-time student. She had paid for his passage home, and had reached London with only ten shillings in the world. The workhouse beckoned, she said, if she had not persuaded her bank manager to give her an overdraft of £10.

> I have practically adopted Laurie, the English boy I rescued from Spain, & he is living here as my nephew. It's pretty obvious that the village, from the rector downwards, are convinced that he is really my son: they say 'your son' and then politely correct themselves & say 'your nephew'. However, they all appear to be sympathetic – especially the rector – & no doubt think he was a 'war baby' & therefore excusable.
>
> He is a very nice boy to have about, most helpful & obliging, & of course I could not live alone in so isolated a cottage. On the other hand, I would not need to live in so primitive a place if I had not made myself responsible for Laurie. But I felt that someone had to do something to make sure that his gifts were not wasted, & there was nobody to do it save myself. Of his three talents, I think his poetry is the most important, but that is not a gift that can be trained, nor does it provide a livelihood; so we decided that art must be his standby.

If she lost her allowance (as she might if the new matrimonial law allowed Theo to divorce her for desertion) Laurie could get a well-paid job as a commercial artist. 'But he may turn out to be too good for that...'

The art department at Reading were impressed by Laurie's originality, and by his draughtsmanship. 'His lines have power & clarity & are drawn with extraordinary swiftness & ease. His fellow students call him the English Picasso,' wrote Wilma, '& the masters treat him with deference & beg him not to think it necessary to conform to their methods if he prefers his own.'

Rosemary Cottage was just three small rooms plus a cupboard serving as pantry and scullery.

> Outdoor earth closet & woodshed; nada más [nothing more] … we cook over the open fire, & keep the door open in all weathers; otherwise the fire smokes. The windows are so tiny that it's impossible to see one's reflection in a looking-glass, so we never have a notion of how we're looking, & the place is so dark that we have lamps or candles burning all day long. It's stuffy on warm days, & bitterly cold & damp on others. There are no shops, so we depend on tradesmen's carts. I don't much like the neighbourhood: it's flat, & I hate flat country, & there are pines, & I have always disliked pines.

Laurie had to walk two miles to catch a bus to Reading every day, leaving Wilma with the domestic chores – 'a deplorable waste of feminine intelligence, and of masculine intelligence too, since Laurie has to do an equal share'. Cooking, pumping water, heaving logs, and the 'terrific business' of keeping the fire going consumed whole days. So the odd couple rubbed along together 'in spite of our loathing of the English climate & of English towns & the English countryside & English people'. Wilma mothered Laurie, insisting on regular nourishment.

> He is liable to faint suddenly in the street or in a bus. One always has warning when an attack is threatened; he becomes very dreamy & rather stupid, as though dazed, & one just has to let him lie low for a day or two & see that he does nothing whatever.

Laurie soon found musical friends and formed a quintet. Wilma's chief amusement was a witchy black kitten that kept her awake at night by springing high in the air and dancing in circles in her bedroom.

Unlike Laurie's briskly organised benefactress, Molly/Mariquita was in an emotional muddle. She was still recalling Stratford (the magical strains of L'Après-midi over the Avon, the nightingales 'pouring liquid silver from their little brown throats'), despite being newly engaged to a scientist at Exeter University, Eric Rothwell from Oldham, whom she had met at Betty's twenty-first. Laurie poured scorn on this bourgeois move, which made her indignant. 'You didn't miss me in Spain,' she accused, 'though who would miss anyone with the sun bleaching one's eyelashes?'

She had been up to Edge, to consult the trees. 'And from every bole, little devil-faces – curiously like yours – grinned and whispered "Semi-detached", "Two children, one maid and a small car!" all in your voice.'

She protested in her defence that she and 'Roth' would be terribly poor. She was wildly jealous of Laurie's 'hovel with acreage'.

> It so vividly fits the description 'A cottage lone and still, With bowers nigh; Shadowy, my woes to still, Until I die.' More than anything in the world I want a cottage – crammed with books and a good radiogram. Is the offer of housekeeper still open? I can make chips, and pancakes – If I 'abscond' in the near future, may I abscond to you please?

Laurie's taunts about Molly's engagement 'ruined' her birthday in October. She had left his letter until last, as it was so fat and prom- ising among her flowers, books and fluffy lingerie. But Laurie had written with acid pen, mocking her cosy future.

By contrast, Laurie made Wilma's November birthday – her fiftieth – highly memorable. She wrote to her sister:

> The day began when I entered the sitting-room at 7.30 a.m. & found a huge fire already blazing & the room decorated with

paper ropes & festoons & union jacks from Woolworths, & my portrait (drawn a few days previously by Laurie) placed on the mantelpiece like a sacred icon, with lighted candles on either side of it &, beneath, a marvellous Spanish effusion of congratulations & affection.

Laurie's 'exotic foreign friends' from the university had arranged a birthday luncheon in Reading. The students presented Wilma with a clock, and made pretty speeches about not having thought her more than forty. 'We raced into Reading in a ramshackle, madly driven car belonging to one of them, & were very gay indeed; we almost forgot that we were in England.'

At Christmas Wilma packed Laurie off to Slad and was 'alone with the kitten, in the immense silence of our woods & swamps'. Laurie had had several bad turns recently, she reported, and had turned rebellious. He had ignored the master of the life class, yet the authorities insisted that his originality must on no account be warped: he must follow his own bent. 'Our sitting-room is hung with his productions; some of these seem to me a little nightmarish, but they are fun.'

Among the friends Laurie visited that Christmas – he did not call on Molly – were Sufi Rogers and her family, who were impressed by his compassion for the people of Spain resisting Franco's fascist forces, and his determination to go back. (Soon, most of the Rogers family returned to Buenos Aires, where Sufi married an Argentine. In 1978 there was a family reunion in Gloucestershire for Sufi's aunt Ethel Rogers's ninetieth birthday, when Laurie presented Ethel with a teapot.)

By January the cold weather and the hovel's discomfort drove Wilma to take digs at 80 London Road in Reading itself, 'a very dull town'. She wanted Laurie to see more of his friends, and not to brood on the Spanish troubles.

He has been talking of joining the International Column & though if I had a son of my own I should wish him to be among the defenders of Madrid, I think the case is quite different when

a boy has a chronic malady like Laurie's and has, besides, his
freakish talents for three arts.

In January 1937, Laurie did attempt to get away to Spain 'through
the proper channels', but was turned down. He told Molly of his
plan and she launched into one of her crazed flights – her heart was
broken into a million pieces, Laurie oh Laurielee, surely he could
not resist the spring? etc. 'You have been the well-loved stranger
within the gates of those who love you... Always we shall be grateful
to the gods for letting us know you.' Could she not come and work
as a nurse in Spain? 'We can never escape each other, Lorenzo mío.
For now, and always, Mariquita.'

By March she had packed her bag, walked out of her job and
given back to Eric Rothwell his emerald engagement ring ('please
don't crow!') Her letters became increasingly intense: 'Life's so
short Laurie – or is it terribly terribly long?' She resumed her old job
in Sutton, helping Mrs Whitelaw with her handicapped daughter.
While Nat Gonella played 'Georgia on My Mind' on the wireless,
she wrote beseeching Laurie to join her and Betty in London, to see
Shakespeare from the gallery of the Old Vic. The three were reunited
in June, and Laurie played the girls his Spanish songs. Betty had
willed it to be perfect, and she always got her own way. Molly, 'a little
mad tonight', imagined herself in Spain, a gypsy woman

> with dishevelled black hair, dark eyes, and a mouth red as the
> poppies in her hair, and brown bare feet, leaning against a great
> rock on a parched hillside singing those songs in a loud raucous
> voice ... Goodnight amigo. The wind will always blow you in
> my direction. Adiós, Mariquita.

But the wind never did blow them together – because Laurie was
about to fall seriously in love.

After his summer term ended, Laurie joined Wilma in July in
her caravan on the site owned by her family, the Lone Pine Camp

at Ferndown, near Bournemouth. She was fighting a losing battle with rats, which thrived on rat poison. She wanted her family to meet Laurie: her niece Rachel recalled him shambling shyly out of her aunt's caravan, looking much younger than his twenty-three years. As he later recalled, 'In my twenties I was thin, hungry, and gorgeous.'[47]

Wilma wrote him 'a stern auntish letter' as she had been trying 'to protect a succession of girls from Laurie's fascinations', including the clinging Molly, who had turned up in Reading. A doctor had told Wilma that chastity was impossible for Laurie: 'all epileptics are exceedingly sensual and passionate, and it's impossible to restrain them'. At the Lone Pine Camp, Wilma introduced him to other cara-vanners, who proposed taking him off to Cornwall.

It was there, on the beach at Gunwalloe on the Cornish coast, on 23 August 1937, that he encountered the beautiful and fascinating Lorna Wishart, and was bewitched.

Early that morning, Laurie was alone on the sands, playing his violin, when Lorna saw him while taking a walk. She stopped and said (like Miss Havisham to Pip), 'Boy, come and play for me.'

'She was married and had two young children,' he wrote in *As I Walked Out*. 'She was rich and demandingly beautiful, extravag-antly generous with her emotions but fanatically jealous, and one who gave more than she got in love.' She was also the sister of Mary Campbell. It seems a preposterously Dickensian coincidence that he should meet by chance a second Garman girl within two years, but there it is.

Lorna was twenty-six, the youngest and by general consent the most beautiful of all the Garman sisters, born 11 January 1911. She was twelve when their father Dr Walter Garman died, at which point life at Oakeswell Hall – piano lessons before breakfast, and prayers with the maids – dramatically altered. Lorna was at boarding school, hating it; she jumped over the tennis net with glee when she heard about the death of her father which meant she could leave. The family had relied totally on Dr Garman's income. His wife was a dreamer;

it was the governess, Miss Thomas ('Tony'), who took over and kept the children fed and clothed. They had the run of their father's well-stocked library, but the younger ones went somewhat wild.

So Lorna, unrestricted by parental rule, enjoyed exceptional freedom in her teenage years, 'roaring about Herefordshire [where her mother now lived] going to dances on the back of boys' motor-bikes'.[48] When she was fourteen, her brother Douglas, who was reading law at Cambridge (along with Salvador Allende, future President of Chile), brought home his friend Ernest Wishart – always known as 'Wish' – and Lorna seduced him in a hayrick. At the age of sixteen, in 1927, she married Wish, and at seventeen had her first son, Michael. Wish was a Communist, but a rich one. His father, Sir Sidney Wishart, Sheriff of the City of London, had extensive farming estates in Sussex. The newly married Wisharts first shared a house with Gerald Barry, editor of the *News Chronicle*, in Brunswick Square, Bloomsbury, and Wish formed a publishing company, Wishart & Co. (later the Marxist publisher Lawrence & Wishart). In 1925 he had founded the literary monthly *The Calendar of Modern Letters*, edited jointly by the radical poet Edgell Rickword and Lorna's brother Douglas Garman.

'My mother, who was almost a child, treated me as a doll,' Lorna's son Michael wrote in his memoirs.[49] Having married so young, Lorna was ready, when she met Laurie, to catch up on the youthful fling she had missed. 'When Lorna discovered her powers,' her daughter said, 'a floodgate opened. She was wild; she was rampant.' For Laurie that summer day in Cornwall, a glance from her blazing blue eyes was enough, as in Browning's 'She should never have looked at me/If she meant I should not love her.' 'We Garman girls all have these eyes,' Lorna's niece Anna Campbell told me. 'They arrest people's attention. They are very large: "Ils dévorent sa figure," as a French woman said of mine. They seem to drive people (and not only men) slightly dotty.'

Men were constantly falling head over heels in love with Lorna. The writer Llewelyn Powys, for one, was locked in adoration. She had an extraordinarily magnetic, seductive power. Molly and Betty, who met her later, found her 'staggeringly beautiful and most unconventional'. (Lorna told the homely Betty: 'I was jealous of you until I met you – and now I'm not.') 'And of course money was no problem to her,' Betty told me, 'while we were all relatively poor. She gave off a flavour of strength, or concentration – like a strong whisky. It may or may not have been goodness, but it was certainly concentrated.'

'I adored my mother,' her son Michael wrote. He remembered lying in bed on summer evenings as a boy.

> My mother leans over me. Dressed for dancing in clinging sequins, which sparkle like her vast ultramarine eyes, she resembles a sophisticated mermaid. Embryonic Oedipus receives the kiss of life. After mother's departure, I bury my face into the cool pillow where the scent of Caron's Fleurs de Rocailles lingers. I listen for the familiar purr of the chocolate-brown Bentley, crunching on the gravel driveway. My mother, always alone, is speeding through the darkling hawthorn heading for nightclubs which assume, in my half-asleep loneliness, vague Xanadus of Kubla Khan…

Lorna had innate style: everything she did seemed to create an aura of romance. 'It was more than charm; she illuminated everything around her,' said her former daughter-in-law Anne Dunn. 'She was a transformer: if she looked at something it seemed to gain merit in one's eyes.' As a girl she had been absurdly shy. But she learnt to intimidate shopkeepers and waiters, and could at times turn almost sadistically cruel. Laurie's diary, later, describes Lorna having words with a restaurant manageress over a dish of curry. 'L's tactics are brilliant, witty, and so unexpected, so unwomanly if you like, that her opponents are invariably annihilated.'

Those who knew Lorna described her as 'androgynous', 'feline', 'lynx-like', 'a tiger-woman'. Later, Lucian Freud painted her in an ocelot coat, which compounded the resemblance. She was tall and lean, and moved with a graceful feline stride: she loped, she prowled, slightly round-shouldered, head down. She was athletic, physically fearless, loved walking, lived out of doors, swam in the sea in winter, had picnics on Boxing Day, rode proficiently and drove fast. Her husky voice had the rasp of gin and cigarettes. Laurie found her irresistible.

Laurie wrote, four years later,

> Her small head is most unusual & really beautiful, half-boyish because of her hair, half-Latin because of her eyes, strong in colour, cared for and yet with a slightly rough casual beauty about it. I feel she should be the wife of a very brilliant artist, or the slave of some old sensual Indian poet. Only such men would properly appreciate her.

A very Garman assumption – that women should be muses and acolytes to creative men.

At first, during the Cornish holiday, Wish and Laurie got on well together. Wish, who apart from his political dedication to Communism loved trees and kept bees, was a gentle, intellectual man of integrity and considerable patience. He was determined to hold the family together, as he watched his wife falling in love with Laurie. And Lorna, ultimately, was dependent on Wish. Having lost her father, she needed a corner of stability in her life; Wish, nine years older, was her rock.

Fifty years later, journalists tried to discover the identity of the mysterious woman who had sent him pound notes soaked in Chanel No. 5 when he went off to the Spanish Civil War. One, William Greaves, asked Laurie in 1987, 'Who is the unnamed woman whose passionate attentions enlivened the weeks between leaving Spain and returning across the Pyrenees to rejoin the Civil War?' 'How devious of you to notice,' replied Laurie. 'I don't think I've ever been asked. It's right at the tail end of the book. What very nice salmon this is.' Had he met her since? persisted Greaves. 'That's another book,' said Laurie, 'which may be written one day.'

'For a septuagenarian with a memory as acute as it is poetic,' commented Greaves, 'Slad village school's most famous old boy has strangely uncharacteristic moments of absent-mindedness.'[50]

One evening soon after they met, Laurie confided to Lorna that he planned to go back to Spain. Perhaps he thought it would be a way of impressing her.

> Of course, I tried to persuade her that I would be doing it for her, but this wasn't true and she knew it. All the same, it was partly our entanglement that drove me, the feeling of over-indulgence and satiety brought on by too much easy and unearned pleasure...

Meanwhile Wilma, knowing nothing of Laurie's new emotional entanglement, was arranging to take him to France, to study at the École des Beaux Arts in Montpellier. He claimed later, in *As I Walked Out*, that 'I worked my way down through France, heading in the direction of the Pyrenees', but in fact Wilma took him to France, and paid his train fare. In September 1937 – just as brother Jack was leaving Slad to attend the Regent Street Poly, and to live in Laurie's old digs in Putney – Wilma and Laurie sailed from Southampton to Le Havre, and took the train to Paris, where they paused to see Picasso's *Guernica* in the Spanish pavilion of the Exposition Internationale, which Laurie found 'incredibly vivid and moving'. The drawings of the war were 'stark scrawls of hate, as if each stroke of the pen & brush were oaths torn from their guts against the marauders'. He felt 'sick at all that has happened and the vast reproach of my having lifted not a finger to help'. Now at least he was going south; he would wait for his opportunity.

At last they were in Montpellier and arrived, exhausted, at Le College des Écossais, a grand folly built by the botanist Sir Patrick Geddes. The barrack-like building, part Scottish baronial and part Provençal château in style, was now a hotel. It had huge libraries and salons and enormous bedrooms, and a meagre staff of housekeeper, cook and gardener, though the garden was like a desert. It was cheap, thanks to the ill-health of the franc. Wilma wrote to her sister, 'The only guests are a mad Russian woman doctor of psychology, a young French engineer, Laurie & myself.'

Laurie launched himself into the French language with bold insouciance. Wilma reported that 'twelve days ago he had not uttered a word of French in his life. He is making excellent progress, having no social timidity whatever, so that blunders do not distress him in the smallest degree.' Old Colonel Russell, the author of *Brighter French*, was giving him a daily lesson for a risibly small sum. The French engineer played the piano to accompany Laurie on his violin, while Wilma and the mad Russian woman listened, 'and the rest of the day, the boy is producing with amazing rapidity more & more remarkable drawings'.

Observers may detect here, as Wilma did not, the frantic energy and glowing aura of a lover with a plan. The sensual weather amplified his 'torturing sexual dissatisfaction'. 'There is the idiotic Lorna frustration,' he told his diary, 'and the frustration of being so near the frontier of Spain and yet so far from being in a position to cross it.' Above all he hated 'living in comparative luxury which is not the result of my initiative. I think I am really more happy chewing on a crust in a ditch, a crust which I have earned in some manner, than I am sitting down to a heavy meal in a clean shirt all of which are the mere products of kindness.' He was due to enrol at the École des Beaux Arts in October. But by then, the hotel's threadbare comforts had lost their charm, and Wilma decided they should move on to Perpignan, though she suspected, rightly, that he might try to smuggle himself across the Pyrenees. She had told him that he was far too late to enlist, that his 'malady' would debar him from any army, that they did not want more volunteers. 'But Laurie will not believe without definite proof that it is impossible for him to cross the frontier & join the International Column.'

Again she declared that if he were her son, and healthy, she would want him to fight. Since he was neither, she felt even more responsible. 'He would almost certainly get shell-shocked, and his health depends on his being well fed and not undergoing any strain.' Laurie had become cocksure, she said, having been persuaded by a doctor that he could control his condition by willpower. 'He forgets that his improvement since last March is due to the care I have taken of him… When he was living the vagrant life in Spain, ill-fed and inadequately clothed, he had many fits.'

To distract him, Wilma typed out Laurie's poems and sent them to T. S. Eliot at Faber & Faber. Eliot replied on 9 November 1937 to Wilma in Montpellier – a model letter of polite rejection:

Dear Madam,

I have read your long and interesting letter about your young friend Laurie Lee, and sympathise with your interest and anxieties about him.

It is with regret that I must say that his poems do not seem to me, so far, remarkable enough to justify our undertaking their publication. This is, however, only the opinion of one man, who often feels that excessive reading of manuscript verse may have dulled his sensibility, and I therefore advise you to make a fresh attempt elsewhere. I suggest your showing the poems to Mr Richard Church of Messrs J. M. Dent & Sons, Aldine House, Bedford Street, WC2. I shall not meanwhile mention to Mr Church the fact that I have seen these poems.

Yours very truly,

T. S. Eliot.

But within days of their arrival in Perpignan, without telling Wilma, Laurie left their hotel and caught a bus, headed not for the Pyrenees but for Martigues. Wilma was utterly perplexed: she had just spent 260 francs on Laurie's carte d'identité and he had left behind the warm clothing she had bought him that very day, in which to travel to England.

But Lorna had telephoned one evening – 'her warm voice is like an electrical disturbance', Laurie writes – and announced that she was coming to France with her mother, Marjorie Garman, to pay a visit to her sister Helen in Martigues.

It was there that Laurie first saw Helen Garman's daughter Kathy, 'a stumpy, wriggly, golden-curled little girl of five, who spoke a slurred incomprehensible French dialect'.[51] Helen, as recounted earlier, had gone out to visit her sister Mary in 1929, and had met and married a handsome fisherman named Marius Polge, a friend of Roy Campbell, son of a Norwegian sea captain. Tall and blond, 'like Jean Marais only better looking',[52] Marius stood out from the other fishermen, who were small and dark; he was 'like a god'.

There is a photograph taken that week in Martigues: of dashing young Laurie holding little Kathy (a solemn, intelligent-looking child) on his knee, in the garden of Helen's house above the Étang de Berres, the lake whose canals link it to the Mediterranean. In the original picture, there was another figure beside Laurie: Kathy's Aunt Lorna.

> I remember the child sitting in my lap … squirming her plump body against me and looking up at me with brilliant slit eyes of squinting blue [which] studied me with intense regard. I don't know who she thought I was – this crumpled 22-year-old English stranger – but it was then, she swears, she decided to marry me.

Laurie wrote this in his 1983 book *Two Women*, a celebration of his wife Kathy and daughter Jessy. He does not say that he and the child's Aunt Lorna were then enjoying an ecstatically amorous Provençal interlude, 'drugged with coffee, sunlight, tobacco, pine resin, fever and l'amour…' as a later diary recalls. In *As I Walked Out*, he describes how his rich girlfriend 'suddenly turned up again' to give him 'a week of passionate farewell. A week of hysteria too – embracing in ruined huts, on the salt-grass at the edge of the sea, gazing out at the windswept ocean while gigantic thunderstorms wheeled slowly round the distant mountains … Our love was more violent than ever.'

Having taken a bus to Martigues, Laurie had waited for hours in a café before Lorna arrived. Suddenly he saw her, 'standing under a lamp in a camel-hair coat with no hat on … She ran towards me.' They sat drinking endless bocs and coffees as

> the leaves of the plane trees fell slowly one by one onto the table like heavy isolated drops of rain before a thunderstorm. Looking at her across the table I caught her eyes as I would catch her hands & she seemed gay & alive and sometimes unhappy and very much in love and prepared to be in love. She was so prepared that I felt completely in love and impatient of café tables and the sight of drink and people.

At Helen's house Laurie met Lorna's sister, and the fisherman husband Marius, and her mother Marjorie. At first Laurie was put up in a coal-storage room under the house, and Lorna crept from her hotel at dawn to join him, startling the several cats purring contentedly on his bed. Suddenly the cats leapt up and shot out of the window.

> I hear footsteps and L comes in. It is hardly light but her eyes are quite distinct & her mouth is like a lamp. She takes off some of her clothes & slips into the bed beside me. My brain is drowsy but my body is fresh & awake. It has been cold under those scant blankets but now I feel I am standing naked in front of a fire. The old iron bedstead creaks & slides against the wall, the sheets are swept into a heap by our active legs. Her hair is sweet smelling, I swim in her mouth & her nails in my flesh are like a bitter wind … am brilliantly aware of my vitality & the vitality of the woman with me. And then Gladys, with a loud clatter of buckets, comes in to collect some coal.

Laurie soon moved to a hotel in the town, giving free rein to their raptures.

We do more than make love. The intimacy of our bodies has already been established. One can achieve that intimacy with a stranger in a half hour of darkness. But we arrive at an incredible intimacy of mind, an intimacy I have never attained with another woman. There is none of that continual combat of lovers, that weighing of words, that thoughtful pre-meditation ... With L there is an end to artifice and feminine wiles.

He felt no need to sift a thought before uttering it to her. Sometimes, Lorna said, she almost regretted the lack of by-play and foreplay: 'But I think our passion is too bloody true to need such artificial stimulus. And she knows it & I know it. I have often written earn-estly before and lived to regret it. I wonder if I shall ever grow cold reading this. I don't think so.'

It was in Martigues that he began to write lyrically about his feelings,

dazed by all this beauty the pale swift greens, blues and yellows outside & the quick beauty of this woman under my hands. She is the dryest tinder and a touch will strike her with more passion than most women could muster in the whole of their lives. She is so extremely ripe and soft yet strong under one's thighs ... There is no brutal struggle in loving her, she is open & warm like a strong wine that is mature. At last I am sexually complete because instinctively she knows the rhythm of my body & can sense the temperature of my desire, she is as deep and as receptive as any imagined woman of the mind, I go down to her easily & mightily and she takes every inch of me, & her whole form is so poised & perfect that not drop of the glory I feel is spilt but she receives me whole & gives back to me all I have outlined in fire & splendour. Her movements under me are a deft delight and for the first time in my life I experience the true measure & grace of love.

This surfeit brought on one of his fevers: Lorna chose to stay and sleep with him in sweat-soaked sheets. The days were timeless and the nights endless, light and dark passing unnoticed. He was aware only of Lorna, soothing him. 'Endlessly I discover her, or does she discover herself to me? What she doesn't tell me with her lips she tells me with her body.'

There is a draft of a letter to Lorna in this 1937 diary: a letter probably written before Lorna arrived in France, warning her of his plans. 'But I might whisper to you that soon I think I shall have to throw up this comparative luxurious way of living for the harsher more vital thing. That person I knew in the streets, he was filthy & hungry & happy. I haven't forgotten him – and I won't!'

But in November, Lorna had to return to England and Laurie went back to Perpignan. 'I shall wait here till the end of the month and then try my luck,' he wrote on 15 November. So in December 1937 Laurie set off alone to Ceret on the Spanish border, leaving poor Wilma in Perpignan anxious, bewildered and very angry.

7

A Winter of War
1937–1938

FOR WRITERS AND poets there is no more passionate interlude in twentieth-century history than the Spanish Civil War. It was never simply a struggle between left and right. A people's government, intent on ending poverty and inequality, and on bringing freedom of the press and education to the masses, was challenged by an alliance of the military, the aristocracy and the Church, with Nazi Germany and Fascist Italy on their side. And they murdered poets. Federico García Lorca was one of hundreds murdered in 1936. The British government remained neutral, and for writers, Spain became an irresistible cause. George Orwell, John Dos Passos, André Malraux, Stephen Spender, Arthur Koestler, Ernest Hemingway, Simone Weil, W. H. Auden and Miles Tomalin all went out to Spain, and wrote about it. Gerald Brenan was already there. Churchill's nephew Esmond Romilly, and the artist Paul Hogarth, went out at the age of eighteen. Julian Bell enlisted as an ambulance driver and was killed in Spain at twenty-nine: his aunt Virginia Woolf wrote to her sister: 'I suppose it's a fever in the blood of the younger generation which we can't possibly understand…'

Enlisting to fight in Spain was punishable in Britain by two years' imprisonment. Yet 2,000 British men fought on Spanish soil, and 500 failed to come back. Volunteers slipped into Spain from all over Europe and North America, most crossing the Pyrenees at night, arriving footsore and frozen, to be greeted by shouts of '*salud*' and '*no pasarán*'. Some were lured by the adventure. But after the

horrific casualties at the battle of Jarama in 1937, new arrivals knew
that death or injury was very likely.

Laurie was neither politically obsessed nor the belligerent type.
He always said that he had gone to Spain because he felt guilty for
having left; he had a debt of honour to his Spanish friends. This was
true. But he was also making a supremely romantic gesture straight
out of the medieval lays of courtly love.

Though alone, Laurie was one of 912 volunteers who crossed
into Spain in December 1937. 'Laurie slipped across the frontier to
join the International Brigade last Sunday,' Wilma wrote to her sister
from her hotel in Perpignan on 12 December, 'but as yet there is no
means of communicating with him.'

She admired the boy's pluck, but she was furious. He was
throwing away his chances, making the last sixteen months a waste
of her time and money. 'He has not behaved quite fairly to me,' she
said, 'for it seems now that his whole object in coming to France was
to find his way to Spain.' She thought he had given up 'the Spanish
scheme', and would return to London with her, 'until', she added
angrily, 'a stupid romantic woman in England, who has fallen wildly
in love with him, telephoned one night'.

> The woman had been telephoning from England night after
> night, to Montpellier while we were there, & to Perpignan
> after we moved here, regardless of expense in the Windsor-
> Simpson style. That morning, we had bought warm clothing,
> for England; that night he was once more determined to go to
> Spain. The telephone conversation that night decided things,
> & my own opinion is that the boy was scared stiff by the wild,
> romantic, preposterous situation created by her, & fled to Spain
> to escape it.

(How wrong Wilma was. Lorna's call that November night told
Laurie that she was coming to the south of France and would meet
him at Martigues.) Six years later Laurie wrote in his diary for 13

December 1943: 'Six years ago, almost to the day, I crossed the frontier into Spain. What proud, muddle-headed days they were!'

As to how he had managed to get over the border, Wilma had learnt that it was 'quite easy':

> One gives a guide a tip to conduct one across the frontier; at night, the guard waits until the French guards have passed, then beckons, and one slips across. At the other side one meets the Spanish guards, gives up one's passport to them and one is sent to Barcelona if one is volunteering for military service.

Wilma's days and nights of misery, imagining Laurie lost in a blizzard, or having fallen and died of exposure, had been, it seemed, 'unnecessary'.

At this point in her letter, Wilma broke off to answer the telephone: it was 'the romantic lady' (Lorna), assuring her that Laurie would soon be sent back, since foreign volunteers were no longer accepted by the Spanish government. But Wilma was sceptical. 'She has made such a mess of things for my poor foolish Laurie,' she added caustically to her sister, '& maybe it's my prejudice that made me dislike her voice on the telephone; I was surprised that so musical a boy had ever been attracted by her.'

Despite her anxiety, Wilma undoubtedly relished the busybody role she now assumed to get Laurie out of Spain. She wrote to Clement Attlee ('Major Attlee was kindness itself. He is all stirred up & ready to insist on your immediate return by the Spanish Government,' she wrote to Laurie) and to Harry Pollitt, head of the British Communist Party, who was leaving for Barcelona. She badgered the Spanish consul, the police, the left committees, and sent letters all across Spain from Barcelona to Valencia, addressed to 'an English volunteer named Laurence Edward Alan Lee', with a description of him in Spanish, and the fact that he carried a violin. She got the Spanish consul to write to Indalecio Prieto, Spanish Minister of Defence, about Laurie's epilepsy. She rang Jack, insisting he go to Laurie's doctor in Reading to get a medical certificate saying he was unfit for military service. Incapable of writing a short letter, she wrote to Laurie at enormous length every day, sometimes twice.

Though annoyed, she made allowances: epilepsy made people volatile 'and also damned obstinate'. 'The boy simply can't help it, and one must accept him as he is: exceedingly troublesome, not always candid, but honest, warmhearted and very lovable.'

Wilma was right to anticipate the likelihood of fits. Laurie had already had two, as recorded in the rather laudatory International Brigades file written at Tarazona on 23 December 1937:

Laurence A. Lee. English. Age 23. Arrived in Albacete 15.12.37.

Father civil servant employed by British Government in their Customs and Excise Dept. His mother's address: The Slad, Stroud, Gloucestershire.

Has no fixed profession, but has worked as a clerk.

Was studying commercial art, with view to making it his proffession [sic]. Was studying at Reading University. Went to France on Sept 18th ostensibly to continue studies, actually to come to Spain.

His own statement:

'I stayed a while in Montpellier, and then moved to Perpignan and from Perpignan slipped through to Ceret and across the Pyrenees on Sunday 5th December.'

He did not come through the usual channels. He had tried to do so in January of this year when things were much stricter and he was turned down. He gives recommendations which seem to show that he is perfectly reliable. One of the men he knows is the present Commander of the British Battalion [i.e. Fred Copeman, strike organiser on the Putney building site, now attached to the staff of the 15th Brigade]. We have not yet been able to check this, however. His reason for avoiding normal channels is that he did not want to be turned down and did not want anybody to go to the expense of sending him out, because he could not be sure of his physical fitness for the fighting out here. He paid his own fare out, and has enough cash to pay his own fare back if necessary.

He was in Spain from July 1935 to August 1936. He was then at Almuneca [*sic*] near Motril. He says that they were then shelled occasionally and this brought on the epileptic fits from which he suffers. Because of this he was evacuated by a British destroyer in August of 1936. His sympathies however were all with the Republic and he resolved to come out as soon as he had recovered. As stated above he tried to come in January, but was turned down.

After a year without any fits, he thought he was perfectly OK and decided to come definitely and here he is.

He had two epileptic fits in Figueras, which he attributes to the increased excitement of being in Spain and of his journey over the mountains.

He seems to be a fairly good violinist and artist. At present he is assisting in the cultural work at Tarazona.

It seems clear that … being, generally speaking, physically weak, he will not be of any use at the front. He agrees that the added excitement would be too much for him.

On the other hand he seems a perfectly sincere comrade, who is very sympathetic to the Spanish Government.

His family at home are making a great deal of trouble at him being here and are demanding his return.

It was on Christmas Day at the Hôtel Regina in Perpignan that Wilma had her first letter from Laurie, written ten days earlier. 'All the loads in the world fell from my mind when I got your letter this morning,' Wilma wrote. 'Darling Laurie, you've no idea what a to-do we have made in our efforts to find you, and how we worried the authorities in England, France and Spain. I had nightmare days & nights imagining you lost in the Pyrenees.' She had now telegraphed Lorna and Annie; and Jack was with Annie, 'but poor Lorna has nobody and her letters are terribly unhappy ... what can I say to console her?' Laurie told her he had reached Valencia, and was going to Albacete. 'I am very much relieved to hear that Albacete is a training centre, and that you certainly will not be sent to the front for several months yet.' She wondered why he had no regimental number, if he had joined the International Brigade?

Once again she urged him to return. In hand-wringing style ('Oh Laurie, my dear, my very dear Laurie!') she blamed herself for bringing him to France. Annie and Jack would never forgive her; only Lorna (now considered 'sweet and brave') understood. If only he would be ill again, so she could take him home. As Wilma told her sister, she was contemptuous of young men such as her Bournemouth nephews, who remained in comfort at home instead of volunteering to fight fascism in Spain. Laurie knew she considered physical courage the most important quality in men. He might even have found it humiliating, she conceded, to be constantly reminded by her that his 'malady' would exempt him.

Then Laurie's doctor in Reading confirmed this: having Laurie withdrawn against his will, he said, might be more damaging to his ego and nervous system than a prolonged exposure to war. 'So I had to send telegrams and air-mail letters all over the place cancelling my demands for his return.'

Meanwhile Lorna had been to see Harry Pollitt before he left for Barcelona, '& he promised to try to find you,' Wilma told Laurie, 'to ask if you could be transferred to non-combatant work. I'd pray, if I had anything to pray to, that this may have been managed.' She might even try to intercept Pollitt at Barcelona Station herself.

The news of the Republican advance at Teruel was 'magnificent', said Wilma. (The battle of Teruel, the grim, walled city high on rocky bluffs, known for its hard winters, had begun on 15 December, in bitter cold, eighteen degrees below zero. A four-day blizzard left four feet of snow: men on both sides suffered frostbite, and lacked water, food and medical supplies, as trucks were stalled and planes grounded. In early January Teruel was taken, a victory widely reported and celebrated.) Perhaps, said Wilma, this would make Conservative circles in England realise that they had backed the wrong horse in encouraging Franco. 'Oh, the harm the present British government has done & continues to do, all over the world! Ethiopia & Spain & China have all been their victims.'

No real aunt or mother could have fussed more over her boy than 'your loving aunt, Wilma'. Was he getting enough to eat? Could she send thick socks and shirts? A good coat with a sheepskin lining? An overcoat and warm trousers would await his return to Perpignan. A medical certificate too, if he wished to be released. If he had lost his violin, she would buy him another. Also a new camera, she promised. She was planning a Christmas in the mountains, with skiing lessons for him. 'You are very brave & splendid, but I'd so much rather you were safe. Bless you my darling! … As soon as you return, we'll move on, don't you think? You see, darling, I am sure you won't be able to stand the strain much longer.'

What was Laurie doing all this time? As the contemporary documents show, he had arrived with a motley crew of International Brigade volunteers at Figueras, and had been taken to Albacete. He had arrived in Spain at a time when the 15th Brigade was acutely short of British volunteers, and the war was running against the Republic.

An undated handwritten report from Figueras says:

> I will say of the whole group of English only about 6 of them may
> be loyal, the rest I class as opportunists and adventurers, they may
> be alright but they need a lot of lecturing, particularly on morale,
> as they dont no [sic] what it mean's [sic], this is the best report I
> can give in plain words, I hope it is satisfactory, I will add that this
> group was a disgrace to all the other comrade's [sic] (foreign) I
> wish you will report the matter to the Party in London…

The report is signed 'Fraternally yours, Comrade R. Doyle'. Bob Doyle was a bold young Dubliner who had stowed away on a boat from Marseilles to get into Spain, and later in 1937 took a party of volunteers across the border from Carcassonne. Over the page he goes on: 'Also I report that Comrade Laurence Lee has on two occasions of the journey taking some kind of fits. I may add that this Comrade's conduct was excellent, that although weak he showed his willingness to comply with regulations.'

On a list compiled by the Figueras Delegation of the International Brigades of comrades sent to Albacete, dated 11 December 1937, are the names of Booth, Buckley, Corbett, Goodison, Kenna, Smith, Tompkins – and Lee, Laurence.

Another report is from Constantino Dubac,[53] also denouncing the drunken and undisciplined behaviour of Messrs Booth, Corbett, Smith and Tighe – 'No political understanding, only adventurists going after three meals a day.' 'Undesirable.' 'Rotten, lumpen element.' 'Now at Pontones with venereal disease.' 'Deserted from Jarama.' 'Rotten, absolutely demoralised element.' His report (dated 15 December) goes on:

> Lawrence Lee [sic] suffers from epilepsy. He has had an attack at Figueras after one year of normalcy. His conduct is exemplary, willing to do his best for the revolution. Politically a communist. He can, I think, be used to great advantage at some base where the work is not strenuous as he seems a responsible person and trustworthy.

Laurence Lee is listed as arriving at the Tarazona base on 16 December 1937. That morning, No. 2 Company was being trained in bayonet practice, grenade-throwing and Spanish. The next day, 17 December, a handwritten report has the following entry: 'Departures: Lee to Culture by Personnel Office.'

On 28 December the Cultural Commission was instructed to send 'Comrade Lee' and others to see the doctor 'between the hours 1 and 4'.

By 1 January 1938, news of Laurie reached Wilma, still in Perpignan. She had now found out that Laurie had 'a very bad fit' two days after his arrival in Valencia, she reported to her niece. She and Jack had renewed their appeals to Major Attlee for his return. Because of the fit, Laurie had been refused admission to the International Brigade, and was now attached to the Spanish Red Cross, or rather, to the Socorro Rojo at Albacete, on the high plateau.

From here Laurie told Wilma, who had warned him what Spanish winters could be like, that the cold was worse than any he'd ever known: snow, sleet, morning fog, terrific winds, and no mountains to give shelter. All over Europe, it was one of the severest winters in memory. Old people in Perpignan were dying of cold, and there was ice all day long in the darker streets. An American woman in Wilma's hotel, whose son-in-law had gone to Teruel, reported on 2 January that two American journalists and one British had just been killed in their car there. (The only survivor was Kim Philby, reporting the war from Franco's side for *The Times*.)

On 3 January 1938 Annie wrote to Laurie from Slad, vastly relieved to have heard something definite from Mrs Gregory (Wilma):

> instead of just thinking of you wandering in sad terrible Spain, exposed to all danger. But now it will be hard enough for you with the Red Cross. I trust that you won't feel the hardships and cold too much – and that your health will be good and that you will be spared to return to us. Dear Mrs Gregory is ... doing all she possibly can for you my dear Son. I have been *so* worried you ought not to have gone to Spain, & cause us all this anxiety & suspense, I have cried so much and many nights I have not slept...

She wished he had come home for Christmas, to have 'music and happy times with us'.

The politics of the situation, Wilma told Laurie, seemed to bewilder Annie – understandably. 'In one breath she asks with horror whether you are fighting for "the Reds" and goes on to express an equal horror at the thought that you are fighting for that dreadful Franco. Has she been reading the *Daily Mail* and some decent Left paper all in the same hour?'

Later in January, Molly/Mariquita resurfaced in Smethwick, in a sober mood, thanking Annie for the news of Laurie, but declaring dismissively that she had ceased to worry about him. He seemed so resolutely against all reasonable advice, 'I feel he must be left to work things out alone. I'm quite sure that you needn't be afraid that it is Betty's impending marriage which has sent Laurie to Spain.' (Betty had become engaged to Reg Farmer, a Cambridge undergraduate she met on a cycling club outing in Gloucestershire.) 'I feel sorry for Mrs Wishart,' added Molly briskly. 'I hope that for everyone's sake she won't do anything stupid. But surely she wouldn't really be likely to forsake her children for Laurie!'

Lorna had indeed left her children, and her husband, for Laurie. She had gone to a flat at 52 Heathcroft, in Hampstead Way, Golders Green, and rang Wilma to let Laurie know her address, but still spoke of trying to get to Spain herself. She had given Jacob Epstein a letter for Laurie – but then Epstein was refused a visa.

Harry Pollitt had told Lorna that Laurie had been taken to the training camp. 'I guess this means you have joined the International Brigade after all,' wrote Wilma resignedly in January. She began to give up hope of his early return, and now referred to herself as 'a tiresome old aunt' whose letters were 'probably only a bother to you'. She would give away his wireless and his fiddle case. If she heard soon that he was coming, she would wait in Perpignan, but otherwise would move on. If he arrived after she'd gone, he was to write to Wilma's bank for money for his fare home rather than try to fiddle his way through France: 'The French, never at any time generous, are especially parsimonious at the present time.'

Laurie wrote reassuring her that nobody was sent to the front after only a few weeks' training. Wilma said she might go to Barcelona to offer herself, her typewriter and her 'notorious eloquence in French, English and Spanish'. Or she might proceed to her cousin in Athens, or to Corsica, or Algeria. But she had to get away from 'this detestable clot of dullness that is Perpignan'. And she did, on 14 January.

On the same day, Jack wrote affectionately to his brother from Werter Road, Putney:

> My dear Loll, You don't know, Loll, how glad and relieved we are to know that you're safe, and how proud we are of you to know that you succeeded in doing what you set out to do – to cross the frontier and show your sympathies towards the Spanish Government in a practical way …

All the girls in Slad had asked after Laurie, he said.

> Maybe this world of ours is a pretty hellspot to live in & you are continually searching for truth & happiness – it may not have struck you I too have similar problems – but you at least have the satisfaction of your own talent and the knowledge that you are dearly loved – yes I have met her Loll – and I most terribly envy you that.

He had been to visit Lorna, found her beautiful and full of heartfelt concern for Laurie.

He reminisced fondly about their boyhood activities, and asked what he should tell Mrs Wishart and Mrs Gregory? 'They want you back – we all do. The question is, what do you yourself want? Well I must say *adiós*! look after yourself old man.' Even Mrs O'Neill's sister, Wid, sent a heartfelt letter: 'Well, Soldier, are you happy now, back in your beloved Spain? … So – you just napped out, eh? leaving a trail of broken hearts behind.' And of course Aunt Wilma, now in Cassis-sur-Mer, kept up her exhausting entreaties.

But at the end of January Wilma's tone underwent a complete volte-face. Two letters from Laurie, written 1 January and 13 January, had arrived, and she suddenly admonished him for what she saw as selfish fickleness. If only he had explained, weeks ago, what he was doing, 'it would have saved an infinitude of anxiety & worry'. He might as well stay in Spain until the war ended, she said. She would take no further steps: 'You are evidently happy, & the risk of air-raids must just be accepted.' Perhaps he might stay and marry a Spanish girl? 'If you could manage to stay in love with the same person long enough,' she added tartly, 'to make marriage worth while.' It would do him good to stay and help reconstruct the country. 'A little less Laurie, a little more citizenship, seems desirable.'

She doubted that he would ever settle down in England, or become a serious painter. As for Lorna, Wilma had assumed that Laurie had gone to Spain to escape from a volcanic situation. Now she concluded that he was 'not big enough really to fall in love with anybody. Just bodily satisfaction, with, of course, some mental stimulation, is an immense fillip to your vanity as a male.' She taunted Laurie for preferring 'short story episodes'.

Wilma's wounded feelings – tinged now with what comes over as sexual jealousy – overrode her normal wisdom and loyalty. Addressing him as 'dear nephew' and 'Lorenzo dear', she said she knew men needed reassurance that they could charm lovely young females to implore them to '*se couche* upon them'. But by the age of forty, she predicted, Laurie would have lost his youthful, 'downy' air, and become 'a stoutish person, with eyes bleared and watery, thick greasy lips, a coarse mouth. Novelette fears of a suffragette aunt? Perhaps…' Physical and mental degeneration, she declared, was what happened if young men had one love affair after another: she cited H. G. Wells, a potentially great man who had dwindled, by his philandering, into 'only a brilliant journalist'.

Lorna, she told him, now appeared to be building her life on a future with Laurie ('everybody else wiped out'). 'She says she does not dare to think ahead, but she *acts* ahead, my dear. W. banished, the home in Sussex abandoned, a tiny flat in London.' And, Wilma added sniffily, 'very little money, I imagine.'

At Teruel, the British Battalion had won distinction for holding up the rebel advance, but the success was short-lived. Its commander, Fred Copeman, became ill with a gangrenous appendix, and the new commander, Bill Alexander, was promoted captain on the battlefield – only to be wounded in the shoulder. The Republicans lost many men and mountains of equipment and munitions. Everyone who had been at Teruel, and lived to tell the tale, was afflicted by the horror, the cold and the bitterness of that eventual defeat.

By the middle of February, Wilma told her sister it had suddenly become very urgent that Laurie should be withdrawn from Spain. The Spaniards were willing to discharge him. 'But the boy refuses to leave, and, when brought to Barcelona to receive his discharge papers, rushes off to Madrid or Valencia without permission.' He was just a nuisance to them, she added, so of course they would not pay for his repatriation. Typically, Wilma had first demanded that a British warship should be sent to fetch him ('a demand which, to my no small astonishment, would actually have been granted had there been a British man-of-war close to Barcelona at that time'). She had deposited money with the British consul in Marseilles, and requested the consul in Barcelona to ask Prieto to order Laurie to leave Spain. She imagined that the Spanish Ministry of Defence had hesitated because so many 'exalted personages', in England, France and Spain, 'consuls, officials, MPs, *diputados*, and other socialist and communist leaders' had been apprised by Wilma of Laurie's existence. She had given 'an exaggerated notion of the boy's import-ance, and they are afraid to offend him by sending him away'.

She and Laurie would now go their separate ways. She had given her warm clothes to the Spanish aid committee in Perpignan ('almost certainly in one of the *camions* which were bombed into fragments in Figueras'), while Laurie's clothes had gone to England, addressed to Jack via a Covent Garden fruit importer. Laurie might be furious with her, but it would be a relief not to have to write dozens of letters each week about him. 'If ever Laurie can be persuaded to publish anything, I have given him lots of publicity, and there must be quite a big circle of readers awaiting him in three countries!'

Either on Wilma's advice or at the insistence of the Spaniards, Laurie did leave Spain after nine weeks. On 14 February 1938 a French visa was issued at Barcelona – '*bon pour se rendre en*

Angleterre avec arrêt de deux jours en France'. He left on 19 February. '*Sale sin dinero*' (leaves without money) was stamped in his passport. Shortly afterwards the battle of Teruel, two months of horror and misery, finally came to an end on 21 February when the government forces evacuated the town.

In Laurie's travel logbook, this is his bald summary of those two months:

'Spain. Crossed frontier over Pyrenees December 1937. Figueras Barcelona – Valencia – Albacete – Tarazona – Madrid. France. Returned via Port Bou-Paris Feb 1938.'

In later years, Laurie spoke of the 'shadowy, deep emotional memories' of his moment of war, and he obviously suffered great hardship. But for many years he gave differing accounts of what had happened to him in Spain. He told Allen Andrews[54] in 1961:

I crossed the Pyrenees at Figueras in December in a blizzard and said 'I've come to fight.' They said, 'You've got a haversack full of books, a camera and a violin – you have been landed from a submarine and you are a spy.' They put me in a room before shooting me. Just by luck the chief of police talked about this prisoner with the violin to an English newspaper man who recognised my description.

This was Bill Rust, a prominent Communist who had spent years in Moscow. (This episode he later transferred from December to February.)

So they let me live.

I trained as a soldier, but I was mainly used in the International Brigade headquarters in Madrid during the siege, making short-wave broadcasts to Britain and America. When I came back I was conscious of having got off very lightly. There were very few survivors from the men who were with me – chaps from Oxford and the docks, Canada, France, America. I have only ever met one of them since, they went in the heavy fighting of the spring.

A year later – 1962 – he talked to a reporter, Frank Entwisle, about having fought in the International Brigade. 'He was shipped out,' wrote Entwisle, 'after a bout of the recurrent pneumonia that has trailed him from his Cotswold childhood.'[55]

By March 1977 he was repeating the Bill Rust story to another reporter, Philip Oakes:

> In Barcelona I could easily have starved to death – not out of brutality, you understand, just neglect. But after three days in the cells my name was mentioned to Bill Rust – a war correspondent who later became editor of the *Daily Worker* – and he had me bailed out within the hour. The military commander let me convalesce in his flat for a couple of days. He was frightfully decent when he realised that we were on the same side.[56]

In *A Moment of War*, published in 1991, the starvation cell episode in Barcelona had expanded to three weeks (not three days) and took place after the battle of Teruel, when Rust happened to have his drink with the chief of police, heard about Laurie, and sprang him from gaol. (Rust, who went to Spain to sort out the problems within the British Battalion leadership, failed to mention his rescue of Laurie in his own book, *Britons in Spain*, published in 1939. But before he died ten years later, Rust did tell Bill Alexander that he persuaded the authorities to release Laurie for a medical examination.)

As is clear from Wilma's letters, Laurie never mentioned to her any of the elements – death cell, etc. – which eventually became so contentious. When his contemporary diaries were stolen in 1969, Laurie's only account of exact events disappeared.

But he brought home not only his diaries and the large cache of letters which had amazingly got through to him, but the graphic and moving poems he had written that winter, including the one called 'A Moment of War', published in 1940 in the fourth issue of *Horizon*:

It is night like a red rag
drawn across the eyes

the flesh is bitterly pinned
to desperate vigilance

the blood is stuttering with fear.

O praise the security of worms
in cool crumbs of soil
flatter the hidden sap
and the lost unfertilised spawn of fish!

The hands melt with weakness into the gun's hot iron

the body melts with pity
the face is braced for wounds
the odour and the kiss of final pain.

O envy the peace of women
giving birth and love like toys
into the hands of men!

The mouth chatters with pale curses

the bowels struggle like a nest of rats

the feet wish they were grass
spaced quietly.

O Christ and Mother!

> But darkness opens like a knife for you
> and you are marked down by your pulsing brain
>
> and isolated
>
> and your breathing,
>
> your breathing is the blast, the bullet,
> and the final sky.

This poem, rightly praised for expressing so vividly what it felt like to be stricken with terror in war-torn Spain, was originally datelined (in *Horizon*) 'Montpellier, October 1937,' i.e. written before he headed back to Spain. The poem called 'The Return' must refer to his trek across the Pyrenees in the snow and his fevered, fitful state of mind when he arrived (the Bahía de Rosas is on the coast, east of Figueras):

> And the day I observed that I was a lover
> crossed the frontier to seek a wound
> And fell with a fever above the Bahía de Rosas
> Letting the mad snow spit in my eyes.
>
> I put her picture against the mountain
> I covered the snowdrift with her scarf
> and lay with her name across my haunches
> chopping the ice in a fit of love...

There is no doubt that Laurie was deeply ashamed of having been sent back to England. Lorna refers to it in a letter in 1941. For decades, he obfuscated his experiences in the Spanish war, vaguely referring to having 'carried a gun, not a stretcher'.[57] When he finally unscrambled his memories to publish *A Moment of War*, at nearly eighty, an old man's book written with a young man's verve and a poet's imagination, it was hailed as a minor classic of the literature of war. No doubts erupted about it until after Laurie's death, when his version of events became a bone of contention gnawed at by historians and poets, who took him at his word, and Spanish Civil War veterans, who did not.

But nobody would ever question the authenticity of Laurie's impressions of conditions in Spain – the chaos and hunger and the biting cold, the wretched suffering of that ramshackle, ill-equipped army, in which so many young men died. There was one certainty: Laurie had been there, had witnessed that war, and never referred to it without a sense of guilt.

When he got back to Victoria Station, Lorna was waiting for him. 'Then I was back in her flat. In high wealthy Hampstead. She drew me in with her blue steady gaze. I remember the flowers on the piano, the white sheets on her bed, her deep mouth, and love without honour. Without honour, but at least with salvation.'

Laurie and Lorna were together for most of that year. Lorna had left Wish in Sussex, and her two boys – Michael aged nine, Luke aged five – with a nanny in St John's Wood. 'Suddenly, my mother vanished for years,' Michael Wishart later wrote. 'I was moved to a house in St John's Wood. I thought it was my fault she had gone. There followed a time of grief and anguish. Then my mother made brief reappearances. They tore open the wounds of her absence.'[58] Lorna rented a flat for herself and Laurie at 35 Mecklenburgh Square, Bloomsbury. Thereafter Laurie often referred to 'Mecklenburgh' as tinged with misery, because after a few months, in November 1938, Lorna decided to return to her husband, and sent Laurie off on his travels again. 'I took my fiddle to Italy and Greece to earn my keep, and spent the winter just before the big war in Cyprus. I didn't know anything about Cyprus ... I'd read the name Famagusta in a poem of Flecker.'

Laurie later wrote of November 1938 as 'the black November ... a day cursed with tender horror', a time of 'suffering so bitter that I wonder now how it was possible to endure it'. When Lorna sent Laurie away, she was four months pregnant.

8

Yasmin
1938–1939

IN THE DIARY of his travels that winter, Laurie mentions walking up a winding path into the little church of Lycabettos on the hill above Athens, where candles were on sale, 'to put a candle up for the three of us' on the altar. By 'the three of us' he presumably meant Lorna, himself and their unborn baby.

On 16 November, the day he left, Laurie was awakened by Lorna with a taxi at the door. 'She brought me half asleep into a cold miserable fog. The flat looked grey & dull but L put the thrill of God into me. Nevertheless it seems I have to make this journey … two thousand miles of distraction and self-inspection.'

On the Newhaven-Dieppe ferry Laurie met a girl art student from California and they travelled to Paris together. He found Paris dull, he was miserable, his head ached. As he caught the Istanbul-bound train, he watched an Italian saying goodbye to his lover, 'stroking her face and gazing at her with tragic eyes'. Laurie left the train at Venice (in 1978, writing about Venice, Laurie said he had not been to Venice for forty years, when he had been 'a young man running from love'). He recorded his Venetian impressions on a misty day: pigeons darkening the sky, the Church of the Salute across the water, the far off blue mists of water from the tower in San Marco, the cries of the gondoliers and their expert steering, 'above all the cold & the silence in the narrow canals'. He took the *Palestrina*, a comfortless Italian steamer, which moved out at midnight past San Marco to the sea, bound for Brindisi and the Adriatic crossing to Piraeus.

Wilma, meanwhile, had been working for a women's anti-fascist movement in Paris; she was paying off her dentist's bill by instalments, having paid 'on the nail' for Laurie's 'jaw-overhaul' the year before. By December, she was back in London at the Grosvenor Hotel: '15s 6d *per diem* for a gloomy room and an indifferent breakfast'. She had a bank overdraft of £10, and remarked without rancour to her sister: 'You see I am still suffering from the eccentricities of Laurie.'

Laurie was by then sailing past the islands to Piraeus, absorbing 'the lovely smell of resin from the pine trees, the rose coloured Bulgarian mountains'. Once in Athens, he took buses to the Byzantine monastery at Daphni, among cypresses and pines, through the dry hills to Elipsis, 'a decayed town with a ruined temple & a large cement factory'. He walked up to the Acropolis where young men in shorts practised for the marathon. 'In the museum are many battered & incomplete statues. All the finest marbles were raped by Elgin. The Greeks can never forgive England, they talk to me reproachfully about it.' He took tea in the English Reading Room, where he heard a woman complain of having 'nothing to read but the *News Chronicle*, of all ghastly publications'. As always, he absorbed everything: 'A smell of stale fish round the docks, the dry crusts the bakers sell for breakfast, the thick bitter coffee, the boot blacks running among the feet with their boxes & little bottles. In the gutter, witchlike crones are picking over a heap of rotting pears.'

Among painted fishing boats with curved prows, and flag-covered barges blowing their sirens for the Feast of St Nicholas, Laurie left Athens aboard the *Andros* – which pitched alarmingly as they reached the open sea. He arrived in Limassol, Cyprus, on 16 December in heavy rain, and found instant brotherhood among the young Cypriot men in cafés; they went roller-skating, played ping-pong and billiards, went to the cinema, and talked of women. 'They do nothing else. In the evening we went outside the town to sing. Singing is not permitted in the streets. Yet the harsh sounds of motor horns blow incessantly all through the early hours of the morning

when the streets are deserted & keep me awake.' The streets of
Famagusta were narrow and choked with camels, mules, carriages
and bicycles. His poem 'Port of Famagusta', published five years
later, is datelined 'Cyprus, 1939'.

> With the archways full of camels
> And my ears of crying zithers
> how can I resolve the cipher
> Of your occidental heart?
> How can I against the city's
> Syrian tongue and Grecian doors
> seek a bed to reassemble
> the jigsaw of your western love?

In Famagusta he took a room with a verandah, hired a bicycle and
went down on sunny mornings to swim in warm water thick with
salt and sand. 'What large breasts these Greek girls have, swelling
through their clothes like a storm in a sail. But perhaps it is my
celibacy that gives them their size.'

On Christmas Day he went with Picton, 'a cheerful old Englishman
with a white beard', to the English church, and 'bellowed carols
with the sun streaming through the windows. Here were gathered
the crumpled sandy faces of my compatriots, and the service echoed
with the rhythmic phrase of the "virgin's womb".' Making friends
was always easy for Laurie. A tailor named Polichronos gave him
Christmas lunch at his house, stopping *en route* at an orange farm for
a small feast of fruit including 'the nispero [medlar] that I knew in
Spain. And a bush with little cream coloured berries which tasted of
bitter ginger. I left the farm loaded with oranges big as rugger balls.'

> I am treated with amazing courtesy. Poli is newly married.
> His baby is three months old. We sit around the table & the
> women bring the food; they do not join us. There are pictures
> of film stars on the walls, all carefully framed, Conrad Veidt,

Marion Davies, an advertisement for Craven 'A', and a picture of Stevenson's Rocket. We have rice soup flavoured with cinnamon, boiled chicken with a salad of cabbage in olive oil, roast chicken & potatoes, coñac & a sweet wine. After lunch, I carry my oranges & a small cake wrapped in tissue paper which Poli's wife gave me on leaving.

Four days into the new year he ended his celibate period by walking past Famagusta harbour, through a gateway into narrow twisting streets.

I was looking for a whore & there were many here ... In a house just off the square, the front door was open, the girl sitting inside was young & when she saw me she stroked her leg softly and looked out to me. I went in and we sat around a bucket of glowing charcoal. There were four girls, a plump one, a fair one, one who was nice to me but had gold teeth, and the young one who had huge eyes & was Arabian. She was silent while the others chattered. A well dressed German came in, coarse in word & gesture. We sat round the charcoal stroking the girls with our eyes yet unable to move. The huge fat mother came in & sat with us, her legs open adding a bright touch of obscenity. The German stroked the plump girl's buttocks and smoked a cigarette. There was a knock on the half open door and a Greek came in & with hardly a word the fair girl followed him up stairs. We sat for a while longer, the fair girl came down again & fetched water. They asked me what ship I was on. Then the mother said, 'You like girl – you go in room' so I stood up & they all looked at me. I pointed to the young one and said 'you'. She rose & went with me. The bed was high & the girl undressed in a corner. She came with a dark smile on her face. I was so gentle I amazed myself, her skin was rough & when I touched her she shivered & her face flashed a dark smile. Afterwards I felt jubilant & warm towards her. She came with me to the door

& waved as I walked up the moonlight street. The city walls were majestic & the eucalyptus trees amazingly fragile & lovely as I went back to the hotel. I felt strong & terrifically alive.

He cycled to the ruins at Salamis:

Broken pillars, blue & white anemones, lizards on the sunny stone. In the road were camels, and carts painted with blue spots ... I pushed through a wilderness of trees & bushes to the sea. Peasants were ploughing a strip of land by the shore, and some were building walls of earth to keep back the sea. The soil was sandy. I went into a potter's workshop. He makes about thirty pots an hour. They sell at one piastre each. He pushes round the wheel with his bare feet. There is no legislation so far as I can see to protect either their hours of labour or their rate of pay. Even the policemen only get about £3 a month.

In this beautiful city are so many oxen and limbless beggars ... The girls are shuttered by neighbours's tongues, they are unable to stir or speak or let down their hair without meeting a pestilential barrier of censorious criticism. There is little love, but plenty of emotion attached to the house of a girl, her plot of land, her capital. Although the sun shines every day with a charitable benevolence, the sea is always cold & cafés are preferred to the poetical streets. The women mourn their wastage in black crepe, hide their beauty in dark corners, and the men serenade their possessions but know nothing of their souls.

The style and flavour of this diary, with its colour and detail, suggest the kind of diaries he had kept in Spain. The Cyprus diary ends abruptly here.

His passport says Laurie left Famagusta on 8 February 1939 and sailed home via Athens, Naples, Marseilles and Dieppe. He left Dieppe by night and arrived in London on 18 February 1939, exactly a year after his return from Spain.

Laurie and Lorna's child was born almost a month later on 14 March 1939 in St John's Wood. Laurie telephoned Lorna in her nursing home, and first heard his baby's cry over the phone. Almond trees were in blossom, and Laurie came and played his fiddle outside in the garden. 'I wanted a poet's child, and I got one,' Lorna was later to tell their daughter. They named her after their favourite poem, 'Yasmin', from James Elroy Flecker's verse-play *Hassan*:

> How splendid in the morning glows the lily: with what grace
>   he throws
> His supplication to the rose: do roses nod the head, Yasmin? ...
> The morning light is clear and cold: I dare not in that light
>   behold
> A whiter light, a deeper gold, a glory too far shed, Yasmin.
>
> But when the deep red eye of day is level with the lone highway,
> And some to Mecca turn to pray, and I toward thy bed,
> Yasmin...

On Yasmin's birth certificate her name is Jasmine Margaret, but Lorna and Laurie always called her Yasmin. There was significance for them in the initial letter 'Y': it represented two conjoined Ls, for Laurie and Lorna. The details of the next few months are sketchy. Shortly after her birth, Yasmin was photographed with her mother by Baron, the Jewish society photographer, whom Lorna had met in a nightclub and fearlessly rescued when he was attacked by a fascist mob. In gratitude, he took the photographs.

Laurie and Lorna and the baby lived for two months at 10 Kenton Street, Bloomsbury, above a greengrocer's shop. But Lorna shortly realised that the impecunious life with Laurie and the baby would be impossible. Wish had told her that if she came home, he would bring up the child as his own – an undertaking he carried out nobly. So Lorna returned to Sussex, and by the end of May Laurie was working as a farmhand at Upper Roundhurst Farm, Blackdown, near Haslemere in Surrey, from where he wrote telling Wilma how much he missed Lorna and the baby. Three marathon letters from Wilma – still affectionate, but no longer doting – are the sole record of what Laurie was doing and feeling at that time. He did not enjoy farming; the hours were long and he felt cut off. And he evidently confided in Wilma his anxieties about how involved he would be able to be in Yasmin's life.

At rambling length Wilma – fed up with Bournemouth's somnolence, filled with nostalgia for Almuñécar and outraged by the Pope's having blessed Franco and his army – tried to instil some sense into Laurie. She reminded him that Lorna was financially dependent on her husband, 'cannot afford to be with you, cannot support the child without her husband's help, and did not, apparently, think of this difficulty till the child was born'. She was not judging them morally, she stressed – 'We all make such a mess of our lives … one can only try not to behave selfishly and not to damage other people' – but economically. Lorna, she reckoned, would need a private income of £500 to £600 to maintain herself and her child.

> And Lord knows I realise how ghastly it would be for her to bring up the child in complete poverty. As things are, it is fortunate that the husband has taken to the child and is willing to bring it up with his own, and it is, of course, very generous of him.

She had expected Lorna to be 'strong and independent enough to stand by you and help you much as Frieda von Richthofen helped D. H. Lawrence.'[59] But she was more dependent on other people than Wilma had supposed.

As for Laurie's seeing his child sometimes, that would be for the three of them, 'especially the husband', to decide. Anyway, did Laurie feel competent to share in the child's upbringing? She was sorry to be grandmotherly, but in the world as it was, 'only the rich can arrange to have illegitimate children without inconvenience'.

He must face the hard facts, she added, and use the talents he was lucky enough to possess.

> Most men can make love and beget children … But very few can write as well as you can, let alone paint. You have wasted a lot of time, and some opportunity, but you have plenty of time still … If you *must* be introspective, why not use that tendency in your work? Write about yourself; not necessarily about actual facts in your life, but a journal or what-not written around them…

She suggested that Jack, who now worked for the GPO Film Unit, might find him a job there. Or since the nation was mobilising for war, the labour exchange might offer work on the army camps now being built. Or she would pay for a *New Statesman* ad, offering his services. 'Don't get depressed; some more pleasant job will turn up soon.'

Her next homily chided him for 'wandering about in an imaginary Arcady and making love to charming shepherdesses (who, at heart, want more solid things, such as a comfortable home and an income, and pretty clothes and a car)'. If Laurie did some solid work it would give 'those shepherdesses and glamour girls' confidence in his power to look after them. She reminded Laurie that 'throughout the ages, wives have "kicked over the traces" and then been taken back by their husbands, who have accepted an illegitimate child and brought it up as their own'. Laurie must regard this episode as closed, cease all communication with Lorna, and fix his mind on 'the very urgent business of growing up: getting one's values right, and putting one's emotions in their proper place (a comparatively insignificant one)'.

In the Garman family, nobody appears to have been exercised about who was the father of Lorna's new baby. Even if they were told, they would not have thought it exceptional. Kathleen Garman now had three children by Epstein, who was still married to his wife; Ruth Garman had several children, by different men. And as Anna Campbell said of her parents Roy and Mary: 'Goodness, they had both led carefree lives before the Spanish influence, and were in no position to censure anyone.' Laurie's mother Annie was certainly told, and was unreproachfully prepared to bestow on Yasmin all the love she had once given to her little dead daughter Frances.

Of course Laurie did not give up Lorna, or put the episode behind him. 'Yasmin, me darlins, has two more teeth! Top ones,' he noted in the diary he began on 16 October 1939, shortly after the outbreak of war. This diary, written more honestly and sparely than anything he ever published, and kept continuously for five years, became principally an account of the love affair that brought him more happiness – and ultimately, more unhappiness – than anything he had ever known.

At the outbreak of war Laurie was back at Mrs O'Neill's in Putney, where the high street shop basements had become air-raid shelters, and Putney Heath had listening-posts and searchlights and walls of sandbags. Lorna was often in London, but the baby stayed in Sussex with her nanny. Epstein's daughter Kitty remembered standing in the hall at Marsh Farm, Sussex, with her cousin Michael Wishart, both aged about eleven, as Lorna departed for London.

> And Lorna looked at us and said, off-hand, 'You are a strange
> pair of children, neither of you living with your mothers, your
> mothers always going off' and I remember thinking, in that help-
> less way of a child, Well we can't help it. It's you who go, not us.

In these early days of the war, when air-raid shelters were being dug and everyone carried gas masks, Laurie drifted. He went to concerts, and with brother Jack's musical friends, made up a quartet. He kept a careful daily record of events, dissecting the newspaper editorials (disgusted by their childish jingoism), and logging events such as the torpedoing of the Royal Oak at Scapa Flow, and the Graf Spee in the South Atlantic. But mostly he just waited for Lorna.

> L came this morning with lilies and some little white flowers,
> their petals beautifully marked with lipstick. She brought

> Sibelius, a Beethoven quartet, a new flamenco & several others.
> We had music and the gas fire and qualities of tenderness that
> exists nowhere outside our bodies. And then to Pritchards for
> tea where she kicked me on the shin for looking at another girl.

(Lorna was intensely jealous: she tore up Laurie's photographs of a
girl he met in Athens, saying, 'The Greeks have a word for it & I have
a word for the Greeks.')

He would meet Lorna on Victoria Station: 'Tall in her dark-
blue slacks and jacket, brown-cheeked, bright-eyed, giggling like a
schoolgirl as we walk arm-in-arm to look for a taxi. It is more than 2
years.' He bought Baudelaire for her at Zwemmer's, and they went
to an exhibition of Epstein drawings: 'Some from *Les Fleurs du Mal*
unlovely and obscene. Several fine portraits of a repulsive little boy
called Jackie [Epstein's son by his model Isabel Nicholas, adopted
by Mrs Epstein unknown to Kathleen Garman], some lovely nudes
of a thin negress, and several variations on love & death.'

The first anniversary of his departure for Greece and Cyprus, 16
November, was

> a day of sackcloth & ashes, a day for anger & expostulation, a
> day to curse. But kinder in itself, quiet & warm, & not the blue
> smokey cold of last year. I would not fast or shut myself away.
> But I hope I may remember it for ever. *Hassan* was being broad-
> cast and we lay dumbly together without speaking or moving.
> And then she went & I remained in that vast room while that
> nerve-wracking second half of *Hassan* continued. You're a
> bloody day and you mark the end of an indescribable year.

Soon, Jack did find Laurie a job at the GPO Film Unit, a reserved
occupation, later renamed the Crown Film Unit. The cream of the
British documentary film world worked there, including Humphrey
Jennings, Pat Jackson and Harry Watt. Jack arranged work for
Laurie in the sound department under Ken Cameron, brother of the

legendary reporter James. His first job was to create percussive sounds for the noise of marching feet in a film about London preparing for war: 'Brian Easedale smiting a radiator with a piece of iron, whilst I tapped two wood blocks together & whistled,' his diary records. 'For dockyard noises we used drums, blew sirens, stirred water in a basin … It seems that 90 per cent of sound is synthetic in films.' When Laurie went to see the trade show he disliked the film's self-congratulatory tone – 'This is how you reacted to the war and very proud you should be of your calmness, good sense & humour. But then, after all, you're British.' But the barrage balloons were beautifully filmed: 'They will always be the symbol of the first days. Great slow silver fishes, shewn shining in the sun, nosing through misty clouds, rising & falling, wrinkling lazily, and drifting dark and strange in front of the moon. Slow, obscene, yet lovely things, faintly sinister yet friendly.'

Over lunch one day, Molly told him Betty was to marry Reg Farmer (who became a distinguished nuclear scientist), a marriage that would last sixty years. And in December, Lorna rang to tell him 'the extraordinary news' that Wilma had come to live in Lorna's home village of Binsted, Sussex. Clearly Wilma was determined not to be discarded from Laurie's life. After all, it was she who had unwittingly led him to Lorna, or as she put it twenty years later, 'I enabled him to meet the most beautiful, aggressive and, as I thought then, most dangerous of his mistresses, who introduced him to the BBC and also to the world of literature, music and art.'

But that came later. For now, Laurie had to report for work at Blackheath, to be instructed in 'the instruments & speakers & panels and dials and switches' of the sound van. The night before, Lorna came, 'in a dark-blue ribbed frock which matches her eyes & makes her all one dark sloe-blue image. We have a coal fire but our day is soon burnt out & Lord knows when I shall be able to see her again.'

The first film Laurie worked on was the story of the voyage of a cargo boat, the SS *Ionian*, from Gibraltar to Famagusta: 'lovely local music – but since the film was made [the *Ionian*] has been blown up & the film retitled "Her Last Trip"'.He recorded Ralph Richardson, whom he found 'facetious but not unpleasant'. Other projects were less exciting: 'To Tooting Bec to record at a Post Office the noises of a teleprinter in action for Jack Chambers' film "How the Teleprinter works".' The sound unit often used Elgar's music for background, to Laurie's disgust: 'it is all as blank and similar as a spool of unused film. He has the windyness of Gladstone, the four-square denseness of Baldwin, and the leisured ease of speaking immaculate nothings which must be one of Chamberlain's greatest gifts.'

On Christmas Eve 1939 Jack and Laurie returned to icy Slad. Annie's kitchen was 'colder and more confused than ever, but irreplaceable in spite of its comfortlessness'. That evening, two frail voices began a carol outside the door. 'A voice from my feet said "Penny for the carol mister." I looked down and there was a little boy and girl hand in hand & both, it seemed, no taller than a bucket.' Laurie asked who they were. 'I be Reg Smart,' said the boy, 'and 'er's my sister. We do come from Stroud.' 'And they went stumping up the freezing bank in the moonlight like a couple of well-wrapped up dwarfs. These singers made my cup quite full.'

After having his annual Christmas fever, Laurie returned to London and Lorna, and played the records she had given him (Bach preludes and fugues), and they went through his poems together and 'primed them again'. 'At least we saw the new year in. Waking in the dark and leaving the warm, enflamed cheeks of Scheherezade is one of the most difficult things I have ever had to do.'

The winter of 1939–40 was said to be the worst for 100 years: at Putney the Thames was frozen. But Lorna brought lilies and orchids, Sibelius and Brahms and they would lie by the gas fire. 'Her return is like the moon, I am struck with familiar surprise and shake myself with joy. She waxes swiftly to a full, heady brilliance and then the dawn sees her face turning away, pale, and disappearing.' 'We lay still & talked and breathed warmth into each other's hair until late in the morning. I cannot think why lovers ever leave their beds...'

In blacked-out London, Lorna glowed: a vision, a free spirit, a scented romantic, bringing flowers, music, wine, and inspiring in

Laurie dozens of poems. In the evenings, when he got back from the Film Unit, he would find her in his Putney room: 'My love was waiting tonight with long slender swords of leaves and dark red roses. We played the Chopin Ballades and the Debussy Quartet. Chopin is definitely the music for desire...' 'L was waiting for me this evening. Again everything was forgotten, she hung her head or twisted her hair, and talking or embracing, there was little to show that I had ever flown to Greece, or Yasmin had been born.'

9

The Green Caravan
1940–1941

THE DANGER POSED by the war seemed to intensify Laurie's affair with Lorna. On fine spring days, they would escape to the Sussex countryside

> and there among the sheep we did make merry and tumbled the shadows and sunlight to brilliant effect. We averted our eyes from war flares and ignored warnings. The sun smote us ... We pitied the sheep, we pitied all men, so lofty were we in the pride of happiness and fulfilment.

They strolled through churchyards 'doped with lassitude & mutual excitement'.

Lorna also opened doors. She sent Laurie's poems to her friend Stephen Spender at his new magazine, *Horizon*, and he and Cyril Connolly took three. Laurie was suspicious; were they publishing him just because he was a proletarian? Spender wrote assuring him that they simply liked his work. 'If we published poems just because they were proletarian, *Horizon* would be the size of a telephone directory.'

He added: 'Perhaps you will not mind my saying how very struck I was by your poems when Mrs Wishart sent them to me ... more struck than by anything I have read for some time.' He found Laurie's drawings 'interesting', but preferred the poems. There was a postscript: 'I shall remember that your name is Laurie Lee and not Laurence.'

Cyril Connolly also wrote, from Devon: 'If you substitute "upper class" for "working class" in your letter, it might have been written by a peer fifty years ago,' he told Laurie. They were pleased to publish him because he was unknown. Besides, Connolly pointed out, merely being working class was

> not much of an asset from a literary point of view. A great many
> of the working class now write, & I do not think they write very
> well ... From the *artistic* point of view your visit to Spain, and
> knowledge of countryside has been lucky ... I hope this clears
> it up & I'm sorry for spelling your name wrong. May I say how
> much I like your poems. Yrs v sincerely Cyril Connolly.

John Lehmann, general manager of the Hogarth Press and ever alert to a new name, offered to publish Laurie in his *Penguin New Writing* series. Laurie rang him – again pointing out that he was Laurie, not Laurence – and typed out three of his poems. He wrote a fourth for Spender 'as ordered' but the effort brought on a fever. The next issue of *Horizon*, no 4, carried a portrait by Lucian Freud, a review of Housman by Spender, a V. S. Pritchett short story, and the poem 'A Moment of War' by Laurie Lee: fee, one guinea. He was paid another guinea for 'Words Asleep' in *Horizon* 5.

By day Laurie was recording the sound of machine-guns and Spitfires for a film on *Ammunition*, and the voice of J. B. Priestley for *Britain at Bay*. He spent his first evening with film people in a Soho pub: 'They all drink and drink – don't they ever go home?' (Laurie had not yet acquired the masculine taste for long evenings in pubs.) Each day he noted the numbers of planes shot down, and of casualties; he logged German advances and lamented the fall of Paris: 'Is there nothing we can do for France, are we so impotent after all?'

In June he took Lorna to Slad for the first time, in a train packed with young soldiers. He noticed how women, Lorna included, eyed the military with approval. 'It is bitter to be a civilian among these men.' They arrived in high summer to find the valley in extravagant bloom.

> Everywhere blossoms, orchids, moon daisies, roses, the garden a heady pool of syringa, the banks and fields vital with scent & sound. Nightingales in the woods. I lay with my face in the grass, or with my mouth to hers. Everything was the beautiful familiarity of home, she and the valley were never divided.

Laurie's poem in the next *Horizon*, later called 'Invasion Summer', reflected this sybaritic rural interlude in the midst of war:

> The evening, the heather,
> the unsecretive cuckoo
> and butterflies in their disorder;
> not a word of war as we lie,
> our mouths in a hot nest
> and the flowers advancing.
>
> Does a hill defend itself,
> does a river run to earth
> to hide its quaint neutrality?
> A boy is shot with England in his brain,
> but she lies brazen yet beneath the sun,
> she has no honour and she has no fear.

On a hot August afternoon when the fields were stacked with corn, Laurie went down to Arundel to see Yasmin.

> They were waiting for me, L holding Yasmin, a plump golden-haired little beauty with the 'greensleeve' eyes of her mother and a chubby comfortable face, the rough lovely face of a country girl contrasting oddly with the rare fine charm of her eyes.

She wonders at me at first, but toddles across the station yard desperately clutching my hand.

They went for tea. 'Yasmin crowed and chatted between us and we fed her, gazed at her, talked about her and laughed at her jokes. We watched her eating and drinking with pride ... for a short while we enjoyed ourselves, a simple domestic trio out to tea for a treat.'

Afterwards they sat by the river 'where herons walk through rushes on dignified stilts' and Yasmin toddled up and down the path 'with furious little steps', picking up pebbles. 'She smiled at me and held her head on the side and laughed ... She was gay and adorable, but she did not know me, which was not surprising.'

One day Laurie played truant from the studio and went down to Sussex.

We drove out on the downs and lay among the white parachute seeds of thistles ... I spent the night at Wilma's cottage. The mooing of heifers in Wilma's garden woke me in the morning. L came down in her scarlet frock. As we walked back up the lane towards Arundel, the all-clear sounded. Wilma left us and we lay in the wood happy but distant. The drone of planes was continuous.

About one o'clock it grew louder, more threatening, like a swarm drawing near. Suddenly the warning went again and almost immediately the ground shook beneath our bodies and the dull thump of bombs sounded in the distance. We walked out of the wood and presently saw English fighters flying back to their aerodromes in threes and singly. 'The raid is over,' said L. Soon the sky settled and the all clear sounded. We walked slowly down the road and entered a different part of the wood. It was hot and green and dusty. Under the leaves with a bottle of beer we lay and forgot everything but the smell of the trees and the smell of the Arun, Martigues, Kenton. The sky was buzzing with anger again but we succeeded in ignoring it, we were as detached, as otherwise intent as insects there among the broken sticks, the trailing thorn ... And we lay together looking into one another's eyes acting our own war and peace, while our bodies listened uneasily.

As we kissed there was a burst of machine-gun fire, loud, in the sky. It rattled across the hills like an oath. With our faces together we waited for the next, our lips were warm against each other, the machine-gun cracked again and with our lips still touching we stared into the sky in each other's pupils, incredulous but without any surprise. Then all around the ground shook, the dry leaves crackled with repeated bombs, machine-guns bred and multiplied, planes tore their harsh parabolas across the sky and the siren split them all with its tragic wail. The sky was full, cut, slashed and shattered with noise. The ground heaved with the throb of bombs. We were still kissing. 'I must see this,' I said so we crept through the undergrowth and I ran from tree to tree to the edge of the wood. I lay in a ditch and watched. The sky heaved and boiled. I saw planes whirling round each other like little wooden crosses tossed up by a juggler. The noise was indescribable. I lay there for some moments my heart throbbing then I ran back to L crouching under a tree. We remained there waiting and helpless, fascinated. The bombs continued to fall with horrible deliberation, so irrevocable. Everything seemed to be directly above us, everything seemed to be aimed at us, we heard the vicious tearing whines of crashing planes coming down straight to us. We were uncovered, our backs tingled as we lay. Presently the sound of battle shifted. We walked down to the road again and looked once more down into the sky ... The aerodrome was blazing. We sat by the roadside and the battle receded into the distance ... We found we were sitting by the gate of the cottage hospital, and very soon the ambulances began to arrive.

... Later we returned to the wood & L drinking beer from an uncorked bottle swallowed a wasp. This filled us with considerably more dread than the bombardment. She had to go and be sick, and then we felt better.

At the end of August 1940 Laurie gave in his notice to the sound unit. He had one more job, at Dover, where he was caught in another air raid. He crouched against a wall watching with awe the sheets of flames left by the crumpling balloons, and pieces of AA shell and tracer bullets striking the road a few feet away. 'Then the raiders were out to sea, and all that remained were the echoes, the gleam of excitement on our faces...' Next day they filmed residents whose houses had been wrecked, to a background of gunfire, dogfights and balloon strafing. He watched bombers flying in formation, fighters wheeling and circling.

> I sat in the shaking trembling van recording it ... They were flying north towards London, they seemed invincible, & it was terrifying to watch. But as soon as they were out of range of our guns, they were broken up by fighters and they began to stream back in twos and threes, making for home.

That evening the hotel was 'bright with the chatter of facetious newspapermen picking over the heroism and unspeakable brutality of the day's events'. Jack was shooting every night in the East End for a film called *London Can Take It!* and actually fell into the Thames with a camera clutched to his stomach.

On 7 September Laurie left the studios. At nightfall fire glowed over the city.

> The damage in the East End was terrific and there were 40 killed and over a thousand seriously injured. Now the vicious bloody business has started in earnest, it is a war of terror aimed at every living thing. We are bombing Berlin. Dead children in Germany, dead children in England, terror and madness in the hearts of the survivors ... The stench of blood and the broken limb drowns the weak voice of humanitarian reason...

The next day Jack and Laurie were returning from the West End by bus when the warning went; they threw themselves to the ground on Putney Bridge. Bombs had fallen in the road next to theirs. The following night, escaping to Arundel ('Next to Slad I could be more at home here than anywhere in England – but I'm like a bloody outlaw'), Laurie was picked up by the police, 'partly due I expect to my Germanic appearance. They rang up Wilma and she vouched for me.' Wilma had indeed been telephoned and asked if she knew a Mr Lee, whom police had found 'hanging about' outside Arundel Station with no identity card. 'Only a Laurie Lee,' as she wrote to her sister, 'would travel in defence areas without his War Office passes.' She told them he was 'an important government sound engineer, and that if he looked queer it was because he was epileptic. He turned up brightly and stayed two nights, and cleared up my rations for last week.'

From Wilma's, Laurie went to Annie in Slad, spending his evenings among the village women whose menfolk had gone to war, playing and listening to music. Feeling like an adolescent again, as he always did in Slad, he saw two local lads, Fred Tilley and Jack Halliday, 'marching up and down dressed as policemen. You feel they are still part of Slad Players dressed for rehearsal.' In Gloucester he saw Molly Smart with her newborn son, looking 'ripe & well, lactic & quite beautiful'. He visited relations, walked up Swift's Hill, dug potatoes. ('Down among the roots & worms & stones & weeds, the damp earth takes me back to old frustration & old contentment. Ringing fork combing the soil, raking the stones, panting with the effort, thick earth sticking to one's shoes, the sounds of the village around, a dog, a cough, a greeting bright & laconic.')

Then Lorna, having just sent her son Michael ('speechless with dread and misery')[60] off to board at Bedales, suddenly telegraphed, instructing Laurie to 'reply to Glebe House and sign yourself Alan' – and arrived at Slad next day. Laurie sat by the kitchen fire with his mother and his mistress.

> Mother is gay for moments without thinking … then she will
> bend her old face across the candles & almost weep that we are
> in love and not married & together. L puts on her nightdress
> with such a soft slow twist of her body that I think of salmon &
> the play of rivers and the gentle gestures of smoke. I sit hunched
> in bed watching her silent grace, a woman, alive, adoring the
> hour, the closed door, my eyes & the promise of sleep. And I
> cannot bear to extinguish the candle.

Proudly he walked with Lorna through Stroud. They took a bus to
Hereford, and looked at a house in the hills 'wild & lost from the
world'. They walked along Slad Road eating fish and chips. They
took sherry up Juniper Hill among the sheep

> & there we lay for a while, half sleeping under the turning wheels
> of the sun. Later we went down to the old stonemason's hut and
> hung festival leaves on the walls and rinsed our teeth with sherry
> … and her body caught glints of autumn, red nipples & long
> bruised leaves…

The afternoon was later captured in his poem, 'Juniper'. 'That
evening we were slightly drunk & in love with the village & miserable that we were leaving tomorrow.'

Back in Putney, John Lehmann's letter waited with proofs
of Laurie's poems for the next *Penguin New Writing*, including
'Music in a Spanish Town': as Laurie noticed, anything on Spain
got a sympathetic reception. He was amazed at the imperturb-
ability of Londoners amid the debris of Shaftesbury Avenue and
Charing Cross Road, bombed a week ago. In Zwemmer's he bought
Lorca's poems and, back at Werter Road, worked on the poems he
had started in Slad, until guns shook the house, 'so down into the
kitchen among the women, the smells, the hideous wallpaper, and
there work is impossible'.

Millions were sleeping in shelters and tube stations. In their basement Mrs O'Neill and Wid were in hysterics, quaking under the table. Laurie would go out in his tin hat, crouching against the wall, hearing the bombs screaming past and thudding into houses.

> Five fell, shaking the ground, and I leapt into the shelter with my head throbbing like a beating drum … Over the next garden, a house had disappeared, & one thought of the crawling, groaning shattered human beings buried by beams & cut with red hot flying swords; suddenly their moment, their bitter personal war, their nameless death, coming upon them with awful tongues of flame, separating them from their cup of tea, their shining shoes, their harmlessness, their sins still unresolved.

By October Laurie had seen a hundred raids. One night a fever came on. He lay sweating and shivering in the kitchen, hearing gunfire like maddened drums. 'The women were terrified … Dolly recited the whole plot of Rider Haggard's *Witch's Head* while I lay on the sofa with a handkerchief soaked in lavender water on my forehead & went gently to sleep.' Annie wrote deploring the destruction of 'that London which for years I have dreamt of exploring with your or Jack's guidance…' and Laurie himself had had enough. He would leave London and 'find a shack to live in', close to Lorna. On 12 October 1940 he took a bus to Pulborough in Sussex and put up at the Railway Hotel. The landlady showed him a dressing-table drawer, full of papers: Sir Arnold Bax, the composer, had asked her to look after them. 'I caught sight of a letterhead, The Dorchester Hotel: "Darling WHY can't you write", signed "Your Jeanie" – & I thought he was an old man.' From his hotel window on market day he watched a runaway cow head down the railway line, leap into the river and swim downstream.

He rang Wilma, who told him she had heard, years ago, about 'someone who was a bit mad & owned huts & cottages near Storrington'. He set off, and found himself in 'another Whiteway'. This was the Storrington Sanctuary,[61] where one Vera Pragnall had erected a cross on the hill and freed the land for settlers to claim.

When Laurie later read Pragnall's book, he decided that apart from her mysticism-riddled generosity and enthusiasm, she was also 'full of the most awful arty-crafty, spinning, dancing-barefooted-in-the-dew clichés…'

He looked at a cottage, but then spied a green caravan 'much more to my taste', just under Chanctonbury Ring, an area shortly to be occupied by the military. Next day, Lorna's grey Bentley took them to Storrington where they walked in the woods, lay in the bracken, and in the caravan found the bed made and oil ready for the lamps – prepared for them by the wife of the landlord, Dennis Earle. 'It was delightful. We went back to Pulborough, talking of the amazement of love, fetched my bags, bought a few things & back to the caravan. How nice to light the lamp and draw the curtains.' After Lorna had gone, he found 'little love messages' scrawled inside the crockery cupboard. 'Sweet beloved, they acted on me like delayed action bombs.'

Laurie quickly settled to his gypsy life. While London raids worsened, he heard owls hooting and a distant bugle: 'I thought of that artist in Tarazona trumpeting his sharp frozen music through the cold white streets…' He cooked sausages, listened to his wireless, and tussled with poems, 'complicated by lack of paper'. In the morning Lorna arrived 'wild of hair & in a green tartan frock with a long line of seductible buttons down the front', bringing books, eggs, tea, sandalwood and honey.

> Bed & sherry & sunlit gloom and smooth pools of eyes in the darkness. Late afternoon crept up like a thief behind our backs. We walked round the wood & picked leaves & teased a snake. As the evening grew blue & dusky she left … In the oily warmth of my van this evening, to the roar of planes overhead, I practically finished my poem.

It was paradise: enchanted forests, shifting mists, groves of silver oaks, stark Nordic pines. In the evening silence, the caravan was bathed in mist and moonlight. Mornings brought hot sun and tropical colour. He went to Worthing 'along the road which I tramped six years ago with my fiddle & a fever & the kisses of Yvonne. How ghastly that town is, what wildernesses of bungalows.' A week later he packed up his belongings at Werter Road. Another bomb fell nearby. 'Mrs O read from D Mirror that Hitler had reached accord with Pétain. Italy has invaded Greece ... Spain too may be forced to become a belligerent...'

As autumn came, bringing storms and gales, the caravan was less cosy and Laurie would ponder on his solitude. 'The evening was macabre & bitter with loneliness – I began to feel scared.' 'All day her beauty has nagged my nerves with frustration. I must get a job.' 'Tonight there is a waxing moon and lust is waxing in my loins. It makes me mad alone here.' 'Depression covered me like a raven's wings, I could not shake it off.' Then Lorna would arrive and drive him to Arundel, to the pictures, or to the Black Rabbit pub to sit over a roaring fire. 'It is a paradox,' wrote Laurie, 'that the best way to preserve the thrill & intensity of love is to put as much distance as possible between myself & the beloved.'

He found congenial neighbours. Hugh de Sélincourt, 'despite his somewhat Punch mentality', was a fan of Blake. Mrs de Sélincourt lent him Haydn records and 'played Mozart with real feeling despite her fat coarse bunchy fingers'. There was a Mrs Brook, sister-in-law of the actor Clive Brook. A Mrs Aggs held musical evenings in a cloistered house with cold stone floors. The resourceful Mabel Mallet lived in a junk-filled hut named Unto the Hills, under a sign proclaiming 'Helping Hand Studios' offering 'typewriting, needle-work, portrait-painting, lyric-writing, car for hire'. Laurie bought a bicycle and went to see films in the village hall 'rather like Spanish village cinemas: hard chairs, screaming boys, cheers & claps'. Lorna would drive him to concerts at the Abbey, where he saw Lorna's aunt, 'a wild old lady of 72 with painted cheeks & charcoal eyes. Arnold Bax sitting behind us.' He walked with Wilma on the Downs. He watched people picking over the bones of a crashed bomber. He learnt the names of the stars, 'something I've not been able to do before'. He bought Beethoven music and tried to read Havelock Ellis's *Soul of Spain* but 'I can't bear to read about Spain, its tragedy is so raw & open & seems so personally symbolic.'

On most mornings Lorna would come, 'like a stroke of good fortune, showering presents on my worthless head'. She brought a tambourine, flowers, paintings, cake, rabbit, mushrooms, goose eggs, bananas, shells and a pretty little carved chessman; Beethoven's Spring Sonata; 'a chunk of apple wood like the fork of a tree and a half-formed woman leaning against it, lovingly carved … L is very proud of the cuts and callouses on her hands, token of her labour'. There was always 'an eddying fragrance of irresistible passion'. She would depart at dusk, to the distant rumble of guns and planes. On frosty mornings he woke cold and desolate, 'my mind ugly and raw, clutching desperately at the precipice' until 'L came again, with a bag of sweet cakes and two bottles of wine'. He played the violin while she cooked him salmon and potatoes, steak or corned-beef hash, filling the caravan with oily aromas.

> We felt secure in the warm shadows of the van. In a nightdress fragrant with sandalwood, her nakedness was transparent in purple light. We shook the storms from our hair and sank in roots of weariness. We crossed the mountain of passion, our eyes roped together, our lips firm-footed in the slopes of darkness. I was easily abandoned in the fierce languor of love.

Annie wrote, wondering how he was faring 'all on your lonesome'? In November the caravan was rocked by gales, whipped by rain. But Lorna came 'looking the very acme of desire'; 'a very acolyte, dressed in all the grace and colour of a premature primavera'.

> She came bringing cakes, and the *Oxford Book of Verse*, her hair becomingly piled up on the top of her head, fixed with a large comb she said was her grandmother's. Her face was fine & lovely under the sleek ebony of her coiffure; but later, when

she had posed and held her head gracefully for me, she became impatient, combing it all out and saying I couldn't get my fingers into it. Which was true, but I did like it. We played some old records (Satie, which overwhelms us with its tenderness). The storms & the tortured trees were forgotten, the afternoon became one with night...

At 6 o'clock we had plates of beans & giggled, making silly jokes that do not bear repeating but we laughed with pride & joy ... And then, with hushed voices we would speak of November 1938. But suddenly digging her fingers deep into the rice pudding she looked across the table & said, 'But Laurie don't you know what suttee is?'

He reflected:

Her head is so small & fine, like a lovely diminutive jewel. When I hold it between my hands it gives to my body a sense of unbelievable grace, my hands are beautiful with this exquisite vessel between them. I marvel at the slender form of her skull, like a rare jar decorated with vivid designs of eyes & lips, slashed with brows & shadows, dreaming & overflowing with the warm wine of hair. I cannot imagine it ever growing old. It has the strong unalterable permanence of a work of art, a piece of statuary, that could be buried for a thousand years & still startle men's eyes with its barbaric beauty. Our love is a recurrent cycle. Lying in the dark intimacy of sheets we talked of it. Later when she stood naked in the candlelight I felt amazement & humility that this stalk of flesh, this passionate totem that had so often burnt my eyes in the desolate days of my adolescence, should now really exist for me.

They cycled up to Chanctonbury Ring. On one occasion they were woken by a shepherd who leaned over them, hands on knees, and asked, 'How d'you like it 'ere?' They affected to despair over their separate lives, but were peculiarly happy. When Laurie was offered a hut on top of the hill for 10s a week, they went to peer through its windows, but decided they preferred the green caravan.

A German bomber flew over the woods, dropping four bombs; Laurie heard the whistle of a splinter beside him, six feet from the caravan, too hot to handle. Bombs destroyed houses, burst a water main, broke the telephone wire. One night Lorna, distracted by flashes, ploughed her car through a hedge and into a ditch. She showed him two great bomb craters on each side of the road near Bury Hill: 'She missed them by seven minutes on her way home from here a fortnight ago.'

There were solitary days of 'horrible nervous terror' and lonely nights 'loud with bombs & planes & tenseness'. But he was fine when the sun shone and she was with him. Then silence fell 'like a deafening wave' and alone, Laurie faced reality.

> The caravan closed in about me and the maddening terror reappeared. Violent pains in my head & a sense of dissatisfaction in my mind. Being with her is like being at the pictures, I am in another world drugged & oblivious to the actual condition of my life. And leaving her is like walking out into the cold reality of the street, the fantasy is over & I must examine the irritating facts of my existence.

As Britain's industrial cities were devastated, Laurie was guiltily conscious of his apparent immunity from engagement. Whole days would pass when he 'made a few drawings, did a crossword puzzle, cooked a stew, trimmed the lamps, played my fiddle, and wrote two poems, one unprintable and the other incoherent'.

His isolation struck him forcibly.

> Buried in my van I grow ever more remote almost to madness. It is a curious situation, with men & women dead, injured, over-worked, faced with all forms of danger, with Europe obsessed and strained by war, I sit in my caravan, make tea, smoke black

cigarettes and play the violin. I am not boasting – I am in some way amazed that I am allowed to do it. My life is more tranquil, more lacking in incident than it has ever been. I only know that it cannot continue so. One of these days, the strain of staring at myself will become too much for me & I shall have to move back into the city of activity. When I find myself making love on sunny afternoons with the sound of battle overhead I can only think there is something marvellously right about my life – or something terribly wrong. Although I like to feel, as I have always done, that nothing but life & love is my business, I have a recurrent breath of suspicion that I have some duty to my fellow men. We shall see how long I can ignore it.

Did anyone know he was there? In December he was asked for his tax return ('heigh ho') but not until March 1941 did the Ministry of Labour write to suggest that he train for munitions, or return to the Film Unit. But almost unwittingly he was now 'a poet'. John Lehmann constantly asked for more poems. When the next *Penguin New Writing* arrived with its note about himself under 'About the Contributors', he regretted what he had told Lehmann. 'One can so easily be charged with exhibitionism even when one is telling the truth. I also made no allowances for the natural vanity of L & my family. Neither she or they will like it to be known that I was an errand boy.' He was right: Lorna was 'mildly furious'.

A seductively scented Russian pianist called Madame Alexeieff appeared next door with two Pekes, a warm stove, and a bath. She offered fragrant China tea,

> giving me the sense of mellow contentment, and a physical luxury as if one were clothed in silk. We played *Daphnis & Chloë* & she talked of Russia with a bitter sadness. Of Chaliapin, she said: 'Yes, I suppose he was a fine singer, but he lived on the Volga & was knocked on the head when he was young, and he was only an errand boy you know.'

Foolishly Laurie mentioned the Russian lady to Lorna. In exciting her suspicions he was playing with fire, knowing that she was prone to explosions of angry jealousy. One day he found her in the caravan looking at his letters and reading through his diary. After he relates this in his diary, there are lines pencilled in Lorna's hand: 'I didn't really lend the Beethoven to be copied but was jealous of you playing it with someone else! I'm sorry if I annoyed you or got on your nerves. I love you.'

'On a germ of truth she builds up vast fantasies of infidelity & guilt. I secretly rejoice, but far from removing her suspicions I only succeed, by protestations & shiftless grinning, to appear hopelessly culpable.' She imagined he spent his time apart from her

> in the arms of revolting blondes. She threatens me with spectac-
> ular infidelities unless I mend my ways. But I have not broken
> them. What more can I say than that I love her? ... Walking
> the black streets she said, 'I feel very miserable – I feel nobody
> wants me.' I said how silly you are when you're the centre of my
> life. I stood and held her in the darkness. 'I don't trust you a bit,'
> she said. Her jealousy is based partly on my poem. She takes 'I
> cannot clear your high gold from my head' to be a reference to
> some blonde!

Winter brought freezing mists and grey sleet; Laurie succumbed to one of his bronchial fevers. He sat hunched, dazed and coughing, his violin hanging from the ceiling echoing each cough and parodying it harmonically, 'like a musical parrot'. The caravan would sway, rock and tremble at the slightest sound, 'poised so delicately on its springs that it seems to shudder even when I lay down my pen'. He had terrible nights of 'knotted nerves, restless mad fancies & sleeplessness'.

Back in Slad for Christmas, he found alien planes floating over the valleys, the woods aglow under searchlights, and guns and splinters bursting over Bulls Cross. But there was a plum-pudding-and-crackers Christmas at Marjorie's, he played games with nieces and nephews, drank port and sherry, visited Phyl in hospital and 'kissed all the struggling nurses under the mistletoe'. He chopped logs, played his fiddle, saw the new year in with Annie, and returned to find his little green caravan dark and chill. 'Poor Tom's a-cold tonight. So cold I can't settle to finish the poems I've been working on.'

When he saw Lorna again, 'burning like the bush of Moses in spite of the weather', he fell on her, 'revoking the realisation of a fortnight's fantasy. I trembled & sang & stamped the cloven feet ... hands probing into scarlet caverns, I reduced her to helplessness & took her, sick with power.' For her thirtieth birthday he bought Lorna a silver chain, and for himself a camel-haired overcoat with shoulders like yardarms.

> L came this morning and caught me all behind as my mother would say. She had just taken Yasmin to the doctor's where he removed several yards of wool from her nose ... sad proof of a hereditary recurrence of the nose-stuffing that has made our family a thing of wonder and fear for many generations.

Plump, coy and lively, Yasmin scrambled about the caravan, blowing notes on his recorder. 'I look at her quaint, charming, homely face, her pretty squat little body and cannot yet get it into my head that she is mine.'

Annie was ailing with 'flu, the cottage's chimney smoked and there was ice underfoot. She longed to see Yasmin ('little soul!') and Lorna,

> poor child, but I don't want her to come to this dreadful dreadful house. I love her & always shall. Did she tell you I sent a little dog to Yasmin & she loves it & carries it about. Oh Laurie darling they are cutting the trees down and I can't bear it. Soon there will be no background to our cottages. First they cut two elms one ash one sycamore then this afternoon they cut beautiful scotch pine, then a spruce. Oh dear.

Laurie was 'still with horror at the thought'.

Then Lorna came tearing up the lane 'splashing the tops of the trees with mud', bringing snowdrops, Christmas roses, champagne.

> I can say I have never seen her looking more beautiful, champagne in her hands and her eyes. Her black sweater & black hair enclosed her face like night enfolding a star. And round her throat hung the silver chain … She tells me she is in love with me again, and her demonstrations do compensate for the rather disquieting knowledge that she was once, then not, in that emotional state which she now professes.
>
> Our difficulties are boundless. I live in a most inaccessible place, petrol is rationed, and her children are sickening for something … After a particularly wild shaking release she sleeps deeply, but I sleep just under the sweet surface of wakefulness. A particularly loud cry of a bird will wake me with a terrific start.

Sometimes he bridled at being the secret lover; he could go to Binsted to visit Wilma, 'but it is forbidden country, Christ al-bloody-mighty. I skulk around the hedges like a poacher & don't begin to whistle till I'm in the bus well on my way to Worthing … When can I take my girl into the open?' Lorna would remind him of her marital commitments, 'fiendishly dwelling on the inevitability of conjugal surrenders'. She told of a nightmare after which she had woken up screaming for Wish: 'How I hate that she should awaken like that.' She showed him the £50 bill for the thick silvery sealskin coat Wish had given her. 'She confesses that she wanted to impress upon me that others still thought her desirable. But I am not in need of such virulent propaganda.' She might sit quietly in the afternoons, darning his socks, but

> I don't know what it is to walk easily up a street with her, or to write her a frank carefree letter. I have never been able to feel 'tomorrow I'll call & have tea with her' or 'tonight I think I'll ring her up'. I have never been able to take her & show her to a

friend & say look, this is my woman: I have had none of those normal domestic gaieties of love. Always we have lived in a state of subterfuge, each second together stolen from the cannon's mouth and consumed under a canopy of uneasiness. For four years it has been like this, for four years I've dreamed about her husband. No wonder the actual state of war in which we are now living, days & nights of anxiety, of restriction, of hand-to-mouth existence, does not seem strange to me.

He brightened, as he always would, with the spring: 'Such a bright singing day I take on quite a different personality. I am myself in the sun, the world has glamour; when it is cold I am a corpse.' He went to London to meet his patron John Lehmann ('tall, teutonic looking and deferential') at the Café de l'Europe. Lehmann praised the richness of Laurie's latest poems and asked Laurie who were the influences on his young life. Laurie declined to write a piece on life in Storrington, but agreed to write something about Spain. Annie sent his Spanish diaries so that he could begin. While in London he went to the Players' Theatre with Jack, where the master of ceremonies, Leonard Sachs, referred from the stage to 'the Masters Lee – or should it be Mister and Master Lee?'

March brought another bone-aching fever,

> throbbing in my tousled bed, sweating, arguing, groaning with thumping head, exhaustion and full of foreboding & nervous strain, aching and rather sorry for myself needing a woman & L did not come. I felt the old slow fires of temper growing inside me. But she had been ill, too...

He dreamed that Yasmin was hurt, and that Wish was holding her in his arms, but had handed her over to Laurie 'without a murmur, as if he understood'. On Yasmin's second birthday he sent a bracelet and a new florin, and spent the day acting an air-raid victim, for a first aid film. When he saw it he thought how old he looked. Lorna told him,

1. Laurie's father, Reg Lee

2. Laurie's mother, Annie Emily Lee, *née* Light

3. The infant Laurie ('a frail lifeless lump'), with elder brother Jack and sister Frances

4. Laurie aged five

5. *top left* Annie's cottage (now Rosebank) in Slad

6. *top right* Slad School: Laurie is in the back row, second from left; in the middle row, fourth from left, is his cousin Rosie Green, later Rosie Buckland, popularly supposed to be *the* Rosie

7. Peace Day fancy dress parade in Slad: Laurie as John Bull, with Rosie Green as a fairy at his right

8. *bottom left* Laurie (back row, second from left) in Slad Wolf Cubs; brother Tony is kneeling, right front

9. *bottom right* A couple of swells: Jack and Laurie in their plus-fours

April 15th 1939

10. *top left* Molly Smart with Laurie, June 1932
(*Betty Farmer*)
11. *top right* Betty and Molly Smart, the girls
from Gloucester, 1933 (*Betty Farmer*)
12. *bottom left* Cleo of Whiteway, in 1934
13. *bottom right* Sufi Rogers, the girl from
Buenos Aires who taught Laurie to say '*Un vaso
de agua, por favor*'

clockwise from left
14. Laurie, photographed in Southampton, having just walked out one midsummer morning: 'a pale, oleaginous shade … his old clothes powdered in dust'
15. Laurie in Toledo, with Mary (*née* Garman) and Roy Campbell, 1935 (*Anna Campbell Lyle*)
16. Wilma Gregory, benefactress and self-styled 'aunt'

17. *bottom right* Laurie in Martigues, with six-year-old Kathy on his knee, 1937
18. *bottom left* A bronzed Laurie and his fiddle in Málaga, 1935

19. Lorna Wishart, mistress and muse

20. Laurie bound for the Spanish Civil War, 1937. This photograph is thought to be the one he used for his International Brigade identity card

21. Laurie, his fiddle, and his two-year-old daughter Yasmin, Sussex, 1941 (*Yasmin David*)

22. Portrait of the poet by Bill Brandt, Bognor, 1942 (*Bill Brandt* © *Bill Brandt Archives Ltd*)

23. Anthony Devas and his wife, Nicolette, with their children Emma and Esmond and (in the foreground) two playmates, April 1945 (*Devas Family Collection*)

24. Anthony Devas's portrait of Laurie with two of the Devas children, Emma and Esmond, and Eileen McKinney, 1945. Eileen was the daughter of Ruth McKinney, author of the *My Sister Eileen* stories (*Private Collection*)

25. Laurie, Crown Film Unit scriptwriter, 1944

26. Jack Lee, film director

27. *top left* Laurie working hard on his film in Cyprus, 1945
28. *top right* C. Day-Lewis and Laurie
29. *bottom left* Rosamond Lehmann
30. *bottom right* Laurie and seventeen-year-old Kathy on holiday in Deal, 1948
(*Devas Family Collection*)

'I'm longing for you to grow old – each new wrinkle on your face is a joy to me – I want you to grow old & repulsive so that no one will want to look at you.' Laurie said, 'I've nearly reached that state anyway.' He was not yet twenty-seven.

One day he met 'a dark man' in the local shop buying rice. Next day 'the negro' visited him, with a girl, to fetch Laurie and his records. He was from Kenya, Laurie learnt, and had been Alexander Korda's technical adviser on *Sanders of the River*, but was 'too red' to be allowed to go home again. It was Jomo Kenyatta – later to become president of Kenya.[62]

> We had tea on the balcony overlooking the downs, and played Ellington, flamencos and Indian records and Jomo trembled and danced in his chair and rolled his brown eyes and jerked his great bearded head back and forth. He has some fine African records. The girl, pale and English and out of touch with all this, preferred Debussy.

Later Laurie went to hear Kenyatta lecturing, in the great hall of a stately home at Little Thakeham, on African colonies: 'We heard all about the black man's burden & joined in reviling the Commonwealth.'

One terrible night in March, Lorna's 'prim, respectful' cook, Rose, was beaten to an unrecognisable pulp by a soldier. 'Wish was marvellous,' Lorna told Laurie. 'He nursed her and bathed her and held her on his knee, but Michael and I nearly passed out.' She was overcome with man-hating fury. 'Just force and lust, that's what it was, I hate the thought of men – I hate soldiers – I hate myself.' 'But as she drove away she said "Love me, love me all the time."' Laurie felt sick and appalled. 'But what can you expect of soldiers from the lives they lead, celibate, disciplined, praised out of all proportion, taught a trade of violence which they are persuaded is the most honourable that can fall to a man.'

One day the caravan's landlord, Dennis Earle, suggested that Laurie might earn his rent by gardening for ten hours a week. Laurie haggled: his rent was only seven shillings a week, and labourers earned a shilling an hour. So he would do two mornings a week, seven hours in all. He blistered his hands with digging. In the evenings he played music with the de Sélincourts or listened to jazz at Kenyatta's where they talked of Nancy Cunard and negro poetry. Annie wrote peevishly, 'If you are able to hold a pen or pencil write & say how the world's treating you. My address above. Perhaps you are very busy, poem writing or something?'

He was poem writing, but had no confidence in his latest efforts and suspected that all the others were 'flukes'. Lehmann found most of them 'too Dylan Thomas'. 'This was a little unfair as I don't read him.' The same week came the *New Statesman* with a warm mention of Laurie's four 'striking' poems in a review. Laurie was also writing his first piece of prose, 'Night in Castelleja', about Spain before the Civil War, for the summer issue of the Hogarth Press's *Folios of New Writing*, though Lorna demoralisingly declared that the subject was 'dead meat ... Hemingway killed it'. 'I am not being modest when I say I don't think it will be any good to you,' wrote Laurie to Lehmann. 'It is just an amplified extract from my diary, nothing more.' It was the account of playing his fiddle for the stomping, politically excited vineyard workers of Andalucía in June 1936. Lehmann said he would make some small cuts 'where I think you overdo it a little (a criticism I sometimes hear of your poetry)'.

A letter from Laurie was published in the *News Chronicle*, on 26 March 1941 (signed L. E. A. Lee of Stroud) in defence of young people toiling in factories. 'A modern war-time factory is no bed of roses, the long hours, day in, day out, tend to stifle the high spirits and craving for simple enjoyment natural to every youth. Consequently they react in violence, destruction and petty crime.'

In April he and Lorna went away for a weekend, but her car broke down just as they were about to spin off 'for a little freedom'. The car was towed away and they caught a series of buses to rainy Petersfield and found a mean little hotel with iron bedsteads, paintings of shipwrecks on the walls, and a maid named Ethel. They went to church, Lorna in a white scarf. An usher asked if they had come for a churching. ('I wish we had been.') Back in the caravan a letter waited, offering Laurie a job as Assistant Director in what was now called the Crown Film Unit, at £5 a week.

> Rang L who is in bed with flu. She wept when I said I might go, so of course I promised her I wouldn't. (I remember once, when we were together, she wept long & bitterly when I talked of leaving her. She couldn't contemplate living without me, she cried, she made me promise never to leave her. But it didn't prevent her from leaving me.)

John Lehmann now wanted up to fifteen poems for the third volume in the *Poets of Tomorrow* series. Four poems were ready for the next *New Writing*: 'Larch Tree', 'Juniper', 'Look into Wombs', 'End of a Season'. He wrote another 'for Lorna' and took it to her. Yasmin, bundled in red wool, was there, 'chattering like a magpie'.

> She played with me but would not kiss me. 'No-o-o,' she said. I watched her, having thought of her as Us, existing through Us and dependent on Us, but I suddenly knew that she was more than that, she was herself, with an independent will & spirit, and not only existed apart from us, but even sometimes looked upon me with the blank eyes of a stranger. Though unpleasantly inevitable I never foresaw this.

Suddenly one day a plain-clothes CID man arrived and told Laurie he was breaking the law by living in the caravan. Annie wrote: 'I think it is rotten the police interfering … you do have adventures Laurie boy.' They packed his stuff into a barrow and wheeled it over to Dennis Earle's spare studio, built a wood fire and Lorna arranged cowslips in a saucepan on the table.

> Walking back beneath the castle to have tea we leaned over a bridge. A duck & a drake circled each other passionately.

Suddenly we heard the cuckoo loud & close. It called three times from the trees above the castle. We leapt into one another's arms. We wanted to hear it for the first time together & it happened.

London was enduring its worst raids. The Houses of Parliament had been hit. Rudolf Hess landed in Scotland. Laurie watched in disgust a newsreel called *The World in Flames*, which ended with shots of London in ruins. 'The commentary reached a crescendo. "Here's to bigger & better bombs!" it shouted.' Churchill's speeches were 'hardly reassuring'. 'Nothing becomes any easier, any less complic-ated, any less hopeless as time goes on.' He would lie in bed reading Plato, or Martial, or *The Good Soldier Švejk* (still catching up on his untutored literary education) and listening to the crack of machine-guns and the roar of engines until his hair stood on end.

As summer came the lovers resumed their open-air lovemaking. 'We stood against the sky touching each other and she looked into my face, laughing and saying, "You are extraordinary, you are really."' This August would be the start of their fifth year.

On the flyleaf of Lorna's copy of *Folios of New Writing*, Spring 1941, Laurie wrote:

Again your lily's dazzling star
revolving in the burning springs
transfixes with its scimitar
my happy fascinated wings
and I am full content that I
should on your perfumed petals die.

There are at least thirty versions of these lines in his notebook. 'She didn't think much of my last opus,' he wrote.

I affected despair at her criticism, lying on the bed with my face to the wall. She came from cooking the stew, leant over me & kissed me. 'Darling,' she said to comfort me, 'you know I think

you're marvellous. I think your poems are the most beautiful
I've ever read.' I laughed loud & bitterly. 'I *do*,' she said coax-
ingly, 'I do really – I said so to Mavin [her brother] & he laughed
too.' Cold comfort.

In June they went back to Slad. They found Annie in her garden, 'wild,
wayward and uncontrolled'. The back kitchen had been whitewashed
and the door painted blue with a bright yellow keyhole. There were
three new kittens, making five cats in all. Lorna and Laurie played
together in frustrated harmony on Annie's horribly out-of-tune piano.
Again it was hot, even in the evening, poppies and peonies blazing,
syringa in bloom. 'The days following were yellow with endless sun
& we were quietly indolent. In the mornings we would go to Stroud,
have lunch, and return to lie naked by the lake or in the woods or the
fields.' Laurie did a drawing of Lorna, sitting pensively on Juniper Hill,
with her hair in plaits, the sun shining so whitely on the paper he could
hardly see. They sat on walls and both drew views of the village. 'Some
of her sketches aren't bad in a childish way ... Her eye is remarkably
simple, perspective is ignored, and nothing has any logical relation
with anything else. Her results, therefore, are remarkably refreshing.'
Laurie also photographed her, lying half naked on the grass, 'white
like a new moon' sitting on the bank of the stream, doing her hair. 'She
looks over her shoulder, sly & bold. It is perfectly French, reeking with
wine, good food, and the flesh.'

'In all the fierce blaze of days we did little but lie among the grasses
and watch the valley. Sometimes a quiet tenderness hung over us as we
walked in the garden, or surrounded us like an extra fragrance as we
lay close in the new summer blossoms.' At other moments 'I felt the
bitterness of never completely possessing the full heart & attention of
this woman ... in the middle of a kiss her eyes open to the sky and her
mind goes back to her children.'

Barrage balloons floated overhead. They lay in Brith Wood at
midnight, among the badgers. Laurie waded into the pond to fetch
pink and white lilies. He carried Lorna up through the nettles to

the attic of the ruined cottage by the war memorial, 'hot with a sort of adolescent lust. The evening was a green and rosy gloom, creepers climbed through the broken lattices almost shutting out the light.'

On the Sunday morning in June when Germany invaded Russia Laurie went to bed with a fever '& I thought of Martigues, but the fever was neither so intense, nor did L sit gazing into my face'. On his twenty-seventh birthday they set off for London, Lorna in a chaste grey costume (such a lady, said Annie), and parted at Victoria. Annie sent a birthday parcel after him – soap, tea, sugar, cheese, butter, margarine, lard, lemonade powder, jelly, biscuits, dates, gooseberries and three roses 'all rather mixed'. 'You do know don't you that I was very pleased to have you & your dear one,' she wrote, enclosing a letter for Lorna, thanking her for 'the lovely stockings and also the "little bit of paper".' Back at Storrington the sun was like a furnace. Laurie hoed potatoes, stripped to the waist, dreaming of Spain. 'L arrived in her old summer frock, scarlet, like a pimento. We lay on the bed in a stupor of heat and the red dress opened down the front and her limbs were cool and white like a sweet vegetable.' By the river at Arundel, Lorna wore a green dress which dated back to Martigues. 'She brought me four eggs, and a weasel stole two out of my bag when we were swimming.' They lay in the reeds, and walked through banks of twisting eglantine. Herons flew above them, fighter planes came and went, waterfowl shrieked. 'I like that sound. You've no idea what it does to me,' said Lorna.

A *Spectator* review of *New Writing* declared that 'Laurie Lee's Lorcan imagery may prove baffling', and some poems of this period might indeed baffle: they present the reader with a succession of idiosyncratic images and impressions, which only really spring to vivid sense in the context of his pastoral adventures with Lorna while battles raged overhead:

Pondering your scented skull
I seek its antique song of peace:

desires uncovered by your tide
are trembling reeds with sea-blue voices.

I wind my hands around your head
and blow the hollow flutes of love,
but anger sprouts among the leaves
and fields grow sharp with war.
Wheat bleeds upon a wind of steel
and ivy splits the poisoned sky,
while wasps that cannot fertilise
dive at the open flowers of men.

Your lips are turreted with guns,
and bullets crack across your kiss,
and death slides down upon a string
to rape the heart of our horizon.

('Song in August', 1940)

In mid-July 1941, the BBC wrote offering Laurie a fee of five guineas
to read his poems on a programme called Turning Over a New Leaf.

I sat on the steps and trembled violently, and thought of fits
and nerves sweeping the words out of my mind in front of the
microphone. When I recovered I wanted to tell someone so I
mentioned it casually to Steve who was building a wall. 'Oh,'
he said, 'my aunt broadcast a few weeks back.' 'What about?' I
asked, deflated. 'Sausage making,' he said.

He told Lorna, and she didn't think he could do it.

Meanwhile, not far away, Helen Garman had brought her daughter
Kathy, now nine, home to England. Kathy had waved her father Marius
goodbye, and he told her the war would soon be over. But she never
saw him again, although Helen had bravely gone back to France to try

to persuade him to leave too. Kathy was sent first to the Dorset village of Moreton to stay with her aunt Sylvia Garman, friend of T. E. Lawrence.[63] One day, a telegram arrived to say her father had died, of pleurisy.

Kathy was taken to Vine Cottage, East Harting, where her grandmother Marjorie Frances Garman provided a haven for her grandchildren: Kitty and Esther, Kathleen's daughters by Epstein, and later Mary Campbell's daughters Anna and Teresa. The governess – Mary Elizabeth Thomas, known as Tony, who had 'the face of a dove and the heart of a lion'[64] – was in charge. Esther and Kitty were superior and unpleasant to their French cousin Kathy, adapting her surname 'Polge' into 'Bulgy'. But in the village lived a Miss Murray, a former governess who liked to talk French and took Kathy under her wing. She called her '*mon loup*'. Helen was working for the Free French in London, so she stayed with her sister Kathleen at 272 King's Road, and both sisters would visit their children in East Harting at weekends. All the girls would sometimes call on their Aunt Lorna at Marsh Farm, where the glamour and wealth of the chatelaine dazzled them all.

That summer, Laurie decided he had had enough of isolated Storrington. He would go to Bognor, which despite mines and barbed wire was packed with cheerful holidaymakers. Deaf, drunken old landladies showed him dark, cluttered rooms. Eventually he found a furnished cottage down Market Street for £1 week. It smelled of gas cookers, like Werter Road, but the wallpaper was the same as in Lorna's old nursery, and the landlady Mrs Savage proved to be another Mrs O'Neill: 'If you feel like having anyone in here all the week, don't think I shall mind.'

On 2 August he worked in the garden for the last time, collected his music from the de Sélincourts, packed his books into Mabel Mallet's car and on a clear dappled morning left the Storrington Sanctuary. 'Everything seemed sharp & lovely and I gazed about me with affection because I am leaving it. I have been lonely but not exactly unhappy here.'

10

In Love and War
1941–1942

LAURIE'S MODEST POETIC output might have been even scantier had he not been galvanised by John Lehmann, whose patronage was both an inspiration and an irritation as he demanded more poems. 'I would like to go on pushing your stuff as much as possible,' he told Laurie. '*Poets of Tomorrow* is going to press, and I shall have to invent something if you don't let me have the goods.' 'I never felt less like poetry but was forced to,' wrote Laurie wearily. When Lehmann told him that his sister Rosamond liked his work, and wanted to meet him, 'I feel almost guilty,' Laurie told his diary, 'as if I'm cheating them all … it makes me uneasy that the stuff I've produced is so slight.'

The day of his broadcasting debut – 25 August 1941 – loomed. He left anxiously for London, where Lorna swept him off to the Café Royal with her Old Etonian painter friend David Carr, who 'smoothly delivered light amusing stories with that languid articulation which is the social genius of his class'. They repaired to the Swiss pub in Old Compton Street where Dylan Thomas was swaying at the bar:

> a young rather tubby man, straw coloured in a pork pie hat, with a snub nose, pale eyes and a small loose mouth. He had two females with him, both blowsy and both rather drunk. One was talking to him in unsteady lurches and calling him 'darling' – the other was his wife. I gave him a drink & a cigarette … He was

bleak, dead & rather miserable, saying he had a wife & child to keep and no job. He looked about him joylessly with wet subterranean eyes as if the whole world was a wet Monday. I thought him flabby and conceited…

Meanwhile a dark veiled figure, thin & gaunt like a spook, had taken a seat at our table and L called to me and introduced this thing. A white gloved hand, cold & rubbery, reached up to me. I saw two huge dark eyes, two thin purple lips and a dusty white face inquiring at me from a pillar of black lace & crêpe. I thought of Kathleen. 'This is the Marchesa,' said L. '[Augustus] John painted her.' I remembered the picture and the eyes. L introduced me as a poet. 'Never live with a poet,' said the thing, half in Italian – 'I lived with D'Annunzio.'

(It was the Marchesa Luisa Casati.[65])

From another corner Roy Campbell appeared.

Bald, trembling & smiling … He was delighted to see us, he said, and sat at the table, stuttering, looking from one to the other, smiling & quivering with apologies. He had been f-for F-Franco in the Spanish war and now it was like having backed the wrong horse. 'I was wrong Lorna,' he said. She laughed and slapped his arm. 'There now Roy, after the way we used to fight, you see?' 'Yes,' he said hoarsely, 'I admit it, I admit being wrong.' He returned to his corner…

Lehmann was waiting at Broadcasting House. In a hot little studio, the clock swept round to zero. Lehmann had told him to read his poems as if speaking to someone in an armchair in the same room. Laurie read 'The Larch Tree', 'The Secretive Cuckoo', 'Juniper' and 'The Armoured Valley'. Lehmann signalled to him to read more. He read 'Winter 1939–40' – 'A gentle dove the icicle is now'. Lehmann said that Laurie's poems put him in mind of the carvings of the Crusaders in old English churches. Laurie responded with his prepared lines about writing in wartime and poetry in general, and was followed by a record of T. S. Eliot reading *East Coker*. 'It was over and I felt gay.' In the foyer Lorna waited, and so did Rosamond Lehmann: 'a handsome woman with large deep eyes and silver hair, and the skull of her brother. I walked down Oxford St with her. She said that she thought my poems really beautiful – so disciplined etc. – I found myself saying how much I loathed women writers.'

At the Café Royal he bought roses for Lorna. They went on to a noisy Lyons brasserie, then to a pin-table dive where Lorna had her fortune told by a gypsy. Laurie's last train had gone, and they found a hotel. 'Suddenly, my weariness left me and a great volcano of delight shook us with joyful flames.' Next morning they bought Stravinsky's *Symphony of Psalms* at the HMV shop, and took the train back to Sussex, where they 'strutted through the streets elbowing away the crowds with our embracing and ate peanuts till we rattled'.

Laurie's broadcasting career had begun. He sent Annie some of his five-guinea fee.

But when Lehmann wired again asking for more poems for *Penguin New Writing 10*, 'I beat my breast in despair. I could think of nothing. I polished up four and sent them to him but I have little confidence in them … they don't blend as they should.'

Becoming recognised as a poet created its own momentum. Tambimuttu[66] reprinted three poems in a Faber anthology. Kaye Webb wired from *Lilliput*: they were sending Bill Brandt down to Bognor to photograph Laurie. Annie was delighted to see his 'phiz' in *Lilliput*. 'You really are becoming famous now aren't you? I had already seen hundreds of copies, thrust in my face by all & sundry. I hope you won't get "swelled head".' On the contrary, 'I was quietly deflated by it all,' Laurie noted. 'I feel as always that the best is passed and I can never do as well again.' The day Brandt arrived, Laurie cleaned his room and lit a fire, and took Brandt and his assistant to lunch and to swim at the beach: 'I felt they were press and therefore had to be entertained.' The resulting picture – one of the most famous of Laurie – made him look 'a rugged and Olympian roué';

the other poets under the headline 'Poets of Democracy' were 'a gallery of hideous morons & gargoyles. Dylan Thomas looks sick in a pub, Day-Lewis screws horrible faces at a newspaper, MacNeice scowls like a greasy witch, Spender is flayed by an overhanging lamp.' Laurie's 'Words Asleep' was printed beneath his picture. 'I suddenly felt it was very easy to write poetry.'

But Lehmann wanted prose too. He suggested that Laurie might write 'some rather personal sketch or story about the Cotswolds, and your early days there' for the *Geographical Magazine*. 'We are anxious to have more articles about England and the English countryside.' Laurie duly wrote an article about the Whitsun Treat outings of his childhood, which was greeted by the editor as 'a little work of art...', 'fresh and full of colour and amusing images' upon which Laurie 'sang lustily'. But Lehmann added: 'If anything, I think it's a little too concentrated, a little too packed with imagery: if you were writing anything longer, I think you'd have to watch that. But ... you really must go on writing prose.'

The *Geographical Magazine* wanted pictures of his cottage, the church, the squire's house, etc. Had Laurie any objection to his village being identified? A photographer was dispatched to Slad. Annie expected him on the wrong day, and left her house keys in a bag of beans at Tony's house. Someone had to break in through a window, it was raining, and the photographer missed the bus and had to walk from Stroud 'and the poor boy is a cripple, did you know? What a pity it was wet & dingy & dull, and the day before was glorious.' She agonised over the fact that she had just had the kitchen painted and there was only one teapot on the mantelpiece, 'so I'm afraid you'll be disappointed about this as you don't like things to be changed'. But his article – Laurie had sent a manuscript –

> Oh my dear, I think it beautiful, your fanciful idea of a children's day of joy in lovely surroundings in beautiful weather. I laughed heartily ... Of course I knew who you meant by the various names. Well dear Laurie will you allow me to rewrite part of it so

that anyone who knew the people in S. could not be hurt in any way. NOT bald-headed Mrs Lewis, put smiling Mrs Grey, and what about 'the village cripple' could it be altered? Please write by return and say I may. It's the names dear.

But he changed nothing, and when the magazine came out with 'bald Mrs Lewis', Annie was reproachful:

It to me marred the whole story and I cannot with pleasure show it to anyone who knows the person meant. I have taken it up to Mrs Brown and told her not to let Mrs Tilley see it or Mrs Oakey ... I read some of the story aloud to Eileen John and Mrs Walters oh they did laugh but Eileen was disappointed that there was nothing about her as she thought she was a school sweetheart.

It was a foretaste of Slad's reaction to *Cider with Rosie* two decades later.

While in the caravan, Laurie had gone to the cinema most weeks; in Bognor, he and Lorna went even more often. They saw *Major Barbara*, *Boom Town*, *Our Town*, *La Femme du Boulanger*, the Marx Brothers, *The 49th Parallel*, *The Maltese Falcon*, *Citizen Kane*, *Hellza-poppin*, *Blood and Sand*, *Scarface*. Afterwards they would take home nine-penn'orth of fish and chips, or Lorna would cook 'evocative' rice dishes, 'full of onions, winkles, tomatoes and oily smells of Spain'. On a newsreel they saw what was happening in Russia: the dead laid out in heaps surrounded by weeping women. 'One felt a fever of fear & horror, one could smell the horrible humiliation of death. We were suddenly in the centre of all this foul business, & felt sick.'

Lehmann's sister Rosamond now made a determined approach to make Laurie her friend. She wrote from Diamond Cottage at Aldworth on the Berkshire Downs declaring that she and Laurie had a bond in their 'mutual dislike of women writers', and that Cecil Day-Lewis would love to meet Laurie; she would fix a date.

Lorna read this letter and was furious. Rosamond was a threat. She was 'an operatic goddess of a woman'[67] with a face of Dresden china beauty (or in Alan Ross's words, 'like a creamy meringue') and a sterling literary pedigree.[68] Her first novel, *A Dusty Answer*, written while she was living in Newcastle married to the Methodist businessman Leslie (later Lord) Runciman, had been an overnight sensation in 1927. Her second husband, Wogan Philipps (Lord Milford), the Communist peer, failed to return to her after the Spanish Civil War. She had published three more novels, all dealing with women unhappily in love. She had two children, and told Laurie: 'I've always thought how satisfactory it would be to pull off being a good artist as well as being a successful mother.' When she befriended Laurie, she had just met and fallen in love with Cecil Day-Lewis.

Bidden to Rosamond's London home in Gordon Place, Kensington, Laurie went first to see the Sickert paintings at the National Gallery, and then wandered in Bloomsbury, past 10 Kenton Street, its balcony covered with flowerpots, and Mecklenburgh Square, where he and Lorna had first lived. 'No 35 had completely disappeared, a black heap of ash and cinders with one wall left standing. Somehow I was not sorry.' He found Rosamond's house 'crowded with pictures and furniture of the decayed gentlewoman type' and Rosamond 'as tender and sentimental as her books'. When Day-Lewis arrived, he and Rosamond sat in the same chair, and Laurie told them about his caravan. Day-Lewis, who was editing pamphlets for the Ministry of Information, was intrigued. He asked Laurie to lunch next day: they talked of Dylan Thomas and Roy Campbell. It was the start of a valued friendship.

Laurie was ten years younger than Day-Lewis and they were 'as different as two complicated men can be'[69] but they became fastly entwined. Day-Lewis was vacillating (and did for another eight years) about leaving his wife Mary and their sons Sean and Nicholas. Rosamond quickly latched on to Laurie as her confidant, as one of the few people who did not date from Day-Lewis's previous life.

Laurie was grateful that a respected poet should take him seriously enough to show him his new sonnet sequence 'O Dreams O
Destinations', and solicit his opinion.

Day-Lewis also put Laurie in touch with the composer Ben
Frankel, his old Whiteway associate ('So our paths cross again aha!'),
who wired to say he needed three Russian songs reworked for his new
play – by the end of that week. Laurie ('Oh Lord') felt overwhelmed
by this commission, and sent them off knowing they weren't right. As
he feared, they weren't: 'I wish I could have pulled it off.' Jack, whose
new film *The Pilot is Safe* had been favourably reviewed, arrived by car
in Bognor one evening; they had fish and chips 'and boasted to one
another'. But as winter approached Laurie felt flat and melancholy.
Lorna calmed him, lit fires and was 'as gracefully voluptuous as of old'.
She told him that when the war was over she planned to live abroad
and have lots of children. Laurie said: 'Oh I didn't know anything
about that.' She added: 'You're coming too – didn't you know?' He
never knew how seriously to take her. He felt uneasy.

> Sometimes my brain and body seems quite sick and raw and
> nothing will heal it ... The moon is full tonight and I am
> empty. Up on the downs, we ate beechnuts and I said some of
> my poems but could hardly make myself heard for bombers.
> Should Yasmin go to kindergarten in the village school? asked
> Lorna. But what has it got to do with me?

After she had gone he was sorry he had not been more understanding. He really preferred living mostly alone. 'I am irritated &
sterile living continually with another person. Alone I can examine
myself and cherish love, and sport with illusions.'

Laurie went back to Slad that October, found Painswick devastated by bombs, walked with aunts and cousins, and played Mozart
and Beethoven with neighbours. 'In the kitchen the clock strikes
unbelievably slowly.' He was roused by a letter from Lorna to her
'violently dearly beloved', full of fury. She had been longing to hear

from him, 'vigilant at the door, pacing to the window, peering through the soapy mists for the girl who brings the letters', but his last letter 'only smelt of Slad and your affection for Slad,' she wrote, 'with a burning last few lines, which felt as though they'd been thrown in as an afterthought just to keep me quiet & sound conventional.'

Why couldn't he think of anything to write for *Penguin 12*? He would be better with her, or near her.

At least when you were you thought of some poem for *Poets of Tomorrow*. Faithless rocket, screaming with brilliance one minute & everybody watching in awe & admiration & how many seconds later are you nothing but a forgotten piece of pinewood with shell of burnt cardboard lucky to be found in the grass by some little boy looking for mushrooms – but you might land on the thatch of my house & set fire to it, in which case it'd take more than the fire brigade to cool me down.

It's one of those days, rare now, when I'm in a state of isolated beatitude and I can hover between here & the church in an exalted coma, smell you in Yasmin's darling curls & pray for Russia & thank who I pray to for giving me the glory of loving and being loved by you. In such a state of mind I used to go into a church at Golders Green & pray that you'd come back from Spain & for the victory of the Spanish people & don't for a moment think that because Franco beat them that I thought how silly it was you did come back.

She had been listening to the repellent broadcasts of Lord Haw-Haw:

He's just like the ghoulish grimace at the darkening window, the hysterical lunatic who frightens children ... Did you hear Rachmaninov's concerto on a theme of Paganini – it was wonderful. When I gave Yasmin your kiss I showed her your letter & she said 'kind Tatarty Lolly gave Yassie a koon.' A koon my Lord, I crave a koon, on bended knees.

In two days, Lorna was in Slad. They took Annie for a picnic on Painswick Beacon, and paid a courtesy visit to Juniper. But it was cold '& L twisted her hair and I thought not of Martigues but of Mecklenburgh. We were not unhappy all the time, but the orange glamour of the previous years was not there. Though the evenings at home with mother were contented.'

He arrived back in Bognor in a blizzard. The latest *Penguin New Writing* and a four-guinea cheque brought no pleasure. His house was alive with mice; he drank hot milk and crept into a damp bed 'haunted by peeling wallpaper & dismal shadows'. He was bent in the cold over a blank sheet of paper when a blue fur passed the window and

> L came in. She said the smell of the oil stove reminded her of the caravan and made her want me. I thought of Carven scent at 2 guineas a bottle and paraffin at 3d a pint. The night closed in & I again felt the need for a circle of warmth.

With winter he was struck down with fever again. Lorna arrived with a dizzy hangover from a night out in Portsmouth. 'I curled up like an earwig while she talked to me of drinking, majors, gins, bars, hotels and all the usual Razzle clap trap.' But then she brought a chicken casserole, a pot of honey, Bach preludes.

> I played the preludes while she prepared a pungent meal and baked a cake. We lay in the twilight and I thought of the good things thrust upon me. 'What a comfort it would have been,' she said, 'if we'd known at Mecklenburgh that in two years I'd be doing this for you.' I wondered.

They took Yasmin to a café where Lorna played Mozart on the pianola

> and Y found her tongue. A fluent dialect of her own, at times genteel and at times pure Sussex. I gave her coloured streamers

on a stick which she waved vigorously scattering bits over the floor. How strong and obstinate & charming she is, her face a common supple rosy visage based, I'm afraid, on a strain quite different from L's fine skull & features.

L was caustic & bitter about Rosamond Lehmann – as she is about almost everyone in whom I have any interest. Her jealousy is a strange rare thing & springs out of the slightest trifle. On the strength of reading one letter she contemplated not seeing me any more ... I feel that if I was once unfaithful and she discovered it, all this fine structure we have built up would mean less than nothing to her. She would sweep it away with a curse, & loathe me for ever more. She'd take her vengeance by an immediate affair with the nearest male. Yet within the limits by which she is confined I think she would like to be, and is, my own.

He was tormented by the thought of her husband making love to her. 'She loved me with fierce abandon as if wild to make amends. But how can she live there and withhold herself for ever and what can I do but lament her in secret?' Sometimes they had to hide when the Wishart family were nearby ('I felt waves of fury'), and once Lorna wired to say that 'the enemy' was in Bognor and he'd better lie low. Once, he saw 'L's children running loose in the town'. He would seize a chance to see her when she was at the hairdresser in Arundel, 'smothered in pins & drinking Guinness', or in Chichester where she was giving a pint of blood: Laurie's first visit there 'since I fiddled in the street on my way to London'.

So they went on: strolling along the shore, watching bombers in the sky, shopping, having tea and scones, sitting over the fire, playing music, wandering among tombs.

She was pliant & soft & tender, we walked encircled, with our mouths together. We thought how nice it would be to go far in a train – we said perhaps we can have a holiday among the Lakes

– and felt secretly that it would be impossible. We shall have to commit ourselves for work sooner or later. We can't ignore what is happening.

What was happening was the escalating war. The Russians had rallied in the face of the Nazi advance on Rostov 'but I keep thinking of Teruel'. After Pearl Harbor he wrote: 'Thus does the whole body of the earth succumb to this violent destructive paralysis. God knows how or when we can ever recover.' That day he was whistling Beethoven in the street when a ragged old man came up: 'May I congratulate you on what you're whistling,' he said. 'It's not often I hear that in the street.'

'And it's not often that I get it acknowledged,' said Laurie. 'This is my small life,' Laurie reflected. 'The world meanwhile is a bloody inferno ... South America seems to be the only remaining patch of earth at peace. The war stretches on over an infinity of years ahead.'

At Christmas Lorna brought Laurie books, cigarettes, exotic jigsaws and a briefcase stamped LL. 'I felt like King Solomon entertaining Sheba. My present to L was very humble – a diary.' He spent Christmas Day with his landlady, eating turkey, plum pudding, mince pies and real cream, 'remarkable food for the 3rd Christmas of the War'. Annie sent a book inscribed to 'Laurie Lee (the Poet)' and beads for Yasmin: 'Little Frances used to like funny little things to play with & I thought Yasmin might be a bit like her.'

His latest reviews for *Folios of New Writing* were encouraging. *Time & Tide* said his 'Night in Castelleja' was 'boldly & vigorously sketched; nothing in this volume surpasses it. Among comparative newcomers Mr Lee is someone to be reckoned with.' Annie wrote 'Congrats old thing!' alerting him to L. A. G. Strong's review of *Best Poems of 1941* in *The Observer*, which singled out Richard Church, Laurence Binyon and Laurie Lee as 'the only poets on whom the war has had an emotional impact'.

Inexorably Laurie was acquiring a literary reputation, without feeling that he could justify or sustain it. On New Year's Eve of 1942 he took the train for London, thick with fog, to meet Day-Lewis. At the door of the Ministry he passed Brendan Bracken, Churchill's Minister of Information. He visited 'aunt-like' John Lehmann at the Athenaeum: 'He read "Pastoral" but didn't altogether go for it – said he couldn't get the rhythm. Again he said I must have a book – but O God! filled with what?' At the *Horizon* office he met Spender, 'very tall, drooping, with a weak lisping mouth and looking like an undergraduate'. Cyril Connolly said: 'You've never sent us anything. Everything seems to go to Lehmann.' He told Laurie that John Betjeman admired his work (and when Betjeman sent his *Selected Poems* to Laurie in 1948 he signed it 'for Laurie Lee, a true poet, by John Betjeman, a lesser one'). They showed him poems submitted in a contest to be judged by Connolly, Spender, Eliot, and Herbert Read: 'I was graciously allowed to pass judgement.' Afterwards he walked to Russell Square with Spender, who said he was tired of being never alone – 'and I said I was tired of being always alone'. In Piccadilly he ran into Alberto Cavalcanti, of the Crown Film Unit, who hoped Laurie would come back to work for them. Laurie said: 'I'm a poet now.' But he caught his bus for Victoria immensely depressed. He found Day-Lewis amiable ('I like this man; apart from his sense of solid worth he is human') but the others 'are so sharp & clever, I don't understand them & can't ever conceive of being inti-mate with them'. It was New Year's Eve: he was in bed, alone, when he heard the church clock strike twelve.

Rations were cut to two pints of milk and two ounces of butter a week (Dorothy sent a cake and six mince pies, redolent of his sisters) and the winter weather was 'balls-aching', the air 'like thick blue ice'. Everyone in the streets looked cold, old and poor. 'The cold draws me into the warmth of a shut room, drawing girls on paper & in my mind…' He made thin porridge and scratched away at thin poems, distracted by noises of children and Canadian soldiers in the street outside. Then Lorna would waft in, scented with exotic 'Inque', making Laurie feel 'a flat spiritless oaf', and take him out for steak and kidney pie. 'We lay under warm blankets all afternoon & she was beautiful and I, empty of feeling or joy. There was a poem on the table but she read it when I wasn't looking & made no remark.' If only she'd comment, he might regain some confidence. Withered, uneasy, he walked by the desolate icy sea after she'd gone, watching the blown snow. But on Lorna's thirty-first birthday he combed Chichester and sent her a chess set, two handkerchiefs, a little pot, a rosary, an anthology, a volume of Nat Gubbins, the *Reynold's News* columnist, and an African bangle stuffed with hair.

But he saw 'something terribly lopsided' in his way of life. He was driven 'into an arctic depression' when Lorna talked of her domestic scene. 'I can get no comfort from her. I am allowed, as it were, a pair of coloured gloves and for the rest I may go naked.' In the station waiting room at Barnham he was smitten with a nervous crisis that left him in a dazed and shivering fever. Mrs Savage brought him soup as blizzards howled outside. For days he sat staring out of the window, 'feeling as old folk must undoubtedly feel, resentful and persecuted. All afternoon I waited in hot feverish misery for a voice or a face to comfort me.' At night he lay trembling and icy cold from sheets and pyjamas soaked in sweat. 'I groaned for the very relief it gave me to hear my groans in that horrible shivering deserted silence at four in the morning.' He saw only duplicity and hypocrisy and humbug all around. At last a wire from Lorna said she too was in bed, with bronchitis, and her son Luke also ill.

When Lorna read these diary pages,

> My, she did storm! I am amazed at the way she … twists [things] absolutely without scruple, and seems to forget that this life is only as she wishes it. She has what she wants when she wants it and everyone else modifies their desires to fit in with her. I don't think she realises the privileged position she is in: she, only, is the one who can say 'Today I will do this or that' while others wait…

He resolved to lock up his diary. Annie's prattling letters arrived almost daily with news of illness and deaths in the village, and that his half-brother Reg had joined up. Rommel was driving on along the Libyan coast. Finally Laurie broke off from listening to *The Lark Ascending* and reading *Don Quixote* and went to the Labour Exchange, seeking a job at a local aircraft engine factory. But he was deterred by the seven-day week. Anyway, there were no jobs going.

> I built up a furious fire and was preparing to go out when she walked in, bringing Christmas roses ... the room grew hot as summer with a roaring fire. We padded the floor & lay on it, forgetting the snow. We gazed at one another through the dusky tenor of Rachmaninov's 'Adagio'. I felt an atmosphere of soft colours & a gentle yearning sorrow, which was not really unhappiness. I felt soothed, in tune with beauty & tenderness, and contented.

But when she left he felt bleak and lost. 'Shall I never write anything again?'

He was utterly in her thrall. This was, in poetic terms, the most productive period of his life, but it was up to Lorna to say if his poems were any good; he resisted her suggestions ('those which are successful are written without endless spadework') but needed her approval. When he showed her 'The Wild Trees',

> She read the first two verses & thumped me on the chest. She read the rest & thumped me again. 'There, that shows what you can do,' she said. But I often envy her power of writing which she doesn't seem to realise is always warm & brilliantly original. She says, 'Luke much better, but has a cough like an old tree.' That is typical.
>
> 'You're a strange boy,' she said. 'But not strange enough,' I answered. 'No,' she said. I suppose she sees through me all the time. Oh, she can be winning & tender, touching to a degree ... She either exults me or deflates me. Today there were all sorts of grey undertones. Money, work & supposed girlfriends. We fought stupidly over two letters that came for me. Then waiting

for the train she stressed the frightful way I am living. All very true.
I am too full of the sense of my own failings to be humble. I asked
her when I should see her again. She said not till I wrote & asked
her to come. This infuriates me. I shall not write – that is my obstinate feeling tonight. We shall see whether she will come or not.

Seven days later he rang her, and she arrived 'in jodhpurs of all
things which had a peculiar effect on me so I made 3 drawings'.

In his crisis of poetic confidence, Rosamond Lehmann reassured
him that his poems were beautiful, rich and melancholy, and urged
him not to destroy anything her brother John disliked: 'He is often a
sound critic, but by no means always, to my mind.' Meanwhile Jack
told him he could write film scripts, and took Laurie in a studio car
to Pinewood, 'the great paint-smelling crumbling mausoleum of
desolation', new home of the Crown Film Unit'. Jack, his colleague
Nora Dawson and the director Humphrey Jennings drove Laurie
through devastated London. St Paul's remained unharmed. Jennings
remarked what a satisfaction he got, 'seeing how all those little City
men got theirs and St Paul's still stood up among it all.' Laurie left
them filming, walked back via Charing Cross Road ('price of sex
books soaring') and went home to watch an eclipse of the moon.

Lorna implored him not to go to Pinewood.

She looked at me across the table with an old look & we
marvelled that Yasmin is nearly 3 & that we've known each other
nearly 5 years. We returned home in a passion and the birds
sang loud round the roofs, and the rain stopped & the sun came
out. I hope I shall never forget her as she looked with the sun on
her face as she lay in bed a few inches from me. Suddenly her
dark beauty was brilliant like a precious stone, her hair sparkled
in tangles of rich blue locks, and her eyes were huge and deep
and full of greens & subterranean blues, and across her cheeks
and her mouth pursed in pleasure at my obvious delight, moved
the most lovely colours from the sky. I knew that this sudden burst

of sun through the window was one of the first fires of spring ... it
seemed that all the tender & exquisite lights of heaven entered the
room and were caught in her face like a crystal.

He inscribed Lorna's copy of *Poets of Tomorrow*: 'To Lorna – "In
your eyes I see/scaffolds of love arising and the most remote heaven
as familiar as bread" – Laurie March 1942.'

On Yasmin's third birthday they took her to the cinema for the
first time, and shopped for a wheelbarrow, a tractor and a tea-set.
Laurie began to realise that Yasmin was 'no dream of a child, nothing
like it, but a twisting, argumentative, obstinate, determined, frightened & winning individual. Wouldn't give me a kiss or say she
wanted to see me again. That's how she is.' He found her capricious
but good-tempered. She amused him by saying indignantly, in a
café where everyone sat in Anglo-Saxon silence, 'All the people are
asleep' and by shouting 'Bo-peeple!' Her first coherent sentences
made him ecstatic: 'I see her so seldom, her talking is like a miracle.'
Suddenly an offer came that Laurie could not refuse. Ian Dalrymple,
head of the Crown Film Unit, proposed that he should write scripts
at £7 11s 6d a week. Lorna was appalled, but Laurie could not go on
ignoring opportunities. Lorna said, 'It's like what I imagined death
must be – coming without warning, cutting short our lives.' Laurie
asked his diary: 'What *am* I going to do for this £7 a week?'

Before he joined the Unit, he and Lorna went back to Slad. Annie
cooked for them and they cleaned up the cottage for her, painted
chairs and a washstand. They parted desolately in Piccadilly with
'tenderness, nostalgia & regrets at this breaking up of our paradisal
existence'. He told himself: 'We have been very happy in this back-
water of compromise – we have seen each other more than most
married people find it possible to do.'

Laurie went back to lodge at Mrs O'Neill's in Putney and resumed
the old life there, but with a difference: he was now invited to London's
literary parties. He met Rose Macaulay, Nancy Cunard, Louis MacNeice,
Rex Warner, and of course Rosamond, Day-Lewis and Spender. At

John Lehmann's grand new flat in Hertford Street he drank orangeade while Lehmann 'leaned against the wall with his lofty diplomatic smile, and dispensed wine ... Everyone talked loudly about the Ballet.'

At Rosamond Lehmann's cottage for the weekend with Day-Lewis, he was fascinated to listen to 'their throwaway conversation, like miniature depth charges to scatter some friend in sparks. Do they all do it?' Looking through Lehmann family albums he saw photographs of Spender, Auden and Isherwood – 'brown smiling Nazi-looking youths posing in Berlin attics'. While the lovers were out walking, Laurie dug Rosamond's garden. 'One feels almost guilty to be here, but they shouldn't have asked me. But we had a gay tea of smoked salmon & they are very nice to me & charming together.' Day-Lewis was 'a rock of sense, humour & easy friendliness'. Rosamond he found 'as gracious and superficial as her brother'; he took her sweetness with a pinch of salt.

When Day-Lewis had left for London, Rosamond sat sewing and confided in Laurie her feelings for her lover. Laurie's friendship with Day-Lewis was mutually admiring: 'What an extraordinary number of things you know,' Day-Lewis told him. 'I respect you more and more.' (Day-Lewis was guilt-stricken that, though a Communist, he did not volunteer in Spain.) They would play at pin-tables in pubs and have Greek suppers. In Day-Lewis's Percy Street rooms they smoked cigars and talked of poets and poetry.

> We discussed the ideal way of living for writing poetry. Day-Lewis wanted a patron; I wanted to be lost in a community living an ordinary life with poetry growing out of it. But that wouldn't work, because in the community the barrier of 'queerness' would spring up and the most important requirement, acceptance, would disappear.
>
> We both agreed in the end that the impulse to write poetry can only really endure so long as one lives a slightly abnormal and physically unconsummate life. Marriage – i.e. happy marriage – is death to a poet.

In this respect, Laurie's liaison with Lorna was fruitful: it was secret and forbidden; it gave all his thoughts and sensations a romantic aura. As she told him, 'When you're away I get terrible feelings of tenderness for you – I could kiss your feet. The minute you step on the train you become a thing of extraordinary glamour.' Laurie reflected on this: 'What is absent is desired through a paradisal cloud of the mind; what is present may still be desired, but through a human aura of toothache, colds, worries and obvious blemishes.'

The day came when he had to start at Pinewood. He was to collaborate on a documentary, *Calling All Peoples*, with a Czech writer, Jiri Weiss, who told him: 'When you make a documentary film it shall be za truce, za whole truce and nazing but za truce!' Their joint venture on the struggle of the oppressed nations of Europe – a subject so vast and complex that Laurie was appalled and exhausted before they began – was doomed from the start. After one day's endless talking with Weiss and the director John Monck, he was sick and longed only to go home. Day after day they worked at Weiss's home in Highgate, or in the Patisserie Valerie in Soho, and it became 'a maze...' 'what chaos!...' 'day at Highgate with Weiss arguing and fighting over mutilated script ... I am depressed...' 'Had to go back to Putney with a fever ...' 'Deeper and deeper into morass over film...' 'Monck has brilliant ideas which confuse everyone ...' 'We are both in a wilderness & both very weary.' One day while in Highgate he walked in the cemetery:

> Ghastly place of stone needles, family vaults & broken 'grecian' pillars. Bombs have fallen and thrown up grave stones. Found Karl Marx's grave, bunch of dead forget-me-nots lying upon it. I wanted to write a poem but instead argued fruitlessly all day with Jiri & Monck who get on one another's nerves.

Eventually *Calling All Peoples* was dropped. 'I am lost & undone,' wrote Laurie. 'A cold wind blows, lilac is out, and yet no birds sing.'

He had a regular salary, but he was 'practically broke thanks to all these train fares etc.' He opened his first Post Office account with five guineas from *Poets of Tomorrow* and 10s 6d from *Tribune* for a poem called 'Barriers'. The Budget had put twopence on beer, 'and fags now a penny each: I can't see myself paying it'. Mrs O'Neill told him that 'tarts which cost 1s 6d, went for 4d if broken. She went into the shop and asked, got any broken tarts? No says the girl, shall I break one for you? and did.' Annie insisted he should not send her any more five bobs. 'I never want you to run yourself short & Lorna sent me some last week. Dear girl she is thoughtful, I paid a bill or two and bought some seeds for the garden etc.'

Over supper of bacon and eggs at his flat, Lehmann proposed a book about either Slad or Spain, and a review of de la Mare's *Collected Poems* for *Tribune* 'and God help me, I promised to'. He wrote a thoughtful appreciation: 'One does not question the charm and fascination of this finely wrought verse; it has a decorative economy, a subtlety of tone which is almost Oriental. But in wartime,' he added, 'the ear … finds it increasingly difficult to adjust itself to such delicate faery music.'

Meanwhile Laurie was himself receiving some crushing reviews for *Poets of Tomorrow*. 'The *Times Literary Supplement* suggests I have genuine feeling, limited experience and at times too melodramatic an image…' 'Desmond MacCarthy in the *Sunday Times* says, "These *Poets of Tomorrow* turn out to be very much Poets of Today with all their faults. The fault is obscurity".' MacCarthy had picked out Laurie's 'Village of Winter Carols' for failing to convey its meaning, and ended: 'The reason I go hammering at these poets is that it is painful to see so much sincerity of emotion and subtlety of observation marred by disregard of the art of communication.' Yet Mrs O'Neill's 'semi-illiterate' son Eric, who worked on the cooked meats counter at Harrod's, told Laurie he had understood 'Winter Carols': 'So much for MacCarthy.'

Worse humiliation was to come.

The review of *Poets of Tomorrow* in *Tribune* accuses me of 'affectation' which is I think one of the most humiliating things

> that one can have said about one's poetry. Worse even than being
> accused of plain bad writing. Affectation, which I loathe more
> than anything else in others! Lorna just roared with laughter.
> But can I go on, after these shocking reviews? I am sure if Woolf
> reads them he'll not be disposed to give me my book whatever
> Lehmann may say.

Cyril Connolly mentioned him favourably in *The Observer*, but
The Spectator reviewer, Sheila Shannon, said the only influence she
could detect on Laurie Lee was that of Edith Sitwell. 'However,'
she ended witheringly, 'to do Mr Lee justice, I think most of his
faults are attributable to a quite original lack of poetic talent.' This
plunged Laurie into a profound gloom. Day-Lewis said the test of a
good poet was to carry on in spite of such reviews; but the heartless
Lorna reported Mary Campbell's comment: 'Extraordinary how
these boys get their poems published – I suppose he writes about
as well as he plays the fiddle.' Mary had been proselytising, trying
to persuade Lorna to become a Roman Catholic like her. 'Are you
an atheist?' Lorna asked Laurie. 'I can't bear you to think otherwise
than I do.' She seemed to Laurie to be guiltily seeking some morti-
fication of the flesh. Lorna said, 'It makes me want to black people's
shoes, or work all day at some humble job or crawl naked over the
doorstep.' Laurie was sceptical of her motives: 'Catholicism is the
religion of repression. It sees celibacy as a virtue. The voluptuary,
tired of too much indulgence is attracted to it by a perverted pleasure
in the state of wanting.'

An author inventing a voluptuary could not have improved on
Lorna, with her flourishes, her gifts, her riches, her flowers. She
rarely arrived in the same outfit twice. She would be swathed in furs,
in tweeds, in tartans; 'in seven different blues (counting her eyes)'; 'in
a scarlet corduroy suit and her hair twisted in thick plaits'; 'in a nice
new divided skirt, blue, very smart'; 'in a wine-coloured coat, which
makes her glow'; 'in her camel cloak which makes her look frail &
pregnant'; 'in a wide black straw hat, in the shade of which she's a

dusky beauty'. In her arms she carried an ever-changing bounty: two great white magnolias; scarlet tulips; masses of lilac; Beethoven's Waldstein Sonata and books of Donne, Stendhal, Chinese poems; ravioli and bottles of red wine. And whenever they met there seemed to be some natural aid to romance – primroses, cherry blossom, a cuckoo, a nightingale.

She talked of a break with her husband, but Laurie suspected she would maintain her congenial compromise for ever. 'L is in an unhappy state over things at home, but as I am not the alternative what can I do?' She spoke of getting a job and living on her own resources. Laurie was rightly sceptical. She would 'twist her curls, on the verge of tears, but she can't leave W because he's so dependent & she can't give me up because she's tried – what is she to do? ... In the middle of this endless discussion I felt very tender towards her.' But 'I am the great fool in all this. Obstinately waiting for a bus which went past 15 years ago.' Lorna had been married for fifteen years.

There was never any serious question of Lorna's marrying Laurie. If the subject came up Laurie made a light response: 'For five days I'd get two meals a day then for five months I'd have to cook for myself.' Yet Lorna persisted in harping on Laurie's imagined infidelities.

'I am blameless but she'll never believe it. Her smile was as hard and sharp edged as a stone. In a wave of frustration I tried to rouse her to some reaction and said "I don't think I want to see you again" and she said "All right darling."'

Four days later she brought peace offerings (flowers, sherry) 'and her nightdress as a flag of truce, and every wave of tenderness was heightened by the fact that we had quarrelled & made it up'. At one moment 'she was all I love, gazing into my eyes, quick, suspicious, adoring'; at another she was 'vague and distant with a forbearing manner I'm sure she uses on her children'.

At Bognor, where Laurie was having his first bespoke suit tailored for ten guineas, fighter planes swept up and down, bombers roared back and forth, guns popped incessantly along the shore. On 1 June Laurie read about the bombing of Cologne. 'One must accept such news with terrible feelings – we are preparing a ghastly future for us all. Newspapers facetious about it: "Woe de Cologne" or "Blow de Cologne".' Jack was making a film about submarines, and was having a submarine built at the studio. Betty Smart was now training personnel at the Hoover factory. Laurie went to see her and found her 'in a red dress with freshly washed hair streaming down. Untouchable though. She is sweet and nice, bright, modern & definitely frank about sex, but I feel rather brotherly towards her.' A letter came from Wilma to say that her husband had been knighted 'so she is now Lady Gregory'.

He went to the National Gallery to see Moore's *Tube Shelter Perspective*, 'bone-grey figures like corpses lying in rows in a long tunnel, twisted, crumbling, inhuman looking. Remarkable.' In the evenings he sometimes joined BBC and film people – Paul Rotha, MacNeice, Humphrey Jennings – at the Players' Theatre. He had been asked for another piece about Slad (on carol-singing) for the *Geographical Magazine*, and to write the commentary for a film called *Eternal Prague* and for another about Malta, to be spoken by Laurence Olivier. For a film about the Battle of Britain, 'I supplied about 3 words. I almost think I shouldn't take the money – I haven't really got the brain.'

On his twenty-eighth birthday Lorna came up to London and they had Spanish omelettes at the Café Condé in Russell Square, an old haunt from 1938. 'We walked round cold blue Brunswick Square into its railless gardens where the leaves were falling & L told me of her three empty years there & how she sat under those trees carrying Michael.' They saw *Eternal Prague*, with Laurie's commentary spoken by Beatrix Lehmann: 'voice harsh & shocking and a disappointing lack of feeling'.

At the end of April Jack, looking 'wild and uncomfortable', suddenly announced that he was engaged to Bim, a girl in Gloustershire: they would marry in three weeks' time. Annie approved: 'Jack will be happier and not so selfconscious when he has a wife – someone absolutely belonging to him. He has given me money to get an outfit for the wedding.' Laurie met Bim at the studio and found her 'stocky but pleasant', but Jack 'seemed as flat as a pancake. Not much apparent love between them.'

Jack's colleague Nora – the future Mrs Jack Lee – told Laurie that Jack was not in love with Bim, but 'couldn't get out of it'. Laurie was horrified. 'No wonder he's miserable but why has he gone this far? And is it too late? Jack admitted that getting married was the last thing he wanted to do. I said should I speak to her on the telephone. He said wouldn't I go down and tell her? He couldn't tell her himself.'

So one June evening Laurie took the train to Cirencester, and Bim came to meet him on her bicycle. They sat on a bank in the sunset. 'She seemed happy. I felt terrible. I told her what I'd come to tell her and she rolled over in the grass & wept. A passing lorry driver leant out of his van and said "Give it to her!" She said there was only misery ahead for her either way but she didn't care, if only he loved her. I had to tell her he didn't.'

'Meanwhile Mother writes excitedly about the wedding, the bride, the announcement in *The Times* etc.'

Next day: 'Unhappy letter from Mother saying "I am quite ashamed of Jack – he ought to walk barefoot – can't you persuade him where his duty lies?" What a miserable mess it all is.'

Annie wrote again: 'Did you advise Jack or influence him in any way? because if you did you should not have done so ... for little Bim is sweet and charming I do think she would have made a lovely wife, *not one* ever to be ashamed of...' Annie had met Bim in Stroud by chance ('poor darling little girl') on what would have been the wedding day, 'and she was so brave & chatty ... Laurie you know you boys have done it on me. I wonder that you think I can stand and keep sane. I do not think Jack is like you say. I know he can be constant. But I wish the wedding had not been fixed up in a hurry ... At the last he was rather rushed into it, and he got bewildered and worried, and now,' she concluded, maternal loyalty triumphing, 'I think it was for the best, and quite a manly thing to do.'

In late 1942 Laurie started researching a film for Jack Holmes on youth in wartime. In broiling heat he went to Paignton by train to meet the boys of Sandridge Lodge, high above the curving estuary of the Dart, where Laurie sat in on classes, lectured on music, played his fiddle and sang 'Ilkley Moor' at a village concert, climbed trees and got up at six in the morning to do PT on the lawn with the boys.

But that night he had an epileptic fit – his first for three years. He returned to London feeling low and lost. 'All my theories have collapsed – this attack was so sudden & I thought I was so well – besides it is still summer.' He was allowed to go home for a week, and Lorna went too. They found Annie on the verge of angry tears, because Reg had cut down her allowance again, leaving only 2s of the 7s pension she was expecting. Annie savoured later the image of Laurie and 'sweet Lorna' walking down the village street and over the fields to pick blackberries and wild flowers for the Harvest festival. It was their last visit to Slad together.

Then in October research took Laurie to Cambridge. He sat by the Cam at the back of King's College as undergraduates arrived for the new term. 'Cafés, tea-shops, bicycles, gowns, halls, scrubbed refectory tables & those lovely dreamlike willows over the placid river – how attractive in the blue twilight it was – how I wish I'd had some of it.'

He spent most of the autumn touring youth clubs in the north of England. This was another doomed project, given Laurie's instinctive sympathy with the working-class lads of Cumbria and the equally instinctive Toryism of his masters. Still, it was an education for Laurie, who had seen more of Spain than he had of England, to see living conditions in industrial Maryport and Workington: he played ping-pong and taught drawing to the boys ('incredibly black, dirty & smelly but enthusiastic'). 'What a sooty, dirty, wet weather town this is,' he wrote of Whitehaven. 'Fields of black grass, cramped children, hideous worried women, coalmines on the hills, and

avalanches of molten slag pouring from the steelworks into the sea.'
He stayed in a vicarage with aspidistras in the parlour, and watched
old women carrying sacks of slate coal picked off the slag heap.

> Looking down the cliff with the grey sea boiling below it was
> incredible to think that this was indeed the land of the proud
> & free to see this black bent old grandmother, dressed in sacks
> & rags, wheeling a pram pitifully loaded with shale through the
> wind & rain.

He took photographs of these sad scenes, until a policeman tore along
on a bicycle to challenge him: 'Whitehaven was mobilised and the
"spy" surrounded. There was much showing of papers … I said it was
my job, so in the end he left me. And some devil made me return to the
high wall and take another shot.' Some devil too made him brave the
steep descent into a coal-mine, Haig Pit, in helmet and Davy lamp, to
be transported in the suffocating, deafening din to the coal-face under
the sea, where men naked to the waist heaved and shovelled. 'Oh the
ingenuity of man, the remorseless, indomitable, sacrificial ingenuity.
I drilled some coal & shovelled it on the belt. Who will burn it?' He
took a bus across the Pennines and in Durham, 'a lovely small city
after my own heart', played the Bach Double Violin Concerto with
a girls' club organiser. Everywhere he travelled, his restless curiosity
unearthed excellent material, and he struck up instant friendships.
During dinner in Newcastle with T. D. Young, 'fat bachelor father
of the city', the news came that the Americans had made landings in
French North Africa, but when he changed trains at York Station (in
ruins) he saw the headline: 'Hitler invades Vichy France'.

Lorna welcomed him back with dinner at the Café Royal, and
they chose prints at Zwemmer's (a Seurat and Van Gogh's *Beer
Garden* for Lorna; Brueghel's *Winter* for Laurie).

> These intoxicating waves of affection she has for me contain a
> taste of bitterness because I know they do not last. The higher

the wave the deeper the trough. As she stares at me in the gas light I can't help being happy but … there is no constancy in it. 'Make me not want you so much,' she says. 'I can't get any peace always thinking about you – I want to be able to live in peace again.' That sort of peace will not be long in coming to her, I fear … I can't fathom her twisted brain.

A damp green mould covered his books and records in Bognor, so the Savages moved him into a cold spare room in their attic, with a view of back yards. 'Lorna told me she'd asked W if I might have a room in their house but he just looked at her.' Rather restrained of him, Laurie thought.

One day in early December 1942 he was dropping in his new poems to Lehmann when he ran into Kathleen Garman and her daughter Esther in the King's Road, and she asked him home for tea. Inside number 272 was a bevy of Garmans: 'lovely Kitty now dark and very pretty; Helen, a doubled-up bright-eyed image of her mother, and graceful Kathy whom I last saw in Martigues'. Kathy had just turned eleven.

With Cecil Day-Lewis, he travelled down for another quiet weekend at Rosamond Lehmann's. Rosamond was 'more superlative than ever. "How perfectly lovely to see you" and "Of course John is *simply devoted* to you." All this is normal I suppose in many people but it is a manner I don't find easy.' Laurie sawed and chopped wood, and after dinner Rosamond and Day-Lewis sang their way through the hymn book with Laurie on recorder; and Rosamond read Jane Austen aloud to the two poets. What may have proved another bond of sympathy between Day-Lewis and Laurie is that Cecil too had in 1939 fathered an extra-marital child by the wife of a neighbouring Musbury farmer who accepted Day-Lewis's son William as his own. One evening that weekend, Laurie told Day-Lewis and Rosamond that he was the father of a little girl. 'Rosamond was most curious. "Were you married then?" "No," I said. "Is the mother married?" I ignored the question. "But is the mother married?" "No," I lied, "& the baby's name is Margaret."'

11

La Belle Dame Sans Merci
1943

ONLY LAST SUMMER, Laurie had been living in the caravan and gardening for a shilling an hour. At the start of 1943 his Malta film was being acclaimed, with Sir Arnold Bax's score and Laurence Olivier speaking Laurie's nobly phrased commentary. His social life was impressive. He dined with Eddy Sackville-West at the Savile Club and saw H. G. Wells there. 'How well they do themselves in these red plush dens. The cold table groaned with pewter weight and opulence. Salmon, hams, vast pies & salads; gulls' eggs at 1s 9d each.' He lunched at the Berkeley with John Wolfenden, headmaster of Uppingham. At John Lehmann's he met Sir Archibald Clark-Kerr, British ambassador to Moscow (who was 'very amusing about Stalin says he likes obscene jokes'). When Laurie took Day-Lewis to dine at the Gourmet in Lisle Street, 'How they bow to you,' said Day-Lewis. 'You must be an habitué.'

Lehmann and Sackville-West were both badgering him for poems, but then he was offered fifty guineas to write a film treatment on agriculture in wartime. 'You come to us with the highest recommendation the British Government can offer. You've got a marvellous subject,' gushed Donald McCullough, questionmaster of the *Brains Trust*, over lunch at Casa Pepe. 'I must say I'm quite black with envy.' 'So the big game starts,' wrote Laurie in his diary, 'without a fact or a thought in my head.'

He started his farming research in the areas he knew: Slad, followed by Sussex. A barley farmer drove him round the bomb-cratered downs. He seized the chance for woodland walks with Lorna by moonlight: 'She wore a balaclava helmet which stretched her eyes & pursed up her mouth and concentrated the gaze on those features which are most beautiful.' In Dover the Grand Hotel was half in ruins. His hotel shook at night with bombs across the straits.

At Bognor at weekends, Lorna ('smouldering & lovely, in her birthday bracelet') still brought flowers and cigars, but she alternated between loving declarations and threats of vengeance ('I will not share you') if he strayed. 'She will not believe. I was cold & hot & wild & cruel.' There were 'terrific explosions' out at sea.

They still spent languid mornings in London, listening to Mozart's Flute Trio, which made Lorna cry, staining the pillow black with kohl and scarlet with lipstick. They lunched at the Café Royal, and saw *Casablanca*. They went to a children's exhibition where Michael had a painting on show along with other pupils from Bedales and Dartington Hall; that night, volleys of gunfire shook Mrs O'Neill's house. 'We bombed Berlin last night so we sort of expected it. Raid lasted till 9.30 when L rang me up with love on her lips.'

Laurie was a devotee of the National Gallery's lunchtime concerts. One day, the all-clear made a curious accompaniment to Beethoven's F Major Opus 139. With Lorna and Michael he queued for the exhibition of *French Nineteenth Century Painting*. The queue, blue-nosed in the bitter cold, stretched to St Martin-in-the-Fields; *le tout Londres* was there. Rose Macaulay muttered, 'There's a new meaning to "queuing for the pictures".' MacNeice walked by, giving Lorna a long stare. Anna, Mary Campbell's daughter, last seen in Toledo, was there, 'now 16 and a mirror of Mary'. The throng quite obscured the exhibits: 'classic Cézannes, ruddy Delacroix, misty Sisleys, putrid-coloured Lautrec nudes, soft-buttocked Courbets, Degas ironing women … and a soft tawny golden oh so golden "Blonde Bather" by Renoir. Dreamy blue eyes and yielding jellyfish mouth against a blue sea with cascades of apple-coloured hair falling down.'

The youth film, on which Laurie had spent so many months, was cancelled, depressingly: his treatment painted a too unpleasant picture of the past and looked 'indiscreetly' at the future. 'What is the use,' he wondered, 'of trying to be either sincere or reasonably free from prejudice and mumbo-jumbo when one is bound to be frustrated by the official mind?'

Diligently, he pressed on with farming research. In Cambridge, Leicestershire, Shropshire and Wales, he saw how previously fallow land had become productive. At crumbling hill farms, he became an expert on potato yields at 1,100 feet. In Oxford he stayed with sister Dorothy and her husband Leslie, who took him to the Morris Radiation factory to see women at work. Laurie was a natural reporter: at farmers' meetings, full of curiosity, he took notes and forged new friendships. At Drayton Manor, Stratford, he visited Sir George Stapleton, a farming baronet. '"Good afternoon Sir George," I said, "it's very good of you to see me." "I had no option," he said.' But within hours Stapleton was declaring, 'I've taken a liking to this fellow' and sent for Laurie's overnight bag. He sat up with Sir George – who wrote books himself – and his lady, until midnight, talking of poetry and carrying on over breakfast. In Manchester he went to a Brahms and Schubert concert and met the conductor Malcolm Sargent ('charming, brilliant, very funny'). In the office of the *Warrington Guardian*, he had a birthday greeting to Yasmin set up in type.

He spent an eye-opening weekend with the eccentric artist Cedric Morris (Lucian Freud's former tutor) in Suffolk. Morris took him through pink-walled rooms hung with 'sickeningly diseased and cynical' portraits. Lorna's painter friend David Carr was there, 'drooping his grecian locks', and there was 'a shaven-headed Nazi type [who] cooked staggering meals'. Everybody seemed relaxed about using words that made Laurie blush. (He was still uneasy among aesthetes. At John Lehmann's one night, he remarked, 'What a bunch of posey young weeds he does gather around him. Squinting up their eyes at pictures & bleating about the ballet. Keith Vaughan in khaki, Leslie Hurry who draws a fine line in masculine buttocks, John Craxton, Lucian Freud's friend … a weary gang.') Before he left, Morris warned Laurie against 'the Lehmann gang' and the corrosiveness of Rosamond's endless soul-searching.

He returned filled with a 'strange uncomfortable sickness'. Lorna was in a cold fury of suspicion having overheard him on the telephone. She was so convinced of his infidelity she said she was ready to give herself to any rough old soldier: 'I felt I didn't care what happened to my body if you didn't want it any more.' 'She suggested I went & got married, but what if I did. This is a tightrope situation I cannot hope to control.'

While his own affair was plainly in trouble, he became further entangled in Day-Lewis's. Cecil invited him home in April to meet his wife and two sons at Brimclose, his house in Musbury, in the Axe valley, with its panoramic views of Devon, on a weekend of golden weather. But back in London, as they firewatched one night, Day-Lewis confided that Rosamond bitterly resented his having done this. 'It is driving him crazy, juggling with the two worlds,' Laurie noted. 'He needs a bridge & said that was partly why he took me.'

Rosamond duly wrote to reproach Laurie. She had thought of him as her friend, 'at the beginning of my new & happy life': Laurie was one of the few who accepted her and Day-Lewis as a couple, part of their shared life. 'The fact that he invited you to see his other life seemed to me (morbidly?!) like an attack on me … I felt I should never be at ease with you again.' Having seen Cecil's other life, Laurie might perceive that Rosamond was 'living in an unreal Paradise'. And that Cecil would retire to the bosom of his family and relinquish her for ever.

One hot April day, wearing blue 'like a spirit of the sea', Lorna drove him to Myra Hess's concert at Chichester, and they lay on the grass among other couples:

The act of kissing in public seemed to increase our pleasure. I know she is mine by the smell of her mouth, the shape of her arms, & that intangible, free flow of her soft body when she embraces me. She said, later, 'I sometimes think with real pride that no one shall touch me but you till I die.'

She told Laurie she had again asked Wish if Laurie could come and live with them. 'Wish had laughed loudly: "Don't be preposterous," he said. "Won't you ever grow up?"' Laurie began to perceive that Lorna was quite blind to normal logic, weirdly incapable of forming any vision of life based on reality:

She prefers to drift like the Lady in a barge of fancy through fabulous & romantic cities. But how incredibly her mind works ... She also made the following astounding proposal: that if I chose the father she would have another daughter whom she would keep secluded for me and when grown deliver to me in place of herself.

Not surprisingly they quarrelled, and the quarrels were raw and harrowing. While he noted the distant events of the war – Gandhi 'still fasting'; seventy Junkers troop carriers shot down in the Mediterranean; our own heavy losses when bombing Dortmund 'almost unnoticed' – he began to ache with a pervading hopeless misery. He was ill, not just with his usual bronchial problems but in a torpor of nervous exhaustion. A chiropractor examined his spine and told him he displayed the symptoms of a man suffering from shell shock. To make things worse, Laurie was told that his agriculture film would not after all be made; his third unmade film in succession. 'And so the long line of damp squibs & misfits goes on.' He could write instead for the Ministry of Information, which produced books written in *Picture Post* style – *The Battle of Britain*, *Bomber Command*, *Front Line* – that sold in millions. It was 'the bleakest, most desultory, most negative period in my whole life'. Jack, by

contrast, was on top of the world with his submarine film finished, and a
new film lined up involving trips to America, Africa, Newfoundland. So
Jack was erasing all his former 'psychological defeats'.

The weekends with Rosamond Lehmann and Day-Lewis were
a refuge. The two men played dominoes, and shot stones with cata-
pults at an old tin. While Day-Lewis worked indoors, Rosamond
sat beside Laurie in the sun and probed heavily about Lorna, who
had the most beautiful eyes Rosamond had ever seen. After dinner
she played the piano, read aloud from her *Invitation to the Waltz*,
and Laurie played his fiddle while Day-Lewis sang his repertoire
of ballads. 'How moving in the lamplight his singing of Lord
Randall is.'

In May, Laurie and Lorna were lying in a Sussex field, listening
to larks and watching the planes from Ford aerodrome, when Lorna
announced she was coming to London, to take a part-time job in a
wartime nursery. Laurie was filled with foreboding. 'In fact I would
definitely rather she didn't come. And the prospect of seeing her
every night! Isn't that queer after all.' He was 'all unhappiness &
nerves & bitterness'. Their affair had so long depended on clandes-
tine trysts, any whiff of change blew like a chill wind.

On 23 May 1943 he went, 'weak with strange feelings', to meet
the 4.30 train at Victoria as Lorna arrived, 'brown, nervous, with
bunches of flowers'. They took a taxi to the second-floor room she
had rented in Bute Street, South Kensington. She instantly made
it charming, filling it with 'vases of flowers, St Teresa, a crucifix,
pictures of Yasmin, pots of face cream, Rilke, Shakespeare and
the Bible full of pressed flowers'. They joined Jack and Nora and
Humphrey Jennings at the Arts Theatre: 'Lorna alternated as usual
between a downcast-eye averted shyness with extreme teasing
taunting familiarity.' She threw him the key to her room. 'At last I was
the visitor. I still don't know how this will work.'

They wandered in London, had kippers in a workmen's café
by Putney bus garage, visited Brompton Oratory, and went to
see *The Count of Monte Cristo*. They took Wilma to tea at the

Waldorf, and to *The Watch on the Rhine* with Anton Walbrook.
One day Yasmin, who had been in hospital having her adenoids
and tonsils out, was brought up to London by her nanny and
they took her to the zoo.

> She's tough and plump and walks with a roll. She's very bright
> & charming now but has caught amazingly some of her mother's
> peculiarities of expression & intonations of voice. Particularly
> that birdlike rising exclamation 'What?' when she doesn't catch
> what you say. On the Underground she was naturally fascinated
> by the escalators & magic train doors opening without hands.
> She asked: 'Do mice have fires in their houses? How do they
> keep warm?'

One evening in June, Laurie went to dine at Eddy Sackville-West's in
Chester Square, in a room hung with John Piper's pictures of Knole.
There was a pile of records on the sideboard which Sackville-West
– 'thin, reedy & sick-looking, curled in his armchair like a half-
starved fledgeling' – presented to Laurie: 'I didn't know what to say
– such richness. Denis Matthews playing Mozart, Schubert's "Death
and the Maiden" quartet, Mozart's violin concerto in D played by
Menuhin, and a dozen others. I was overwhelmed.' They listened
to records in a room surrounded by a vivid Graham Sutherland, a
Constable drawing, a Picasso stencil, two Ivon Hitchens and more
John Pipers. Sackville-West had chosen four of Laurie's new poems
to broadcast. He asked what sort of voice Laurie wanted to read
them. Laurie was momentarily nonplussed since Sackville-West
spoke in 'a quaint aunt-like voice', precisely the kind of 'intellectual
sissy whine' he most hated. He replied: 'Something rough – and
unmetropolitan – if you know what I mean.'

Laurie left Sackville-West's at about 10.30 p.m. and went to
Lorna's room. 'She had been out with Lucian Freud and had had £2
stolen which doesn't surprise me.

'A terrible cold grew upon me.'

Lucian Freud became 'a dark presence' in Laurie's diary from that moment. Freud, born in Berlin in 1922, was already, at twenty, a boy wonder of the art world, known for his remorseless, psychologically penetrating portraits. 'People who met Freud in his teens,' as Lawrence Gowing wrote of him in 1982,[70] 'recognised his force immediately; fly, perceptive, lithe, with a hint of menace.' Gowing wondered who was the woman who first appeared in a Freud drawing in 1943

> in which the mood of preoccupation, anxiety perhaps, haunting
> a face, similarly and sympathetically occupied the image. Two
> years later there were little paintings of her, cut like sculptured
> busts by a table edge, each with a flower, a daffodil or a tulip,
> under her gaze, with eyes wide-open, devouring, or else turned
> inward, half-closed, brooding.

This latter was *Girl with Daffodil* – in which Lorna looks decidedly cross.

Gowing asked Freud who she was. Freud answered quietly, without revealing Lorna's name, 'She was the first person who meant something to me.' Later Freud added: 'I wanted to explain that she was the first person I was really caught up with.'

Lorna found Lucian beautiful and fascinating and became his muse, bringing him things to draw, just as she had encouraged Laurie's poems and shown them to Stephen Spender. For both of them she was a catalyst and an inspiration. 'She was a symbol of their imagination, of their unconscious, she was nature herself,' in Yasmin's view. 'Savage, wild, romantic, and completely without guilt. She used to say she didn't know what guilt meant.'

Laurie ached and sweated and was full of nameless fears. Lorna cooked for him, but he got up and staggered home to find the women in Werter Road asking him to kill a rat; they looked on shrieking as he went at it with a brick. One evening he went out with Lorna and her brother Mavin to a Polish restaurant. As they saw Mavin off on the bus, Laurie said to him, 'Let's meet over the weekend.' 'L was furious. "I'll go with Lucian!" she shouted, and was surprised at herself.'

Struggling through his 'flu, he finished the first chapters of the *Land at War* book and took them in to Day-Lewis. He sent Annie money and she thanked him for 'the pelf, nice pelf'. 'Dear Laurie if you have any more to spare I am really stoney ... I was very poorly on Whit Sunday. Did not go anywhere and no one came ... I loved to read about darling Yasmin. Her hair must look lovely, so did darling Frances's.' When friends congratulated Annie on Laurie's poems, 'there is hardly any pleasure,' wrote Laurie, 'to compare with her sentimental appreciation of my few successes'.

Lorna, by contrast, 'contaminated' his latest broadcast poems by listening with an icy smile. She had found a card from Rosamond, and over dinner with Rosamond and Day-Lewis 'L sparked at R, & she became very distant'. On his twenty-ninth birthday ('God help me') he went down to Rosamond's cottage and found himself telling her and Day-Lewis more than he wanted to about his problems with Lorna. Rosamond was all sympathy. She thought Laurie was amazingly tolerant: 'You are the first man I've ever met who ... furiously beset – did not counter with rudeness, indignation, self-justification, sulks, silence, plain male rage, ending in the paralysing act of getting up and going away – but just went on being gentle, affectionate and agreeable,' she wrote. 'A man in a thousand! Tell her so, if necessary.'

Two days later he called at Lorna's room and she was not there. 'Honeysuckle which she had brought from Sussex was thick in the air. I lay on the bed & slept. She did not come in till dawn.' This happened again. It was his turn to be filled with wild suspicions. 'Lorna went out with a fellow but came in at midnight after I was asleep.'

Land at War was a torment to write. He escaped to see Rosamond's actress sister Beatrix Lehmann in *Ghosts* – 'terrible play' – and next day met Beatrix by chance at Ben Frankel's 'Hotch Potch' concert at the Albert Hall. Eddy Sackville-West took him to hear the pianist Clifford Curzon and Benjamin Britten playing the first performance of Britten's *Scottish Ballad*. One night he dined at 'one of those posh irritating restaurants' with Lorna and a girlfriend, and over several gins the two girls

> talked of gigolos and Bentleys, a world as unreal as hell. I thought the leaden heart of woman here reached the lowest depths of ignominy. I sat and watched them in a sort of arrested disgust, seeing the one as it were for the first time, and the other a creature of unbelievable folly.

He left them 'in a paralysis of anger'.

Night after night he waited for Lorna with a tight dull feeling in his chest.

> I could picture her face, stricken by that fixed slightly intoxic-ated smile which carries her through the jokes, the innuendoes, even the frank obscenities of whatever hangers on she has with her. I could picture her thinking perhaps for a second of me & smiling that deathly smile to herself ... All this is so worthless, so ignoble, yet I find it very difficult to put out of my mind...

Should he just withdraw and let her give herself completely to that other world? Or fasten himself like a leech and guard her, receiving the cold comfort of that smile?

'Whatever I do, no more self-immolation, subjections, humilia-tions. I have done enough.'

One day Lorna summoned him. At the Savoy the night before she had lost her wallet with £8, her post office book, five books of clothing coupons, sundry letters and photographs. 'I'm sure she was robbed. She gets so hazy dazy after a few drinks she just doesn't notice.' Laurie found her asleep, woke her to 'a miserable drowse, lamenting she would not say what, but feeling remorseful about something. She confessed that she was unable to resist those nights.

I would much rather she was in the country. I can not watch her all the time.'

This impasse went on for weeks. Lorna went her own capricious way and Laurie felt he was going mad. He would work leadenly, and pace up and down, waiting for her telephone call. Finally he would go to her room and find only the traces of her recent presence – fresh flowers in the vases, petals on the floor. One night he rang and found her at home.

> She answered in a hard cracked voice. 'How are you?' 'Oh very well.' 'When can I see you?' 'Thursday perhaps.' I rang off and ran for a bus. I was coiled up with anguish like the pain of poison. The bus stopped every 2 yards. She was in bed placidly reading a book. She smiled her distant smile. 'Why are you doing this?' 'What?' 'You know very well.' 'But I don't.' Laughter. I have never been so tortured, hopeless. I have never had less pride or cared less for pride. But still she only smiled & laughed & said 'I must get some sleep.' At last she says, 'But what's worrying you? What d'you want to know?' (smoothing her hair with her hand). 'I'll tell you anything you want to know of course' (looking at ceiling & tapping her foot). Of course she'd tell me nothing – except 'Well actually I've just no feelings about you at all. I don't feel anything. I wish you'd stay the night. I don't like being here alone.'
>
> I stayed. But her indifference, the iced friendliness of her voice! I never want to feel like this again. I lay thinking of the future and the bloodless torturing game it would be. Never have I loved so much and so fruitlessly, never has she so coldbloodedly let me torment myself. 'I'll do what I like, go where I like, with whom I like. See?' There have been quarrels between us before, but not this. I have never before doubted that we should survive them. Now I do.

Lorna appeared to have become addicted to her nightclubs ('those putrid dens') and to Lucian, and told Laurie she was going to go on doing the same, so he'd better leave her alone. Work became impossible. Sleep eluded him. His whole brain, 'its order & capacity to interpret feelings & events seem to have broken down'. All he could think of was that Lorna was somewhere in London, with someone else. One night when he had waited for her all evening she turned up on the last train, 'a bit tipsy', and was very sick; he watched over her all night.

At breakfast the next day, Lorna caught sight of Rosamond's last letter and fury broke out again. As she left to catch her bus for work, she asked Laurie for the key to her room: 'I don't want to have you walking in when I've got someone there.' Laurie dumbly followed her.

> Passing a block of flats she got off. I followed. She rang a bell and a weak-looking golden-haired boy stumbled from his bed to let us in. A friend. A kept boy of some rich man. He looked pampered & corrupt, blinking through sleepy eyes. She was glad for me to see him. I went with her to the nursery. I was dumb with pain at this new horror. I never thought I was capable of being so completely possessed by pain & misery. Deliberately, she commended me to the devil.

That night he saw her with Lucian Freud.

> She had promised to see me at 9. I waited in her room. At 9.30 she rang through. Again at Piccadilly. It was raining hard & I knew she had no coat. I said I'd meet her at the Underground. She arrived with that dark decayed looking youth whom she has been playing with. They didn't see me. They walked slowly along the pavement hand in hand, his head inclined towards her shoulder. That moment was the worst in my life. I went cold as death. I trembled from head to foot. I walked up to them & threw her coat over her shoulder. The boy did not look at me – but slid across the road to the bus stop. L turned to me.

'Where did you come from? What's the matter? You're white with fury,' she laughed. I made to follow the boy. 'Don't,' she said. 'Don't be silly.' She saw me go & ran round the corner & hid. I wanted to hit the boy hard. Instead I merely spoke a few words to him – I don't know what. He gave me a mumbling look & jumped on the bus.

I joined L. She was sure I'd hit him. I assured her I hadn't. She held my hand which was trembling uncontrollably and I walked somehow to her room.

I sat on the bed unable to speak. She lay down. She said her head was splitting. She said she'd been to see Cecil, they'd had a merry time talking about me. 'Don't take it out of the old boy any more,' he'd said to her.

She watched my face, my trembling hands. She smiled. 'Now you know how it feels,' she said.

She lay telling me bits & pieces about the evening. Her conversation with the boy. Idly she said, 'The trouble is he's falling for me. It isn't fair of me I know.' She said all this quite normally, either not knowing what it did to me or revelling in it. 'Why did you flaunt him in front of me?' I said.

'Oh, I only wanted you to know where I was so's you shouldn't worry.' Is she a child or what?

Again he watched over her all morning. Her ability to fall asleep when with him struck him as 'almost defensive'. Both of them were in fact becoming ill. Laurie took to his bed with fever; Lorna had jaundice in Sussex. In 'blackest despair' he filled his diary with war reports: of the fierce fighting in Sicily, the bombing of Rome. 'The fire-eaters cheer in the press – they think it is a virtue, a sign of strength to be able to bomb such a place. It would have been a sign of strength if we had been able to refrain from doing so.' The battle for Catania, five days old, was raging and he felt too weak to continue his own struggle.

I am all exposed – I seem to have no defence left. As I sit, sweating in my dressing gown, the sky is overcast & the windows rattle with an unnatural wind. Disaster overwhelms me and in spite of the deepest feelings I have for her it seems I can do nothing to prevent it. What does she feel? Cold blooded retribution, what? I feel my brain going, I have no trust. If this goes on for another week I shall have to resign my job anyway.

In this weak and wretched state, Laurie went to see his father in Morden one Sunday, hardly in the right mood for filial affection. He waited outside St Paul's Church, where Reg played the organ.

He came at last, driving a little car, wearing a pinched serge suit, looking shabbily parson-like, brown-skinned and old. The first time I'd been with him in nearly eight years.

We drove through those awful stretches of Wimbledon & Morden to where he lives (ghastly place, furnished with toy dogs). And there, very bright and brittle was Mrs R – who likes to be called Auntie Topsy, whom Dad refers to as Bill or 'Lady' & whom I can't bear.

For she is hard & hideous, vain, talkative, & without the slightest vestige of humour. Her conversation is a continual assertion of herself. 'I did this & that – ain't it good.' Dad asks me a few questions, we converse a bit about ourselves & personal matters – she sits with her sunken eyes & thin loose mouth listening & interrupting – 'That's my nephew – he's not really my nephew but I like to think he is – he rang me up. "Hello darling" I said, I thought well I'll be nice to him & call him darling – I don't mind being nice to him even though he ain't my nephew – he likes his Auntie Tops.' Then a little boy came in from next door. 'Who made your trousers?' she wheedles. 'Who made them? Auntie did, didn't she? Ain't they lovely? Ain't they nice?'

I am horrified that my father should find such a companion

adequate – but he does. How limited he is. He writes hymns which are just a succession of traditional churchy chords & is proud as Punch. He plays waltzes loudly, & adores Eric Coates. The veriest echo of brother Harold, he talks continually about himself & his doings. To have been a 'pukka' civil servant is the pride of his life. His life is finished now – and his brain is bricked up solidly by this suburban life.

The next day Laurie went to Brompton Hospital to have his lungs X-rayed. After six hours he was told his lungs were weak, would always be subject to bronchitis and might be tubercular.

'But oh, the depression of those poor souls waiting, sick & thin, with hazy eyes & greasy feverish faces.'

When he reached Lorna's room, all her clothes had gone.

Laurie went on tormentedly wrestling with *Land at War*. He felt he was cracking up.

Christ how can I live in this state? Or work? I wish I was a stonebreaker or something … This aching hopeless pain returns in sickening waves & grips me till I tremble like an ague. As night draws in it gets worse until I go to bed like a crazed thing & turn with exhaustion & think & think. But not sleep.

Annie had no idea of the state he was in. She wrote breezily, just off to Whiteway to pick fruit, wondering who was the friend to whose son Laurie had recently stood godfather?[71]

I hope you will hear him say his catechism now and again. It is a spiritual responsibility and I hope you'll regard it as such and be good yourself. What is it like in London now? You did not *jump* at the offer I made to come & visit you … Spose you did not want the old countrywoman to come up to see the smart youth of 1943, the poet etc. I'm only teasing Laurie, but I would have come if you had seemed at all eager … How is Lorna? and

> where is she? & Yasmin … and Jack, have you seen him? Tony
> came, I was glad to see *one* of my sons.

There was a blinding heatwave and Laurie was going out of his mind.
'If I get no relief soon, I don't know what madness I shall commit.'
When he finally got through to Lorna on the telephone he could
only babble like an idiot.

> And she, as she did when I was working at Haslemere, apolo-
> gised for being so offhand but said she couldn't help it. I wonder
> that she has no pity.
>   The world is a grim & shrivelled place … I see no mercy
> or solicitude in her. I cannot help feeling that it is terrible that I
> love her, terrible that I can be neither free of it nor derive content
> from it. If this empty madness is all the future has to offer I
> would be a fool to live.

The heatwave ended with a terrific storm. He wrote for twelve hours
a day without eating; what he produced seemed 'terrible, exhausted,
flat and written in a poverty-stricken vocabulary of about 100 words.
Took it to be typed by Enid and Mavis at the MOI; it looked even
worse typed.'

The next day he was standing on Victoria Station when Lorna crept
up and kissed him. They went to Soho, to the Swiss, to Oddenino's,
to the cinema, and home. Lorna challenged him: 'Why should you tell
me how to live? I won't be bound down.' He realised he wanted total
commitment, and she did not. 'Hers is the urge for irresponsible adoration. She leans to the stranger who will demand nothing, with whom she
can lose herself without committing herself. But O God I want something to call my own.' She left him the next day in her brightest dress.
At the studio, he was praised for his work on a film script on torpedo
boats: Jack Beddington said he did not realise Laurie had such a sense
of humour. 'But Lord, I am a dismal type these days. Something's gone
out & closed the door & I am damp, unlit & cold.'

On her next visit, Lorna brought her son Michael with her and also her niece, 'strapping Kathy from Martigues'. Laurie went with them to an 'impossibly vulgar' film about Madame du Barry. 'Well I don't know,' said Laurie. 'The evening passed. It was pleasant being with the children.' The next day at the Redfern Gallery Lorna picked up *Sunita*, the Epstein she had bought, they lunched at the Gourmet and took Michael to a revue at the Ambassadors – 'but all this falls very flat with me nowadays. Drained empty of everything except pain.'

When he was seeing them off to their train he snapped. Lorna was 'heavy as thunder' and seemed to be clinging with suspicious tenacity to her handbag. Laurie lost control, snatched the bag; Lorna screamed with rage and they fought. Laurie collapsed, trembling. They drove in silence to the station. He was appalled by the state they had got themselves into.

> But she has no care for me any more & will not allow me to persuade her back to sanity & happiness. For myself, only I can save myself. I am alone & that I must do. I am quite unable to turn to her any more. She assured me distantly of her affection – but her words have a hollow ring. This is the depth now.

It was a relief to spend an evening with Day-Lewis, Sackville-West and Benjamin Britten. 'For once I thought, here is a group of chaps who are talking about something I can understand', discussing poetry and 'all sorts of amiable gossip. Britten, a nice scholarly young chap with every visible sign of normality about him, is *the* composer of the day I think.' In the next few days, still intensely depressed, Laurie called on Betty Smart and her new baby. He suggested a new film to the Foreign Office but it was turned down. He discussed other scripts with Jack Holmes, brother Jack, and John Mortimer, the tall, slim Old Harrovian who was then an ineffectual assistant director with the Crown Film Unit. In Mortimer's memoirs he recalls Laurie as a 'small, sly Pan', piping sweet, melancholy music on his recorder in the corridors. When Mortimer took out Mavis, a 'hugely desirable' secretary, she talked endlessly of Laurie.[72]

Lorna had gone camping with the children under a harvest moon on the Downs. 'Inexpressible regret that I cannot be there. Who knows how many more moons we have?' The blisteringly hot 23 August 1943 was the sixth anniversary of his first meeting with Lorna, 'what was once referred to as "the final enchantment"'. He bought her a Spanish crucifix, and some crimson gladioli, and when he arrived at her room found that she had bought some too. 'L has now an incredible number of little charms, gestures, glances, silences with which to wound me.' John Lehmann wrote to ask when he would be bringing in his poems for publication in book form. Rosamond, agitated by Laurie's silence, wanted to know the results of his X-ray, and implored him to come for the weekend: her children were longing to see him.

He was sent to Weymouth on a job for a week, and on 4 September he returned by train,

> through the old lands steeped with past associations, Poole, Bournemouth, from which I left to go to Cornwall 6 years ago, travelling the same line to Southampton on my way to France, then up to Esher & the forests where we slept in midsummer. How sick the world appears. Happiness depends on being not so much in love but in faith with a person. But to achieve that were very heaven.

Waves of bombers crossed overhead.

> The night is like sustained thunder, like a headache, like the deep groaning of all the world. The house shakes as I write & yet I think of her all the time – O God I hope, I hope – but there she is somewhere in this city destroying me and all that ever was. I shall look at these days sometime and wonder what was the point of living them.

On 7 September he went to see Lorna, and she confessed to what he had suspected, about Lucian Freud.

> This mad unpleasant youth appeals to a sort of craving she has for corruption. She doesn't know how long it will last. She would like to be free of it but can't. Meanwhile she says she loves me. Oh I can't express the absolute depths to which this has brought me ... I pray she will get over it but I don't know, I don't know. She is tender enough towards me but devastating with her tender confessions. She goes to him when I long for her, and finds him in bed with a boy friend. She is disgusted but she still goes to see him.
>
> And tonight she says she is going to Cornwall with him ... Can I be patient & endure. Whatever I am I still have to endure.

Freud's biographer, William Feaver, says that Freud found Laurie's behaviour hysterical, but that all three of them tended to exaggerate the melodrama. Lucian did go with Lorna to Cornwall, where he was working on the sets for a ballet. He was as deeply affected by the free-spirited Lorna as Laurie was.

On the ensuing days,

> word by word she builds my grave, word by word she sweetens it with flowers. In the Swiss tonight she looked at me through a haze of rum & tobacco smoke over her beautiful eyes. We went home & she fell fast asleep. In the morning we made brief love. 'That is your province you know,' she said.

That Saturday, 11 September,

> I was sitting on a wall when a policeman came up to me. 'You're thinking about a woman. Or is that a personal question?'
>
> 'Yes,' I said. 'It is a personal question.'

'Well, don't you worry. That's my advice. Never run after a woman or a bus. There's plenty more behind.'

'Perhaps there's only one bus going the way you want to go.'

'Maybe you're right,' said the copper.

On Sunday 12 September, the streets were full of autumnal thundery mists.

> I can think of nothing but this, the recurrent smell of betrayal, the pendulum of reassurance, the sickening of remembered disasters. I tremble and am full of mad arguments, bargaining with fate over the fall of a card, the flight of a bird, the frequency of lightning.
>
> At night in fact there was incessant lightning. I am going mad. I watched it, I shook in bed, I planned, I remembered this afternoon.
>
> This afternoon some music was playing. The Dohnányi Quartet.
>
> I took a razor blade to my throat. There was a dazzling burst of light, a sense of the good life calling. I put the razor down, put my head on my hands and sobbed as I have never done since I was a child.

This was the penultimate page of his diary of that bitter summer. On the last page, he said he had been working with brother Jack,

> but if I pause for a moment a helpless, hopeless desert surges into my heart & brain & fills my whole skin with a hot burning agony.
>
> She rang just now while I was writing this. She has been with him, has been drinking, says everything I say is true, says if only I could convince her of the futility of what she is doing, says she loves me. But she has been with him. The image of that torments me with a strong odour of absolute wickedness & grief. I am trembling so much I can hardly hold this pen.
>
> But I suppose I must add that it was announced today with fanfare that Italy has surrendered unconditionally to the Allies.

> This means that now they will be bombed by the Germans
> instead of us – and the fighting will go on…

Laurie was on the verge of a breakdown and Rosamond Lehmann came to his rescue. She wrote confirming a weekend at Diamond Cottage, telling him her daughter Sally had particularly asked him to bring his fiddle. She added that if Laurie wanted to get out of London altogether, he could be her lodger in Aldworth for the autumn: her son Hugo's bedsit was empty '& you would be properly independent & needn't even sit with me in the evenings unless you choose to – and as for Mrs Wickens [her housekeeper], she'd burst with maternal love for you. There'd be a pile of wood to saw!'

Even Day-Lewis did what he could: he took Laurie to the Arsenal v. Fulham match (Arsenal won 4–3) and at each goal threw his hands in the air and howled. 'My nerves,' Laurie writes, 'were not at all good.' At the end of September, Laurie began a new notebook. He had decided to give up his old style of journal,

> written in day to day agony and weariness. The long summer is
> ended, it was very long, distorted with heat, fever and torment, but it
> is over and I can hardly remember what has happened to me. Nature
> is already busy suppressing those human horrors which brought me
> to my praying knees in a state of almost primitive abandon.
>
> Now I have given everything up, my job, my frenzy. Everything,
> that is, save a dim hope and a vague will to continue the struggle
> somehow.

He had handed over his scriptwriting job to John Mortimer, having first set Mortimer the test of writing a film script about Watford Junction. Inspired by *La Femme du Boulanger*, Mortimer invented a tale about a station-master's wife having an affair with a GI. In later years, Mortimer said that Laurie, rattled by his successor's tireless literary productivity, would always grumble when they met, 'I wish I'd never sent you to Watford Junction.'

Laurie felt

> assailed by friends, eager to do things, to assuage, listen, to give
> me warmth. But they have come too late. For three months I
> had desperate need of that, but I need it no longer. Too much
> has been destroyed I cannot begin to estimate it. The more
> destructive instincts, revenge, suicide, abandon, anarchy, they
> have inevitably triumphed … It has all been too acutely a sign of
> the times. The potentiality for beauty, the warm gesture, happi-
> ness, trust has just been thrown away, as we have all thrown away
> the opportunities of this terrific century.
>
> All that is left to me still is that obstinate itch to work for the
> most painless possible peace. But it is hard when human contact
> is so treacherous, doubtful & faithless, when words are so false,
> false as the bishop's text or the slogans of nations who burn and
> wreck and say that it is for good.

Lorna did not disappear, however. She invited him to the Café Royal
and was 'warm and guarded. Released, at least temporarily, from the
devil. She even spoke of going to Slad, even in a negative despairing
way of leaving everything and going with me to Ireland. This was
like vinegar to my parched lips.' They went to Day-Lewis's place and
played Beethoven. 'She anointed me with inexpressible warmth &
adulation. My frozen flesh began to stir with its old workings.' Over
dinner at the White Tower, Lorna told him that she could not bear
it if he left London, which made him realise he should go. But 'I can
never have enough'. So when she rang a few days later, he met her
again, and they walked in the park under a sky 'like oily cotton waste',
but Lorna threw out even more confusing signals. She told him she
was too romantic, said she wanted the impossible; that London was
a drug, that she could never be contented again. Laurie wished he
had followed his earlier impulse and gone away. Finally on 7 October
he left London for Rosamond's. For him it was just like November
1938: 'The dismal wandering out begins again. I am alternately sadly

fatalistic, & furious that this should be forced on me again.' There were raids in London every night. 'I might have known it. Into whose keeping will it force her now? I can't go back whatever happens.' When he rang Putney they told him Lorna had been on the phone, asking about him. Rosamond Lehmann's son-in-law, P. J. Kavanagh, heard from Rosamond that Laurie would sit day after day typing one word over and over: 'Lorna Lorna Lorna Lorna Lorna…' But he managed to finish *Land at War*, a lively and original little book despite its official propaganda purpose. Day-Lewis applauded it and Rosamond congratulated herself on enabling him to get it done – 'though the fight for self-discipline and mastery over the powers of disintegration was yours alone, my poor pet'. After six weeks away, Laurie returned to London. A bomb had fallen on Putney High Street, killing many in the dance hall.

Rosamond had found those weeks 'a strange and happy interlude'.

> I have never in my life felt such perfect ease, affection, lack of friction with any member of the opposite sex. You are my brother, and I love you. You don't realise to what extent you helped to steer me through *my* nasty crisis. Next year, if we can have the little house, things will be better. Please think *seriously* of taking a share.
>
> Best love darling. *Don't* be down. How I hope you'll see Lorna soon, & that all will be well. I feel it will.'

In December *Horizon* carried Laurie's new poem, 'Equinox'.

> Now tilts the sun his monument,
> now sags his raw unwritten stone deep
> in October's diamond clay…

The Hogarth Press sent a contract for his first book of poems: Day-Lewis had made the selection, and jokily suggested he call it 'Laurel Leaves'. Laurie recorded three of his poems for the BBC.

'After the programme I felt very empty, there is nothing so trans-
itory, so over and done with as a broadcast. L didn't even hear
them, Jack fell asleep before they came on, our mother had 'flu.'
Stephen Potter – 'tall, sandy, half bald, refreshingly normal' – asked
Laurie if he'd care to have a shot at a radio script. 'I just can't
believe I could ever write a radio script, any more than I could
write the King's speeches.'

He thought of Lorna constantly and knew it was madness:
writing out declarations, condemnations, appeals, far into the night.
The letter he drafted is tucked into his journal.

> To my love: I have no wish to criticise you. Whatever you are
> is my happiness and my grief, and I know that it is precisely
> because you are as you are – strange, lovely & unpredictable
> formula of woman, that I am born to love you & I would no
> more wish you altered than the moon.
>
> And I have only one desire & why should I not tell it? My
> desire is to be true to you, to tear from this twisted, faithless,
> blood-sodden world one clear immaculate image to which I can
> bind my heart, to which I can turn in prayer, in declaration, in
> all such moments of excitement and peace as are left to me in
> this life. It is the duty of every man to declare his faith once he
> has discovered it whether in the face of cynicism, mockery or
> doubt. Therefore I declare that to you I will be true as long as I
> shall live, and that I will fight to keep that faith and will preserve
> it with all my strength. I will be true in heart and flesh, publicly,
> secretly, wherever I am, with you or if necessary alone. True I
> can be, and I defy the whole damned world to scorn this prot-
> estation, and it is an indescribable exultation to make it.
>
> It is possible you may laugh. Beloved I do not care. I have at
> least the comfort of my own religion. It is a good thing to have.
> It is a glorious & responsible thing, something to be cherished
> with a real & militant passion.
>
> In time you may fade from my eyes and become only a

ghostly shadow which inhabits the books & pictures of my room, a half-remembered fragrance rising from the blankets of sleep, an idea, a theme of strange beauty which I can only repeat to myself. But whatever you become in the sly hands of imagination while you are out of my sight, to this I am devoted, to Lorna, this cherished image, & I will protect it with all the will & resolution of my heart and all the steadfastness of my body.

Laurie was never quite the same man again. Decades later he was still dreaming of her, 'dark, brilliant, beautiful, with locks of hair woven into a dark crucifix at her throat'. Thirty years later he wrote in his notebook, 'The betrayal & desertions she was capable of making in her passion for you never warned you that she would eventually do the same to you for another. You were too young, too secure in the sovereignty of your flesh.' He was damaged; and was determined never to be rejected again. He would protect himself. He developed a carapace. It made him suspicious and pessimistic. He could disguise it, and some never guessed it, but the sweet youthful optimism had gone. He would 'never give all the heart'. He had given it once, and that was enough. He wore Lorna's signet ring until the day he died.

12

'No one at home'
1944–1945

THE AFFAIR WAS 'finished, but an unconscionable time a-dying'. Lorna still summoned Laurie to Sussex, and he could not resist going, partly to see 'that lovely child to whom I'm more than a stranger now'. On a wintry day with a cold wind blowing from the sea he packed up his things from Bognor. They sat by Mrs Savage's fire and Lorna told him: 'I can't help it. I love you – but you must just leave me alone.' It had now been nine months since the intrusion of Lucian Freud, but 'this paralytic sleep of winter has not been a forgetting at all. Old wounds smart with all their hideous first pain. I have given up any desire to struggle with this any more.'

At first Laurie kept his new address from Lorna when he moved in with Cecil Day-Lewis and Rosamond at 41 Hasker Street, Knightsbridge. Day-Lewis occupied the sunlit and graceful upstairs rooms, Laurie the 'grim & grimy' basement, calling himself 'the King's Provost' – the chaperon who prevented their liaison appearing adulterous under the old divorce laws. (The King's Provost had been instrumental in the granting of a *decree nisi* to Edward VIII's mistress, Mrs Simpson.)

Laurie's diaries in those months are punctuated with shattering roars, deafening explosions, clanging fire-bells. Descriptions of air raids were monotonous, so full of clichés they were almost pornographic, he decided. But his apocalyptic tableaux of the city with the red glow of fires above, the fear and trembling below as jagged lumps of hot shrapnel showered down, were never dull, as he ventured out to scenes of destruction and mayhem. One night a factory and a furniture warehouse down the Fulham Road were hit. Laurie made his way there, helped to fill buckets of water from a trickling tap and climbed to a roof for an awe-inspiring view of flames flying up fifty feet in great gusts from the now roofless warehouse 'like a box of molten slag'; from the tobacco factory came loud explosions of buckling girders and breaking beams. By the time fire engines arrived, the buildings were gutted.

> I walked back through the streets with a soldier from Tobruk who, worried about his wife & child in Putney, had stolen leave from his barracks in Colchester and was walking to Liverpool St. He had to be back by 5 a.m.; he had left his wife hysterical & his child howling.

Laurie's contribution to the war effort was another narration for Laurence Olivier to deliver at the Red Army celebrations in the Albert Hall, for a fee of 35 guineas. When Laurie submitted his script, Malcolm Sargent read it aloud to the braided band chiefs of the three services, pausing at the line 'his crippled eagles brood in their own blood' to smack his lips and comment with an 'apish' grin: 'Fine stuff this … Isn't it fun having a nice tame poet working with us.'

> The Service men laughed & looked at me uneasily. We were later discussing my introductory stanza – 'Now let us rejoice' to the Hallelujah Chorus. 'Dare I suggest that you write in "let us give thanks to God"?' Sargent asked. I declined firmly, though smilingly. 'I'm not so tame as all that,' I said. The Service men laughed again, this time more easily.

'I adore your narration,' Olivier told Laurie, 'but can you cut the references to Fascism. I don't like having to say them.' 'What is this squeamishness?' asked Laurie.

When the day came, 23 February 1944, Lorna came up, 'lovely in her white lambskin coat' and they shared a box at the Albert Hall with Vivien Leigh, Ralph Vaughan Williams and Sir Arnold Bax. Towering above the assembled 5,000 was an 80ft painting of a Red Army soldier, 'his face rather like Tyrone Power, a tommy gun the size of a howitzer in his hand, his boots the size of tanks'. On the stage sat the London Symphony Orchestra, the band of the Coldstream Guards, and 350 members of the Royal Choral Society. On balconies were the bands of the RAF and the Royal Marines. In the Hall were nurses, firemen, policemen, landgirls, miners with lamps on their heads. Around the stalls sat mayors in golden chains. In the boxes, ambassadors, admirals, generals and cabinet ministers; in the Royal Box, Herbert Morrison. After the National Anthem, the lights dimmed and the spotlight beamed on Olivier. 'In absolute silence he began my prologue. He spoke it magnificently.' Vaughan Williams and Bax talked loudly through Laurie's stuff, so Lorna and Laurie talked through their music ('very English, like stale lavender water which hardly fitted the ranting histrionics of my narration') and they all glared at one other. The audience was restless – 'coughing drowned a good deal of my verse' – and Morrison's speech lasted forty minutes: 'Everyone was fed to the teeth. L & I dived out before the end, after exchanging a few words with Vivien Leigh who apologised for Olivier's performance which I praised. Cheap, pretty face she has, with the spiky selfish personality of a vixen behind it.'

That night there was another air raid. He lay in the coal-hole and watched the sky.

> Flares, welling from the dark blue gloom overhead, seemed like huge drops of blood dropping from a wound. Tracers floated in slow arcs to meet them. Rockets rushed upwards like flocks of darting silver birds … The roaring noise they make as they fly upwards is terrifying; at first it melts the very marrow with alarm. But one's ears grow acute in an inferno of noise and can separate each sound & identify it: rockets climbing, various

types of guns firing or their shells exploding, the sharp crack of tracer guns, the hiss of incendiaries, the sound of a nightfighter from one of theirs, the wicked hum of falling shrapnel which has many sounds from a piercing whistle to a low savage beating of swan's wings.

As I walked along Fulham rd the silence returned and was beginning to bring people from their shelters ... When I arrived the street was a shambles, brilliantly lighted by the flare of a burst gas main. Glass lay everywhere, bricks scattered over the road. Rows of houses nearby, their fronts battered in, were full of people in their thin night-things groping around with candles.

The all-clear went & youths from nearby shelters came whooping & shouting down the street to see the show. But the houses that had been hit were a terrifying spectacle. A few walls stood propped up with fantastic debris through which flames were savagely spreading. The cries of people trapped below in the basements, covered as they were by piles of rubble and the fierce crackling fire made one sweat to hear them. A woman said there were ten people down there. The rescue squad arrived, firemen slowly unrolled their hoses, the crowd watched, the cries could still be heard. A neighbour on the verge of furious tears said, her face convulsed with anger, 'And they call us brave! We're not brave – we've just got to bloody well put up with it, that's all!'

Through the black smoking hole of a basement window I helped with the first casualty. I could not tell his age: his face was covered with white dust & his hair was grey. His eyes flickered sightlessly & he moaned & shivered. There was a cry for blankets but there were no blankets. We piled our coats on him and I took a handle of the stretcher & we picked our way over the glass & the bricks ... & carried him half a mile to the nearest hospital. Women & children sat in the passages dripping with blood. Doctors were walking with torches, some, aliens, unable to make themselves understood. The windows of the ward were out. Our charge was suffering from shock, but when I took the coats off him I saw he was only a child, he was curled up as if still in the womb, dressed only in a shirt which at the back was torn to shreds & thick with dried blood. The stretcher bearer with me was stuttering hysterically. Other casualties were coming in, lying still or moaning; people walked in silently with very young children in their arms who were either asleep, or unconscious, or dead.

He was still incensed by newspaper coverage. The day after 19 February, the heaviest raid since 1941, 'The headlines, in their infantile way, say: "London AA barrage beats raiders." To eight million people such headlines are an insult both to their intelligence and courage.'

On a visit to Oxford to see Dorothy he saw his father. They played music together, and quarrelled: Laurie criticised Reg's piano-playing and Reg said 'he had it on good authority that an accompanist's job was to lead'. It was the last time Laurie ever saw his father.

Living with Cecil Day-Lewis brought London literary life into his own home. One night Raymond Mortimer was there, talking in 'a loud silky Bloomsbury voice' on subjects beyond Laurie's ken: Valéry, Compton-Burnett, Stephen Tennant.

About 10.30 a raid starts and Raymond's voice booms above the guns. Cecil grows pale & we cock our ears & mark the long trailing path of a bomb. C goes on his knees, Raymond & Rosamond spring to the corner and crouch on all fours & I am left trembling like a jelly on the sofa – and RM's voice goes on booming without a break, telling us of the exquisite Stephen Tennant caught in a raid while a green flare drops overhead. 'Oh dear,' he says, 'this is death to one's complexion.'

Still he went down to Sussex when summoned by Lorna, to lie 'among the cold primroses & violets' in a wood above Horsham.

A sudden peculiar little blazing up of her hot star of older days has illuminated the week ... Regretfully, but uncomplainingly, she tells me to be careful whom I sleep with – taking it for granted that I do. Yasmin is 5 – and further away than ever. There seemed no point in sending her anything ... each year I feel it more pointless.

This spring has no destination – L waves frantically or dutifully from carriage windows, but we have changed trains & no longer have similar destinations.

In June it was a year since Lucian Freud's arrival in their lives. 'I am dogged by an evil shadow.'

Every letter from Annie ended with the refrain: had he seen darling Yasmin, and sweet Lorna? Laurie went to Slad for a weekend of freedom before starting work, on 17 April 1944, with Day-Lewis in the MOI Publications Division in Room 614, Russell Square House, Bloomsbury. This was a congenial office. As well as Day-Lewis there was Nicolas Bentley, the cartoonist, and Joan Hunter Dunn (celebrated by Betjeman) to serve lunch. Laurie became the resident clown (later caricatured in one of Day-Lewis's crime novels.) At nights he firewatched with Day-Lewis and they played chess and talked into the small hours. One night when he and Day-Lewis and Rosamond went to hear a new work by Britten, he suddenly saw Lorna. 'Uncontrollably my blood turned to sand, my mouth dried up – later I felt I had been soundly beaten all over.' When he went to play Beethoven with Ben Frankel and girlfriend Anna, and afterwards the conversation turned to jealousy, 'I was amazed to find how much I've changed, holding fidelity a high ideal,' Laurie noted, 'which they reckon to be weakness, primitive & possessive & narrow.'

On 4 June a girl called out in the street: 'Have you heard the news?' The Normandy landings had begun. The night was full of strange sounds. 'Some infernal machine was being launched from the N. Coast of France, and coming in numbers off the South Coast

of England. Papers said radio controlled, speed 240 miles per hour,
& full of explosives…'

A few days later he was in the office when he had his first sight of
a flying bomb:

> It was like an incredible toy; fascinated I watched it streaking
> towards the tower of the University. Just as it seemed it would
> crash into it, it hesitated, spurted flame from its tail, and fell
> slowly upon Tottenham Court Road. I lay by the radiator and
> then, after the explosion, saw a great tower of grey blue dust rise
> up. Slept in the ministry this evening, with Cecil. Flying bombs
> came in a steady stream. We got little sleep.

Two nights later when he returned with Day-Lewis from a night in the
country, they found that a bomb had come down right in the middle
of Russell Square. Leaves were blown off trees and lay thick over the
roads among heaps of glass. All the windows in their office had blown
out and the door hung from its frame. All day they heard the sound of
glass being swept up. A proof copy of Laurie's first volume of poems,
The Sun My Monument, had been lying on Laurie's desk. The book
is inscribed: 'The small cuts in the cover of this book were caused by
glass splinters from flying bomb blasts in June 1944.'

Dedicated 'To Lorna', this volume forms a poetic account of his
life since 1935. 'Music in a Spanish Town' is about playing his fiddle
in Cordoba just before the outbreak of the Civil War; 'A Moment
of War', with the dateline now 'Spanish Frontier, 1937', and 'The
Return' ('And the day I observed I was a lover/I crossed the frontier
to seek a wound…') were brought home from the Civil War. All the
poems written for *Horizon* and for John Lehmann reflect the years of
Lorna's passionate embraces in the midst of war; for example, 'The
Armoured Valley':

> No festival of love will turn our bones
> to flutes of frolic in this month of May,

> but tools of hate shall make them into guns
> and bore them for the piercing bullet's shout
> and through their pipes drain all our blood away.

Publication day was Tuesday, 27 June 1944, the day after Laurie's thirtieth birthday. There was a bomb warning that day, and from the office window Laurie watched it crash near Regent's Park. He lunched with Rosamond Lehmann, and in the evening her brother John held a party at his flat: guests included William Plomer, Rose Macaulay, Eddy Sackville-West, Louis MacNeice, Henry Green, Peter Quennell, Lawrence Durrell, and of course Rosamond and Day-Lewis who took Laurie to dine at Oddenino's. Laurie's diary says:

> This might have been an excruciating anniversary [i.e. his birthday, one year since Lucian Freud took Lorna] but am too dead to feel it.
>
> I am a bit depressed about my book now – it seems so slight. At the party people were picking it up and putting it down as if it were a month-old *Evening Standard*.

It was some months before he received a forthright criticism of his poems from Wilma. She told him her sister Sybil, 'a 67-year-old woman who lives in very dull surroundings', admired them: but Wilma was harder to please. 'It's the pattern or design I'm doubtful about; i.e. as to whether there is one,' she declared. 'I don't want a story, but I do want a theme, & it seems to me you lack this. Beauty of rhythm, certainly, & an amusing clash & grind & romping ugliness of words which is often exhilarating. And sometimes beauty there too. But I still ask for a theme.'

Louis Aragon's poems had themes in plenty, she said, and Lorca's, and Day-Lewis's and Spender's. Having been born in 1886, she added, she supposed her opinions were out of date. But 'I still hold that theme is to words what design is to painting. Toss your glittering words on paper, & they might as well be left in the dictionary, if they're not expressing a subject. So it seems to this ancient, now condemned to heresy by her weight of years.'

He had plenty of emotion, she allowed, but had he yet begun to think? 'I doubt it.' For good measure she enclosed a poem by a contemporary Spanish poet she did admire (Pedro Salinas) and hailed Rosamond Lehmann's *The Ballad and the Source* as a master-piece. She added that she had been to Binsted and seen Lorna, Michael and Yasmin, 'who were all looking very well & seemed in good spirits'.

In August 1944 Rosamond, inviting him for a weekend ('Beatrix is here. We'll have a laugh'), was puzzled to find Laurie distant and secretive. She sensed that he was forging new friendships, as indeed he was. His MOI colleague Daphne Hardy – who had just ended her affair with Arthur Koestler, whose *Darkness at Noon* she had trans-lated – ran into Laurie in Malet Street, just when she was buying his book. Laurie took her address, and visited her: rather embarrass-ingly, as she was already living with the designer F. H. K. (Henri) Henrion.

Then the novelist Betty Askwith, who was broadcasting a review of his poems ('You've got the real thing haven't you? The sensation of fear that comes across in "A Moment of War" is physical and terrifying') introduced Laurie to Virginia Cunard. Tall and elegant Virginia, who was doing St John Ambulance work, was one of the six Cunard sisters who were to feature almost as importantly in Laurie's life as the Garman sisters did. Virginia found Laurie charmingly naïve: 'He asked me to meet him at Piccadilly Circus: nobody had ever asked me to meet them there.' As they walked home, guns began going off and shrapnel fell. 'And he pushed me down the area steps and held a dustbin lid over my head like a modern Walter Raleigh.' He recited a verse featuring the names of wartime generals:

> Hark hark, Mark Clark, the Kesselrings
> It is the Eisenhower

The general Patton of events
Has made old Monty sour
His Spaatz are fitting Bradley
And he Rommels as he runs.

She was enchanted by Laurie, and fell hopelessly in love with him – as everyone did, she said. 'He had charisma. That was the word for Laurie.' Her sisters Laura, Veronica, Barbara, Penelope and Grania all took to him at once. The Cunards had grown up at their family home high in the Cotswolds at Notgrove, where their father, Cyril Grant Cunard, grandson of Samuel of the Cunard Line, was known as the Squire. Soon Laurie was escaping from the flying bombs to stay in Surrey with Grania Cunard and her husband Val ffrench Blake at Nalderswood, at the gates of a house belonging to another sister, Barbara Charrington.

Laurie rapidly became like one of the family, Grania said, 'just part of all our lives'. Her husband Val, a tall and handsome officer with the 17th/21st Lancers, had been wounded in North Africa the previous year. He and Laurie had a musical alliance, playing Brahms and Beethoven and their *pièce de résistance*, the César Franck violin sonata. Laurie also encouraged Val in his oil painting: Val was impressed by Laurie's 'sensible and instinctive judgement, quite unclouded by any fashionable dogma which he might have picked up from his artist friends'.

The artist friends had arrived in his life through a gilded couple, Nicolette and Anthony Devas, whom he met at a Chelsea party that summer. Nicolette's sister Caitlin was married to Dylan Thomas; their father was Francis Macnamara, the wild poetic Irish friend of Augustus John. Nicolette – small, stylish, shapely, fair-haired and amber-eyed – had been at the Slade where she had met the strikingly handsome Anthony Devas, now much in demand as a portrait painter. Nicolette and Anthony were house-sitting off the King's Road at 6 Markham Square (home of Georgiana and Noel Blakiston), which had a studio on the top floor, with roof garden; the

Devases made it into a bohemian but civilised gathering place for artists, models and poets. Augustus John, Nicolette's adopted father, would frequently call. Laurie, whom she found 'a romantic-looking young man who measured up to the popular idea of a poet', immediately asked Nicolette if he might become their lodger.

Nicolette hesitated. Realising that Laurie was on the same wavelength – 'inflections and half sentences tell a saga as fast as the wink of a cat' – she told him: 'We don't want lodgers who want to be friends.' Undeterred, Laurie asked again. At his third or fourth plea ('Laurie could charm the birds off the trees and argue the hind leg off a donkey') she gave in, and he was allocated a sunny attic room with a view of the trees in Markham Square.

Later, Laurie told Nicolette that her reluctance had made Markham Square all the more appealing. He too wished to keep himself to himself. In their house the artist's need for solitude was respected. Laurie would hole up in his room unless Anthony persuaded him to come down and join the family. In Laurie, Devas found a soulmate. Both liked snooker, tricks and pranks. Laurie's speciality was balancing a tangerine on his head, letting it fall and catching it on the point of a kitchen knife. From his attic he would shoot peas at the ankles of passers-by: one day he caught Paul Potts, a poet who lived in the basement across the square known as Poets' Kitchen, presided over by the beautiful, sad-faced Elizabeth Smart (known, after her novel, as 'Sat-Down-And-Wept').[73]

Nicolette perceived that there was a winter Laurie and a summer Laurie. In winter he looked sickly and haggard with bags under his eyes. 'At the first ray of spring sunshine, he relaxed like a lizard ... turned his face up to the sun and baked his skin brown ... Sunburnt at midsummer, he deceived himself and felt robust.' His eyes lightened, he became extrovert, interested in women, and played cricket with the children. When the Devases's son Prosper was born in 1946, Laurie became his godfather. At Markham Square, Anthony Devas painted several portraits of Laurie – one, first exhibited at the Leicester Galleries in November 1945, hangs in the

National Portrait Gallery today. But Laurie's face was a challenge: it was 'like water', wrote Nicolette, 'never the same, mastered by the weather with a change of colour and texture; glass smooth, ripples, dead sulky. His weather was his moods.'

Devas, who was the local ARP warden, would hustle the family into the Anderson shelter during air raids, but Laurie remained in his bedroom, playing his fiddle. So during lulls in the raid they would hear the consoling strains of Mozart down the stairwell. The violin, Laurie said much later, is a solitary instrument, but it had always been his solace.

> You can stand in front of a window and play, and it absolutely destroys time, like making love. There seems to be no beginning and no end. You start in the early evening and you're still playing at midnight, and you don't know what has happened in the meantime.

He had always found it 'a deliverance from time's winged chariot'.

The war, Nicolette wrote, gave artists a free-wheeling independence. Money was short and ambition pointless, 'so the artist got on with the job of being an artist ... people like Anthony and Laurie, who were in a position to pursue their art during the war, never had it so good.' One day Nicolette took Laurie to see a house in Cheyne Row whose façade had fallen into the street after a landmine. The interior was open to the street, with paintings still hanging, and an eiderdown hooked on the chandelier. Walking by with her son Esmond in his pram, Nicolette heard the hooting of an owl, bringing food to its young in a nest in the corner cupboard. Laurie made this the subject of his poem 'Town Owl'.

When Rosamond Lehmann wrote, urging Laurie to 'come next weekend & gladden our hearts' and to take her son Hugo out ('Just say no if it's a bore. You know how my children dote on you, but I don't want them to suck your blood'), she added: 'I did not realise you were *chez* Devas. I do hope you're happy.'

He was not exactly happy, but he had found his milieu. Chelsea was more congenial than Putney or Knightsbridge, and his colleagues at the MOI were excellent company. In October 1944 the woman who researched the pictures for *Land at War*, Olivier Popham – later Anne Olivier Bell, Mrs Quentin Bell, editor of Virginia Woolf's diaries – shared Laurie's small sunless office, where Laurie and Day-Lewis 'would carry on hilarious commentary with hoots of laughter'. 'Laurie was sometimes poorly and subdued,' Olivier said, 'but jokes and fun were the leitmotif of our daily life.'

Lorna had now temporarily vanished from Laurie's diary, except that on 12 October he wrote: 'This morning, I considered for the first time the possibility of killing her, without rejecting it immediately.' Perhaps this is worth remembering in the context of his later poem 'My Many-Coated Man', who 'hooded by a smile, commits/ his private murder in the mind'.

Instead of this drastic step, he devised another strategy. From his vantage point in Markham Square, Laurie was perfectly placed to find himself a new Garman girl. There were three of Lorna's beautiful nieces now in Kathleen Garman's house at 272 King's Road: Epstein's two daughters Esther and Kitty, and Kathy, the child Laurie had dandled on his knee in Martigues in 1937, daughter of Helen Garman and Marius Polge. The four-storey house was one of a Regency terrace later pulled down for the new fire station, in a parade of junk shops, cafés, art stores and greengrocers. The houses on either side stood derelict. Kathleen's house had gracious fireplaces and was stuffed with works of art: 'bronzes, drawings and gouaches by Modigliani and Epstein, amid the marvellous Benin heads and furniture which Epstein and Picasso had collected in their student days'.[74] Kathleen's Steinway piano was in the first-floor drawing room, with its tall shuttered and balconied windows.

Laurie had already spotted Lorna's niece Kathy in the King's Road, 'nubile, arms swinging, straight and tall, her limbs clad in a tight blue frock ... sturdily curved and comely'. She was indeed precociously shapely and long-legged, but she was only thirteen. Her less robust cousins Kitty and Esther were 'each of them a heart-stopping beauty'. The girls' upbringing, as Epstein's second family, was singular. Epstein – who continued to live at Queen's Gate with his wife and the two children he had fathered, adopted by his wife – would visit his mistress Kathleen and their three children, Kitty, Esther and Theo, twice a week. Kitty recalled his arrival at six on Wednesdays, with a bottle of wine and flowers or fruit.

> He'd look at us in a benign way but there was no real rapport; I once heard my brother Theo calling him 'Papa' and it made me cringe with envy. On Saturdays my mother would be got up in evening dress with silver shoes and a wreath in her hair, and they'd dine at the Isola Bella in Soho, or the Ivy, and he'd come back for the night. Sometimes they'd take us with them, to things like the Ballet Russe. I remember feeling hot and teenagerish and left out and never having the right dress.

Kitty and Esther were shy, nervous, slightly fey and other-worldly in Garman fashion. 'We cultivated being pale and interesting to the extent that we were called the Magnolia Girls. Most young men weren't glamorous enough for us. We were tremendous poseurs,' Kitty said, 'reading poetry and playing Debussy. Kathy was more down to earth.'

Within the year of 1945, Laurie took out all three Garman nieces. Esther, graceful and swan-necked at seventeen (as sculpted in clay by her father), was taken by Laurie to Yehudi Menuhin's spellbinding performance in aid of Jewish relief at the Albert Hall in July 1945: Epstein had been given tickets, and passed them to Laurie. In a powdered, bejewelled gathering, Laurie noted in his diary, 'no one looked more beautiful than Esther, whose long plaits hung down like tassels of black silk'.

But there was also Kitty. When Laurie asked eighteen-year-old Kitty out, she was surprised – 'he had seemed like a romantic kindly bohemian uncle' – but flattered: he was a sophisticated older man (thirty-one) and a poet, therefore glamorous. She went back to his room at the Devases's, and when Laurie made advances Kitty did not reject them.

> Partly from curiosity, and a kind of fatality. But I thought the things he said were rather corny. He put on the *Rite of Spring* and said, 'How does this make you feel?' It didn't make me feel at all erotic. I was embarrassed and I didn't really like it.

But he gave her a pretty bracelet and wrote her a poem, an acrostic on her name.

> And then he rather brutally broke it off, quite sensibly, saying, 'I don't think this is right.' And of course my self-esteem was bruised, and I made a painful scene, thinking I wasn't passionate enough, saying, 'You can't leave me, please love me again, you can't,' like any distraught and tearful girl of eighteen with her first lover. My mother went to see him, because I was so upset, and he denied it through and through.

At some point that year, Lorna stepped in. At a party at Roy and Mary Campbell's, Lorna pointed to Kathy – beautiful but also tough – and said to Laurie, 'Try that one. She'll do for you. She'll be strong enough.'

Kitty felt she wasn't made of stern enough physical stuff for Laurie, who had hinted darkly at illnesses which she would not understand. But she was jealous when Kathy was taken out by Laurie. She claimed he sent Kathy an almost identical acrostic to hers, 'using the same words, except that mine began "Know the green wells of the sea"; and hers started "Know the blue wells of the sea" (her eyes were blue and mine were green).'

In fact Kathy's acrostic, spelling 'Kathy Polge', which she still has, dated 26 August 1945, is different:

Keep in your hair that summer golden crop
And never shall its corn-flushed harvest go
To fill death's sickle or the grave's grey mill.
Hold your heart's rose in bloom, and blossoming
Your youth, its life, shall have no need to die.
Provençal child, in whose deep eyes I drink
Outpouring wines of blue Iberia,
Live in my vision, burn its northern frost,
Grow like the sun that rises heaven high
Each year returning summer for our joy.

Kathy was in her Parson's Green School uniform when she saw Laurie leaning against the gas stove in the basement kitchen of 272 King's Road. She was no longer living with her Aunt Kathleen, because her mother Helen had fallen in love with a charming old Italian law professor, Mario Sarfatti, who had left Mussolini's Italy as a Jewish refugee. Helen and Kathy went to live with 'Sarfi' at 10 Kensington Church Walk. Laurie began to visit Kathy there and would take her to the pictures – Olivier in *Henry V*, *Jane Eyre* (which they saw three times). When Laurie wrote Kathy the acrostic, she had already decided that he was the only man for her.

Her cousin Kitty took a while to get over Laurie. She left home and went to stay with a Garman aunt in Herefordshire, got a job in a school, and 'began going out with all and sundry to make up for it'. The bizarre postscript to this brief affair is that Kitty's next serious boyfriend was her Aunt Lorna's other ex-lover, Lucian Freud. He too, after Lorna left him, had gone in the same pursuit as Laurie. Lorna saw what was happening and realised that pursuing her nieces was her rejected lovers' way of staying close to her. She appeared to accept that if they couldn't have her, both Laurie and Lucian would want one of her nieces. 'It was a confirmation of her psychological power over them,' Yasmin said. 'Also, as her nieces, they weren't threats to her.'

Kitty was naturally conscious, with both Laurie and Lucian, that she was following Lorna, and felt inferior to her. 'She was so glamorous, and rich, and we were all so poor. Also Lorna had, like my mother, great physical courage. Physical discomfort meant nothing to them, while I wasn't intrepid; I always wanted to be warm and cosseted, catching a cold on the least provocation.' She said she truly went into both affairs in complete innocence,

> naïvely assuming that because Lorna had now become a Catholic and went to mass every morning, and said she'd given her heart to God, that she had given up both Laurie and Lucian: but she hadn't inside, of course, at all, and she made me feel treacherous, which I wasn't.

After two years with Lucian, Kitty became his first wife, just before their daughter Anna was born in 1948. She left him four years later, after he painted her in one of his most famous portraits, *Girl with a White Dog*, in which Kitty gazes apprehensively ahead, wearing a yellow dressing gown with one breast exposed and a white bull terrier lying with its head on her thigh. Kitty met and married the economist Wynne Godley[75] soon afterwards.

Rosamond Lehmann longed for Laurie to confide in her about his 'new girls and activities'. She felt affronted by his secrecy and was convinced he was unhappy. 'I know you like covering your tracks, mystifying the world – but we'd got beyond that once, and trusted one another. Now I can only try to read your face and form conclusions from what you *don't* tell me – from the expression in your eyes.' Was he avoiding her because of having revealed so much of himself last year when he was so miserable?

'I can only *guess* that things never did come right between you & L – I can't ask ... I waited for you to say "All is well again" or "All is over." That is all I wished to know.' She would rejoice if he had found someone to be happy with; but she suspected he was wrapping himself round with crowds to hide himself, the popular young man about town. 'When I knew you, really knew you, you were alone. I so admired & respected your plan for life.' She signed herself: 'Your loving Rosamond.'

Having received a 'sweet' reply, she added:

> I think you are, without perhaps deliberately meaning to be, rather
> a dangerous person for women! You seem to expand with such
> warmth & freedom towards them, it goes to their heads – it's such a
> rare pleasure for them to find so much subtle understanding, sens-
> ibility & attentiveness in the male sex. They think you need them as
> much as they need you. Then suddenly they discover they've come
> to a walled enclosure with a sign: Keep Off. Keep Out. No Visitors.
> No Inquiries. No One At Home. And they get upset.

Rosamond was right: Laurie's charm remained, but his carapace now made him dangerously immune to commitment and he
was glumly conscious of hurting people. He wrote in his diary in
February 1945: 'I have been regaled all round by offered love. I have
been without heart.'

That snowy new year of 1945, Annie wrote listing the deaths in
the village; she had missed Laurie's broadcast poem on Christmas
Eve. 'I kept looking at the clock trying to make up my mind to go up
to Mrs Brown's but the noise of the rushing 40 m.p.h. wind deterred
me.' Reg, she had heard, did not think much of Laurie's photograph
in the *Radio Times* – 'but he is always finding fault with everything'.

Lorna's elder son, Michael Wishart, now sixteen and about to
go to the Central School of Art, did hear Laurie's poem and wrote –
decorating his letter with an exquisite Grecian head and laurel leaves.
He admired 'Words Asleep' and 'I think at night my hands are mad'
('Night') and drew a naked lady. 'I can't say anything in a letter to
you, Laurie. I shall give you a painting which will say all I have to
say. I have been painting and am empty now. With love, Michael.'
(In his autobiography Michael wrote: 'I have always painted what
I could not express better in words.') Invited to choose any picture
from Michael's first exhibition, Laurie chose one of magnolias,
which Michael framed for him in plain gold. He also promised to
design the cover for Laurie's next book.

'Be always occupied,' Michael advised Laurie, endearingly, 'because I have discovered it means being happy. Boredom is misery.' Laurie was certainly busy; he was about to take the traditional recourse of those wounded in love. He was going abroad, for the first time since he had left Lorna on that black day in 1938: and again, he was going to Cyprus.

One dark, grimy day, 'when the war had been on six years and the face of everyone had a jaundiced look', Laurie walked into a pub and found Ralph 'Bunny' Keene, who told him: 'I'm going to Cyprus to make a film. Aren't I lucky?' Bunny was an Old Marlburian who ran a documentary film company called Greenpark Productions. Laurie told him he knew Cyprus from his pre-war visit. ('True, I was only there for a few weeks, but nobody knew that.') So he was signed up to tell the story of the island under British rule. He bought himself a safari suit and on 9 April 1945 was issued with his second passport, this time described as 5ft 10in and 'Government Official'.

He saw Lorna, who wrote a chatty letter ('Our little angel has chicken pox … I do hope you feel better, my sweet') hoping they might have lunch before he left. She referred to 'undividable you & me'. She had been listening to Rachmaninov's *Rhapsody on a Theme of Paganini*:

> Do you know the slow movement? He has a sad haunting truth in his music which never fails to give me gooseflesh … Did you hear the Poulenc Cantata – with Paul Éluard's poems & Laurence Olivier reading them, I thought he read badly. I think it's a mistake to put music to poems, true poems should be & are music & especially as the only sort of poem one could set to music is the lyric & that is essentially musical by itself don't you agree.

She had been planting Madonna lily bulbs. 'I adore gardening it's about as far removed from any form of neurosis as any pastime I know. I was so happy to see you again my darling let's try & meet before you go or on the day Love me Lorna.'

In a postscript she rhapsodised over his latest poems in *Penguin New Writing*, 'so new & exciting do write some more my darling & PLEASE send Tang of healing herb [poem] to *Horizon* let me know the result. Love & XXXX from us.'

She also sent him a totem she had carved herself:

> I wanted to send you a great big Chinese agate which looks like a cow's eye but it was too big for you to carry in your pocket & the whole point is to have it everywhere you go, so I'm sending you this [a little wooden madonna] as I have the other one which makes it more of a totem because there are only 2 and you & I have them. This spring is certainly very lovely & you're right when you say about it having no heart when one's young – but now it has the richest heart never to be forgotten. I played romance for C Sibelius last night 1st time for many moons. It's so lovely darling love, have no fears – I swear I'll look after you. Y all better Love & kisses from us both. I adored the post cards send me some more for goodness sake.

Lorna had also carved a huge wooden madonna which she placed in the grounds of a deserted eighteenth-century house near her home. She had covered her madonna with a scarlet hooded rain-cape to protect it. Michael was in the post office one day and heard a woman saying: 'Mrs Wishart's become very peculiar: she stands out for hours in the rain just staring into space.'

Laurie departed from Hurn airfield by Dakota in April. After a stopover in Cairo – 'hideous, lemon-coloured, hot, mercenary, and plagued with black kite-hawks that spun like bellicose flies over the city's rank-smelling carcass' – he took a pretty white biplane for the last lap over Sinai, Palestine, Syria, Beirut, and arrived in Nicosia with a week in which to prepare the script. A mad Turkish driver named Achmed, who could kill snakes, sing and 'do the stomach dance', tore 'like a ball of mercury in a frying-pan' through squat brown villages, scattering mules, goats, poultry and people. In a café one night Laurie found Nikos the handsome farmer and Vassos the villainous-looking goatherd, who became the film's main characters. 'They lived their story before the camera, arguing with a natural passion that was completely unselfconscious and childlike.' Feasting on pickled sparrows, goat's cheese, honey and rough wine, enjoying the singing and dancing, absorbing Cyprus's legends of Aphrodite, St Paul, Othello, St George, Laurie was happy. One night a man came running down the street in Nicosia, while Laurie was at a film-show, shouting out that the war was over. In his book about the experience of making the film, unthrillingly entitled *We Made a Film in Cyprus*, a beaming Laurie is photographed basking on a bed of oranges. The easy friendship with Bunny Keene developed into a fruitful working partnership.

Laurie arrived back, lean and brown, on 13 May 1945. Sister Marjorie had written to him in Nicosia, 'Oh to be in England, now that V-day is almost here', having climbed up the steep hill to the cricket field on 'a warm sunny evening with a strong scent of hawthorn in the air'. Laurie went home to Slad in July, and carried away armfuls of lilies.

In London Laurie now enjoyed a reputation as 'a real Don Juan'. He drifted in and out of his room at the Devases' house as he pleased. Frequently, he lodged with Virginia Cunard at 21 Raphael Street. 'The telephone never stopped ringing for Laurie,' Virginia recalled. 'He had more people in love with him than anyone I've ever met, and all the girls thought they were the only one.' Laurie got on especially well with Virginia's housekeeper, Bessie, a Gloucestershire girl with a country brogue, a strong personality and a staunch view of morality; she thought Laurie a bit of a lad, but respectfully called him Mr Lee. Virginia's flat was burgled while Laurie was there, to the fury of Annie: 'So the wretches took your clothes & suitcase – I wish I could help you but I have used all my coupons. It seems to me people are doing that sort of thing all over London & getting away with it.'

Another Cunard sister, Penelope (Pen), began to invite Laurie to stay. Her husband was Brigadier Nigel Dugdale, who had been wounded in North Africa like Val ffrench Blake, and now worked in the War Office in public relations. In the summer of 1945 Laurie spent his first of many weekends at Bushton, the Dugdales' Georgian manor house near Wootton Bassett. Their elder daughter, Antonia, then aged five, recalled the excitement of Laurie's first arrival on their doorstep, delivered by her aunts Virginia and Veronica. 'He lay sleeping in the sun in the garden, and we tiptoed around because nanny said, "Mr Lee has been ill and mustn't be disturbed. He has to have his rest."'

Pen Dugdale was a natural hostess who loved filling her house with guests, and could organise things so that an atmosphere of ease and plenty was conjured with no apparent fuss.

Her sister Virginia said

> Pen was totally unsnobbish. She was a Gaitskellite Socialist; Attlee and Jim Callaghan were among her guests. She would never invite people because they were grand, only because they were interesting, so she preferred writers or painters. When anyone asked 'Are you one of *the* Dugdales?' Pen said, 'No, I'm afraid I'm not.'

She wrote doggerel verse ('Lord Tennyson's cry went up to the sky in the year eighteen hundred and nine; No doubt his mama and perhaps his papa said I've ne'er seen a baby so fine'). Her husband Nigel was a tireless joker, carrying a wig, moustache and false teeth in his pocket at all time, and kept a fairy cycle at the War Office, to ride up and down the endless corridors.

As the privileged eldest, Antonia was not banished to the nursery but was allowed to dine downstairs and to taste the wine – her father always produced 'something special' from his cellar like a Chateau Latour 1934 – and to absorb the electric atmosphere caused by Laurie and Nigel Dugdale's battle of wits. Laurie would 'go into thought mode, brew up some *jeu-de-mot*, whereupon my father would cap it'.

At Bushton were the kind of toys Laurie liked – guns and bows and arrows, and croquet. One of Dugdale's eccentricities was tying cotton around the waists of wasps, and letting them go with a cry of 'Thar she blows!' to locate a wasps' nest. Laurie could make coins disappear, and produce them from behind his ear; or perform with a tremendous flourish the egg trick, standing three eggs on match-boxes on three glasses of water, taking a broom and knocking the tray away, so that the three eggs fell unbroken into the glasses of water.

Yet Laurie felt he was 'in a very bad state and unable to absorb much' of Britten's *Peter Grimes* at Sadler's Wells with Rosamond Lehmann. He disguised his low mood from Annie, telling her only about his forays into the *beau monde*: 'Glad you sat on the settee with Lady Louis [Mountbatten] and the other great ones,' she wrote. 'I'd love to have seen you.' Laurie had been to the salon of Lady Sibyl Colefax where Day-Lewis sang, and he suspected that most guests, like him, felt faintly ashamed to be there but were 'unable to resist the compliment'.

Laurie and Day-Lewis would often go to Long Crichel House in Dorset, where Eddy Sackville-West, Raymond Mortimer, Eardley Knollys and Desmond Shawe-Taylor conducted their literary salon. Annie loved reading these names. 'How did you enjoy your weekend with E. Sackville-West? He is not one of the Sheepscombe Wests is he? You descended from them on your great grandmother's side.' She was dismayed by the 1945 election results: Stroud had fallen to 'Dirty Labour'.

In the midst of street parties and VJ Day celebrations Annie was cast down by having seen 'that man' (Reg), '& that as you may imagine always upsets my nerves. *He* seems all right – well, cocksure & conceited.' Reg had set off for his son Harold's in Stroud, and en route called on Dorothy in Oxford where he found Annie. 'He got a nasty shock to see me there I know ... he had Mrs R with him in the car "Tops" she is called by the family...'

Rosamond and Day-Lewis had decided to found a new *Horizon*-style magazine to be called *Orion*, and commissioned Laurie to write about his childhood in Slad. In December 1945, Annie wrote a helpful letter of reminiscence. 'What about the beating up of the poor man who was not found till the next morning and it had been a frosty night? He eventually died of exposure. The men who did it were a heartless lot, no conscience or anything.' So Laurie began to write the article which would become, fifteen years later, a chapter of *Cider with Rosie*.

13

'Warm thoughts of warm nights'
1946–1947

THE COTTAGE OF Laurie's childhood was no longer quite so picturesque. 'Oh our home is abominable,' wrote Annie in December 1945, on her usual scrap of old envelope. It was cruelly chilly, sunless and damp. When Laurie went home he found the kitchen 'like a hollow in the wood', with moss on the dank walls, black leaves and ferns and twigs on floor and furniture. 'Annie lives like a squirrel, hiding away little stores of treasures, & losing them. Wrapping herself in scarves, blankets, curtains & pieces of flannel, ready to roll herself into a ball.' Annie's dream was to live in the kind of rural retreat that would lure her boys back to stay with her. Couldn't Laurie borrow money? ('I don't think you are stiff-necked are you?')' A house would be 'for you boys for the future, not entirely for myself... You can have the bakehouse-cum-schoolroom for your own private sanctum for writing or painting or music – and how glad and happy I should be knowing you were in there, oh! please God, let it come true.' Laurie and Jack did bid for a cottage in an auction, but it went for £1,200.

She wondered if Grania ffrench Blake might buy 'a nice place going at Sheepscombe called the Brooklands with buildings etc. attached, including a cottage which she might let to me'. But Grania bought a farm in Cornwall instead, at Tokenbury, which became another refuge for Laurie. While Val went back to command his regiment in Italy, Laurie would go down to stay with Grania with romance in mind. The letters from ffrench Blake were remarkable,

Laurie thought, for their 'felicity of phrase & fancy' so he always replied with a self-conscious flourish, possibly indicative of guilt. 'All the clumsy knots and neuroses of London untied themselves as if by magic,' he wrote in February 1946 after a weekend staying with Grania, shifting stones and clearing out gutters and ferreting for rabbits. He assured Val that Tokenbury would make a first class dairy farm, with its sloping sunny fields and good grass. 'There's a health in the air, a sweep of grandeur in the country that makes one feel superhuman ... What lovely country for the flesh & the spirit.'

Laurie was now an expert on the open spaces of Britain, having spent a month travelling 100 miles a day, researching for an MOI film. From the Brecon Beacons he was driven to 'the wild Pembroke coast with its great cliffs and bird-islands and crimson-coloured castles; snow-bitten Snowdon where the car got stuck in a pass; the Peak District and the Pennines & the Roman Wall; and the lovely Lakes, wine-dark, under snow-capped mountains sparkling in the sun like Christmas cakes'. In letters he was already drafting his script, promoting the idea of National Parks.

The resulting film panned over urban streets, chimneys, power-stations, railways, the voice-over lamenting 'the crowded generations living ... and dying' in cities. A girl leaned out of a town window on a summer evening, with a pot of geraniums and a bird in a hanging cage. 'Is there any country under this sky?' asked the voice.

> There was country here once. Green fields and free-growing flowers. They once made hay on the ground beneath that railway, snipe flew from the wild marshes drained for that power-station ... And London – this great crust of smoke-blackened chaos – was once a small city standing alone in its fields by a country river. The land is too much lived in, too used up...

But if Britain had protected areas called National Parks, there would be somewhere to go on Sundays. There would be footpaths and cycle tracks, youth hostels, and farmhouse catering; beauty spots and ancient monuments open to all. Famous voices – Clough Williams-Ellis, Professor G. M. Trevelyan, Julian Huxley and Augustus John – spoke of man's spiritual need for country life. (Ten National Parks, as mooted in 1945 by John Dower, civil servant and rambler, were set up between 1951 and 1957 in all the areas Laurie visited.)

Laurie's flourishes of poetic reportage for documentaries were widely appreciated: the Prime Minister's secretary sent a note to say that Mr Attlee had 'particularly admired' the commentary in the Cyprus film, *Cyprus is an Island*. It had fine photography by Bunny Keene, and good music, Laurie told Val, '& a lush pagan commentary written in those round ripe full-blooded numbers for which Lee is so notorious'. There were spinoffs: the book, *We Made a Film in Cyprus*; a wireless interview on *In Town Tonight*; a lecture to the Geographical Society before an audience 'grey, rustling & deaf'. Though disliking his own radio voice ('husky, nasal, with intonations of my brothers'), Laurie began to be known as a natural broadcaster in 1945 after a graphic talk called 'Journey through Spain'. In the BBC canteen after the recording, by a neat coincidence, he found Roy and Mary Campbell. It was his first sighting of Mary 'since I walked from her house in Toledo, heading for Madrid, nearly eleven years ago. Now she is like an oldish Spanish woman, but with extraordinary facial inflexions that are Helen/Lorna.'

Laurie was now thoroughly at home in his metropolitan milieu. John Lehmann took him to the French Embassy to meet Madame Odette Massigli.[76] Ushered in by a liveried retainer in white gloves, Laurie presented the lady with a his poems (at Lehmann's whispered prompting, 'like a court plotter'), signing it with a conceit about the roses of April. '"But charmant!" she cried with her soft scented eyes.' He started collecting pictures: he bought one by the war artist Leonard Rosoman; and his favourite painter, Matthew Smith, now almost blind, gave him a portrait 'in violent greens & blues & russet browns' in exchange for his poem 'To Matthew Smith':

> Oil is incendiary on your moving brush;
> your hands are jets
> that crack the landscape's clinker and draw forth
> its buried incandescence.

One evening at a literary soirée he watched Stephen Spender acidly introducing three Soviet writers who discoursed interminably until 'Stephen drooped in a jelly of anger'. Another evening, in Cheyne Walk, Spender hosted a concert in memory of his brother Humphrey's wife. In the long elegant room where Whistler once painted, with snowdrops heaped on tables, they listened to Spender's pianist wife Natasha Litvin playing Bach, Beethoven and Schubert. Spender, 'lisping ... thunderous', read his poems; Peggy Ashcroft read 'The Lady of Shalott', a Shakespeare sonnet, and some poems by Day-Lewis: 'As Peggy read "The Album", a love poem written to Rosamond, the charge in the air made my hair stand on end,' Laurie recorded.

> But when it was over R leaned to me & whispered 'How d'you think she reads?'
> 'Pretty bad,' I said.
> 'I think awful, such a mechanical declamation.' And as she spoke Rosamond caught Peggy's eye & two of the sweetest and falsest feminine smiles passed one to the other.

Laurie was still snarled up in Day-Lewis's tangled web. In March 1946, Rosamond announced 'a miracle': Cecil had finally told his wife about her, but Mary was behaving as if nothing had changed, saying things like: 'Next year we must have a wire fence here.' 'You will appreciate the grim symbolism,' wrote Rosamond. Laurie's article about his childhood, for their new magazine *Orion*, was considered by Rosmond 'beyond even my high superlatives' and Day-Lewis, paying him twelve guineas, urged him to write a book-length memoir of his childhood, never imagining that it would take another dozen years.

Laurie's poetic muse-in-chief had departed, but poems about the natural scene still sprouted 'like rare and sickly orchids' at unlikely moments. He wrote 'Day of These Days' on the top deck of the number 11 bus, en route to Yates's wine bar in the Strand, where he bought his his Portuguese rosé. Forty years later he remembered:

> It was such a wonderful morning that this poem began almost to dictate itself. As I drove through this golden light, images came of my village on an autumn day, a kind of *alegría* of atmosphere, and I began to write, 'Such a morning it is when love/leans through geranium windows/and calls with a cockerel's tongue./ When red-haired girls scamper like roses/over the rain-green grass,/and the sun drips honey.' And there I was hacking away, and the conductor came along and saw I was writing and didn't even ask for my fare, which was threepence.[77]

He escaped to the country regularly. He and Bunny Keene went to stay with the actress Ann Todd and her husband Nigel Tangye on the Welsh coast, where they watched a drowned man dragged from the sea. He went home to Slad and watched his contemporary John Teakle being carried in his coffin up the steep churchyard path under a stormy sky. Yet another rural retreat beckoned when Rosamond Lehmann bought an Oxfordshire house, Little Wittenham Manor, with the £40,000 she had made from Hollywood for her novel *The Ballad and the Source*. While staying there, Laurie rang his mother, who was at Dorothy's in Oxford. It was the first time Annie had ever used a telephone. 'Did you think I spoke distinctly?' she wrote. She had just 'lost' one of her sons, as Jack had married Nora Dawson, his colleague on the newly released feature film *Children on Trial*. Laurie went to a screening in the presence of Queen Mary, who 'sniffed heavily throughout the film, which endeared her to me'.

In hot and steamy June, Laurie went back to Slad again and took Kathy, his 'dearest girl' with him. Wise old Annie guessed she was Lorna's niece. 'I think she was very nice & really such a child.' Kathy was only fourteen, but looked older: 'so pretty, with a sometimes conscious childishness, yet not innocent', said Laurie's notebook, recording how they spent days and evenings lying in the grass among wild strawberries, hearing the cuckoo's song. 'Down to the lake in darkness. We lay by the green-smelling reeds. I found a glow-worm which she had never seen before.'

Later, in *Two Women*, Laurie described how he had known 'this lovely girl' for years, 'steering her through adolescence'. 'Her mother seemed to have accepted my role of instructor and pathfinder and gave us unusual freedom.' The Garman family example encouraged precocious amorous licence: Lorna had met Ernest Wishart at fourteen and married him at sixteen. Someone sent Laurie a Valentine that year: 'No spring or summer hath such grace/As I have seen in one autumnal face.' 'Ah, time!' wrote Laurie. 'That I am loved for my white hairs.' (He was nearly thirty-two.) He would take Kathy in her school blazer for walks after school, through the bombed gardens of Kensington, 'like Carthage or Pompeii, a wilderness of wild cats and scented jasmine' or by the Thames, with the moon reflected on the water, and the distant noises of families in the thin-walled riverside prefabs. They flew Laurie's kite in Battersea Park until 'rigid & strong as a swan' it came down in a tall tree; Laurie climbed a ladder but could not dislodge it. Kathy would prattle companionably. 'Are you brave?' 'D'you like the sea?' 'Will I be taller than you?' or sometimes, 'Can't come out tonight – I've got to do 53 theorems.'

That August of 1946, Helen Garman decided to take Kathy back to Martigues and asked Laurie to accompany them 'as their acknowledged but ambiguous protector'.[78] They took a tin of coffee and fifty cigarettes to barter for three nights in a Paris hotel, arriving just as the peace conference was taking place. Paris was 'grey-blue, empty, expensive, sad with ennui'. Most restaurants were closed but they had beefsteak and managed to get seats on a night train to Marseilles. They stayed at a farmhouse just outside Martigues on the Istres road, because Kathy's 'huge, waddling grandmother' ('with swollen mouth, legacy of a bottle-fight in Marseilles, greasy black dress and big boots') was living with her lover in a one-room shack. Laurie and Kathy walked among pines, bathed in the still green lake, ate bouillabaisse with their fingers, watched fishermen winching in their catches and American soldiers behaving like conquering troops. On 21 August, the anniversary of the Liberation, there was a seven-course feast. Seeing the welcome Kathy received from the Provençal villagers, who exclaimed at her beauty, enveloped her in their embrace and wailed about her *pauvre père*, Laurie said he first 'truly noticed [Kathy's] clear gold beauty, and the depth of her eyes ... She had no guile or suspicion of treachery.'

Laurie was reaching a peak of professional creativity when he took part in Cyril Connolly's *Horizon* symposium in September 1946 on 'The Cost of Letters', which asked writers how much they needed to live on, and what they considered a suitable second occupation. (John Betjeman said he would be 'a stationmaster on a small country branch line'; Connolly himself replied 'a rich wife'.)

Laurie wrote: 'The commodity most necessary to the writer is not money at all, but time ... long avenues of it stretching far away before him.' He did not recommend second jobs: 'A he-man's job as a woodcutter or crane-driver, with a couple of hours' writing in the evenings? Romantic fallacy! ... A State job, then – Ministry propagandist or BBC hack? No; they fritter and stale like nobody's business.' ('It will be a black and evil day that lures me into an office again,' he had told Val ffrench Blake.) As for a State pension for writers, Laurie declared that hardship and near-starvation were no bad thing for young scribes: 'Let younger writers first serve this apprenticeship, and show something for it...'

He had no shortage of commissions that year. Uys Krige, friend of Roy Campbell, editor of the South African monthly *Vandag*, asked him for essays (at three guineas per 1,000 words) on Spender, Day-Lewis, MacNeice, Dylan Thomas. But Laurie was too busy writing a BBC talk called 'Free Trade in Poetry', on how the Spanish war had inspired British poets:

> Shelley, Browning and others fed lustily upon the sun and
> flowers of the Mediterranean. But ... they were inspired by its
> classical nostalgia, its static past; never by its present agony or
> possible future. Those native poets of ours who wrote of the
> Spanish War were, I think, the first to see Europe alive.

Annie listened to his talk at the house of a neighbour, Mrs Warner, who had been moved to tears.

Laurie had now also written his first radio play, in blank verse, and it was a small masterpiece. *The Voyage of Magellan*, produced by Rayner Heppenstall for the Third Programme in October 1946 with Frederick Valk and Bernard Miles, was a reconstruction of Magellan's first journey round the world to the 'spice islands' in 1519. In his preface Laurie remarked that man's first circumnavigation was 'as revolutionary to the human mind, perhaps, as anything that has ever happened to it' and he wrote like a man inspired. He seemed to have dredged from his seafaring Lee ancestry a folk-memory of ship's rations, salt-meat and scurvy, and borrowed the narrative device of Coleridge's *Ancient Mariner*, having a surviving sailor tell the tale to a blind beggar. In rich, evocative language – 'heightened towards poetry ... aiming first to capture the eye' – he brought to colourful life the clamour of sixteenth-century Seville, the reckless courage and daring of the voyage to Tierra del Fuego, the mutinous fury of the sailors, the violent death of their captain.

> We did not love Magellan, – but he was a captain.
> Beggar, we were all blind at the dawn of that journey,
> but with his black-eyes he led us – five ships,
> five creaking worlds in a green universe of ocean.

In its evocative power the play is closer to Browning's dramatic monologues than to his own poems. It was published by John Lehmann with drawings by Edward Burra, and is now almost forgotten, but it remains one of the best things Laurie ever wrote.

Magellan was regarded as a landmark in radio drama (the *New Statesman* ranked it with Sartre's *Huis Clos*), yet a decade was to pass before Laurie wrote another. A note in his diary suggests that he felt radio plays were a dying art. He and Rayner Heppenstall had talked over coffee of 'the last sweet days of blind radio. Literature will go out of radio when television comes in.' Also, Laurie had little confidence in his own creativity. In Day-Lewis's new detective novel *Minute for Murder* (under his pen-name Nicholas Blake), set in an office based on the MOI, there was a character named Bryan Ingle, caption writer, purveyor of purple prose and office joker: 'I have all the creative writer's equipment, except creativeness,' Ingle says. 'Curiosity, exuberance, spiritual stamina … But I can't invent. So I write flaming captions.'

All Laurie's curiosity, exuberance and stamina were deployed that autumn when Bunny Keene invited him to accompany him to India for two months, to write two films for the Tea Board: one on the tea planters and pickers, one on local customs. Nobody remains less than overwhelmed by a first trip to India, and Laurie returned with a notebook so crammed with stories and impressions he could have written a book – as one of his colleagues, the future novelist Emma Smith (then aged twenty-two, and on her first trip abroad), did, making India on the eve of independence the background to her second novel, *The Far Cry*.

Keene, Emma, Laurie and two cameramen, George and Teddy, embarked on 5 October 1946 on the SS *Andes* for the voyage to Bombay, which took two weeks. 'Laurie chases all the girls one after the other,' Emma's diary noted on the voyage out, 'talks to them, lies on the deck, plays deck-tennis, and deserts them for another.' A passenger named Vivien was going out to marry an Army officer she barely knew. 'V fears India and her marriage,' wrote Laurie. 'She lies in my arms and says I shall drive her mad.' When they disembarked, 'Vivien spots her John – a weak-looking officer with whiskers. She is in tears.' Laurie was also in demand to play his fiddle on board for singsongs, concerts and dances: 'kissing of hands and the girls in raptures,' observed sharp-eyed Emma. He had a running contest of puns with the cameraman George ('I asked the Captain this morning if he'd washed his Andes…')

On the night *The Voyage of Magellan* was broadcast, Laurie was in the straits of Gibraltar, huddled over the ship's crackling radio. He pronounced the production 'hammy' and preferred to be out on deck watching the lights of Tarifa and Cape Trafalgar, Ceuta and Tangier. When they eventually arrived in Bombay's teeming streets, they saw shrunken children with legs 'like rusty knitting-needles', horses 'thin as latchkeys', 'a boy without eyes led by his brother', endless bargaining and begging ('Memsahib, memsahib, baksheesh'). The searing heat felt like being hit on the head with a flat-iron, as Emma's vivid diary records. They travelled 1,200 miles by train to Calcutta and chose a bearer named Babu, 'bright & crafty as a mongoose', to go with them to Assam. Both Laurie and Emma were repelled, in those dying days of the Raj, by the English colonials' arrogant assumption of superiority, and horrified by the Indians' unquestioning cringing servility. When they played tennis at the Burra-sahib's bungalow in Nazira, there were twelve uniformed ball-boys, and everywhere teams of turbaned servants handing round tea and sweetmeats, while empty-headed tea-planters' wives appeared to do nothing at all. They were all caricatures. The men talked of nothing but sport and none had an inkling about humour or irony, so 'one must be always on guard'. Emma was more scathing: 'The awful creatures at Dibrughar, ordering whisky after whisky in the middle of the day, lolling at the bar in their shorts and boasting to each other of past drinking bouts – looking so silly, their lives just one string of parties and polo and rubbish.'

Laurie told Val ffrench Blake (an old India hand) that India was more astonishing and even more beautiful than he'd expected; Calcutta on the eve of partition was 'chaotic & in the grip of panic: no buses or taxis, stabbing in the streets [on the night of 27 October seventeen people were killed and ten injured with knife wounds], Bren guns & sten guns, & the station knee-deep in refugees from southern Bengal'. With Hallam Tennyson and his wife they watched the Kali Puja celebrations, with fireworks and music and singing, little oil lamps in tiny boats sent floating down the Ganges, and ritual sacrifice of young goats.

He heard from Lorna, and wrote sweet letters to Kathy, childlike in style: 'Calcutta is a tough place. We got no milk yesterday morning because the milkman had been murdered. There is stabbing every day, so I carry the knife I bought in Marseilles ... Keep warm,' he told her, 'by thinking of warm things, warm thoughts of warm nights among the jasmine bushes.'

Their journey north to Assam was held up when the rail track was washed away by a flood, but after the heat and violence of Calcutta, Nazira seemed idyllic. They occupied a handsome white bungalow on a bend in the river. Laurie rhapsodised over the misty green Naga hills, the light cool sun, exotic flowers, falcons and eagles, beautiful children riding buffaloes through the paddy fields, brilliant butter-flies, and constellations of fireflies at night. At the gold-topped temples of Sibsagar he was struck by the grace of girls in draped white saris and long thick plaits. He watched vultures fighting over a dead calf, and in the luxuriant jungle 'caught a whiff of something rank like goat – it is jackal'. Everything was photogenic, from water hyacinths to cow dung in the yard. They began filming by bringing down some Nagas (a sturdy people: 'no shrinking or servility' about them, noted Emma) and reconstructing a forest fire and a flood. Laurie went pigeon shooting every morning, ate bananas by the dozen, and one evening, when there was a circus, he got the fire-eater to teach him the trick of eating fire.

He noted the 'pathetic' grace, contentment and patience of the peasant women, and their prodigal but poverty-stricken fertility. The thin land, the tiny cows with spindly calves producing trickles of milk, mothers with wrinkled babies, hens laying minuscule eggs. While Keene and the others went on filming, Laurie returned to Calcutta, wandering the streets and markets with their 'multitudes of coloured visions – girls with their garlanded hair & flowing mists

& silks', struck by 'tragic children in rags & the smell of ghastly cooking, some hideous mess that fills me with a strange atavistic sorrow & fear'. The English, striding through the Taj hotel, were 'painful to look at, such disasters of form, feature ... and their skin – is it lack of sun, too much carbolic, or what. The wearing of shorts by all ages incongruous.'

Everyone he met warned him of the coming bloodshed after partition. Mr Wadia of Indian PEN told him Pakistan was 'biologically, ethnologically, economically impossible'. On 11 December 1946 Laurie steamed out of Bombay for the homeward voyage, suddenly lonely and feeling sour and empty of poetry. 'It would not be so bad if the crowd weren't so lifeless, or if there was some privacy. We move at a crawl through the tropic sea.' The hours hung heavily, filled with 'morning baths & changing for dinner – things I have never done regularly before'.

But at the ship's carol service he played his violin, learnt a new carol (Christina Rossetti's 'In the Bleak Mid-Winter'), won game after game of deck tennis, and stopped off at Mombasa where the East Africans looked to him much happier than the demoralised and fearful Indians. From the still Red Sea they crossed the Suez Canal into the teeth of a gale, pitching violently, green faces all round while Laurie played picquet. He dressed as a pirate on New Year's Eve and was dancing with a 'Nell Gwynne' from Arundel when 1947 dawned. On 3 January he again beheld the 'haunted' coast of Spain. With borrowed fieldglasses, he scanned the barren foothills at sunset. He could see Almuñécar and the pass through the snow-streaked sierras to Granada. 'It is 11 years since I last looked there. What a longing I have to return.'

He arrived back at Markham Square on 7 January 1947 to find 100 letters and £100 in cheques. Just as he was unpacking,

> comes lovely K, her corn hair stooked on top of her head, her
> blue eyes swimming. I showed her my treasures, gave her her
> presents, shoes [he had taken with him an outline of Kathy's size

five foot, which is still tucked into his India diary] and turquoise
jewellery, & we were happy.

The next day they went to watch 'dark, sweet' Anna Campbell,
daughter of Roy and Mary, now twenty and dancing with the Anglo-
Polish Ballet, rehearsing in a dim basement. 'Lovely to watch these
slender girls leaping in a brisk Russian dance. The director walks
up & down, puffing a cigarette & inventing steps with a twirl of
his hand.' That day, a telegram arrived from Annie: 'Ring Dorothy
re dad's cremation tomorrow.' Reg had become ill while cranking
up his old Morris, and died peacefully in bed on the day Laurie
arrived home.

Jack drove Laurie to Streatham crematorium. All the men of the
family attended: the three brothers, including Tony, the youngest,
'ageing, hollow-cheeked'; half-brothers Reggie, now 'old', and
Harold, 'nearly bald, pale in his factory mackintosh', and the sisters'
husbands Leslie, Harold and 'dear Maurice, overcome & weeping
copiously from his one eye'. A few days later everyone gathered for
the reading of Reg's will – a solemn assembly in Harold's front room,
relieved by a scream when the floor cracked and the sofa beneath
Dorothy and Harold sank into the floorboards. Reg had left five
pounds to 'Mrs R', the rest of his estate to be divided among his
eight children. Annie was glad: 'I feel that dad has acted in a very
good & fair way. As Marjorie says it is right, you are *all* his children.'
Jack remembered inheriting £180.

Annie was overcome with forgiveness and remorse and self-re-
proach, wishing her boys had seen him more often, wishing she and
Reg had been reconciled, and that he had spoken kindly to her 'for
I always loved him'. She was glad Laurie had mentioned his father
generously in his *Orion* story: 'I only wish *he* had lived to read it,
poor old boy.'

After Reg's death, Annie declined. Mothering had been the
purpose of her life, and at sixty-eight she had no one to mother. Her
boys discussed what was to be done with her, that day in Stroud.

They paid the outstanding rent on the cottage, but Annie wrote
from Dorothy's at Oxford, beseeching Laurie not to condemn her
to going back there. 'If I were only 37 as I was when we went up
there first, when I was strong and had you all round to help me, how
different it would be.' If she had known then how strong she could
be, she might have hung onto Reg. 'It is a great miracle,' she added,
'you have all done so splendidly.'

They decided that Annie must be looked after; the cottage was
cleared of its detritus, to her consternation, and she was moved into
Steanbridge House, which now took in the infirm. From there she
wrote happily that she was 'living the life of a lady in bed, warm &
comfortable & being waited on, not a dream but true...' Her room
had a view of the lake, and for the first time she had an electric fire and
electric lights, walnut furniture and pictures on the wall. She was effu-
sive in gratitude and full of guilt about not having to do the housework.
It was Annie who sent Laurie news of Yasmin: she had been given a
Shetland pony for her eighth birthday. 'The little girl is going to join
the Catholic church,' Annie told him. 'Lorna says she is now a Roman
Catholic and wants me to be, but I don't know.' She was impressed by
her two elder sons' activities: Jack directing a film with Ursula Jeans
(*The Woman in the Hall*), Laurie dining at the Garrick with Henry
Irving's grandson Laurence, going to the opera. At the first night
of *Carmen*, in a jewelled *galère* he saw Queen Mary, 'her hair full of
diamonds', Mrs Winston Churchill and Sir Alan (A. P.) Herbert.

It is true to say that the entire prose output of Laurie Lee's life had
already been commissioned by 1947. John Lehmann had long ago
proposed a book on his childhood. In March 1947 Cecil Day-Lewis
offered an instant advance from Chatto & Windus, where he was
now working, for the story of Laurie's Spanish wanderings. He
could have a clause in the contract to say he need not deliver for
three years, so that he could write for Lehmann first. If Laurie had
gone ahead as commissioned, he could have completed his lifetime's
opus by 1950. But he was quite exhausted, having completed a new
play in blank verse. This was *Peasants' Priest*, commissioned for

the Canterbury Festival that summer. He had used the story of
Wat Tyler's Peasants' Revolt over the poll tax of 1381, when the
preacher John Ball led his rebels in the march on London to storm
the Tower. Echoing Eliot's *Murder in the Cathedral*, Laurie's play
opened with a prologue by a chorus of one figure in a tragic yellow
mask, and another in a comic green mask:

YELLOW MASK:
It was yesterday, it was today,
a black winter and a red summer;
a blackened death, a crimson birth;
it was today, and yesterday…

Dramatically and tautly, it relates the story of the murder of the
Archbishop of Canterbury and others through characters named
Barfoot, Flint and Skelp. It ends with John Ball – 'lean as a stave,
rough as a wolf, and brilliant of eye' – being led away to his execution. As in *Magellan*, Laurie displays extraordinary imaginative gifts,
a flair for rhetoric, a remarkable grasp of the idiom of the medieval
mystery play, and an intuitive skill in incorporating political and
religious themes: hypocrisy, redemption, the plight of the common
man. As Ball is led away he says:

The end is not far off. What have we won?
Like foxes creeping from our holes, we've proved
the sun is up, that angels walk the grass,
and there's still heaven to be won on earth
when we've the trick of love to win it.
So with that lesson learnt, let's back to darkness,
to hide in holes till faith shall let us out.

Day-Lewis found Laurie in a slough of despond after finishing the
play. But he hoped Laurie was 'pulling out of the pit, & taking up the
pen again', because a dispute had arisen over who was publishing

him. Eric Gillett of Longmans had mentioned to Day-Lewis that he was publishing Laurie's Cyprus book, his Canterbury play and his Spanish travel book. "'Just a moment, Gillett,' I said coldly. "I am publishing the Spanish travel book.'"

'What am I to tell Mr Chatto & Mr Windus about this?' Day-Lewis asked Laurie. Leonard Woolf himself then wrote formally from the Hogarth Press, part of Chatto & Windus, which had published Laurie's poems, reminding him that they had first refusal on his next work. 'If you do not want to become a bone, with angry publishers snarling over you,' warned Day-Lewis, 'you had better retire swiftly to your Italian villa.' This was the house where Kathy had gone to stay, on Lake Garda at Torri del Benaco, owned by her mother's companion, Sarfatti. Later that year Helen Garman married seventy-year-old 'Sarfi', and so Kathy acquired a charming, steady and rock-like Italian stepfather who rather resembled Edward VII, 'with a lovely twinkle in his eye'. Kathy's stepbrother Walter Sarfatti was born in May 1948.

From this point on, Annie's letters became increasingly nostalgic – 'gone are those days' her refrain – wheedling for news and longing for visits.

> I haven't seen any one of my children since last Sunday when Jack & Nora came also Tony & Ruby [Tony's wife], Marjorie & Diana also came but they never stay long. Have you seen sweet Lorna & Yasmin lately? I wonder if I'll ever see her again and I wonder if I'll ever see Yasmin. Is anything wrong dear Laurie that I do not hear from you…

Laurie did go, with Virginia Cunard in her car, and they took Annie for a drive, but he was suddenly flung again into the Rosamond Lehmann–Cecil Day-Lewis maelstrom. Day-Lewis wrote an SOS from Devon urging Laurie to come down.

> The hideous, destined thing has happened. I've had to write &

tell Rosamond we must part; God knows if it's the right decision
… And it has just about finished me. So do come if you can
(wire to Colyton 126 telling me what train to meet). But I shall
perfectly understand, Laurie dear, if you don't feel up to it.
Love Cecil.

Laurie went. It transpired that Day-Lewis had finally tried to tell his
wife Mary that he was leaving her, but as they drove to the station
she wept so heart-rendingly that he told her to turn the car round.
So Rosamond was to be jettisoned instead, and Day-Lewis was in
despair. Laurie arrived with a violent toothache, an abscess, which
provided a diversion as the Day-Lewises had to drive him round to
find a dentist. This eased the situation, but the upshot of Laurie's
visit was that he and Day-Lewis decided to take a holiday abroad
together. Their fortnight in Denmark in July 1947 was the first
time Day-Lewis had been abroad, apart from a pre-war weekend in
Paris. They sailed to Esbjerg, stayed at the Hotel Cosmopolite in
Copenhagen, went to Elsinore and to the Tivoli gardens, and came
home in high spirits. When Day-Lewis's next collection of poems
came out (1948) it was dedicated to Laurie Lee.

Rosamond was grateful for Laurie's vivid letter – Cecil's letters,
she said, told her nothing. But she was still impatient for commitment. 'I am sick, *sick* of hearing him say "I can't face" – or "daren't
risk" – etc. etc. I am sick of hearing him talk of his "roots" – as if
roots were always healthy, as if they didn't often bind & strangle.'
She decided Cecil was frightened of Mary, and couldn't bear failure,
including in marriage. 'And now he feels he must simply go to earth
& write poetry about it.'

Laurie, at the ffrench Blake farm in Cornwall where he was sick-
ling and scything, appears not to have been exasperated by all this.
Rosamond's agitated histrionics contrast strikingly with Laurie's
happy and loving letter to Kathy that same month. Writing in the late
summer twilight in his attic room, he was longing to see Kathy again
and to dance with her 'before I get gout'. 'Grow, grow, my golden

girl, grow & be strong & cook a nice apple pie … & look at me with your blue eyes that say swim with me through the dark waters of night, then it will be all right.'

A month later Laurie accompanied Kathy, her mother and Sarfi on another holiday, at a farm near Aberystwyth. Kathy remembered rushing across a Welsh field shouting, 'I've passed my school certificate!' The extra significance of this milestone might be explained by a quotation from Kathy in Laurie's diary earlier that year: 'Wait till I've passed my school certificate.'

14

Kathy Come Home
1948–1949

'CHARM IS THE ultimate weapon, the supreme seduction, against which there are few defences. If you've got it, you need almost nothing else, neither money, looks, nor pedigree,' wrote Laurie, in his perceptive analysis of charm in 1978. He had always been a supreme practitioner of the art of effortless attraction. Men, women and children fell under his spell, and part of his appeal was his boyishness. The families Laurie collected – or the families who collected him, inviting him to their country houses and on their holidays – fell into a definable pattern. The father was clever and amusing (often Etonian), the mother lively and beautiful, the children agreeable. Laurie sang for his supper with his stories and music, his enthusiasm for food and fondness for competitive games and pranks; and he wrote rapturous thank you letters. 'I always feel frightfully well after a day or two among your mole-hilled mountains,' he wrote to the ffrench Blakes in January 1949.

He invariably brought some new toy, like the exploding matchbox he took to Beatrix Lehmann's one weekend, which gave people an electric shock whenever they struck a match. He infuriated John Lehmann by letting loose a clockwork creature under the feet of Elizabeth Bowen, the Sitwells and other grandee guests. Such foolery captivated children: the Devases' three, the Dugdales' three, the ffrench Blakes' two, and Rosamond's children Sally and Hugo Philipps. Sean Day-Lewis remembered that unlike most of his parents' guests, who engaged in impenetrable literary or political discussions,

'Laurie Lee alone was able to become a boy again, initiating games, making bows and arrows, giving out intimations of mischief.'[79] When Anthony Devas painted Laurie surrounded by children, Annie wrote: '*What* a very jolly picture. You look a very happy "uncle" – you remind me of my old grandfather, Uncle Tom, and even my mother. This is all to praise you, for they were all kind and loved children.'

Emma Devas remembered her parents saying, 'Laurie can't go on for ever being Peter Pan.' In the summer of 1948 they invited him on their holiday at Deal in Kent. Laurie brought Kathy ('a Wilson Steer child in a blue dress wading thigh-deep in the waves'), renting rooms in a house next door to the *Reynolds News* columnist Nat Gubbins. The artist Rodrigo Moynihan was there too, with his wife Elinor Bellingham Smith and son John. This was the start of an almost unbroken series of six blithe summers with the Devas family at the seaside.

Laurie had begun 1948 in hospital, having a sinus operation. He wrote to Val ffrench Blake from his bed at St Thomas's, saying that the BBC had commissioned a new poem for Epiphany, and one for Easter, puzzlingly, since he was plainly on the side of the pagan deities. He was home in time to hear Roy Fuller giving a constructively critical analysis of his second collection of poems, *The Bloom of Candles*, on the Third Programme.

This volume, published at the end of 1947, was the one dedicated to Annie. It included 'First Love', inspired by Kathy in Martigues ('her heart revealed by the wash of summer/sprung from her childhood's shallow stream'). John Lehmann had the book printed in New Zealand because of the British paper shortage, and shipped home with a meat cargo so it arrived 'ponging of mutton fat'. It was only twelve pages and twelve poems long. 'No more vivid use is being made of English today,' said G. W. Stonier in the *New Statesman*.

Roy Fuller had some misgivings. He said in his broadcast,

This poet's interest has never been the contemporary world. The distinction of his poetry has resided in an innocent lyricism, a sharp eye, a striking use of colourful and strong words. In almost every poem there is a word or image which gives that pleasurable shock without which lyric poetry can never rise above the third rate. And once or twice, in 'Bird' and 'First Love' for instance, Mr Lee shows signs that he can give his poetry the more complicated organisation which alone will enable him to bridge the deadly chasm which yawns for all poets round their thirtieth year.

But the danger, as he saw it, was that Laurie's colourful and strong words might not be adequately supported by the content of the poems. He quoted from 'Summer Rain':

Where in the valley the summer rain
Moves crazed and chill through the crooked trees
The briars bleed green, and the far fox-banks
Their sharp cries tangle in sobbing shades.

'This, I think, is sound and fury. For rain to be crazed, for briars to bleed and cry, for shades to sob, there must be a very dramatic and very plausible situation. But, in this poem, Mr Lee does not present it. There is rather too much whipping-up of language in the whole book ... One is asked to give a larger response than the poet's emotion deserves.'

Sometimes, Fuller said, Laurie descended to the mock-pastoral. He cited 'the cheeks of girls are as baked-bread to the mouth': there was 'something half-baked' about it. 'I would like Mr Lee to dare much more – dare to be complicated, dare to write of other things than nature, dare to use more verse forms, more rhyme – dare, perhaps, to write about the world as it impinges on us in 1948.'

It was fair comment, Laurie conceded, writing to Fuller the next day from Virginia Cunard's flat. 'In fact it made me laugh ... I especially liked your "half-baked" crack, though if you were here I'd ask you to come out into the back yard and repeat it.'

However, Laurie faced Fuller's challenge to him to write differently.

'You dare me to eschew nature,' Laurie declared. 'I shall dare to be more natural. You dare me to be more complicated but I shall dare to achieve simplicity. I have no desire to cater for a brief unhappy fashion of intellectual confusion...' Laurie had rehearsed this ringing apologia in his notebook first.

A jocular rivalry between the two poets had begun in 1944 when Cecil Day-Lewis reviewed Fuller's *A Lost Season* along with Laurie's *The Sun My Monument*, and preferred his friend Laurie's work. Then a fan letter to Laurie arrived, misaddressed, *chez* Fuller. 'My cup is full,' he wrote to Fuller. 'The normal pleasure which any fan mail brings is heady enough; how much more intoxicating is it when it has been read by one's dearest rival.'

Cecil Day-Lewis now urged Laurie to get on with writing about Spain, and invited him to share his office in William IV Street. But days would be frittered in conversation and games of chess, and nothing emerged from Laurie except more poems. Kathy, who was looking after her baby half-brother Walter, had by now fixed on Laurie as the man she would marry. But Laurie still saw himself as the uncommitted bachelor. 'Sometimes I used to dream that I was, in fact, married and I'd wake up with a violent start. I needed the company of men, but I required isolation even more.'[80] Moreover, in November 1948, Laurie swanned off to Paris again, for a fortnight, taking Jennifer Gault, eighteen-year-old daughter of a cousin of the Cunard sisters. Jennifer's mother had sent her daughter to see Laurie to be 'cheered up' after a break-up with a boyfriend, perhaps not realising that Laurie was, like Dickens, extremely partial to girls of seventeen or so. He had kissed Jennifer among the wheatsheaves at her parents' house. The Paris interlude, while her mother was away, was Jennifer's first visit there.

They stayed at the Hôtel d'Alsace, where Oscar Wilde died, and went to the Louvre and the Deux Magots. Jennifer knew there was no future in the affair. 'But Laurie was a wonderful influence in my life,' she said. 'He opened my eyes to all sorts of things. He had great charm, and was very secretive. Well, he had to be.' Her liaison with

Laurie continued sporadically for several years; when she became Mrs Hunter-Blair they remained friendly, Laurie becoming a godfather (again) to her son Tom.

Annie was now in a nursing home run by Nurse Critchley at Painswick. No woman was less suited to life on her own.

> It seems such a long time from morning to night, alone, no one pops their head round the door and says Hello, let alone come inside to have a chat, so I'm a dull old stick ... Marjorie is coming on Sunday, but there is the rest of the day and tomorrow and Saturday to get through.

The isolation of her declining years was relieved by the generosity of the Cunard sisters. Virginia and Pen had already invited her with Laurie to Bushton Manor in the late summer of 1947, and she went again for the next two Christmases. She had been dubious – 'should I be an intruder in the magic circle?' – but they loved having her. Virginia and Laurie collected her from Painswick and drove her to Bushton. They stopped at a garage which said 'No Naked Lights'; 'Mother,' said Laurie, 'you'd better put on some clothes,' which Annie thought hilarious. They gave her a room with a four-poster bed, and she was enveloped in the bosom of a family again, with 'music & singing & the games & the crib'. She was at Bushton for the baby Sam Dugdale's christening. Laurie sent a telegram: 'Three cheers for young Sam/Three cheers for his Mam/With love and good wishes/From Larry the Lamb.' 'Isn't he a ridiculous old thing?' wrote Annie to Kathy. 'But Laurie was always like that.'

In the new year of 1949 Laurie arranged for Annie to have a longed-for visit to London – staying with Virginia Cunard at Raphael Street, in the care of the sainted Bessie. It was another fulfilment of her dreams. She yearned to see pictures ('I don't mean films I mean paintings') so they took her to the Royal Academy and to the Rossetti Studios, where music was played and Cecil Day-Lewis sang and Rosamond brought flowers. 'I liked so much Cecil Day-Lewis's singing and his looks. I've never met people so good and kind before. Bessie was an angel to me. I have been overwhelmed with kindness.' But she swung between appreciation and maternal reproach. After a birthday telegram from Laurie in February she wrote: 'I was so glad you had not forgotten me, I know you have been very busy and active in the social world with your friends, Cecil Day-Lewis etc. so I will not bother you, but nonetheless I'd like to have a letter.' The dependable Bessie – 'I wish I had a daughter like her' – loyally kept her informed of Laurie's activities:

> Bessie says you have been enjoying yourself with parties and going to the theatre … Well dear boy good for you and may your happy times continue … No one has come this afternoon, now it is five o'clock I wish one of my sons would walk in and sit by me in my room and talk…

In fact, Laurie had been busy moving house. The Devas family had just moved along the King's Road into 12 Carlyle Square, and Laurie naturally went with them.

In May, Annie sent him £1 as he said he was off to Paris again. This time he was taking Kathy, en route for Italy. Her mother Helen had been having shattering migraines, the early signs of what proved to be a brain tumour, which eventually robbed her of most of her sight. Sarfi was taking Helen to a surgeon in Milan. At first, Kathy's cousin Esther went with them to help with baby Walter, but Esther missed her lover Mark Joffé and his young son Roland (the future film director), whose mother had run off. So Esther went home, and Helen summoned Kathy to Florence, in the care of Laurie.

In Florence they met up with Laurie's friends Daphne Hardy, his former MOI colleague, and her husband Henri Henrion. Kathy went off to see a friend in Siena, and Laurie in a rash moment of bravado followed her on foot through Chianti country. 'The heat was terrific & I was carrying about 30 kilos on my back,' he told Val ffrench Blake. 'But I did the 70-odd kilometres in two days and terrorised the local peasants on the way with my wild blond looks & Nordic tongue. They took me for a German; old women & children fled into the bushes at the sight.' He had tramped through wheatfields full of poppies, slept under olive trees and honeysuckle hedges to a backdrop bedlam of frogs, crickets, cuckoos, dogs and nightingales.

He had watched the sun slip into the Arno from San Miniato, slept in the monastery of Fiesole, picked syringa from the gardens of the Roman theatre among pillars and Etruscan tombs. He had been entertained at vast, echoing, rose-clustered villas. He was stuffed with impressions of classical landscapes and gorgeous glowing frescoes. The Henrions had driven him to San Gimignano, not yet tourist-infested, 'on a hill surrounded by wild oak woods, & creaking with medieval secrets, nothing can have changed here for 600 years. Thirteen great stone towers clashing their bells & fresh memories of Dante at every step.'

Kathy and her friend Charissina, daughter of Sarfi's fellow internee, the philosopher Leone Vivante, were sitting outside a café in the semi-circular Campo in Siena when suddenly Laurie appeared, bronzed and fit, his back scarred from the weight of his pack. He found Siena an exquisite city, just his size and colour. He had seen the 'violently exciting' sculpture of Donatello, the 'sombre, human, exquisite' paintings of Duccio. 'These, & the Botticellis in Florence are what I came to see, I feel.' He played his pipe in cafés, and went on to Assisi, Perugia, and back to Florence.

Kathy, in her seventeenth year, thought that after his romantic gesture in walking so many miles to see her, Laurie would ask her to marry him then; but he didn't. She was installed instead in the great oak-panelled apartment of her Uncle Gualtiero and Aunt Eloisa in Florence, and stayed for another eight months. She learnt to speak Italian, joined the university club and took up dressmaking.

Lorna still kept in touch. She was on a pilgrimage to Lourdes, as her mother had died and Yasmin had been ill with appendicitis. Her postcard of St Bernardette said: 'I am going to the waters for you tomorrow July 2nd' and was signed with a cross. The card was tucked into Laurie's India Diary, at the page where he noted that he was reading *The Song of Bernardette*, finding it 'curiously moving, inspired & eerie – passages of her vision brought tears to my eyes'.

This was Laurie's last summer of bachelordom. He enjoyed a wildly sociable season, not just at Bushton ('sun, flowers, games, sweet company and the quiet indulgence of the senses') but at less familiar country houses. Annie was baffled by names she knew only from newspapers. 'You say you were in the swimming pool of the Whitney Straights who are they? I seem to have heard about them in a former life are they Americans? you mention Roosevelt's little granddaughter in the same breath and Lady Winchilsea – who is she?' And on 21 July 1949 he went back to the seaside, to Tenby in Pembrokeshire, with the Devas family. They were all invited by Geraldine Lawrence, a spinster of independent means, the daughter of a rich pit-owning family. She was a woman of presence and character, a pillar of the community, a JP, a formidable figure to the children ('The Ogre of Lexden Terrace' in the Devases' 'Holiday Book'), but also an accomplished artist. She loved having artists to stay, and had commissioned Anthony Devas to paint her nieces. She lent them Little Rock House, next to her own, facing the sea: a tall white bow-fronted Regency house with green-shuttered windows, crammed with books and paintings. And she provided a full larder and a bottle of gin on arrival. 'She was the hostess everyone dreams of,' the artist John Ward said.

Steep cliff steps led down to the sandy beach with its rock-pools. Every day guests took paintboxes and picnics on to the beach and competed to find the biggest prawns. These were cooked in a pan of sea-water, and eaten for lunch with hot bread from the nearby baker. At the house the children were encouraged to make apple-pie beds, causing shrieks of rage. After supper in the evenings everyone gathered at Geraldine's for entertainment: one of the 'payments' she expected was a singsong round the piano, and costumed charades.

Geraldine was an inveterate traveller, forever off to Paris or to the racing at Chantilly. But most of all she loved southern Spain and its fiestas, bullfights and *romerías*. So when she met Laurie they fell upon one another with reminiscences of Andalucía. Over many years, every letter she wrote Laurie arrived in a vividly hand-painted envelope, with a watercolour of a bullfight, or of the brawny straw-hatted and tough-booted peasant women in the fields between Seville and Jerez, with 'tough forearms and leathery faces, like tortoises'.

The Devas family's Holiday Book is a priceless record of the Tenby summers. Everyone contributed; even the au pairs wrote poems ('Le chanson de Tenby') in charming franglais. Artistic endeavour was obligatory. Nicolette and Anthony's guests had to join in painting beach scenes and sea-shells and wild flowers, sketching one another and writing limericks, as well as snorkelling, harpooning and competing for the biggest catches of fish. Emma Devas, now Lady Monson, said that underlying the fun and games was a strictly professional anti-dilettante attitude. 'My father would insist on punctuality and proper dress. None of his children was allowed to behave like my mother's family, the wild Macnamaras.'

After this sybaritic summer even Laurie had to admit defeat when invited to Cornwall again by the ffrench Blakes in August.

> There's nothing I should like better than a trip to the Tokenbury tin mines but alas … I can't possibly go off on the loose again for some time. I have been burning the summer at both ends; a month in Italy, a month in Pembrokeshire and so little work done I blush to think of it.

In fact he was collapsing with pneumonia, and spent two months convalescing at Dorothy's in Oxford, reading novels in which (as he told Pen Dugdale) 'practically all the characters contract pneumonia & most of them die of it'. His doctor was

> the one who saw John Masefield through a bout of pneumonia back in the spring when we were all so busy choosing a new Poet Laureate. He is dying for me to get better as he wants me to

teach him how to blow fire from his mouth, and he approaching 60, too.

Annie wrote recommending George du Maurier's novel *Trilby*. Cecil Day-Lewis sent commiserations from 'Wystan, Stephen, Edwin Muir, everyone in Venice' where they were attending a PEN conference, with 'interminable, egotistic, bawling, exhibitionistic, abstract, sententious speeches'.

Laurie told Pen Dugdale in October:

> This started as a weekend and nearly finished as a dead end. It was high, sweltering summer when I was driven to bed & now it's autumn ... I wanted to write when I was up and about again, but I am still only half up & half about. And yet the fascinating thing is that these weeks of bed, of contemplation laced with fever & lightheadedness seem to have changed the whole course of my life. I wonder if it is really so.

(It was so. He had begun to think of marrying.)

By November Annie, now scarcely able to get out of bed with rheumatism, heard from Bessie that Laurie was better and 'back at your London Haunts', and had enjoyed Guy Fawkes night with children. Did he recall being frightened by a banger Uncle Sid brought back from abroad? His Uncle Fred, her youngest brother, had just retired in Perth, she told him, with an encomium from his boss: 'All who knew Mr Light spoke of him as a gentleman: he was one of nature's aristocrats.' That's where Laurie got his manners, Annie added.

Annie's letters in these months, her last year of life, read sadly, but they reflect her motherly nostalgia, her loving nature. Pen had been to visit her ('so kind of her to come & see the old person') and had posted off Laurie's Christmas gloves for her: 'better not have red gloves,' Annie told him, 'as I am afraid Chelsea is a hotbed of Communism.' She longed to see Jack's 'dear old smile', but he was away in Germany, making *The Wooden Horse* with Anthony Steel.

Did Laurie remember the days of the old Sunday school treats? She recalled the entry in the parish magazine:

> 'Miss Eileen Brown at the piano and young Laurie Lee played selections on his violin'. I always thought of Young Lochinvar come out of the West... But you are the son who has led a life of contrasts – such contrasts – A book of your life would be very varied, interesting & lovely, because many people love you & many more would if they could know you & see you & hear you talk and hear you play.

In December that year, 1949, she was again invited to Bushton for Christmas.

> Isn't it sweet and kind of them ... I can't help crying a bit when people are like that, for I am terribly lonely here & so often cold. Wish I was in that lovely four-poster at Bushton. In *Picture Post* there are lovely pictures of children Christmas shopping. Oh to put the years back & to get to town with some money & to take you three little boys up to Barkers or some other nice shop & do some lovely shopping, but what useless wishing.

If Laurie was concerned about his mother, he was also thinking seriously about his own future. He had done precious little productive writing that year. In July, HM Inspector of Taxes had written asking him what income he had apart from Casual Literary Earnings, which had been £120 in the last year. In his book *Two Women*, published in 1983, Laurie related that during that autumn of 1949, 'intimations of a sterile death moved upon me. I also missed the presence of that acquiescent and radiant girl who seemed to care for no other company but mine.' He decided to telegraph to Kathy's mother and ask her to come home. She told him to send the money for Kathy's fare, which he did.

Early in 1950, an equally momentous decision was taken by his friend Cecil Day-Lewis. He finally left his wife Mary – not for Rosamond Lehmann, but for the young actress Jill Balcon. As Rosamond put it, bitterly, in a letter to Laurie, 'he transferred his overnight zip bag from my bedroom to Miss Balcon's'. (The couple had fallen in love after an exchange of fan letters and a dinner with Epstein, who was sculpting Jill's head.) Laurie said, in much later retrospect, he was not entirely surprised. 'Rosamond's pressure on Cecil to marry her had been emotionally wearing. I did not see how he could get out of that dilemma. He was tugged between these two loves. He couldn't decide who to desert. The only solution was to take a third and not choose either of them: to betray both.'[81]

Rosamond was in utter despair. 'We shared ten years of what I thought the deepest and most permanent commitment. He broke our mutual vows, and laid waste my life, and also his wife's.' And at just the time when Rosamond needed him most, Laurie was himself distracted by mid-life decisiveness. At thirty-five he was about to shake off the Peter Pan image: take a proper job, move into a flat of his own – and get married to Kathy.

15

The Festival Jester
1950–1954

'I FEEL LIKE a murderer; but for Jill I could do murder,' wrote Cecil Day-Lewis to Laurie. He was 'absolutely committed to' Jill, and in love with her, but Rosamond was suicidal, and he himself was 'flying through a very low cloud'. He had promised Rosamond, who thought he was off his head, that he would not see Jill for three months. Would Laurie take her to lunch? 'It would be your Good Deed for the Day ... You always seem to be helping me out of crises, & I hardly ever ditto you.'

He added: 'I do hope your reunion & plans go well.'

The reunion was with Kathy, at Victoria Station. Laurie had last seen her in Siena, 'a shapely, tight-limbed, flat-bellied young beauty'. After eight months of spaghetti and idleness she seemed 'more radiant than ever, but twice the size'.[82] Laurie led her straight to the weighing machine, saying, 'If you're over twelve stone, I won't marry you.' She was eleven stone twelve pounds. Laurie was still living in his attic at Carlyle Square, but they took a flat together at 37 Collingham Place SW5, up five flights in a West Indian house overlooking the railway. (Laurie claimed he carried Kathy over the threshold but collapsed after one flight and she carried him up the rest: 'She's a very strong girl.') Though 'beset by fevers' Laurie had found a salaried job, the last he ever had.

He became chief caption-writer for the Festival of Britain, the jamboree to mark the end of post-war austerity set up on twenty-seven acres of bombsites on the South Bank. With the Skylon, the

Dome of Discovery, the Guinness Clock, the *Reclining Figure* by Henry Moore and Epstein's *Youth Advancing*, it would epitomise new artistic ideas, modern standards of design. The fastidious Roy Fuller thought the whole concept 'self-consciously bright and bragging and English'.[83] Looking back twenty-five years later, the architect Sir Misha Black said the Festival's only influence on popular taste was to release 'a flood of the worst kind of modern architecture the country had ever seen'.[84] But for Laurie it seemed 'a kind of Xanadu'. And his contribution to the Festival, by common consent, was 'the quirkiest and most timeless'.

On Tuesday 17 May 1950, without even noting it in his diary, Laurie married Kathy at Kensington Register Office. Cecil Day-Lewis and Jill Balcon were the only witnesses. Jill remembered that Laurie was sucking a peppermint and Kathy, clutching a tiny spray of lily-of-the-valley, looked like a Renoir: 'She had a down-to-earth kindness, an unvarnished quality, with skin like a peach.' She also looked 'so young we thought we'd be accessories to a felony' (she was eighteen, and had a special licence signed by Sarfi; Laurie was twice her age, a month away from thirty-six). Kathy's eyes had a shine, Laurie later said, that he only ever saw again when she won a steam-iron on stage at the Walham Green Empire.[85] After the wedding the quartet fell into the Prince of Wales pub among some dustmen and a newspaper-seller. A barnacled bottle of champagne was produced; the dustmen raised their glasses and said: 'Here's to a long life with plenty of trimmings.' On leaving, Day-Lewis and Jill looked into the estate agents Marsh & Parsons, spotted 73a Bedford Gardens for rent, and took it as their first joint home.

They lunched at Elytis in Soho, then Laurie went back to work at the Festival office, at 2 Savoy Court. Kathy went to the fishmonger and asked for a nice piece of sole for supper 'because I've just got married'. Laurie sent a telegram to his sister Marjorie: 'Have married Kathy. Let the family know.' He told Jack's wife Nora, 'I've decided to make myself responsible for Kathy,' which struck her as a curious way of announcing one's marriage.

He wrote to Val ffrench Blake, 'Yes, I went & got married. It was sudden, like falling down a man-hole, but my seat on the coals is quite comfortable. No one knew about it save Day-Lewis who was raised from his bed to be witness. But I was charmed by your letter, it made me laugh both ha and he.'

Col. ffrench Blake had sent him a spoof army charge sheet, which Laurie filled in:

> Name: Lee. Occupation: Poet and/or Peasant.
>
> Brief Description of Residence: Flat in Negro Quarter of Earls Court ...
>
> Lee pleads Guilty to all items indicated on charge sheet.
>
> Future movements: Earls Court to Festival of Britain, Festival of Britain to Earls Court – till further notice.
>
> Tokens of esteem etc: Gratefully accepted.

(The ffrench Blakes sent a charming table.)

There was general astonishment that Laurie should marry at all, since he had for so long enjoyed the comfortable patronage and favours of 'grand ladies who gave him lodgings'. Most of his friends had never even met Kathy; but once they did, they were captivated. She was so young and sparklingly beautiful, and completely under his spell. It was her idea to marry. Laurie had told her: 'I warn you, it's going to be very difficult. I may not be able to be the person you want me to be. I may do things that hurt you. I may not give you enough love.' But she felt 'a sense of dedication'. After all, she did come from a very strange family. The Garman girls were sexually magnetic and muse-like in their devotion to artistic men.

> I told him, 'I want to look after you.' I said I had enough love for both of us. I knew it was a challenge, I knew about the true love he'd had before. But I was protected by a kind of confid-ence, almost arrogance. I felt sure of my ground, quite powerful

and invulnerable. Partly because I was an outsider. I didn't feel
threatened by the other women, at all.

To show how much she trusted Laurie she would allow him to put
an apple on her head and aim darts at it through a blowpipe.

On the day they married, Kathy said, Laurie wrote a letter to the
Inland Revenue 'saying he couldn't afford to buy his wife a broom'.
But within days he was sending a donation of £2 10s to Bernard
Miles towards his Mermaid Theatre – 'at least equal to £222 10s
from a rich Philistine!' said Miles, requesting names of others who
might subscribe: 'e.g. address of Jacquetta Hawkes?' Mrs Hawkes,
the archaeologist, later Mrs J. B. Priestley, was enthusiastically
checking Laurie's Festival captions, having been struck by Laurie's
poetry and also by his name: 'as improbably euphonious as mine is
angular'. (Laurie always said he was lucky in his memorable, alliter-
ative name, which was widely assumed to be invented.)

A fortnight after their wedding Laurie took Kathy to Bushton.
Antonia Dugdale, who had proposed to Laurie at the age of six,
and had been accepted, was expecting to hate 'the woman who had
stolen my man'. 'But five minutes later I was in love with her too.
She had such beautiful eyes, a lovely complexion and corn-coloured
hair.' During that weekend, Laurie told Kathy about his epilepsy. 'I
wasn't scared,' she said. 'I was very strong; I was always able to hold
him tight when it happened.'

Laurie was at his most fulsome writing to Pen Dugdale afterwards, one of many such bread-and-butter letters. He claimed to be

> still drowsy with the honeyed richness of my weekend, still
> fatted with cream and flushed with strawberry ices, still tinkling
> with the music of your piping laugh & sweet-voiced flute …
> Bushton endures in the flowers we carried away, in the lilac's
> purple sunlight & the lilies' cream-green shade …
>
> Dear friend, we did enjoy ourselves. You could tell that
> by the faint frenzy in my eye … But then Bushton is as full of

pleasures as an egg is of meat … thank you for all your bounty;
for your eternal readiness to sport & play, for that lovely room
& luscious bed, for your gorgeous meals, your ever-delightful
company & your complete domination of the weather.

'*To think I don't even know her*!' cried Rosamond Lehmann of his
bride, writing from a nursing home where she was trying to recover
from 'the most cruelly dealt, the most utterly unexpected blow of my
life'. She reminded Laurie that he had been 'deeply knit' into what
Day-Lewis had destroyed. She could not bear the thought of Laurie
continuing to see her former lover. Laurie gently told her he could
not be a judge of Cecil's behaviour.

Rosamond replied that although it would be a hurdle for her to
see Laurie, she wanted her children Hugo and Sally not to lose him:
'They are so devoted to you, & have gone on asking me, poor things,
how you felt about it.' Rosamond's affections were restored when
Laurie took out her daughter, 'my heavenly Sal', who 'came home
starry-eyed from her blissful day with you. Oh, I am so *glad* she has
got you back.'

Annie, meanwhile, was fading. In her last letters she still hankered
after her old cottage, and her mislaid belongings, including Laurie's
published stories: 'Your stories are *you* and I loved them for that.
No one ever finds them for me. So I can't help feeling sad. Yes,' she
added, 'I saw that Aly Khan & Rita Hayworth's baby was called
Yasmin. I had a card from Lorna: she does not forget me ever. Have
you seen her lately?'

Annie died, aged seventy-one, on 30 August 1950, and was buried
in Slad at the top of the churchyard, near her four-year-old daughter.
Laurie placed a poem inside her coffin, and a photograph of Yasmin.
Her gravestone 'In memory of Annie Emily Lee (née Light)' reads:
'She loved the world and all things in it.' Laurie's diary for this time
is blank. But about thirteen years later – in his Mexico notebook – he
recorded one of his long, disturbing 'dreams of truth & the dead'.

Mother. Dorothy telling me she is dying. Go on, I say. Aching with emotion. Family gathers. I won't go with them – walk off, remembering her alive.

Overhearing them say Good riddance – he'd spoil the party. Party, I cry.

I hear them telling truths of me. 'He's no longer of the family.' It's true.

A spirit of gaiety prevailed at the Festival of Britain offices; and Laurie, in tweeds and pipe, was its resident jester, sometimes to be found twanging a guitar and singing 'a rumty-tumty Gloucestershire calypso ... Beer was flowing, of course...'[86] He was surrounded by old friends: Hugh Casson, Alan Ross, Lionel Birch, John Piper, Stephen Potter, Henri Henrion and Daphne Hardy. Laurie's small team furnished 'tens of thousands of descriptive words ... brilliantly written and edited', of which only a fraction were ever read. Still, it was an opportunity for florid and orotund phrasemaking.

Facing the main entrance, on stone, were these words:

Land is the blanket of Man's birth;
His launching-ground to the stars.

A geological history of Britain for the Land and People pavilion was narrated in Laurie's richest prose, on which the unmistakable influence is of Jacquetta Hawkes's best-selling 1951 book, *A Land*. 'Britain's crust, like a cloth, has been dipped in the ocean, soaked, rinsed, and hung up in folds to dry. At one time it was part of Europe ... And from the rising seas, when the ice-caps melted, Britain emerged an island.' Limestone was formed from 'skeletons crusting the sea floor'. Birmingham was once 'an inferno of blown sand'. 'The Lincoln marshes crawled with crocodiles ... the Kentish Weald rose and fell like a breathing island.'

Laurie's text eulogised British craftsmen, British freedom, British justice, parliamentary democracy. The English Tongue, it proclaimed, 'writes sonnets, talks shop, sings music-hall, and speaks volumes. Once the dialect of a handful of islanders, it is now the mother-tongue of 250 millions.' 'The English Bible ... put the Divine Word into common speech and inspired the native genius for language.' In the Lion & Unicorn pavilion, which celebrated the Briton's characteristics of strength and individuality, choice texts were emblazoned: 'In the Beginning was the Word, and the Word was with God, and the Word was God.' 'We are such stuff As dreams are made on, and our little life Is rounded with a sleep.' 'The English man of letters is a giant gorged with words. With the English Dictionary in one hand, he has written three million books with the other.'

And so on, in what Desmond Fitzgerald (in the *World Review*) designated 'Festival English': a didactic, Arnoldian style of prose, reminiscent of Georgian poetry and William Morris wallpaper, eulogising a 'forever England' of greenwoods and larks arising, mixed with 'documentary or *Picture Post* English, suitable for conveying information that might be a bit "above" the reader' – in short, exactly the kind of stuff 'turned out by poets, often good ones, who are driven by circumstance to work in the BBC and in government propaganda departments'.[87]

It was Nigel Dugdale who suggested that a corner of the Lion & Unicorn pavilion should reflect the eccentric side of the British character. Laurie's 'fantastic cast of mind'[88] made him the ideal 'Curator of Eccentrics'. He launched an appeal in the *Times* in November 1950 for 'curious, unusual or ingenious objects of eccentric conception'. The press loved the idea of eccentrics rallying to the call of 'Mr Laurie Lee, the poet', for something rich and strange. His office became a museum of crackpot oddities. 'He sauntered into my office one day,' said a colleague, 'with a violin and mandolin made from used matchsticks, and gave a spirited performance of a Telemann concerto.'[89] Someone offered a brilliantly engineered machine, 20 feet square, with the sole object of blowing out matches. There was a staircase with weighted steps to give the feeling of going upstairs when going down; a deflatable rubber bus for low bridges; a brick mousetrap maze scattered with pepper so the mouse bashed its brains out with sneezing: 'But you cannot have six months of mouse massacre,' said Laurie, 'just for the fun of the thing.'

Early in 1951 these objects were selected for the showcase:

The Cuthill Smoke-Grinding Machine
A Roundabout of Eggshells
Davoren's Self-Wiping Motor-Cyclist's Goggles
A Nose-Guard for Drinking Tea
A Tea-Set of Fishbones
A Mandolin Made of 10,000 Matchsticks
The Archives of the British Snail-Watching Society [90]

A life-size Emmet-built replica of Lewis Carroll's White Knight presided, standing alongside a screen showing cartoons by Tenniel, Lear, Pont. An extra device – the 'Morale Raiser' invented by Lt Col. Nigel Dugdale – was strapped to the back of the White Knight, who was looking gloomy. An electrically driven, velvet-gloved hand patted him on the back and said, 'You're a wonderful fellow ... you're so attractive', etc. The King, it was reported, visiting the Exhibition in the pouring rain when it opened in May 1951, seemed 'nonplussed' by Eccentrics' Corner.

In 1951 Kathy and Laurie moved from their Earls Court flat over the railway to 49 Elm Park Gardens, a tall brick Victorian house run by Chelsea Housing Improvement Society, which provided homes for impoverished artists. They should take paintbrushes and canvas along to secure their tenancy, advised Emma Smith's local councillor husband, Richard Stewart-Jones. The Chelsea/Fulham border was still essentially a working-class area, and the square had an almost Mediterranean evening life – doorsteps spilling with families, children running in and out of the gardens. No. 49, a former ambassadorial residence, was divided into five flats. Other

residents included Jane Lloyd, a painter, with her husband the artist
Jeff Hoare, and the sculptor Elisabeth Frink, brigadier's daughter,
with her fine strong bony profile and helmet of hair. Her flat was
a shambles, 'the muddled aftermath of endless parties'.[91] But her
studio was 'a white, quiet place, littered for action', with 'a scribble
of notes and images, and the various bits of homely junk, plaster,
wire, old newspapers and firewood, which she uses to build up her
figures', as Laurie said on television nine years later. The Lees first
occupied the ground level, and later moved up to the top two floors,
with their high ceilings, tall windows and fine plasterwork.

In the spring of 1951 Rosamond Lehmann wrote from
Goldeneye, Ian Fleming's house in Jamaica, where she was enjoying
Noël Coward's 'enchanting astringent affectionate society'. By May,
Rosamond and Laurie were reunited, with cuckoos and nightingales
in attendance, 'a moment of such pure happiness', said Rosamond,
'that it has given me back my life'. At her son Hugo's wedding that
autumn, Rosamond finally met Kathy ('so sweet') and Laurie played
the piano. That evening Laurie, Rosamond, her daughter Sally and
Willie Mostyn-Owen went to see *Caesar and Cleopatra*. Kathy was
sure to understand, Rosamond said: and of course she did. She
knew she had to share her husband with a wide circle, and must
slot into his busy social life, or stay at home while he was out with
old friends.

Anyway Kathy soon had a job which occupied her evenings.
Nigel Dugdale owned a French restaurant named Père Auguste in
Gerrard Street, for which he wrote droll ads in the personal columns
of *The Times*. Pen had decorated it in dark red striped wallpaper
with gold cherub wall-lights and a vaulted ceiling, and Nigel rightly
envisaged that the nineteen-year-old blonde Kathy would make an
alluring barmaid in black stockings and pinafore. She earned £3 10s
a week plus tips. It was an amusing place where Dugdale would hold
court, inventing puddings like Shusha Baskusha, a concoction of
meringues and exotic fruits, borne in aloft with four lighted spark-
lers stuck into the meringue peaks.

During the Festival summer of 1951, Dugdale went on television to publicise Eccentrics' Corner as 'Major Oswald Murgatroyd, M. O. W. (Master of Wasp Hunting)', the character he had invented in *Time & Tide*. Laurie took all his friends' children – Dugdales, Devases, ffrench Blakes, Philippses – to the Skylon and the Big Dipper, which he loved. A set of plates, printed with Laurie's five lyric couplets on the seasons of the year, were on display:

'Four seasons square the rounded year,
And all in Nature's glass appear.'
'With leaf-green eyes, and lips half-curled,
Spring leads a white lamb through the world.'
'Butter the hedgerow with cream-fat roses:
Gorged with his garlands, the Summer dozes.'
'Ancestral Autumn, with hands of brass,
Shakes the last apple on the grass.'
'The Wintry crow creaks home to hide
And frost locks up the countryside.'

One afternoon in April Celia Kirwan (later Goodman) was looking into a delicatessen window in the King's Road when Laurie approached her: he had mistaken her for her twin sister Mamaine, who was married to Arthur Koestler, and whom Laurie had accompanied home the night before from a dinner at the Henrions'. Celia and Mamaine, the Paget twins, had been unusually cultured débutantes. Celia was a pianist, and she and Laurie soon discovered that they were on the same musical wavelength. They began meeting often to play music at the house of Celia's friend Ralph Jarvis, a cultivated and musical banker. So Doddington, the Jarvises' haunted Elizabethan manor house in Lincolnshire, became yet another of Laurie's weekend refuges. And throughout his life his affection for Celia was unfaltering.

For that summer's official 'Festival Holiday', Laurie and Kathy went back to Geraldine Lawrence's house at Tenby with the Devases and other artists, John Ward and Norman Hepple and their wives. The 200-mile journey from Chelsea to South Wales took two days in the Devases' car, with an overnight stay at the Imperial Hotel, Hereford, and long enough stops *en route* to paint watercolours. Laurie took charge of logging the weather, the mileage, and prawning records, noting each day's tally in his italic hand. Every excursion and mishap became an event in the Holiday Book: 'Michael's cow-pat'; 'the crash'; 'Esmond's bad foot'; 'Tragedy' (Anthony accidentally shot dead a seagull with his airgun). John Ward and his wife were drawn swooning at the beauty of Little Rock House; Ward also drew Geraldine, breakfasting in her swan-shaped bed, among her Dufys. Laurie drew everyone going in to bathe, and wrote a poem in heroic couplets called 'Pembroke Evening', ending –

> For years to come we shall recall this scene
> When tongues nostalgic speak of Geraldine.

Laurie was in his element at Tenby. 'He adored good company; it stimulated him,' John Ward said. 'He had none of that grim Cezanne lack of communication fashionable when I was a student.' On the last day of the holiday Laurie got up at 6 a.m., at low tide, and wrote 'I LOVE GERALDINE' across the sand, which she would see when she got up at 7 a.m. to feed her pet seagull, Lucifer. She was ecstatic.

In August Laurie and Kathy went off in the Henrions' car to Martigues, desperately seeking some sun. 'For six days we sat & watched the Mistral blowing up the sea while I drank absinthe & grog & shivered,' he told Val ffrench Blake, 'and then we got involved with a forest fire which burnt out 150 acres of hill scrub & pine trees & warmed me up for the first time this year.' They joined the Jarvises for a further two weeks in France, but were back in time to hear Laurie's talk on the Home Service, 'An Obstinate Exile' (produced by Gilbert Phelps, an old university friend of Betty Smart's husband), about his reluctance to live in London. London might be the greatest show on earth, Laurie said, but it wouldn't impress the villagers of

Slad. Its flowers had no scent, its mushrooms no taste. 'Fancy having to buy flowers anyway. I can never get used to it.' But why, Emma Smith wrote to him, didn't he write that book about his childhood he'd started years ago? (He had read aloud to her the first chapter, the *Orion* article, in 1947.) 'It's a crime not to, and if you don't do it soon you never will.'

But Laurie's procrastinating years had begun. He had already had almost all the experiences he was ever to use as a writer, but had yet to sit down and write them. There was a 'prolonged uncertainty' about his health, said Rosamond. By September he was 'deep in the hands of the medicos'. A series of chest X-ray appointments at hospitals would delay their arrival at Tokenbury in Cornwall until mid-October for 'sun-lit days and full-moon nights punctuated by regular doses of cream & honey'.

Laurie was obliged to start planning a book in earnest when John Lehmann told him the Society of Authors' Travelling Scholarships Committee had unanimously nominated him to be awarded £200, 'and the only condition is that you spend it abroad ... Just immediate banishment, & nothing more severe.' Lehmann hoped that the journey would produce 'a flood of poems – and prose galore'. Laurie decided to take Kathy to Andalucía, and to write the book which became *A Rose for Winter*.

Before leaving, he made a schools broadcast on Madrid. 'Madrid first came into being when King Philip II stubbed his finger into a map and said: "I want a new capital, and I want it there – right in the middle of Spain" ... And that is exactly what he got.' He vividly described from memory a day in Madrid's life: the boot-blacks shining shoes as bright as chestnut conkers; the market with live chickens, and great flat loaves of bread like cushions; the cafés, the donkeys, the boys singing for pennies; the din everywhere; the deserted siesta hour, the bullfights, the flamenco dancers, the evening *paseo*.

After a glamorous appearance at the Chelsea Arts Club Hallowe'en Ball, Laurie and Kathy sailed from Tilbury for Gibraltar.

They stayed in Algeciras, in Seville, in Écija with its towers, in Córdoba, and spent three snowy weeks in Granada (including a week under the blankets when Laurie had a bad fever, and lay close to death until he heard voices gathered round his bedside saying what a beautiful widow Kathy would make). In Granada, too, Laurie heard that he had been appointed MBE for services to the Festival of Britain. He had cards printed which came out as 'Laurie Lee Mbe' – 'that well-known East African grocer'.

Laurie's Spain had not yet changed much since the 1930s, but 'how hard the baked ground of the olive groves looked', he noted. 'Ground to which my body used to cling in a very drunken rapture of sleep.' He enjoyed being Svengali, introducing Kathy to everything. Her goldenhaired, olive-skinned glow was complimented every-where, and the chambermaids taught her how to respond with dignity. 'When men call after you, you can giggle if you are unmar-ried, but if married, never.'

In January they reached sunny Almuñécar, with fruit blossom in the fields, and oranges & bananas ripening. They stayed at the Hotel Mediterráneo, where Laurie was still remembered, 'though the golden boys of my youth are now pouch-eyed & fat,' he told Val ffrench Blake, 'with strings of children & invisible wives.'

Wherever Laurie went, he made friends. He could not enter a bar without talking to people, hearing their life stories, sitting up till 2 a.m. He practised his guitar every day, learning new songs from the carolling chambermaids. Kathy quickly learnt to speak better Spanish than Laurie and was a great success with her dancing. As a Provençal child she had watched Spanish dancers and gypsies; she danced flamenco, Sevillanas, Malagueñas and Sabateados to the manner born. In Córdoba they were told: 'But you're Lorenzo and Catalina! There's a song about you.' This song – '*El sol se llama Lorenzo* y *la luna Catalina. Cuando se acuesta Lorenzo, La luna se levanta Catalina*' (The sun is called Lorenzo and the moon Catalina. When Lorenzo goes to bed, the moon Catalina rises) – became Kathy and Laurie's party piece.

Suddenly they were summoned by telegram to North Africa, where brother Jack was making a film melodrama called *South of Algiers* ('a piece of old hokum', Jack later called it). He needed Laurie's help with the script. As Laurie told Pen Dugdale in a letter:

> We were lying watching the sun & moon drift over the classical blue sea, watching the fishermen each dawn raking the still waters for their tiny catches of scarlet fish, listening at night to the guitars and the girls singing, and not expecting to stir until it was time to take the boat from Gibraltar, when suddenly all the cacophony of the high-pressure film world broke upon us and in less than no time ... we were in Africa among the ghostly Moors.

It was a long train journey through unexpectedly lush green fields, among camels and white-robed Arab women, to the sophisticated city of Algiers, 'a town of which I have always dreamed'. The 'vain and florid actors, beetroot-coloured with makeup', amused him vastly. 'Oh they are continual entertainment, sitting all day in the lounge of the hotel, sticking each other with sly verbal pins, quarrelling with poor Jack, wheedling me to write them extra scenes.'

Desert life was new to Laurie, the landscape of naked rock and sandstorms, the snow-tipped blue mountains, and the wild unseen voice of the muezzin calling the faithful to prayer at dawn and at noon. Bou-Saada (the city of happiness) was full of gaunt bearded men with faces like mountain goats, 'and the women are so heavily veiled that they look like bundles of washing with just one dark eye peeping out'. When King George VI died in February they observed the two minutes' silence out in the desert.

> We had eight Arab soldiers dressed as bandits for the film. At 2 o'clock they formed in a line and fired their rifles into the air and stood rigidly to attention. We were among great bare hills, and as we all stood silent the echo of the guns went roaring and rolling all round the mountains.

They arrived back at Tilbury in March. Rosamond Lehmann welcomed them with 'inexpressible joy' from her new flat in Eaton Square: her daughter Sally had just won a scholarship to Oxford. Kathy set about making a flamenco dress, with sixty yards of white flouncing and as many yards of Woolworth's lace. She was performing at the Albert Hall ('Olé!' cried Laurie) where she danced a magnificent solo. Laurie was suffused with pride: 'I am always fascinated by technique and efficiency – even in games like billiards,' he had told Val ffrench Blake once, after Val had taken him to see the passing-out parades at Sandhurst. When Kathy mastered flamenco, he boasted of her faultless precision.

Laurie's mysterious illness persisted, and in July, when they went again to Tenby with the Devases, Laurie was told he must have a lung removed (hence his later references to himself as 'Wun Lung Lee, the famous Chinese poet'.) Before his operation they went to Doddington and to Bushton, and on 16 September 1952, they were at the Farnborough air display, where they witnessed the terrible disaster of that year when a prototype de Havilland DH 110 jet fighter plummeted into the spectators, killing twenty-six. The Lees and the Devases were near enough to feel debris falling all around them, and Rodrigo Moynihan, who was also there, wrote to his son praising Laurie's bravery as he sheltered six-year-old Prosper.

Laurie described the disaster to Val ffrench Blake.

> We were in the line of flight and the cockpit fell in front of us while the engines passed over our heads and hit the crowd behind us. From the moment he [John Derry] began his dive 8 miles up till the shock waves exploded and the aircraft fell to pieces a kind of smooth pattern of almost classical tragedy seemed to emerge; the triumph of breaking through the barrier; the clap of thunder which followed the aircraft, and cheers, and death. Perhaps the greatest moment was when [Neville] Duke took off while they were still carrying away the bodies and climbed to eight miles & did the whole thing again.

After his operation, Laurie went to recuperate in Cornwall. Typically, he became even more competitive with only one lung, and even listed 'holding his breath under water' as a hobby.

Over Christmas he wrote his first account of crossing the Pyrenees into the Spanish Civil War as 'A True Tale of a Spanish Adventure' for another BBC schools programme.

> Some years ago, when I was a young man ... a cruel Civil War broke out among the peoples of Spain. All war is terrible, but a civil war – which is a sort of murderous family struggle on a large scale – is probably the worst kind of all ... When I heard the news of this war it made me very sad, because I had a lot of friends out there, and more than anything else in the world I wanted to try to help them.
>
> All the sea-coasts were guarded by ships, and the frontiers by soldiers ... and the northern part of Spain is joined on to France by a great wall of snow-covered mountains called the Pyrenees, which are just like battlements, only thousands of feet high...

Later, a detailed 1,500-word report arrived, from a BBC education officer who had heard the talk in a school class. He described the children's intense concentration, their laughter and enthusiasm for 'one of the most exciting stories they had ever heard'. A useful secondary career, recycling experiences as talks, had begun. The following September Laurie did another schools broadcast, on 'Village Life in Cyprus'.

Laurie's attention to schoolchildren's inquisitiveness is clear from a long, handwritten letter that spring to an O-level student, Sue Wheeler, who requested an explanation of his poem, 'Bird', even though he felt that 'to coldly & logically explain a poem is to begin to destroy it'.

> This poem is a poet's vision, written in the grip of an intense mood ... to describe how the bird carries the poet to his own

private world ... The bird is killed in the last stanza because
one must destroy to create, because life needs must nourish
itself upon death, because without death there can be no new
growth of life. This to me is a haunting truth which is both
tragic & beautiful.

That April of 1953, Laurie took Rosamond Lehmann's daughter
Sally to Paris for a week. Rosamond seems to have trusted him
(despite his susceptibility to girls of that age, which she surely knew
about) to be an honourable and avuncular companion to her golden,
glowing eighteen-year-old daughter. 'They had a marvellous time,'
said P. J. Kavanagh, the poet and writer whom Sally later married.
'Laurie was hailed everywhere, the two Roberts, Colquhoun and
MacBryde,[92] sitting outside Le Dome, calling out "If ever I saw
blessing in the air" ... as Sally and Laurie passed.' It was soon after
this interlude that Sally captured the heart of Kavanagh, a fellow
Oxford undergraduate who had lived in Spain. Through Sally,
Kavanagh became a lifelong friend of Laurie.

On the wet and cold day of the Coronation, 2 June 1953, Laurie
and Kathy were at Doddington Manor in Lincolnshire *chez* the
Jarvises. The villagers watched three television sets mounted in the
church. Laurie noted:

Silence & smell of mackintoshes. Children's tea in granary then
grownups tea of ham & tongue salad. Anthony Jarvis [Ralph's
son] planted a tree by the school. Then I played fiddle for children's maypole dance in stable. Judged fancy dress dance. At
midnight I lighted bonfire [Laurie had cut down a dead holly
tree for it that morning] – good blaze.

Next day he and Kathy watched the Queen drive along the Fulham
Road in an open car in a white hat. A round of summer drinks,
dinner and garden parties and receptions, with music and singing,
ensued. They went to the Derby and drank champagne; to Lord's

with Hugo Philipps; and at Bushton and other country houses they enjoyed the novelty of watching the Test match on television. Kathy danced at El Patio, and at the Festival Gardens. Laurie dressed in Field Marshal's uniform to stand in for Viscount Alanbrooke for an Anthony Devas portrait.

Some were mystified by their weekend disappearances. Laurie had no money, no car: Kathy still rode a pushbike. Where did they go? Answer: Laurie and Kathy's double act meant they were constantly invited. In Kathy's view, they simply made a good couple – and she was 'quite pretty and not unintelligent'. 'With you two I always feel it is the hosts who should give thanks to you,' as Bryan Guinness, later Lord Moyne, wrote,

> as you bring so much of – happiness yes but it is *not* the word I want – blessedness is the word, in the sense of the Baraka – an Arabian conception of Blessedness which my friend John Hamilton of Egypt (who so much wants to meet you) found in the Sudan. Anyway you have it … & leave it behind you like John Aubrey's spirit that disappeared with a melodious twang – but we wish you would not disappear.

Guinness, a poet himself, had met them at the Dugdales'. He was so 'stirred' by *The Bloom of Candles* that he invited them to stay. So Biddesden in Hampshire, one of the most beautiful houses in England, with Arab horses and peacocks in its park, became yet another weekend refuge for Laurie and Kathy.

They were back in Tenby that summer, every episode of the journey in the Devases' car being noted by Laurie: the Oxford bypass café with poisonous pork-pies; Laurie falling in the Thames and being saved by Prosper; the picnic in a hayfield on the Wye; the shooting of air-guns at bottles and mushrooms; the puncture five miles from Tenby. Once again there were intense prawning competitions (Laurie bagged 105 prawns on 14 July) and the usual jolly mishaps, sketched or painted for the Holiday Book: a burning motorbike drawn by Esmond Devas; Laurie's drawing of two chickens, one called Catalina, one called Lorenzo; an old lady and dog terrified by one of Laurie's fireworks. 'A Wet Day' depicted everyone lolling indoors in armchairs, children drawing on the floor.

Laurie's old patrons were still demanding new work. Stephen Spender launched his magazine *Encounter* with contributions by Day-Lewis, Auden, the Sitwells, and unpublished letters of Yeats, but 'It would be lovely to have something of yours ... We pay £10 for 1,000 words & corresponding rates for verse.' John Lehmann wanted Laurie's 'wonderful visual freshness and sparkle' for the *London Magazine*. With Rex Warner and Christopher Hassall, Laurie was editing the PEN anthology of 1954. They sent out letters to established poets, soliciting material. Clearly Laurie (in bed, ill) was unimpressed by the results, and told Hassall, 'I do not see why we are bound to accept inferior work.' 'But think,' asked Hassall. 'Would you send back a poem to de la Mare which you yourself had solicited?'

That year de la Mare, aged eighty, was awarded the William Foyle Poetry Prize *in absentia*. The *Daily Express* diarist covering the event reported: 'Three poets told me they are making less than £100 a year from poetry.' Laurie was one of them. He certainly could not have existed by poetry alone; but poems, he was discovering, are endlessly recyclable in anthologies and readings.

His poems were written for the voice. 'They are not intellectual poems, they are sensual. They celebrate sound and colour and smell and light.' The poet Adrian Mitchell, then an undergraduate at Christ Church, invited Laurie to perform for the Oxford Poetry Society, along with Anne Ridler. Mrs Ridler told Laurie that her pleasure in his poems had been intensified by hearing his reading 'as a light is doubled in a mirror'. 'I have always envied music its temporal advantage – its easier transport, so to speak, making its heaven here & now & hailing us all into it. But poetry well read aloud can do that: yours makes the visible world exist – "the round world is filled with exultation" as the Whitsun sentences express it, "& that which containeth all things hath knowledge of the voice".'

At Bushton, after-dinner singsongs ('On Top of Old Smokey', 'The Streets of Laredo', 'Ae fond kiss, and then we sever', 'Ye banks and braes o' bonny Doon', 'Barbara Allen') were *de rigueur*. Laurie would sing his variation on 'It Takes a Worried Man' – 'It takes a married man to sing a married song … I'm married now, but I won't be married long' and 'It takes a curried lamb, to sing a curried song…' In the early 1950s these impromptu soirées developed into organised concerts by 'The Barnstormers', in the village hall, Val ffrench Blake at the piano in side-whiskers and a high collar. All the relations (Charringtons, ffrench Blakes and Hanbury-Tracys) joined in, even Sam Dugdale aged three. Five Cunard sisters, dressed in 1920s flapper dresses and beads, performed the Beverley Sisters' song 'Sisters'. Antonia Dugdale danced a ballet solo; Veldes Charrington played violin; Kathy danced flamenco; and Laurie played recorder with Kathy and Antonia in a trio.

Laurie, court jester, could make spaghetti grow through the cracks in the dining-room table. He could eat fire. He would lead the children Pied Piperishly to the shooting ranges at the Wootton Bassett fair. Antonia recalls,

> When they discovered helium balloons, Laurie's idea was to weigh down a balloon so that it would travel along level with us. He tied his keys to the balloon, and we walked along with the keys alongside us, until suddenly a current of warm air lifted it up – and we all leapt up, but it floated out of reach, and it was goodbye Laurie's keys.

Some of his friends wondered, what on earth did he do all day? His appointments diaries were full with lunches, dinners and music recitals. You could draw a line from Chelsea through Pimlico to Belgravia and Mayfair: that was the London of Laurie's social circle. Also, it took time to keep daily accounts of cash in and out (he had learnt book-keeping at evening classes in Stroud) and of letters written and received. He recorded his weight each day. He checked

his thermometer and recorded the highest and lowest daily temperatures, in a book labelled 'Hot/Cold', with complicated graphs. Like
many writers, he gazed out of the window a lot. He watched over his
window-boxes ('2 November – Four geraniums still blooming') and
the trees in Elm Park Gardens: 'leaves falling steadily'.

But he was also writing *A Rose for Winter*. He wrote the opening
chapter ('We had come to the southern city of Algeciras…') as
a radio talk for the Third Programme, but suddenly he had no
publisher for the book. John Lehmann had been booted out of his
own company by his majority shareholder – 'sacked like an office
boy,' he told Laurie. Other publishers came to the rescue and on 11
October 1954 Laurie signed the contract for *A Rose for Winter* with
the Hogarth Press, who would pay £75 on signature, £75 on publication. Then André Deutsch, who lived just off the Fulham Road,
was introduced to Laurie by Nicolas Bentley. 'Like most people I
instantly fell in love with Laurie,' Deutsch said. 'Because of his
personality, his attractiveness, his mind.' Deutsch agreed to publish
Laurie's next collection of poems, if he could manage to make the
number up to twenty.

That summer Laurie had taken his fifth holiday with the Devases,
again to Geraldine Lawrence's at Tenby, Laurie drawing en route a
swollen, staggering, goggle-eyed rabbit, dying of myxomatosis. Back
from Tenby, Laurie made two trips abroad in August and September.
With two of the Cunard sisters, Virginia and Veronica, he and Kathy
motored to Chartres, Orléans, Pau, then briefly into Spain. At
Christmas he was back at Bushton with the entire Cunard clan. 'You
are the spirit of Christmas both,' he wrote to Pen and Nigel, 'and
a Christmas without Bushton doesn't seem a Christmas at all…'
Antonia remembered that Laurie kissed her under the mistletoe that
year. She was fourteen – which (as he told one close woman friend)
was his favourite age.

16

'Write about your own life'
1955–1958

> Now he has the right life for him; knows all the bright young
> writers and the foremost painters, hears all the literary scandals,
> is given free tickets for the best concerts and, every year, finds
> benevolent friends who enable him to spend a few weeks in
> Spain or some other foreign country.

THUS WILMA GREGORY, in a letter to her sister, accurately summarised the life Laurie was leading by 1958. Not yet famous, earning little, Laurie enjoyed the esteem of fellow poets, and had plenty of 'benevolent friends' providing a full social life and, long before packaged foreign travel, prolonged summers in Mediterranean villas.

In the mid-1950s anyone distinguished in the arts – writers, actors, poets and musicians – knew everyone else. At the Apollo Society's evenings of poetry and music Laurie would read with Spender, MacNeice, Day-Lewis and Jill Balcon, Marius Goring, Peggy Ashcroft. His diaries remark the beauty of Natasha Litvin (Mrs Spender) as she played Liszt, Dadie Rylands's reading voice 'like sunwarmed terracotta', Irene Worth's 'actressy listening pose'. At one Apollo evening he met the young guitarist Julian Bream, and he and Laurie became comrades at once 'through the Iberian connection' as Bream put it, and of course his guitar, 'the old plonk box' which Laurie played intuitively. Laurie liked Bream's referring to his art as 'the old gut-plucking lark' and the fact that he could play C. P. E. Bach, Sor and Villa-Lobos beautifully even when apparently drunk. Bream lived near Laurie at 20 Bolton Gardens. So they drank at the same local, Finch's in the Fulham Road (and later at the Queen's Elm, following the charismatic publican Sean Treacy, an ex-pilot from Galway), and both had a passion for fireworks. The effect when Laurie tied two rockets together at Bream's 1957 Guy Fawkes night party was never forgotten.

As a poet Laurie reached a pinnacle with *My Many-Coated Man*, his third and last volume of new work, published by Deutsch on 8 May 1955. He dedicated it 'to W. G.' – despite Wilma's harsh reaction to *The Sun My Monument* in 1944 – 'out of affection and gratitude,' Laurie told her, 'for all you did for me'. It contained half a dozen of his best loved and most anthologised post-war and post-Lorna poems: 'Town Owl', 'Twelfth Night', 'Boy in Ice', 'Apples', and the sinister 'My Many-Coated Man' itself.

'Laurie Lee is one of my favourite poets,' wrote Cyril Connolly in the *Sunday Times*. 'He has not a great deal to say, but a most delicious way of saying it.' He linked Laurie with Blake, Clare and Lorca: 'He never tries to be a philosopher ... but is content to portray changing moods and weathers in simple lyrical form, relying on a sharp eye and an exquisite ear.' He said Laurie invited comparison with Dylan Thomas, 'but the one is a Van Gogh, the other a Samuel Palmer, a maker of ravishing verbal woodcuts'.

His book became the first Poetry Book Society choice. Vita Sackville-West praised it and so did Bryan Guinness ('every page has the shining, thrifty concentration of a jewel; every phrase tells & burns its way into the imagination to set it on fire'). Atticus in the *Sunday Times* admired Laurie's bohemian credentials: 'Mr Lee, unlike most of our poets, has never been bureaucratised. He has never taught, never lectured, never taken political orders, never worked (or almost never) in an office – never sold out, in a word, for respectability.' 'I don't know quite how I exist,' Laurie told Atticus. 'It's a miracle really.'

In the spring of 1955, while brother Jack was in Indonesia directing *A Town Like Alice* with Virginia McKenna and Peter Finch, Laurie was in the bars of Madrid with Bunny Keene planning a film. They took a train through fields of caves – still inhabited – and reached Cuenca for the procession of the Virgen de la Luz. In this charming medieval town perched on an outcrop of rock east of Madrid, Laurie was still fondly remembered forty years later by Alejandro, former patron of El Sotanillo bar, as 'Lorenzo', a '*desgarbado*' (slovenly) figure who would spend hours in his bar, singing and playing the guitar and chasing girls with live crabs. 'Cuenca I loved, and next to Cuenca Alejandro of El Sotanillo,' wrote Laurie to his fellow poet Ted Walker, who visited Cuenca in the 1970s. 'Ask him what he did with the ten shilling note I signed & which he nailed to the tavern wall. I always mean to return & get it back.' (It may still be there.)

From Valencia, Barcelona and Gerona, Laurie joined Kathy and the stage designer Jocelyn Herbert in Provence. *A Rose for Winter* was dedicated 'to Cathy & the Benefactor' – Laurie by then had changed Kathy's name to Cathy, which he preferred, although she later reverted to her original initial – but on the publication day they were still away in Martigues. And perhaps it was as well to be out of the way. *The Spectator* reviewer was Kingsley Amis at his most acidly xenophobic. Amis deplored 'Mr Lee's vulgar and sensational little book' along with all writers who lyricised 'abroad' and gave the impression that 'the other fellow's grass is greener'. He saw Laurie's poeticism as an indecent degeneration from the more elaborate and unfashionable graces of prose. He declared the book to be 'a string of failed poems – failed not very good poems too'.

As for Laurie's impression of the Spaniards, 'so far as this can be debarnacled from rhetoric, generalisation and rhapsody', Laurie seemed to interpret 'their instability or hooliganism as gaiety, their coxcombry or self-pity as unselfconsciousness'.

The critic John Davenport sprang to Laurie's defence: 'Spain is hard and unsentimental. Mr Lee does not sentimentalise it. He

respects the rock-like integrity individual Spaniards have retained.'
He hoped that Amis might soon gain some tolerance of 'furrin
parts', since Amis had just won a Somerset Maugham Award: £500
to spend on travel abroad. Robert Conquest weighed in, supporting
his friend Amis in 'the important task of giving hell to "poetic"
prose'. Amis then responded himself, writing to *The Spectator* from
Portugal to say 'I'm not being grumpy about furrin parts, only about
people being silly about them.' Privately he told Conquest he was all
for escapism,

> but people should … not try to inflate their pleasure-etc trips
> into a spiritual pilgrimage AND THEN COME AND TELL
> ME ABOUT IT in a travel-book … Lee's book was notable as
> much for bloody stupid *ideas* as for crappy style, and these ideas
> are shared by other craps (Davenport & his 'rock-like integrity'
> etc.). I really do mind the ideas more than the style, bloodiest as
> the latter undeniably is.[93]

Laurie would never be admitted to Amis's gang. So it is interesting
to mention at this point, with the advantage of biographical fore-
knowledge, that a few months later, Laurie was having a romantic
holiday in Spain with Elizabeth Jane Howard – who was to be the
second Mrs Kingsley Amis.

Throughout that summer, Laurie's literary friends rallied. Rose
Macaulay ('Goodness, what a book!') found *A Rose for Winter* 'funny
and delicious. How unerringly you alight on the right words that sing
& clang & shine, & set the scene to music! the smells & the flavour &
the dusty tang which is Spain' and 'Oh Manolo, I should like to meet
him!' Elizabeth Jennings was 'appalled by Amis's ludicrous lack of
intelligence and taste' and Emma Smith found the book 'absolute
heaven … As for Kingsley Amis and his dastardly stuff I would like
to wring his neck, except poor man I feel sorry for him … all his own
writings must have seemed so mingy murky dingy in comparison,
he was just EATEN UP with envy.' Sarfi wrote from Italy to say that

Hemingway (whose *The Sun Also Rises* he had just read aloud to Helen) 'is nowhere beside you as a writer'. Even Wilma, in hospital in Aylesbury having two toes chopped off, confessed to enjoying it. After a lengthy discourse on Liberia (she had a Liberian nurse), she wished she too could revisit Almuñécar, 'especially because I, unlike you, was on friendly terms with the small farms, cottages, villas, well away from the *pueblo* ... Salud to your Kati. She sounds a person.'

Laurie was much too busy holidaying to record any of this. He went to Guernsey with the Devas family, replicating Tenby with added sunshine, shooting fish underwater and executing some good drawings including a portrait of himself looking pleased with a net full of mullet. And after a weekend with the Dugdales at Bushton, he set off on 4 September 1955 for Spain with Elizabeth Jane Howard.

At thirty-two Jane was a celebrated beauty with her intense dark eyes and hair drawn tautly back from her high-cheekboned face. Trained as an actress, she had married the naturalist Peter Scott at nineteen, had a daughter, and bolted; she had modelled and worked in publishing before her first novel, *The Beautiful Visit*, won the John Llewellyn Rhys Prize in 1950. She had met Laurie through Cecil Day-Lewis and found him 'instantly companionable'; he made her laugh and she loved his mobile expressive face. That summer, Jane was unhappy after her affair with Arthur Koestler ended. 'Laurie suggested I go with him to Guernsey, but the Devases couldn't have us, so he said never mind, we'll do something else, just the two of us.' Jane had never been to Spain before. They had an exhausting all-night train journey from Paris (with nothing to eat or drink for twenty-four hours) via Toulouse, Carcassonne and Perpignan. 'And at Gerona Station there was a crowd of people we knew, like Rodrigo Moynihan and Elinor Bellingham Smith. Our holiday wasn't a secret so it didn't matter. It was a very happy time.'

Laurie had not read Jane's novel. 'We were sitting on a rock one day, when he said, "Someone who looks like you can't be any good at writing," and I pushed him off the rock into the sea. The bravest thing I ever did with Laurie.' She signed her next novel, 'For Laurie, admiration, gratitude and love from Isabel.' Laurie had renamed her 'Isabel' because in Spain, 'Jane' is unpronounceable. 'Sometimes he called me "A Typical Kurd" – a reference to travel books which have a picture of a peasant in a blanket squinting into the sun and the caption "A Typical Kurd".'

'Yes, we were lovers,' Jane said, 'but it wasn't meant to have a future. We have always been loving friends. Always.' They stayed in cheap *pensiones*, explored villages by local buses, visited a guitar-maker to order a guitar for Julian Bream, saw a bullfight and went on to Estartit on the coast. 'A troupe of children would follow Laurie everywhere. They were enchanted by him.' On the way back they stayed overnight in Orléans and in Paris.

Kathy's tolerance of Laurie's trip abroad with Elizabeth Jane Howard may seem surprising but Kathy said it was not at all remarkable, at that time. Laurie remained very affectionate towards Jane throughout his life. Twenty years later he was writing to her and remembering Gerona:

> your long, exhausted, exquisite shape, face down, sleeping in
> your stifling room after the two days' train trip from London
> ... your face half lit over the table at the beach with the dark
> sea behind you, the unexpected euphoria around us, the game
> of love that kept on refusing to believe it was a game. Panic,
> protection, most of all freedom, happiness, and always your
> extraordinary beauty.

Laurie's visit to Bushton that August turned out to be the last of its era. On 6 September, while Laurie was with Jane Howard in Spain, Nigel Dugdale died in a terrible accident. He was swimming with his daughters Teresa and Antonia at Weymouth, when he dived off a diving board – unfortunately with his hands behind his back – hit his head on the sandbank, and broke his neck. When his daughters dragged him out he was already dead. He was forty-eight; his son Sam was only six. Fifteen-year-old Antonia had to attend the inquest and was asked whether her father might have intended suicide: the notion was absurd.

Laurie wrote the obituary in *The Times*: 'Nigel Dugdale, professional soldier, sportsman, humanist, bon vivant and wit, was one of the rarest and most unclassifiable spirits of his age ... one of the great English eccentrics,' he said. He praised Nigel's kindness and humour, his restless and agile imagination.

> With a toy, or a trick, or a turn of phrase, he could melt the most brass-bound of conferences or restore the spirits of the shyest child.
>
> He was also a poet – a poet of words, ideas, appetites and friendship ... One sees him now, bright-eyed ... moving among his guests and anointing them all with his cherished wines and rare good spirits. We were all his guests, and the party is now over.

That Christmas, their first without Nigel, Pen Dugdale and the children were joined once more by Laurie and Kathy.

Having hardly been in London during the summer, Laurie still recorded a 'Letter from Britain' talk for the BBC World Service about the prolonged heatwave he had missed: 'London's usual summer is sweet and piercing short, as temporary as young love. But this year has been unbelievable, historic, something to write poems about...' A month later he broadcast another letter about Guy Fawkes night, by which time he had left London again for a wintry visit to Warsaw to celebrate the centenary of the death of the Polish poet Mickiewicz. Laurie had never heard of Mickiewicz, but he was curious to experience life behind the Iron Curtain, and the trip made excellent *Encounter* fodder. Typically, while breakfasting on pork and eggs, Laurie spied Graham Greene at another table. Greene received him with 'detached warmth, as though it were the Savile Club', and asked rather testily, 'Shouldn't you all be at meetings or something by now?'

The following spring, Laurie took Kathy back to Andalucía. The weather was dire. Laurie filled two notebooks, observing 'the snob habit of wearing sun-glasses – in a people who have been able to look at the sun since Creation...' and commenting on 'the fat young wives producing those exquisite classic-faced children, so quick of smiles, of wit, of grace, for what? to become fat, worn young wives – what are these beautiful children for?'

But the best word-picture of Laurie and Kathy in Spain is given by Geraldine Lawrence in an illustrated letter to Nicolette Devas. That May of 1956 Geraldine was at the Hotel Reina Cristina in Algeciras, where her sketches were on show. She found Laurie and Kathy, who had been lashed by rain and wind for four weeks, 'poor dears', on the quayside. They were waiting for 'The Girls', Virginia Cunard and Pen Dugdale, to arrive on holiday.

> You know, Nicolette, I had so longed to come across Laurie & Cathy in Spain and I can't tell you how delightful it was ... Laurie knows Spain better than I do, yet he has such delicacy of enjoyment, and of sharing his pleasure; he never for one moment lets it be thought that he knows it all better than anyone else.

Off they all drove – Geraldine with the Stewarts and the Campbells from Gibraltar, and the Lees and Cunard sisters in a rackety hired car. The destination was Almorrhama, where there was a *fête champêtre* or *romería* on the first Sunday in May. Geraldine reported:

> And it all went like a dream. Laurie and Cathy practically stopped the fair. It is a delicious scene – cork woods, swings in the trees, booths with lemonade, hot shrimps, olives, where we sat down to our chicken and salad picnic ... We suddenly heard a pipe playing and along came Laurie ... He was enjoying it all so: the warmth, the sun, and the arcadian little fete was just what he loves.
>
> Joan Stewart said: 'Everyone in Gibraltar wants to know what Cathy is like.' I said, 'Well she's very beautiful and very artless

too: I mean she takes her own beauty quite coolly, she doesn't play up to it, but if you walk along with her all the Spanish men are sighing and moaning like the flowers of the forest...' Then a most wonderful thing happened. A *huge* moving crowd slowly came over to us, about 100, with Cathy dancing and Laurie playing & everyone enraptured: they surged around us, everyone yelling Olés and encores.

From then on, those two really *were* the *Romería*. News spread among the people who had come over from Gibraltar ... As we drove away people put their heads into the car and said, 'I say, is Laurie Lee the writer here, because Lady Mary Walker does so want to meet him, and so do the Brinton-Lees.'[94] I said, 'Well look here, d'you see that green dress with white spots in the crowd, that's Laurie Lee's wife and he's behind with the wicker wine bottle.' 'Oh thanks frightfully,' they said and scurried away. They really had everyone *longing* to know them ... John Hastings said afterwards, 'You know Geraldine, I'd always heard so much of Laurie Lee and I don't think I have ever met anyone whose charm so held one under a spell.'

On another evening they all went into the hills to see cave paintings, and their guides took them back to their little *cortijo* and out came the sherry and brandy and guitars, and everyone sang in the lamplight, and a young mother with babe in arms played castanets. 'This is how life should be lived, isn't it?' said Laurie happily. Later they were in the sailors' quarter of Algeciras, 'where a hideously ugly man sang deep flamenco and Cathy brought down the house by dancing wonderfully – she flings her whole self into it,' wrote Geraldine. 'She has got the static, still-footed part of the Spanish dances now, and of course her beauty, her hair in a plait & the fact that she was English sent all their temperatures up.

The hideous man rose and bellowed out a song to her, from the depths: 'Ah, if I had a woman!' he yelled – 'a woman, such a woman as you, I would not walk in the streets in the sunlight, nor under the stars – I would live deep, deep down in a c-a-a-ave and you would be my sun and my stars and the air I breathe.' Cathy listened, her eyes modestly cast down, while all the men wrung Laurie's hand & told him what a man he was having this pearl, this woman without compare, as his wife.

Kathy, who had been taking flamenco lessons in St John's Wood, said this was the time in her life which she and Laurie 'really shared'. Laurie was so proud of his lovely young Provençal wife.

He was very particular about doing things to a certain standard. So he was pleased with me. And in one way it was wonderful. In another way it was exhausting. We were always on the move or among people. If he had a dark day, and had to lie low, I would go out on my own, past the war-wounded and out of work men who spent all day leaning on the wall, and they would shout '*Guapa!*' The hotel maids teased me if I got upset. They told me: 'Remember we are far superior to them. Walk with your head held high! Be proud!'

In September they flew to Nice to join the house-party of Audrey and Jeremy Harris, who had a villa with cantilevered pool at Cap Ferrat, and were keen on boules and charades. Laurie harpooned himself in the ribs while snorkelling, but they took a few days in Martigues, and returned briefly before Laurie flew off yet again on a journalists' trip to Greece, sailing around the Aegean on the *Semiramis* as a guest of the Greek government.

Between travels, Laurie was writing the script for *Journey into Spring*, a now classic half-hour documentary film which Bunny Keene directed for the British Transport Commission. It was shot around Gilbert White's Hampshire village of Selborne, with Laurie's words ('This is England, hanging on the lip of spring…') spoken by Stephen Murray. Edgar Anstey, who had commissioned it, was so pleased he suggested a fee of 100 guineas instead of the 75 earlier proposed. The film was nominated for a Hollywood Academy Award in 1957. But when Laurie went to see it he commented, 'Many sloppy bits in the writing I must say.'

They were back at Bushton for Christmas 1956, made memorable by Laurie's carrying in the pudding, flaming with brandy, and dropping it. There were bits of pudding all over the floor with flames dotted about. 'Everything went with a bang,' wrote Laurie to Pen, 'including the pudding. Laurie's not so handy/With puddings fired with brandy/For flaming puddings floor him/O come let us abhor him.'

The Lees seemed to be at every party, such was their popularity, and nobody minded that they never gave parties themselves. In jest, Laurie would say, 'We don't return hospitality, because that might look as if we didn't like it.' But he increasingly did mind being unable to reciprocate the luxurious offerings of weekends where everything was arranged with lavish style and grace by unseen hands. By 1960 he was noting, 'There is a natural level of squalor in this flat, little sense of comfort, no visual imagination ... Curious feeling of no food in the place too.' Their more sensitive friends perceived that there must be a darker side to Laurie's sunny personality, that he must be difficult to live with, being so often ill, and unquestionably self-centred. 'Don't discover anything about self except black now,' was an enigmatic diary entry January 1957. But the uncomplaining Kathy seemed a blithe spirit, who supplied whatever he needed, and centred her life around him.

Social life was punctuated by the occasional funeral. 'What drives these young men to suicide?' Laurie asked his notebook. He listed five, including the artist John Minton, who killed himself at forty.

> Rosamond writes of the doom of them & asks 'any idea why'.
> I think it is the unbearable plurality of experience which bombards us now, too much expected from the artist, no safe leisure of sensation, too many people; impossibility of finding

in the flood any substantial moral or immoral rafts to cling to: breakdown, breakdown.

In March 1957 Laurie found he needed glasses, though still able to observe a comet at sunset, and to count the buds unfolding on the sycamores in the square. Did the eye test bring intimations of mortality? That month, an English teacher, Neville Smart, who had first been struck by Laurie's poetry in *The Bloom of Candles*, invited Laurie to come to Kingsbury County School in north-west London, to address the sixth form about poetry. Laurie courteously replied:

> Dear Mr Smart,
>
> Thank you very much for your letter & for your flattering suggestion. I simply couldn't do it though. I feel I've no right to lecture anyone about poetry, particularly the young. You can teach them far more than I can.
>
> Roberta was a remarkable girl & I congratulate you upon her. She had a strong & original style of writing, but there wasn't much I could tell her. She lectured me, rather. I think she'll do well.
>
> Forgive me for not being more helpful, but this isn't the first time I've had to find excuses.
>
> Yours sincerely, Laurie Lee
>
> PS I sent Roberta a copy of '*The Bloom of Candles*'. She wrote to say she didn't think much of it.

Roberta Green, the girl mentioned, had written several highly accomplished poems in the school magazine at Mr Smart's previous school, Willesden Grammar. In the fourth form, she had written 'Warning to Prospective Lovers':

> Like a bee
> She softly purrs with honeyed words,

Fluttering gossamer wings;
And like a bee
She stings.

Roberta (now Mrs Nigel Planer) recalled that when she sent Laurie her poems, he invited her out to dinner. She did go, but it was a tense occasion, as her strict Jewish grandmother insisted on coming too, fearing that Laurie might carry Roberta off to the white slave trade. What the incident reveals is that Laurie, aged forty-three, was willing to make a dinner date with a seventeen-year-old schoolgirl poet.

That May, Laurie made another foray into reportage and proved himself adept at the craft. He went to Cannes to cover the film festival for *Encounter*. On the first evening he was refused entry to a screening because he had no dinner jacket. He wrote to Jean Cocteau, the Festival's president:

I am an English poet ... Last night I was thrown out of the evening show because I was not wearing 'smoking'. I came to Cannes to study the films, not to take part in a dress show. May I, in admiration to your president, supreme poet, imagist of my youth, & as one who would not care much for the dictatorship of clothes, protest against this petty law?

Cocteau replied: '*Mon cher Laurie Lee: Faites comme moi. Venez voir les films à 7 heures – ainsi j'évite le smoking et je me couche le soir. De toute manière je joins une feuille de passe-bien ... Salut fraternel de Jean Cocteau.* The girl at the Hôtel de Paris desk translated this for Laurie, and said, 'Is very good that – you must keep it.' 'Is very good & I will keep it,' wrote Laurie in his notebook.

He also kept the *feuille de passe-bien* on Carlton Hotel writing paper: '*Monsieur Laurie Lee est venu à Cannes sans son smoking – mais avec son coeur. Vous serez tres aimables de le recevoir comme il le mérite. Jean Cocteau.*' Laurie tried flaunting this the next evening:

superiors were sent for, tongues clicked, and he was told, 'Well, monsieur, you must wait even so till the lights go down.'

His notebook absorbed everything in Cannes: the palms and pines, the white-gloved gendarmes, cormorants plummeting into the sea, the scent of 'sun-sickened' lilies, the price of white wine, the posing starlets, the prowling men, the atmosphere of big money and the power of the photographers, the evening sun that gave everyone a halo. He congratulated Maria Schell 'on the miracle of the eternal summer in your smile'. 'She embraced me & said, have a ham sandwich.' One morning 'in this city of sensuality and materialism', he suddenly heard the Archduke Trio in a deserted bar. His notebook says:

> It was ten in the morning. The tears streamed down my cheeks. 10 days of solitary confinement in this paradise suddenly unexpectedly broken by the notes of Beethoven so clean & spirit-borne. If they did this to me in prison – and this I believe they do – I would break down & betray all & everyone. I know my weakness.

He also had one of his dreams of Lorna.

> Dream: Slad. It was green light of country summer dawn. I was restless on the big kitchen bed. My young wife was busily talking in her sleep. Somewhere above a creak of boards, a presence. Then, horror, from the bedroom above, footsteps descended the wooden stairs to the kitchen. Who could it be. The stair-door opened. It was she, beautifully dressed, horrifying white. She took off clothes & lay on my side – the incomparable body. C asleep now with her lips open. Breakfast – half-naked – she looks winningly at me, asks me to spend the day with her – then Lewis Eyers[95] begins to fit a chain across the kitchen window. Why should he choose this morning? The sun shines. Village servants bring coffee & join us. I know I can't escape or be alone with her.

He wrote his Cannes article at speed – despite distractions including the Test match, an eclipse of the moon, and a glittering Savile Club dinner for Robert Frost. His report was perceptive, witty and sharp. It drew praise from Rosamond ('Laurie how like an angel you do write. You are a veritable Lorelei: more Lorelei-like than angelic, full of the most seductive guiles and wiles…') and from Cecil Day-Lewis: 'I read all about you & the starlets, bless their little cruppers & fetlocks.'

In July Laurie and Kathy embarked on a month-long Grand Tour of France, Italy, Switzerland, Lichtenstein and Austria. The trip was organised by Tom [T. S.] Matthews, former editor of *Time* magazine under Henry Luce. Matthews was an American aristocrat: born in 1901, son of an Episcopalian bishop and a Miss Procter, an heiress of Procter & Gamble, he was trim, stylish and witty, educated at Princeton and at New College, Oxford. He had four grown sons, and now lived in Chester Square with his second wife, the war reporter Martha Gellhorn, former wife of Ernest Hemingway. Matthews, meticulous and disciplined and from a background as different from Laurie's as could be, became one of his most valued friends. Both men had an extraordinary gift for friendship.

Matthews drove them across Europe to Portofino where he had rented Il Castelletto, a glorious villa high up the steep hill, with a flower-decked terrace overlooking the bay, where they sat at sundown or in the moonlight among fireflies. There were spectacular storms and blazing hot days, visits to Ann Queensberry in Rapallo, and on the feast of St Peter, brilliant fireworks. Matthews, who was a poet as well as a journalist and author, wrote every morning, finishing his book on press barons, which Laurie considered 'an excellent job, taut as a bowstring, shafted with arrows and most winningly aimed'. Galvanised by Matthews's example he completed two poems and a radio script.

The day he got home, Laurie heard that his brother Tony – of whom he had been fond, calling him the visionary of the family –

had died on 2 July, of cerebral meningitis, leaving a widow and a young daughter, Anthea. He was forty-one. At Stroud hospital, where cousin Marion Light was matron, Jack had found Tony in a darkened room, blind and dying. It was almost ordained, Jack said. 'Tony was a sweet boy and he never had a chance.'

Almost without pause, Laurie was away for the rest of the summer. Kathy went to Martigues, while Laurie drove with the Devases to Tenby once more, recording and sketching. After judging the Guinness Poetry Prize, Laurie flew off to Greece in September again as 'a fancy guest of the Greek government with other writers of several nations', he wrote from Athens to Tom Matthews. 'I don't know why they do this.' They cruised the Aegean on SS *Philippos*, and had a few days on Hydra.

'If all the year were playing holidays, to sport would seem as tedious as to work,' as Prince Hal said. Laurie was understandably conscious of being too busy playing to get any writing done. When he wrote to Roy Fuller (a close second for the Guinness prize) looking forward to Fuller's *Collected Poems*, he added: 'I could collect *my* lot on an ash tray. A bit envious I am.' Fuller dedicated his volume to Laurie. 'I never cut your throat much in the past,' said Laurie, 'but you've certainly become my favourite poet now.' Their friendly rivalry continued and when a second fan letter to Laurie was misdirected to Fuller's Dulwich flat, Fuller sent it on with a note: 'TO L. LEE – WARNING. My flat must no longer be used as an accommodation address for what is doubtless an amatory or subversive correspondence. Your rival, R. Fuller.'

By the end of 1957 Laurie had become 'rather sick' at his scant productivity. 'It makes me want to kick the wall,' he told Matthews, who had finished another book of poems. 'Do you write them at night, or in the can, or walking home drunk through the streets?' All Laurie had written lately was an introduction to Epstein's work, praising his massive and controversial *Ecce Homo*:[96] 'Squat, square, the totem of our crimes, he stands before us in a pitiless, blinding light. No chisel was ever less compromising than Epstein's in this work. Ten thousand churchfuls of sentimentalised Christs are denied forever by this raw and savage figure.'

It was now almost ten years since the Hogarth Press had commissioned *Cider with Rosie*. What propelled Laurie finally into writing it was editorial director Norah Smallwood's offer to pay him 'to give up all other work and get on with it'. Laurie named what seemed to her the astonishingly small sum of £500. So in November 1957 he resumed his journal-keeping habit (a reliable sign of self-discipline) on the day the second Russian satellite was launched, carrying 'Little Lemon', a Samoyed dog, spinning around the world fourteen times a day. Laurie was riveted by all things astronomical, especially space travel; five months later he was rushing home from seeing the Marlon Brando film *Sayonara* to catch Sputnik II. He stood on a roof, in bitterly cold wind, determined not to miss it 'until a bright star glided silently south-east, passed almost overhead, quite fast, purposeful, with its dog in it, heading for final extinction in the atmosphere. It was extraordinarily moving.' He did not share the Canine Defence League's fury about the dog, which had died in space on 10 November.

He did not renounce his continual party-going. His journal featured a cast of 1950s gossip-column fixtures: Lady Dufferin & Ava, Lady Oranmore & Browne, the Tynans, Randolph Churchill, Willie Mostyn-Owen with his 'pink marble shining face', 'delicious fat old Russian Moura Budberg'; Gerard Hoffnung, Edgar Lustgarten, Woodrow Wyatt; Enid Starkie ('admired Cathy in obsessed lesbian way "like my niece – brainless girl – beautiful eyes"'). Dr Jacob Bronowski talked to Kathy for an hour, Laurie reported, before she asked him his name.

The gossip was of Caitlin Thomas 'almost in the madhouse'; George Weidenfeld 'divorcing his wife, ex-Mrs Cyril Connolly, and naming Mr Cyril Connolly' and 'the new sack dresses behind whose shapelessness men can imagine their ideal figure'. Anthony Devas was painting the Queen, 'stiffly encased in a dress the colour and texture of half-eaten trifle'. (During sittings 'HM discusses bosoms of film stars which she deplores'.) The banker Michael Behrens took him often to the opera. He heard W. R. Rodgers speaking about Yeats: 'Said Yeats thought poetry should be able to be shouted across the street to a friend (I said: "AND PEACE COMES DROPPING SLOW!") and that he couldn't write with anyone else in the room, even a child. (Me neither.)'

He spent several long evenings talking till 2 a.m. with his favourite painter, Sir Matthew Smith, in his Chelsea Cloisters flat, reverently recording the old man's reminiscences. Laurie had first met Smith years before, with Lorna. 'Remembered your name,' said Smith. 'Beautiful – "Laurie Lee". I thought of the Rhine.' Smith was a modest, unassuming man. He told Laurie.

> It was Churchill got me my knighthood. Never met him. I never met anyone. Too shy or proud or something. Could have met Derain, could have met Matisse, Picasso – all those. Never did. My fault. Too negative ... But I was in a room with Churchill once. I went up to him & said, 'May I shake your hand, sir?' A young man said, 'Sir Matthew Smith, sir.' Churchill said, 'I know, I know, I know, I know!' I think he was cross with me. Being too negative.

Exuberant with creativity, Laurie wrote his longest ever letter to Rosamond Lehmann's daughter Sally, who had sailed with her new husband P. J. Kavanagh to Jakarta, where Kavanagh was lecturing for the British Council. Laurie advised Sally to keep journals, and Kavanagh to 'put on his Willie Maugham face and plan a wicked book'. He was sure the young couple had made the right decision, in their twenties: 'What you see won't be seen again.'

He told them about the Guinness prize-giving: 'Never, since Warsaw, have I seen Poetry so richly sponsored. Uniformed footmen, chandeliers as big as haystacks, gallons of Black Velvet, hundreds of sparkling brimming glasses with a poet's nose in each.' He mentioned Enid Starkie 'biting & bibulous' ... gripping my hands and weeping over long-lost friends'.[97] 'Plump Socialist Naomi Mitchison was also present. She straps down her bosom in order to present a united front.' At the Colin Crewe/Sally Churchill society wedding, there was 'a good negro band, some close dancing, and a lot of sick young girls running for the cloakrooms. Oh, my friends … you've no idea how Gomorrah begorrah we are.'

He was, he added casually, 'on chapter 3 of a book'. He later claimed to have spent that winter happily 'cloistered in my snug, paraffin-reeking, sooty-windowed garret seven days a week' scribbling away with his 4B pencils on the back of old BBC scripts (Laurie did not believe in buying writing paper; he felt stationery should be something you came by.) His childhood days returned 'in pavilions of sound, and pavilions of colour', moving him to tears and laughter. He told Wilma he had 'moods of staring at white paper', but she told him he was lucky in not having his mind cramped by classical models: 'Whatever you write is bound to be original, entirely yourself.' In fact *Cider with Rosie* was slotted in between parties and bouts of 'flu, and seeing Mr What win the Grand National, and counting daffodils, and recording the temperature. Downstairs, Kathy was looking after the children of Jill and Norman Hepple, their neighbours. 'As Cathy tries to keep them subdued her shushes are much louder than their noise.' By the time he finished his first draft he was broke, he said: 'I took my fiddle out into the streets and made £4 15s one afternoon.' Luckily Jasper Gilbey of Gilbey's magazine, the *Compleat Imbiber*, rescued him by paying him for two poems with 20 guineas' worth of gin and crates of wine at trade prices.

The new Guinness prize entries, he told P. J. Kavanagh, included 'two excellent poems by Ted Hughes & Roy Fuller'. Hughes was a new name to Laurie. Lehmann had taken him up, but his *London Magazine* was in financial straits. Laurie was not surprised: the magazine had a repellent format and a heavy pedagogic solemnity. 'John's forewords sound like a brisk rapping of canes in cold morning classrooms: "Enough of that fooling boys! To the task! To the task!" In fact what is wanted is a little *more* fooling, more iconoclasm, more wit, more irreverence, more warmth. Even the outsider boys read like prigs & pets.'

Wilma, now seventy and living in a cottage near Aylesbury, was also writing 'a weirdish, probably idiotic book' which might be 'a ponderous bore'. She was right. Even her friend Rebecca West declared that Wilma had 'no gift for writing in an entertaining manner'. Wilma asked Laurie whether he felt sick about politics now: she was as scathing about Gaitskell as about the dull Tories. Laurie had just made a rare political foray, to the first Ban the Bomb rally on Good Friday 1958 in Trafalgar Square, hearing Philip Toynbee, Canon Collins and Michael Foot. Laurie marched with the demonstrators as far as Marble Arch 'among the beards & pony tails, duffles & slacks, horn-rimmed specs, the uniform of the *New Statesman*/Third Programme minority, with whom I am clearly identified'. But he asked, 'Why Aldermaston? Like marching to protest to an arrow-maker's hut – why not to the homes of statesmen & generals?'

Further financial salvation arrived from another Society of Authors travel award. Laurie tried to discover the identity of the donor. She replied to his letter anonymously, revealing only that she was female, a writer, over sixty, 'belonging to the Protestant north rather than the Latin south'. She hoped he would use the money to get away, 'forget your worries and enjoy yourself'.

So Laurie and Kathy went off on 23 April 1958 to the little-known island of Ibiza. From Majorca they took a six-hour slow boat and arrived just in time: an airfield and 'lunchbox villas' were sprouting, and a year later the island was tourist-packed. But in 1958 there was still 'an unearthly silence, bad roads, empty beaches, very little traffic', he wrote to Tom Matthews, and the islanders were 'proud & distinctive'.

They took a furnished house (an ugly concrete box) with a roof terrace, for a guinea a week, just outside the walled medieval village of Santa Eulalia, five minutes from the beach. Nearby was a fresh-water pool surrounded by oleanders where nightingales sang. He told Matthews that it was '65 degrees, landscape flowery but not ostentatious; many resident painters and their women, all very bearded and serious'. It was not Ischia or Capri, but there were friendly natives working in the fields looking like Bible figures, and the local absinthe, called *palo*, was four pesetas a glass. Matthews arrived with his friend the artist Cathleen Mann, former Marchioness of Queensberry, bringing tea, coffee, alcohol and cigarettes. Every morning Laurie and Matthews stayed in their shuttered rooms with white wine kept cool in buckets of water. In the afternoons they swam, and in the evenings they drank under the trees. There was nothing to do but work, drink and swim. Laurie did not even shave, until a man in a bar said, 'I encounter your beard very ugly,' and turned out to be the local barber, who shaved him forthwith.[98]

Matthews too was writing a book (entitled *Name and Address*), about his childhood, his over-protective mother, and his irascible Trollopian father; in America his book was eventually reviewed in tandem with Laurie's. After Matthews had gone, Laurie reported stormy skies and strong winds making doors bang like paper bags. Laurie had walked up a distant fir-covered hill and sent Matthews this triolet:

Lee climbed up that hill;
We all knew he could do it.
So steep it could kill
Yet he climbed up that hill;
There's a cairn for him still
On the top, marked: 'Rest! Poet.'
Lee climbed up that hill;
We all knew he could do it.

On 11 June ('4,600 pesetas left') Laurie and Kathy took the night boat to Barcelona, and a bus to Calella on the Costa Brava, to meet Virginia Cunard. From Gerona on Midsummer Day he wrote a nostalgic card to Elizabeth Jane Howard – 'to Isabel the dark and the beautiful' – before they travelled on to Figueras, Marseilles and Martigues. They were away for nearly three months.

At Easter, Rosamond Lehmann had written of her anxiety about her daughter Sally 'in that beastly Djakarta'; Rosamond had sold her Utrillo in order to pay for a visit there later in the year. But first she was off to the US on Good Friday. 'God speed and Good Flyday,' Laurie had replied breezily. When Laurie got home from Ibiza on 1 July, for the third time in three years he returned from abroad to learn of a premature death. On 22 June, the golden Sally had died suddenly in Java, of polio, at the age of twenty-four. Laurie could never bear to talk about it, her husband P. J. Kavanagh said. Kavanagh translated his grief into the haunting memoir *A Perfect Stranger*; Rosamond wrote *The Swan in the Evening*, in which she said that Laurie was 'one of the most passionately resentful of all those who loved and mourned her'. Laurie certainly never forgot Sally. Whenever he described a particularly appealing golden-haired girl in his diary he would add, 'like Sally'.

By August, he was paring down his third draft of *Cider with Rosie*. Kathy went off to her mother in Italy while Laurie carried on writing, between excursions to the Oval, to a PEN party for James Thurber, to dine with Peggy Ashcroft and Julian Bream, and to a weekend at Bushton. He spent a musical weekend at The Cedars, Crondall, Hampshire, home of the former Celia Kirwan, now Mrs Arthur Goodman. Of all his friends' country places, Laurie said theirs was the one he most coveted. The Cedars was in the heart of a village, 'two steps from the off-licence and three pubs, and 5 minutes from the boggy beech-wooded countryside'. When he made his break with London, he said, this was the kind of place he would like.

It is truly remarkable that he ever had time to finish his book that summer. He also made a tour of the Western Highlands with the Henrions, twice visited Bryan Guinness in Dublin, once with MacNeice, to thrash out the Guinness poems ('I drank 23 Guinnesses the first day and rode round the wet city in a horse and trap'), and wrote to Barbara Castle about the Cyprus problem.

Finally on 28 October he could record: 'Finished Typed Draft of Book Cider.'

Leonard Woolf wrote him a sharp little note saying he did not really care much for this kind of book, and did not encourage the writing of childhood memories. 'But I think in your case we will publish it,' he ended grudgingly. The letter was 'dictated by Leonard Woolf and signed in his absence'.

Elizabeth Jane Howard, now Mrs Jim Douglas-Henry, gave Laurie the manuscript of her own next novel, *The Sea Change*, and he responded admiringly: 'Dear Artist Isabel. To read these pages after my own is like watching a dolphin swim.'

With his book at last finished, the mood of Laurie's notebook became more than usually jocular (after an evening of Scottish songs and Brecht's songs at the Arts Theatre, he wrote 'A braw Brecht nicht') and full of dreams. Sometimes he would wake himself up laughing at the puns in his dreams: 'Talking to a Dr Blow about illegitimate children, then saying "Bye, Blow."' On 18 November 1958, after meeting the young writer Jeremy Sandford, who knew Yasmin (now aged nineteen), he had a dream about his daughter.

> It was arranged for me to go to see her & they were both in riding kit. She was not very beautiful but had a fresh bright face & blue clear eyes. She was very friendly & chatty. She had a slight pock mark on her nose (like mine) & an injured middle finger, slightly twisted, owing to some childhood accident. She gossiped. 'My father makes a hobby of Opel cars,' she said. 'He doesn't, you know,' I murmured, sotto voce. Her mother laughed knowingly with me.

In 1958, the new arts magazine *Motif* appeared, featuring his neighbour Lis Frink, with an introduction by Laurie that expressed the earthiness and eroticism of her sculpture: 'It is spontaneous as an ejaculation of lava, a round of images shot into the air by the convulsions of buried truths.' For Laurie, Frink was the striking embodiment of primitive woman, 'a hoarder of myths, a familiar of spirits, a courage-giver, a buckler-on of swords' ... Her beauty was archaic, finished in gold-bronze like 'some oracular Delphic presence' and he summed up her iconography as 'brutal, uncompromising, virile and sharp as knives'. Laurie's words, as Frink's biographer Stephen Gardiner commented, 'read like a love letter to her art'.

One night Laurie was in Soho with the Cockney writer Frank Norman, learning all about rhyming slang and porn shops, when they ran into the poet Philip O'Connor, whom he hadn't seen since Putney in 1935 'when we were young men congratulating each other on our genius'. O'Connor said he'd been in the madhouse. At the end of a wildly sociable week in November, Laurie was knocked down by a lorry. He was just saying to himself the lines of the psalm, 'Like as the hart desireth the waterbrooks', when he stepped off the pavement and

> I was hit & spun round twice & rolled in the road & got up all in one smooth movement. Nobody moved or approached me, or asked about injuries. They just stood staring in fishy groups. I staggered to the pavement feeling sick & exhilarated. My trouser was split from thigh to ankle. I had missed death closely. It should cure me of absentmindedness.

The year ended with yet another premature death on 21 December. Laurie and Kathy had been out seeing Orson Welles's *Othello*. When they got home, 'Emma Devas was there & from her face I knew her father had died.' Anthony had begun a portrait of his twelve-year-old son Prosper that morning, and the two had then walked in Hyde Park. Later, Prosper found his father slumped in his chair. 'But he died in an instant,' noted Laurie, '& it was better at home.' Devas was forty-seven. Christmas Eve 1958 found Laurie at Putney cemetery, as one of the bearers of Anthony's coffin.

From the funeral Laurie and Kathy went on to Bushton where, minutes after they arrived, the real candles on the tree were lit, and the whole tree and its cotton-wool snow went up in flames with a great whumph. Everyone stood transfixed with horror, but in seconds Laurie had opened the french windows and pushed the flaming tree outside, where it fell into the snow with the sound of glass balls shattering in smithereens.

That Christmas Laurie wrote another acrostic for Kathy:

> Could I in verse iambic
> Appraise your gentle aura
> Then would I in one sonnet
> Hoard all your beauty's wealth.
> Yet such neat-rhyming trickery
>
> Could only freeze in aspic
> All your live warmth and *alma*
> These lines are yours – and yet,
> Heart of my married hearth,
> You make a wilder poetry.

17

Back to Slad
1959

Dear Mr Lee:

I am a factual person who dislikes mystery but I am also in
a predicament about giving my name, so I must ask you not to
speak of it. You see, I write books myself and I don't want myself
as author to be mixed up with the travel award.

THUS WINIFRED BRYHER, historical novelist, succumbed
to Laurie's second inquiry in January 1959 and wrote from her
Bauhaus home above Lake Geneva, revealing that she was the
mysterious benefactress who gave money to the Society of Authors
to enable writers to go abroad. Laurie had received two benefactions.
Winifred Bryher[99] was the pen-name of Winifred Ellerman, lifelong
companion of Hilda Doolittle (the writer H. D.). Winifred's father
had left a fortune from newspapers and shipping, and since money
gave her complete independence, she wanted other writers to share
it. In the 1920s she bought Edith Sitwell a house, and gave James
Joyce a monthly allowance in Paris. 'I think you respond to the sun
and the Latin south,' she told Laurie, 'so I am enclosing a cheque to
help you to return to Spain or wherever you would like to go.' She
herself preferred the icy wastes of Greenland: 'Mountains as high as
the Alps, icebergs of fantastic shapes, gay, laughing Greenlanders. I
don't know why the North always calls me. It is something against
which there is no struggling. Have a good time in the south.'

Cider with Rosie was ready for publication in the summer of 1959, and his publisher Norah Smallwood expected it to have a modest success, selling perhaps 800 copies. She asked John Ward, then a *Vogue* artist, to illustrate it. Ward knew Laurie from Tenby, and they had played cricket together in Putney. Ward recalled,

> I went to see Mrs Smallwood in her eyrie where I once heard her saying on the telephone: 'Mr Jones, what I don't know about photolithography can be written on the side of a black-currant.' Leonard Woolf sat there like an old prune. Norah told me that if they broke the bank they could pay me £175. I had a wife and four and a half children to support, and a mortgage of £11 a month. But I had an instinct for commissions that were worth doing.

Ward too was a countryman, from Herefordshire. 'I grew up in those cottages. I knew the Sunday school treats, the wild flowers, the kitchen ranges, the pitchers of milk, the flagstones on the floor.' He asked Canterbury art school to find a student to be his model, so eighteen-year-old Pamela Kay posed as Annie, Crabby, Granny Trill. 'One feels such gratitude,' he told me, 'towards anyone who can catch a character and hold a pose.' His Cotswold-dwelling sister lay on the carpet to pose as the drowned Miss Flynn. For the Uncles he drew men from his army days. He used his own son William for Laurie the sickly boy.

Laurie was just back from a trip to Tangier for *Queen* magazine when he sat with Ward in the garden of the Chelsea Arts Club, commenting on his sketches. Laurie had jotted down a few points of detail about the dim cottage interior, its pools of lamplight and deep evening shadows, the need for more litter on Annie's bedside table: books, vases, flowers, candles. He had noted,

> Mother looks absolutely right in the servant sketches. She was perhaps heavier later in body and face, wilder hair. The old

granny making wine should be more shrivelled, bent, half witch-like. The little girl's face is lovely, but body not perhaps childish enough. The drowned girl would be mostly concealed by water reeds, though her face – staring, and haunting, and masses of floating hair, could be seen. I do like these though ... I think they're splendid.

Laurie told Wilma he originally thought drawings unnecessary 'when the writer has taken pains to create a scene in the readers' mind ... But John Ward knows the country, has an eye for wild flowers, and his impressions of me as a child are remarkably like.'

That spring, Kathy went into hospital to have the ovarian cyst removed which had prevented her from conceiving after nine years of marriage. Their childless state had been as mystifying to them as it was to their pitying friends. Each had collected several godchildren, Laurie's latest being Emma Smith's daughter, Lucy Rose Stewart-Jones: 'Collecting godchildren is so clearly your vocation,' Emma wrote, adding that Laurie need not send presents: 'The thing is for you to fly kites or stand on your head or take her to the zoo or teach her to sing.'

In Kathy's absence Laurie wrote his account of Ibiza for *Encounter*. John Lehmann wrote regretting that *Encounter* was also publishing an extract from *Cider with Rosie*, 'rather than your old friends on the *London Magazine*'. Was this not 'the book which I managed to rescue for you from the debris of J. L. Ltd?' he asked. But the warm reception for *Encounter*'s extract (the 'Grannies' chapter) gave a hint of the success to come, which justified all his 'wintry labours and dark hours at the desk', he told Wilma.

Kathy emerged from hospital with a pretty little scar, and departed for three months' convalescence on the Greek island of Hydra. Along with the bereaved Rosamond Lehmann and her son-in-law P. J. Kavanagh, she joined the house-party of Barbara, formerly Lady Rothschild, to look after Lucy, her daughter from her marriage to the classical scholar Rex Warner. Laurie would have to stay behind in England for the summer publication of *Cider with Rosie* – delayed for four months by a printers' and bookbinders' strike.

On the day Kathy left, Laurie went off to Barcelona with Julian Bream, introducing him to Los Caracoles restaurant where you could get a plate of eponymous snails and a glass of wine for elevenpence. Laurie took his fiddle, Bream his guitar. 'Laurie saw the dramatic potential of the situation,' Bream remembered. 'He knew that the Spaniards thought nobody outside Spain could play the guitar. So we would pretend we were just a couple of fellows with instruments, and we'd start to play … Laurie loved to observe the expressions on people's faces.' It happened just as planned. 'J crouched on his stool & played some Albéniz,' Laurie wrote in his diary, '& the bar was reduced to a whisper, & the gypsy guitarists from the cabarets fell on their knees & clutched his ankles in agonies of pleasure. Even the fat old patron cynic Caracoles himself came to listen, astonished, & crying out afterwards, "And of all things, an Englishman!"'

Laurie was to spend the rest of the summer back in his home village. He had been offered a 'furnished hut', Woodside Bungalow, a cottage in the corner of Slad called The Vatch. On the rainy first of July, Nicolette Devas delivered Laurie there. In the local pub, the Star, they talked to an old man who the very next day was carried out in his coffin. 'Talk about omens,' noted Laurie gloomily. On his first weekend he went to a lunch at Peggy Phillips-Birt's dove-covered cottage nearby. Peggy, preparing the salmon mousse, suddenly said 'Bloody cat!' and handed Laurie a dying dove, torn at the throat. 'Had to kill it. Talk about omens,' noted Laurie again.

It was an extraordinary summer. He discovered how much (and how little) life had changed in his village. In the butcher's he was saluted by old familiar schoolboy faces, now fat and bald. But the place itself had not changed at all: 'the smell of herbs, distant sound of crowing cocks, dogs, owls, children's voices, train whistles, heavy smell of jasmine in twilight – even with my eyes closed I know I am here'. The conversations in the Star were noteworthy: 'Got a rabbit the other day. Big 'un. An' would you believe it. 'Ad a wire round his neck I'd lost two months afore. Buried right in 'is fur. Don' know 'ow 'e lived I'm sure.' … 'Wuss thing I ever seed – rabbit in a net with 'is eyes gone, pecked out, still alive…'

He rode to Stroud on his ten-shilling bicycle and, as of old, had a puncture. He walked with his sister Marjorie and niece Anthea across Rodborough Common to hunt for rare bee orchids and found five. There were days of thunderstorms when he needed his 'snakepit' boots; then blinding heat and heavy July greenness. The sun was alluringly brilliant over Swift's Hill in the mornings. There were chattering magpies, butterflies, snails bright as liquorice. He dined at Steanbridge House, now a guest-house owned by Mrs Collier and her daughter Gwyneth. Most Friday nights he took the train to Bushton Manor, the place he loved best 'next to this valley'. He liked to say, in letters: 'I live near a wood called Madding Grove, far from the Budding Crowd.'

To Kathleen Garman, now Lady Epstein, he sent condolences on the death of her husband. Epstein's last years had been stricken with loss: Theo, his son by Kathleen, had died in his twenties, and their daughter Esther had committed suicide over Mark Joffé, leaving young Roland Joffé to be brought up by Lady Epstein. '[Epstein] was the greatest of them,' wrote Laurie, 'a mountain among scratching moles. I think of you & feel the loss of him but join in gratitude for the riches he left us.'

One August afternoon Laurie was sitting out on the steps in the heat, when he heard the sound of a galloping horse and a cry from the field above him. He found a girl lying face down in the grass, blue-jeaned leg twisted, face bleeding, shirt torn. It was Gwyneth Collier, who had been thrown and dragged by her horse. She had been on her way to ask Laurie to play his guitar at a barbecue. Laurie propped her unconscious head in his arms: he was quite alone and nobody ever passed by, so he shaded her with branches, ran down and stopped a car, and an ambulance was summoned. She had a suspected skull fracture and a broken femur. 'I felt tender but awful. The smell of her blood stayed on my clothes.' Five days later she was still semi-conscious. The local paper told the story of how 'no less a person than Laurie Lee, the poet and writer'[100] had gone to Gwyneth's aid. 'Miss Willa Gibbs, American writer of historical novels, who lent the horse, has got rid of it through guilt.' (And twenty-five years later Gwyneth, now Mrs Jeffries, met Laurie in Gloucester at a book-signing, and told him he had saved her life.)

'The summer has been the kind I have always remembered,' Laurie told the paper, 'a gold sun each morning and slow hot days.' He'd dislocated a thumb playing cricket for Sheepscombe, got blown across the room by an exploding stove, and sliced a finger with a potato knife. He wrote to Kathy in Hydra about the finger. 'Lord, how it bled. Who would have thought the old man had so much blood in him? (*Macbeth*, Act II, scene ii.) It was like a murder: blood all over the floor, the walls, and quite a bit on the ceiling.' He told her he was living on sausages and home-grown vegetables supplied by the villagers, that the local cider was very strong, there were thirty-eight pubs in Stroud, and 'some beautiful girls in Stroud paper shop'. 'I was looking last night at some coloured pictures of you. Yum yum. That is all my news. Signed in blood, Your redhanded L.' His thermometer recorded a variation of 20–30 degrees in a single day ... 'It's sexy weather, the sort of weather for my long languors in attics.' But he assured her he was quite solitary in his 'Woodside Monastery' and was not tempted too much by provocative shapes from his window.

He was covering his tracks. One August night it was 'hot & lavender hazy, and a moon past the full rose red' when Pen's eldest daughter, Antonia, now a lithe nineteen-year-old Royal Ballet student dancer with 'dusky Alexandrian face and gold earrings', came to visit him. She had loved Laurie since the age of six, and the conviction that she was in love with him had not waned. Laurie had observed her springing about 'like a sleek young cheetah' while at Bushton, and now she came 'bouncing on her heels with frank young wanting'. Laurie knew well how romantic those green valley slopes on summer nights could be. He had sent her a proof of *Cider with Rosie.* 'She came a hundred miles, carrying three bottles of wine, helpless with love...' The late summer brought continuous baking hot golden days. Sometimes Antonia would visit in the afternoons, or they arranged to meet in London. Their relationship was to continue intermittently for many years.

Julian Bream came down to stay before departing on an American tour. From the States he wrote letters full of grief about problem guitars with whistling strings, and audiences who would listen enraptured to the opening G minor chord of the 'Lachrimae Pavane', but would then repair to the bar to play 'heathenish neurotic synthetic juke boxes, blaring at full blast'. He said he would give every dollar he'd earned to be back in Los Caracoles with the gitanas, or with Laurie in the Queen's Elm. His new Mönch guitar was 'no bloody good. Sounds like rusty tin tacks being shoved around in an old baked-bean tin.' Would Laurie write a letter in Spanish to Ignacio Fleta in Barcelona 'to work the old magic & produce a real box for me'? (Laurie did get his Spanish doctor in Chelsea, Dr Martinez, to write a letter, with noble Spanish flourishes about *luz, alma y vida.*)

Late that August, Norah Smallwood wrote to say that *Cider with Rosie* was to be the Book Society choice for November. Laurie was incredulous. A fluke, surely? He'd thought his book was 'disjointed and quite old hat'. Now he began to hope he might cover his advance. He also began to realise his own appeal as a native son of rustic Gloucestershire. One August day he took a bus to Stratford-upon-Avon, to read his poems at Hall's Croft, as part of the Shakespeare Festival. The enchanted reaction of a local reporter – 'He captivated our hearts, and sent us away as though Puck himself had poured an unction on our eyes' – suggested the kind of reception he might expect in his home territory.

> Laurie Lee is a shy, slow-speaking, modest man. His voice is born and bred of the country. It breathes the scent of summer hay, the wind, the autumn moon and the soft voices of the

woodland … It is good to know that such men as Laurie Lee
still spread the gospel of the country to the world.[101]

After his reading Laurie dined with Shakespearian scholars and on the
way home stopped at Gloucester to visit Gwyneth Collier in hospital.
He took her three roses, three peaches and a goldfish in a bowl.

From his sister-in-law Nora came a letter to say that Jack wanted
to divorce her and marry another. Jack had first met Isabel Kidman
in 1956 while he was in Adelaide working on *Robbery Under Arms*
with Peter Finch. Isabel, the rich grand-daughter of the legendary Sir
Sidney Kidman 'The Cattle King of South Australia', was married
with two young children. She had opened the door to Jack and for
her, it was love at first sight. Now she had come to London. Laurie
wrote in sympathy to Nora, and in the light of his own new situation
it is interesting that he voiced such anger with Jack, and with Jack's
proposed way of dealing with a 'cliché situation'.

> Sometimes, somewhere, there's always another woman, but
> civilised people have always been able to cope with that one. It's
> not new love but a projection of the old one, and doesn't count
> a damn compared with a marriage. But here they go, asking for
> divorces, and thinking that happiness can be founded on the
> ruin of two families, as though that kind of happiness was one
> of the Rights of Man and that such a solution is somehow frank
> and honest. I wonder when we'll learn that it's the children who
> have the rights and always have had, if parenthood makes any
> sense, and that nothing counts against their claims, and how one
> can contemplate solving a temporary or personal problem at the
> cost of incalculable permanent damage to two families … strikes
> me as absolutely crazy.

It was to be another three years before Jack did leave Nora for Isabel.
Laurie was back in London, in the Queen's Elm, when he saw the
headline 'Cathleen Mann found dead in bed'. He should have dined

with her and her lover Tom Matthews the week before. Sleeping pills
were found. 'It was impossible to expect this,' he wrote to distraught
Matthews, 'with her bright voice and that active face and her aura of
life and vitality.' Matthews, writing from St Louis, rebuked himself
for sins of omission. Laurie agreed: 'We remain so little aware of a
friend's troubles, unless they actually scream for help, which they
seldom do.' In any case he would remember Cathleen as she was,
'all life & sparkle and dotty rainbow dresses dispensing cheer with
either hand.'

Laurie was with Antonia at Elm Park Gardens on a warm
September night when the nine o'clock news announced that the
Russian rocket Lunik II was nearing the moon at two miles a second
and would hit the moon in twenty-one minutes.

> I made two omelettes, and the moon was out of the window,
> buttery golden & half full, like an omelette turned over... we
> turned off the lights, sat in the window, and watched the sky
> with field glasses – the moon waiting, clear & dusty ...
>
> I counted 60 – the moon never changed – did I expect dust
> or disintegration? 'Another minute,' I said, 'to allow for speed
> of light' – the wireless was linked with a Jodrell Bank telescope,
> & we held our hands, hearing the last bleeps of the rocket as it
> raced to the moon's white skin. Behind the rocket's signals were
> the gravel sounds of space & the raw Midlands accents of Prof
> Lovell's assistants. Then the signals ended abruptly. The rocket
> had struck.

The next night Laurie met Kathy, home from Hydra, at Cromwell
Road air terminal. She was deeply bronzed and wore a pink dress
and her hair was 'quite gold, & fine gold hair on legs & arms'. They
had a quiet reunion, drinking brandy till one in the morning. His
notebook says: 'It's nice to be accompanied, but marriage is a kind
of schizophrenia. I can only concentrate when alone...' This was
true: Laurie increasingly saw himself as someone who preferred to

be solitary, but with creature comforts attended to when he wanted them. It was not long before Kathy knew about Antonia. Such was the generosity of Kathy's love for Laurie, she excused this development: she had been away on Hydra for four months after all, and said she was pleased, for Laurie's sake, that he was being looked after while she was having 'a marvellous time'. No wonder their friends spoke of Laurie's good fortune in finding Kathy. And nobody was ever to know how she felt in her heart about it.

A few days after Kathy's return, they were at the funeral of Sir Matthew Smith. Laurie had gone with Cathleen Mann the previous year to visit Smith in hospital ('v yellow, old, like Chinese poet') when he grasped their green grapes in wonder: 'Aren't they beautiful – beautiful – the shape of them – feel how heavy they are.' The mourners were 'like a scrapbook of old photographs'. 'The gaunt South American Indian cheekbones of Lady E[pstein] – and little Kitty a gypsy beside her ... He was buried at noon. There was also an eclipse of the sun.' Afterwards he saw Augustus John hobble out and stick a black-tarred boater on his head.

Two weeks later he heard that 'dear Matthew', whom he hadn't seen for a year, had left him £350 in his will, 'to Laurie Lee (poet)' plus a portrait of the glamorous and fascinating Ann Elwell.[102] When the cheque arrived the following March, Laurie bought a plot of land in Slad – near the war memorial, the site of the derelict cottage where Joseph and Hannah Brown had lived, the old couple in *Cider with Rosie* whose removal to the workhouse was one of the book's most moving episodes. It was also the cottage where he had taken Lorna on their golden afternoons. In fact, Laurie sold the plot some years later, without ever building on it – but Smith's money planted the seed of the return to Slad that was vital to the next stage of the Laurie Lee legend.

The day after the Tories won the October 1959 election, 'Election over & lost,' Laurie noted, 'we came back to Slad as the clouds gathered. Fields bare, scorched brown like India.' He brought Kathy

to Woodside Bungalow to introduce her to Slad village life. With
her, or alone, he walked for hours – from the Camp along Calfway,
down Catswood Lane, through Fletcher's Farm, along the fields to
Jones's pond, savouring everything. 'Found wild hops growing up
the lane by the Rifleman. Last blackberries. A badger flat in hedge
like a rug, run over, decayed, but with his fine head. Many paths
grown over now – rabbits & children gone. Full moon at dusk, large,
orange, hunter's.' In grey rain, with trees dripping, and rainbows of
oil on the roads, and cows still and steaming, 'the place looks as it
ought to look'.

He filled pages of notes from bar-room conversations, with
their snatches of country lore and local stories. Why trap badgers?
he asked Fred Green. 'It's for the skin an' the fat, Laurie. Worth
a lot that is, the skin. They makes shaving brushes wi' the 'airs,
the bristles, Laurie. An' they 'as this fat just unner the skin, shift
anything that will Laurie. Catch 'em in the morning, boil 'em in a
copper for the fat.'

'Once when Fred Green drunk, they tied a foal to his bike. "Drat
you, get away, stop followin' I."' In local brogue, people said 'you' for
emphasis at the end of sentences. 'He got more money than I you.'
'Then 'e made a mistake you.'

Early in November Laurie's radio play *I Call Me Adam* (his last,
as it turned out) was broadcast on the Third Programme. It was the
story of Fletcher Christian and John Adam, the *Bounty* mutineers,
setting up a new society, 'a patch of Eden' with eighteen Tahitian men
and women, on the uninhabited South Sea island of Pitcairn. 'One
or two good moments,' Laurie noted. 'C & I did our best to keep
awake.' He thought Wilfred Babbage, as Christian, 'stiff and awful,
stuffy officer type, clipped, engendering no pity'. But it was a superb
play. Like *Magellan*, it is hauntingly atmospheric to read: evoking the
heat and fertility of the tiny island, the labour of building, the gradual
souring of ideals, the growing rebellion, violence, death. Laurie had
an extraordinary ear for dramatic dialogue. Yet there is no reference
in his diaries to the research or the writing. The play was never

published and (in common with *Peasants' Priest*) it was not even
listed by Laurie among his works in *Who's Who*. It was eclipsed, like
everything else, by *Cider with Rosie*, which immediately afterwards
took over his life and made him, at forty-five, seriously famous.

This happened almost overnight. So the account he then gave
of his previous life was the one that stuck. Laurie Lee was launched
as a memoirist of a rural childhood, with 'lively blue eyes and a
Gloucestershire burr', a fellow of modest desires ('All I want from
life is £10 a week and no questions asked') but possessing a colourful
past. His legend, as issued that month in publicity handouts, was
repeated endlessly ever after: 'At twenty he ran away from home
to make his fortune, went to Spain with £2 in his pocket, because
someone had told him how to ask for a glass of water, and travelled
from Vigo to the South playing the violin ... He later went back to
fight in the Civil War – "when it wasn't yet fashionable to oppose
dictators" ... After being nearly shot as a spy, he fought for the anti-
Franco forces and broadcast from besieged Madrid' ... 'On the
Marseilles waterfront he met Cathy, the barefoot girl who danced
to his guitar and later became his wife. "I fell in love with him at the
age of nine," she confessed. "But of course we had to wait."' So the
muddled half-facts took root.

On publication day ('Same day as *Lolita*,' he noted glumly) Laurie
was in bed with a cold. His publisher Norah Smallwood had written
to booksellers saying if this book didn't sell she'd eat her hat. Laurie
noted in his diary that he had £445 in the bank, £210 in the post
office and £50 in premium bonds. From his sickbed, feeling 'woozy',
he sent a book to Wilma, 'my best and severest critic': 'I can't hope
that you will altogether approve' (but she did).

He told Tom Matthews he felt low because the early reviews were
'rather flat'. The first was Isobel Quigly's in *The Guardian* and she
inclined to the Amis view. 'Laurie Lee's prose is of the kind that has
turned "poetic" into a dirty word. Lush, strained, top-heavy, and
quite painfully unsuited to most of the functions of prose, it alternates

between half-embarrassing felicity and overblown, over-flavoured selfconsciousness.' But then came Harold Nicolson in *The Observer*, who pronounced it 'a first-rate work of art'. H. E. Bates called it 'a prose poem that flashes and works like a prism'. Margaret Lane in the *Daily Telegraph* said that although writing about childhood could be a snare, Laurie had managed to take the reader 'straight into humble hedgerow, cottage and village' without falling into the sentimental heresy that country childhood and poverty were paradise. And perhaps most influentially, the prolific J. B. Priestley, in *Reynold's News*, declared:

> I have only one complaint against Laurie Lee – he does not offer us enough of his work ... he produces so little that we are in danger of forgetting how good he is.
>
> Often he trembles on the very edge of affectation and over-writing ... But always ... he dances out of danger, and coins phrase after phrase with which to delight us.

Elizabeth Jane Howard ('I'd rather please you than anyone,' he told her) asked to interview Laurie for her television programme *The Bookman*. 'No one I like talking to better,' said Laurie. 'You make me feel easy always ... let's meet in a bar, on delicious expenses.' In the Teddington studio on a foggy day in November, they recorded the interview and he recited his poem 'Apples', but forgot the words and had to be prompted by Jane, who knew it by heart. Afterwards he sent her the poem with only the first word of each line, the rest a series of blanks: 'Love to Jane, who filled the gaps with her eyes.' Alan Ross sent a note: 'You'll be a filmstar yet, you old TV charmer.'

'One pleasure, come what may,' wrote Laurie in his notebook, 'is lying in bed with a beautiful young girl and hearing The Critics say nice things about one on the wireless.' 'Aren't these every man's dreams of paradise?' he asked his journal. 'What have I done to deserve them?'

One night, the doorbell in Elm Park Gardens rang at 2.30 a.m.

Drunk young Irishman barges upstairs. 'I wanted to see the
man who wrote the most beautiful poem of the 20th century,'
he says. 'You look like a farmer, not a poet. What are we going
to do about your appearance?' He then deliciously misquoted
'April Rise' – 'where did you get the words, the words?' Drunk,
coherent, dotty, unshaven, young. Thought we'd be stuck with
him all night. He just as suddenly left us.

Day after day came auguries of success. Foyle's Book Society
ordered 100,000 copies. Siriol Hugh-Jones gave him a rapturous
review on radio: 'This astonishing, entrancing, shining and sparkling and glittering book...' Peggy Ashcroft, visited in her dressing
room at the Royal Court, said, 'Why don't you write a play about
it, & I'll play the part of your mother?' Christopher Fry wrote a fan
letter. So did Mrs Mary Wilson, wife of Harold. It was Book of the
Year for Harold Nicolson and, in the *Sunday Times*, Dilys Powell,
despite the fact that she usually found childhood reminiscences 'a
thundering bore'. Laurie was cautious and bemused. 'It is selling
about 250 a day. I wonder for how long?' He told Wilma: 'It is a very
light & local book and I find its present success a freak of coincidence for which I thank good fortune & don't pretend to understand.'
He always attributed his success to having written his own dust-
jacket notes ('sure to become a classic') and to the printers' strike
and the lack of competition: 'At Christmas there was little else on the
shelves. It was either me, or James Pope-Hennessy's *Queen Mary*,
or bath salts.' (In fact it was a highly competitive bestseller list that
winter – including Jessica Mitford, Lady Diana Cooper, Nevil Shute,
C. P. Snow and Nabokov's *Lolita*.)

The question of how true was his picture of his childhood
village soon erupted in literal-minded local papers. Several set out
to investigate Laurie's story of the 'forty-year-old unsolved crime'
– the braggart who boasted in the pub one night of the riches he
had made in New Zealand, and was found next morning frozen
to death, having been beaten up and thrown over a wall. Annie,

back in 1945, had reminded Laurie of this story. The *Cheltenham Chronicle* found the villagers of Slad still closed in a web of silence. But some remembered what had happened 'and some even said they knew who did it'. Charlie Green, now eighty-four, remembered the victim as 'Albert Burt, a wood turner from Small's Mills at Pitchcombe. The money was his army gratuity.' The *Stroud News* declared: 'It was exactly as Laurie Lee said' and even named one of the culprits.

Anyway, who cared? In one single day, 15 December, *Cider with Rosie* sold 1,600 copies and shops ran out of supplies. Three days later, suddenly cavalier about money, Laurie took Kathy to Paris for a weekend at the Hôtel Voltaire. (After one lavishly expensive dinner they reverted to the old favourite, Le Chop Danton, opposite L'Odéon.) And on New Year's Eve Laurie took a party to the Chelsea Arts Ball: Nicolette and Esmond Devas, Norah Smallwood, Janey Ironside, Norman and Jill Hepple, Tom Matthews and his wife Martha Gellhorn. Laurie apologised to Matthews that it was so uncivilised: everyone packed in 'like potted brawn'; a cold supper distributed, of '1 polythene-wrapped baby chicken, 1 tomato, 1 roll, 1 sheet lettuce' and 'glasses ritually smashed & trodden on floor. Many scant-dressed girls.'

Cider with Rosie's brief preface – 'The book is a recollection of early boyhood, and some of the facts may be distorted by time' – was a caveat, but it did not save Laurie from a libel action. A man in a mackintosh arrived one morning at Elm Park Gardens and handed Kathy a writ from Bentleys, the Stroud Piano Company of Woodchester, which objected to the line on page 272: 'There was a fire at the piano works almost every year, it seemed to be a way of balancing the books.' Bentleys had been making pianos for fifty-four years, although Laurie had no idea of their existence.

So 1959 ended with *Cider* heading the lists of Christmas bestsellers. But Christmas at Bushton was ruined, says Laurie's notebook, by the withdrawal of books from libraries, the absence of books from London: '& the book is poisoned'.

18

Annus Mirabilis
1960

LAURIE WAS AT top table at the Foyle's 'To Greet the Sixties' lunch in January 1960, with *Cider with Rosie* top of the bestseller list, sales nudging 100,000. The new decade boded well. Publishers and magazines clamoured with contracts. Soon, a small ad in *The Times* offered 'Furnished cottage and 5 acres woodland high on remote Cotswold hill overlooking "*Cider With Rosie*" valley.' Rosie even became a *Times* Crossword clue: '28 Across: With her, cider (5).'

But there were clouds in Laurie's blue sky, and not just from the libel writ. 'I stopped walking on air and started wading through protests. A chill wind blew from the west...'[103] Writing about one's family is always a minefield, and Laurie's Aunt Alice and cousin Frances were deeply upset by his tales of Uncle Sid's fake 'suicides'. Laurie had to draft craven letters. He wrote to his aunt ('dear Auntie I could weep') saying he was 'grieved to the uttermost'. He wrote to his cousin too:

> What I wrote was written purely out of pride & affection for a remarkable man who was also my favourite uncle. Don't you realise that your father has always been a great legend in the district, admired & respected by all ... and that he was the hero of my boyhood? The last thing I wished to do was to hurt any of you. I have always loved your family. I may not have shown it, & you may not believe it, but it is true.

> Your letter has made me almost sick with unhappiness.
> I cannot bear ... to have unwittingly been the cause of your
> anger. I only hope that you will live to learn that my affection
> and loyalty has never wavered for you all, & never will. Laurie.

Jack acted as intermediary, and saw that peace was restored. But
then there was the libel writ. Laurie's instinct was to go down to
the piano factory and apologise in person. His publishers urged
him to do nothing: their solicitors would handle it. But the resulting
apology and disclaimer (describing *Cider* as 'a novel') appeared in
Hogarth's name only, not Laurie's. 'The piano works, infuriated by
what seemed a deliberate withdrawal on my part, went for me with a
personal writ demanding heavy damages.' They were asking £5,000.
'This is literary success,' noted Laurie drily.

But in other respects 1960 was an *annus mirabilis*. The writer
Margaret Lane, the Countess of Huntingdon, who had reviewed *Cider*
so warmly, held a glamorous dance at her house in Roehampton. Lady
Selina Hastings, the elder daughter of the house, wearing her first
off-the-shoulder black dress, told Laurie she loved *Cider with Rosie*.

> He was so seductive. He said 'I'm no good with all these soph-
> isticated people. I'd much rather be with you.' And spent the
> whole evening with me. I fell completely in love with him. We
> danced, and sat in the garden, and he held my hand and said,
> 'May I kiss you?' and kissed me very gently, and then asked me
> how old I was; I said fifteen, which I wasn't until March. It was
> my first kiss. He wrote to my mother afterwards, 'Selina took
> wonderfully good care of me and I have some crushed gold
> baubles in my pocket as a memento.'

(She didn't see him again for thirty-five years, when he had a book
launch at the Arts Club in Dover Street. Laurie was at the top of the
stairs, leaning on his stick, almost blind. She went up to him and said
softly, 'Laurie,' and he said at once, 'Is that Selina?')

But at the ball, all other eyes were on Kathy, dancing in her shimmering grey-green gown. Laurie's wife was in her prime at twenty-eight, a decided asset. She was declared to be among London's most beautiful women and was frequently painted and sculpted.[104] At the Dorchester for the presentation of the Foyle's Poetry Prize to Robert Graves, Laurie sat next to Dame Sybil Thorndike and wore a piratical eye-patch. On his souvenir programme he wrote to Kathy, 'I can see with only half an eye that you're the best girl in the room.' Mrs Laurie Lee was described by *The Guardian* next day as 'the Alexandrian type' of beauty.

But to a Spanish journalist, Rafael Pineda, Señora Lee was 'a woman with exquisite Saxon beauty, reminiscent of the sublime models of the painter Bainsborough [*sic*]'. Pineda interviewed Laurie for *El Nacional* about '*Un Vaso de Sidra con Rosie*' and addressed Laurie throughout in the formal Spanish style as '*Poeta*'. 'Poet, permit me to congratulate you on your extremely beautiful wife,' he began, whereupon 'Cathy, in a pose of classic serenity, vibrated delicately.'

When asked, 'Poet, what is the dominant note in modern English poetry?' Laurie replied that it was the neo-puritanism of young poets frightened of language '*genuino e incandescente*'. Amis and Wain – '*Los Jóvenes Furiosos*' (angry young men) – suffered from a British disease: fear of sentiment, resort to satire or esotericism. Asked to define linguistic puritanism, Laurie replied: 'The fear of using words whose temperature exceeds 35 degrees Fahrenheit.'

That spring, *Cider with Rosie* was launched in America as *The Edge of Day*. Laurie had not wanted the title changed, but his publishers (Morrow) assured him, 'There is no sale of cider in the States. The closest thing to your cider is applejack, and that has a rather low standing in the minds of American drinkers.' Then D. C. Jarvis's American book *Folk Medicine* came out, advocating cider-and-honey as a panacea, and *The Times* reviewed it under the headline 'Cider with Jarvis'. Laurie sent off this review to Morrow. They would not be persuaded: Jarvis's miracle remedy was 'not cider at all but cider vinegar, a very different thing'.

Anyway, the American reception was ecstatic. Even Dorothy Parker found it 'an entirely delightful experience'. 'Charm is a word that it is as well to keep away from, if possible, and so is beauty, but I think both are needed in speaking of *The Edge of Day*. This is not to say that parts of it are not exceedingly funny.' Elizabeth Janeway warned that it was almost too warm and glowing, and might provoke sceptical readers to seek out an old copy of Stella Gibbons's *Cold Comfort Farm*. Tom Matthews, whose own childhood book *Name and Address* was also out, wrote in the *New York Times*: 'Laurie Lee has done it. Blessed be his name.'

Laurie kept notes on the effects of success. No longer did people respond, when introduced to 'Laurie Lee, the poet' by asking him if he'd known Dylan Thomas. Writer friends would say: 'Ah, rich now, eh?' 'as if I got away with the slate club funds'. His family were 'kindly but cold'. He had blown the gaffe on their poverty and this must have been galling for his siblings, he conceded, who had spent thirty-five years building up relative affluence. As for the villagers, some avoided him, some bought him drinks, but everyone had a different version of the stories he'd told. His writing energy went into answering letters, more than twenty a day.

'Are you enjoying your celebrity, or does it leave you no time for your work?' wrote Wilma perceptively, from a hospital bed in Devon, having had her appendix removed. She suggested that before long he should write about 'your months with the International Brigade'. It was three decades before he took Wilma's advice. But meanwhile, the *Evening Standard* asked Laurie to reminisce about his youth, so he related, for the first time in print, a brief resume of his wanderings in Spain and his unwitting arrival at 'the heart of the '30s tragedy'.

> The Spanish civil war found me trapped in a village on the coast near Malaga. Through the dust of battle came a neat British destroyer to take off its nationals. Tattered tramp though I was, bearing no more than a fiddle, I was piped aboard to a salute of officers.

Wilma, by now living in London – within a mile of Laurie, in Redcliffe Gardens – read this tale in the *Standard* with justifiable indignation. There was no mention of her vital part in his story, or even her presence! She wrote to him denying that they were 'piped aboard' the destroyer, and questioning his version of his adventures. Laurie replied the following day:

> My dear Wilma: You do pack a wallop I must say. You are right of course, yet quite wrong. There was nothing in that article that was untrue, but there were important omissions which I had to make, including yourself. A short newspaper piece was no place to bring in everything. You must wait till I write a book about it.

The eventual book, *As I Walked Out One Midsummer Morning*, still made no mention whatever of Wilma. In the episode of his evacuation by destroyer from Almuñécar he said he was accompanied by 'an English writer', anonymous and genderless. But by the time he published that, Wilma was safely dead.

Freedom to travel, Laurie said, was what *Cider*'s success brought. Laurie and Kathy seemed to enjoy plenty of this freedom already, yet in the summer of 1960 they broke even their own travelling records. They went to Portofino again, returned to Martigues and to Andalucía, and in the autumn made their first trip to the United States. But first, at Easter, they were invited to Wolfsgarten, a sixteenth-century hunting lodge near Darmstadt on the Rhine, with peacocks and golden pheasants, and wild boar in the forests.

Celia Goodman had introduced Laurie to her friend Peg, *née* Margaret Campbell Geddes, now 'Princess Peg', wife of Prince Ludwig of Hesse.[105] The Hesses combined good works and arts patronage with lavish hospitality on a truly royal scale at their several castles. Despite a horrendous start to their marriage – an air crash had wiped out almost all Prince Ludwig's family who were en route to attend his wedding in England in 1937 – 'Lu' and Peg ('Lupeg' to friends) were a singularly joyful and devoted couple. Laurie and Kathy took the Trans-Europe Express to find a liveried chauffeur waiting at Frankfurt, at the start of a 'mad royal Easter'. The music was exquisite. The company included European royalty, 'all related to Queen Victoria & Tsarina of Russia'. Their bedroom was huge, hung with tapestries and Van Dycks. It was the first of many visits to Wolfsgarten, since 'Lupeg' were quite smitten with Mr and Mrs Lee.

Hardly had they returned from Germany when they set off for six weeks in Italy, France and Spain. The first stop was Portofino again with Tom Matthews and Martha Gellhorn. Laurie and Tom flew to Milan, writing silly quatrains en route: Kathy arrived from Lake Garda. Again porters hauled their bags up the steep climb to Il Castelletto on a hot thundery night. Matthews, disciplined as ever, worked each morning, but was sick and low-spirited. Laurie spent many wakeful nights, 'disturbed by T walking the terrace'. After dinner one night, Martha Gellhorn wanted to go dancing but 'T already rather far gone'. Matthews fell heavily on the uphill trek home by torchlight. Laurie accompanied him to a doctor in Genoa, who put him on the wagon. The Mistral came roaring in, 'a smooth metal-grey porridge of cloud'. Then it was Laurie's turn to be ill, with a fever, and disenchanted with 'characterless' Portofino: 'It's like living in A Present from Polperro – the deadness of people who have always lived only for tourists.'

Things cheered up with the arrival of Julian Bream. After Portofino's annual million-lire firework display, Bream drove Laurie and Kathy through Provence to Martigues. Then they took trains and buses to Barcelona and Albacete, hitched a lift to Jaén and eventually reached Málaga. From Málaga they took a bus up to Churriana where the writer Gerald Brenan, 'Don Geraldo', the doyen of British exiles in Spain,[106] held court 'like a mandarin, facially reminiscent of Henry Miller,' noted Laurie. 'Wife charming slow-spoken Southern American bit like Auntie K [Kathleen Epstein].' Under a broad nispero tree, *gambas al pil-pil* were served in a garden blazing with blue jacaranda and scarlet catalpa. A coterie of the 'Gargoyle

Set' from the Soho drinking club were there, including Henrietta Moraes, who had lived with Michael Wishart, modelled for Lucian Freud and was a painter herself ('no talent really but GB encourages with all conviction of old man lusting for young girl'). Everyone prattled of parties in Marbella and Torremolinos, 'all threatening to go to Rocio – ugh,' wrote Laurie. It was a foretaste of what was beginning to destroy his beloved Andalucían coast. Torremolinos was already 'like Peacehaven, based on the cheap peseta'.

They next got off the bus at Estepona and finally reached Laurie's favourite town, Algeciras, where their old waiter friend Manolo served plates of snails and *callos* (tripe), and they went with Geraldine Lawrence to a bullfight. At the kill the matador 'stared at bull as though at angry father in family crisis'. During the evening *paseo*, in the little white streets near the brothels, children sang and danced for them: 'erotic pushing of hips, perfect foot stamps, serene proud smile, arms up; what freedom, confidence these children have – slapped down only for bad manners to strangers'. They saw Francis Bacon, 'seedy and sinister', in a bar.

Laurie was not well in the fierce heat of June. 'I haven't written a word,' he wrote to Tom Matthews from Gibraltar. 'I wish I had your discipline.' Gerald Brenan sympathised: 'One doesn't write well in this country. The mind goes to pieces. One just indulges one's sadness and one's euphoria and one's bent for frivolity.'

The Stewarts of Gibraltar[107] had long urged Laurie to come to the Romería del Rocio before tourists ruined it. A new easy road had just opened. 'Original *rocieros* like us, who drove through rivers to get there and slept on the ground, feel aggrieved,' wrote John Stewart. 'What about all that lovely lolly that must be pouring in from your golden book?' wrote his wife. 'Take a handful and come. Our *coche* awaits … *Cariñosamente* Joan.'

Out to the dusty plains they drove next day, with Geraldine and the Stewarts and the Searles,[108] pitching their tents near Puerto Santa Maria, and talking under eucalyptus trees over demijohns of red wine until they realised that it was no longer sunset but sunrise. Mrs Searle (dark) and Kathy (blonde) made a striking pair, dancing Sevillanas for the crowds. But in the middle of all the excitement, possibly brought on by by the noisy clapping, clicking and stomping, Laurie had an epileptic fit. Luckily Dr Toomey of Gibraltar was on hand.

Laurie had missed the Royal Academy summer exhibition which included *Concert at the Chelsea Arts Club 1960*, by Paul Wyeth – a group portrait including a fur-hatted Laurie playing his recorder. He had also missed the BBC arts programme *Monitor* on the sculpture of Lis Frink, featuring his commentary. Her *Bird Men* (one of which Laurie had bought for £100) 'might have been bred for Edgar Allan Poe. They are no springtime choristers, they are augurs of death,' he said. 'If they sang they would spit out splinters of iron.'

By then he was back in Slad at his bungalow, playing music with old friends including Arthur Swain at Painswick, basking on Swift's Hill on midsummer day among moon daisies, purple orchids, thistle and vetch. Blackbirds and pigeons were loud in the mornings. He was filmed in his old haunts for a BBC programme: he knew exactly where wild strawberries could be found, and stood on Painswick Beacon, saying, 'This is where Charles I walked up the hill to hold his parliament in Painswick, and looked down on the Cromwellian troops in the valley.' He umpired cricket and opened the first of many village fetes, at Woodchester, where he made a speech about the lost rural world, deploring the commercialisation of everything: 'We are a starved society living in the midst of plenty; our possessions are many, our satisfactions few.' He had become, he told Tom Matthews, the valley's favourite son. 'They began to treat me with sardonic pride. I spent much of the summer weighing marrows and tasting cakes.' On his forty-sixth birthday he was presented with no fewer than three old cider horns.

This return-of-the-native act in Slad helped to create the Laurie Lee legend. As he said, 'Every branch of every tree, every curve of every field, and every twist of every hedgerow is the mythology of my life.' In retrospect he thought it took courage to go back: he had returned as 'a bag-eyed poet who had written a book about them

314 THE LIFE AND LOVES OF LAURIE LEE

all, and broken taboos' by revealing local legends. 'This upset them in the way that tribal Blacks can be upset by somebody taking their photographs. They are still wary of me. They put a finger to their lips when I come into the Woolpack and say "Careful what you say, he'll put you in a book."' Nevertheless, what they said in the pub filled enough notebooks to furnish another *Cider* volume, if he'd wanted to write one. 'Old Wally Bishop now in pub every night. His brother had just drowned in a water tank.' 'Met old Bill Tuck (84) in his green Elcombe corner. Did the stonework of Uplands church, the drywall at Bulls Cross.' The young village girls wore short stiff-petticoated bell-like frocks, 'their bare legs glimpsed in the high grass'. He struck up a close drinking companionship with Frank Mansell, who worked for the telephone company but also wrote poetry, 'as Cotswold as a dry-stone wall'.

Though Laurie was writing no new poetry now – his output to date was sixty-seven poems – he was still known as a poet who had written a book, rather than (as later) a prose writer who had formerly written poems. In June, a Pocket Poets edition of Laurie Lee was published in a Vista Books series priced at 2s 6d that included Rupert Brooke, Edward Thomas and Gerard Manley Hopkins. Laurie's fore-word said that he 'scarcely recognised' his early verses but was 'not yet prepared to disown' them. He dedicated this little book 'To Y'.

The libel case was eventually heard in the High Court on 19 July. Helenus Milmo QC declared that the piano factory fire was an imaginary episode; Laurie recognised that he had written something untrue and damaging. He was to pay 'substantial' damages of £5,000, a cost shared between himself and Hogarth. He told Wilma that the libel had 'clouded much of my pleasure in the book's reception & also I feel polluted it in some way'. The offending paragraph was 'merely a jaunty little fantasy which mentioned pianos because I like them ... I didn't even know this firm existed any more.' None of the publishers' lawyers had foreseen the danger, hence his irritation. Wilma assured him that 'Your wonderful book has NOT been polluted by that wretched libel case; nothing can tarnish its beauty nor shake its lasting value.'

The lasting value of first editions, of course, was increased by the libel. In later editions, piano factory became 'boiler factory', and the sentence 'It seemed to be a way of balancing the books' vanished altogether. Years later, when Val Hennessy showed Laurie her first edition with the libel in it, Laurie 'grabbed it from me and I almost had to fight him to get it back'.

But argument persisted over the question of using fictional stories in biography. On one side of the debate were those who felt that one untruth dented the reader's confidence in other episodes. On the other sat Laurie's defenders who said all autobiography was recollection in tranquillity, and did not need to be true 'in the sense that a legal document is true'. Laurie weighed in to say his book was simply 'an attempt to give the *feel* of my early years, of a countryside & people'. Hence the disclaimer in the preface.

'Memory can be more real than events,' he wrote in a notebook. 'Details may differ but the shape, the feeling remains. If all my friends who shared that life wrote their recollections I think not one version would agree with another.' Later still, in an essay on auto-biography, he declared that 'the only truth is what you remember'.

Another piece of Laurie mythology was developing too: of leading two separate lives, in town and country. London's social life was vital to him, and he could work best there. He began to see his Gloucestershire valley as 'like a novel in which you're present throughout the year, a kind of unfolding of a long tale … through lives, deaths, childhoods, and so on'. London, by contrast, was 'a kind of anthology, almost a bedside book of snippets of life and gossip'.

Often, when he went to London, Antonia would meet him at Paddington Station, ready to drive him to poetry readings or literary luncheons. She was happy to be at his service – once a week or fortnight. 'The strain of pleasing him was so great, it could never be relaxing: one was always trying to get it right; but you felt wonderful if you did.' And he was appreciative. He knew how lucky he was. Kathy conceded that theirs was a marriage 'against the odds', but she continued to send Laurie sentimental Victorian Valentine cards signed 'Madame Lee'. She had, after all, both an inborn Garman family attitude, like her aunts Kathleen and Mary (beautiful wife serving the needs of a genius husband), and a Mediterranean acceptance of a woman's place. Life with wandering Laurie still offered plenty of amusement.

When they sailed from Southampton on the *Mauretania* for New York in August 1960, Laurie was at first dismayed by the 'chaste silences' on a great liner, but was cheered by the Irish influx in Cork Bay: 'boys in blue serge suits, just like the boys in Stroud – violins and accordions playing & the older boys drinking and singing'. Kathy won the shipboard quiz and their first New York stops were the Empire State Building, though Laurie hated heights, and Fulton's Fish Market ('My wife's a fisherman's daughter.') American reporters found Laurie, with his violin and guitar, 'a highly unorthodox character'. *Newsweek* recounted his 'peripatetic 46 years' and mentioned his volunteering in the International Brigade. Would he go on with autobiography? Laurie replied that the Spanish Civil War had been 'done to death'.

They jetted home in time for the presentation of the W. H. Smith award, worth £1,000, more than Laurie had earned in a lifetime of poetry writing. In a televised ceremony in the Lincoln Room at the Savoy, he received the cheque from Peggy Ashcroft's elegantly gloved hands. (Afterwards, 'Cheque went round pub, kissed, creased, covered with lipstick, had to be ironed.') Laurie played up his peasant credentials, said he wasn't going to go mad and spend the money on wild women and fast cars; he would use it 'to buy freedom and confidence and time'. He thanked his publishers, 'whoever they are' (still disgruntled about the libel), and said, 'Little did I think when Rosie first led me under the hay wagon ... that she was leading me to these glorious halls, and to this illustrious company...' On stage was a cart of apples, and at the end of the evening he let off a party popper that showered streams of coloured paper over a distinguished audience that included Leonard Woolf, Yehudi Menuhin and Ian Fleming.

The judges were C. V. Wedgwood, William Plomer and Harold

Nicolson. Twenty-four years later Dame Veronica Wedgwood declared that her 'austere literary mind' had no doubts about the book's quality: it had a magical freshness, every page was written with affection, and it was 'so enormously alive; you can hear the voices'.[109]

The following day Laurie wrote in the *Evening Standard* about how success had changed his life. Few poets, save the dead, make a living today, he wrote. A writer needed free time as a painter needed canvases. He had written only two books of prose, apart from his poems. 'Without some form of patronage to buy me the time, I doubt that I could have written either.'

Laurie had reached an unimagined pinnacle of fame. At a party he met T. S. Eliot, whose attitude to publicity was the antithesis of his: *Life* magazine, he told Laurie, had made his life a misery in St Louis by following him wherever he went. *Cider with Rosie* was parodied in *Punch* ('Raindrops glittered on the whitethroat-happy hedge in shifting opalescent arabesques and the leaves were a filigree of chrysoprase against the washed Aegean-blue of the over-arching sky...') 'Laurie Lee' became an answer on *Round Britain Quiz*: 'Who was paid £1,000 to buy freedom, confidence & time?' They guessed it.

But nothing that marvellous year could compare with what happened to Laurie at the end of November. It was his habit to call at the Queen's Elm on the way home. In Sean Treacy's pub, famous for 'the best conversation in Chelsea', he could always find friends, have a game of snooker, play his fiddle or recorder, and stay after hours. 'Dropped in at Queen's. Drink till 2 a.m. That's a pub,' as he noted one night.

On 28 November 1960, while Kathy was visiting her mother in Italy, Laurie was playing his violin in a quartet at a friend's house in Old Church Street. This is how he described the evening in his notebook.

> Left at 8. Looked for Satellite Echo in frosty sky. Called at Queen's
> Elm. Sean there, James Cameron, wife & daughter. Showed me a
> write-up in *Harpers*. Fetched out fiddle. Played two quick reels. Bar
> not very full. Caught sight in mid-reel of rosy-cheek girl, watching

me, curled mouth, shy sly smile, loose dark hair, fringe. But the eyes blue & red mouth. I felt an astonishing shaft go through me. Not thinking I felt it, I knew. In a moment the girl had gone through the door. I had to follow her & called. She turned, smiling faintly. 'What's your name?' I said. 'Why?' 'Well, I'm sure I've met you before.' (Corn.) Still smiling: 'You have, once. My name's Yasmin.'

21 years old. So like Johnny Lee [Jack's son]. Working for a flower shop, lodging Notting Hill. She stood looking at me. Smiling. I still had my violin in my hand. 'Stay here. Don't go away. Promise you won't go away.' 'I promise.' I dumped the violin. Came back. She was waiting.

Off into the cold night. She chattering. Amused, quick, young, old, nervous, shy, excited. Meal at New Assam. Drink. Walking. Me shivering with pleasure. Holding arms. She talking. Mother's inflections. How she'd planned to do it. Nearly lost her nerve. Saw thing in *Harpers*. Made up her mind. Knew there was something. Had suspected for years. Asked her mother right out. 'What d'you think?' said she. Back home. So natural. Lay on the bed till 3 a.m. Me half asleep. Happy. She still chattering, chattering, filling up 20 years ...

Morning. Coffee at Lyons. Which she likes. As her mother & I did. Smiling with I swear love. Promising to see me again. Soon. The greatest occasion of my life? Simply was. But will she?...

Two days passed. He began to think he'd been a fool to let her go. She might write and say, 'I'm sorry. I was crazy. Goodbye.' He was changing to go out at 6 p.m. when she rang.

It was all right. 'Don't worry,' she said. We talked on and on. We should both have been somewhere. 'What have we been doing all these 20 years?' she said. She hadn't eaten much since Monday. Could I meet her midday Friday? It didn't matter what we did, or where we went, did it? We ought to see a lot of each other ...

'London suddenly seems to make sense,' he noted. 'At parties, not caring, smiling to self.'

Yasmin said that in her teens she had had a growing feeling, in her heart, that Wish was not her father. After Frensham Heights School she had gone to Worthing College of Art – where Laurie had watched her one day, he later confessed, coming out of college. When she bought the little Pocket Poets edition of Laurie's verse, and saw the dedication 'To Y', 'It was just too odd. I thought, this means something.'

'I really didn't think, when I went to see him, that anything would develop between us,' Yasmin told me. 'I didn't know that he would be so quick, and would recognise me at once. It was hilarious in the Indian restaurant. He just glowed. And he introduced me to poppadums.'

At home, Yasmin went for a walk with Wish, wondering how to broach the subject of Laurie, 'and he was very sweet, and broached it himself'. He said he had always thought that Yasmin should have been told when younger, but was advised that it would complicate things in an already dramatically charged family. The differences between Wish, the committed Communist, and Lorna, the Catholic convert, had been exacerbated by extreme passion on both sides. 'Their politics and religion had polarised them.' Wish had been a totally loving and accepting father to Yasmin. But she was Lorna's child. 'I wanted a poet's child, and I got one,' her mother told her.

Lorna was a bit taken aback when Yasmin found Laurie. It made her feel insecure, Yasmin suspected.

> She was quite possessive: her things were her things, and I was her daughter. She didn't show any great joy, I must admit. She was having her tonsils out at the time. But after she'd had time to process it she was pleased for me. Then it became very normal and civilised.

Laurie and Yasmin began going on outings, walking round London together. They sent Lorna a postcard of Nelson's column. 'What I loved about Laurie immediately was his capacity for enjoyment. My family were lovely but they did not have that sense of freedom that he had.' He took Yasmin to the point on Battersea Bridge where he had thrown Lorna's letters into the Thames and watched them come bobbing back on the tide. They went to Westminster Abbey, and to Brighton.

'Darling Yasmin: I loved our day by the sea,' he wrote. 'I told Cathy last night and of course she doesn't mind & was very moved by it all, and you must meet soon.' As Yasmin's cousin, Kathy knew, of course, that Laurie was Yasmin's father. Elated, Laurie confided in Pen Dugdale. All his atavistic feelings were released. That which was lost was found. He even told Yasmin about the carapace he had been enclosed in since 1944.

> I adored seeing you … Thank you dear love for your red-sealed letter & all you said in it. It is meat & drink, red wine & beef, to have these thoughts from you. I, too, have a shell, though it's not as pretty as yours, and I've been in it for years. But we don't need shells any more in fact, unless it gets stormy & then we'll share one together.
>
> I'm glad we wandered into the Abbey … the vanity of the rich dead, who want to be remembered, is rather touching, like the poor who scratch their names beneath the rich men's tombs. But most of us want it really, and I wanted it through you, and never thought I had it till now, and that's better than any old Abbey.

He sent her his childhood pictures, and one of himself playing the fiddle in the pub,

> a memento of you know what – that wonderful miraculous chancy Chelsea night which I shall treasure until I die. Sometimes, waking in the night, or in moments of panic during the day, my mind used to fill with moments of past horrors. Now it fills with that occasion, and the sheer happiness of it, the unbelievableness of it, is like salvation floating ashore in a bottle.

19

Rose Cottage
1961

'DON'T DESERT ME whatever you do,' Laurie wrote to Yasmin. 'You are the one spark in my shadowy life.' Dark feelings lurked behind Laurie's surface conviviality: disappointment, guilt, old torments of Lorna's rejection, failure to have a child with Kathy. Now he was rejuvenated: Lorna had left him, but Yasmin had come back. Her letters, cherished by Laurie, were wax-sealed with a 'Y', and Laurie said she must use red sealing-wax. 'The silver, though elegant, looks like something raked out of the Aga on a grey morning.' He sent 'oblique love to mum'.

Yasmin showered him with presents just as her mother had: 'candles & purses of gold, a bagatelle table, and a musical box'. He called her his Christmas angel. He wanted to seize the time they had left together. But he was, as usual, going away. Princess Peg had invited Laurie and Kathy back to Wolfsgarten for 'a genuine old world German Weihnachten Christmas'. With Julian Bream and his guitar they left for Dover, Laurie writing to Yasmin as they raced through Kent, 'where all the black leafless bushes stand in rows of Ys'.

On Christmas Eve there was 'a banquet of Princes (Hanover, Bismarck, Metternichs & Hesses)' but Laurie missed it, being in bed with a fever. 'Then in the middle of the night,' as he told Yasmin, 'the castle burnt down. Drunken firemen were called from their Christmas parties, and we were forced to flee into the snow carrying the princess's jewels.'

It was true. Julian Bream was sleeping in the guest wing, where he woke up to hear '*Feuer*!' (He was later held responsible 'in a most friendly way' for starting the fire with his cigarette.) A grand ball-room, with priceless furniture, books, Venetian mirrors and royal busts and portraits, was threatened. So everyone set about evacu-ating the treasures wrenching them off the walls as the rain poured down. Prince Ludwig gave Bream an overcoat that had belonged to Edward VII. Laurie, shivering with fever, made notes: 'Fabergé, present from Tsarina – flames & sparks blowing across house … Firemen drinking schnapps – Cathy extricating herself from drunken fireman's clutches.' Bream and Laurie tried to rescue a cabinet of ancient coins: Bream told Laurie to take one end, but he was so weak all the coins spilt on to the floor. Laurie said: 'Heads it's mine.'

Prince Ludwig watched the blazing roof with a wonderful insouciance and said he 'never did like those bloody windows anyway'. Princess Peg said she'd had nightmares about fire for twenty years and was almost relieved now it had happened. Everyone joked over breakfast next day about the 'housewarming'.

'I'm getting worried about Christmas,' wrote Laurie to Pen Dugdale. Three years before, at Bushton, he had dropped the flaming Christmas pudding. Two years ago the Bushton tree had caught fire. Last year, he'd had the libel threat over the Piano Works fire. 'And now the burning schloss. Next year, if I live, I shall spend the festival in a cold bath wearing an asbestos suit.'

He told Yasmin about Wolfsgarten fare: a whole side of venison, 'with chocolate cakes the size of cartwheels, & Rhine wines as delicate as summer air which even you could drink with innocence … Darling, I have thought of you every day, and dreamt about you, and sent you messages by mental pigeon post … I simply adore you.' Yasmin knew that a few years earlier, he might have found her as awkward as any father finds a teenage daughter. They had missed out the difficult stage.

Sometimes he would tell Yasmin ruefully, 'If only you'd come and look after me.' Since her cousin Kathy was already looking after him devotedly, this made Yasmin cross. He told her he no longer wanted to go away so much, now that she had found him; but in January he was off to the Caribbean to write for *Mademoiselle*. His letters to Yasmin reflect a mood akin to that of a man newly in love and wanting to share everything. He wrote to her from Port of Spain, 'with hot & cold Caribbean winds blowing & hot rum to drink'. He was surrounded by 'hot scarlet flowers, ibis, humming birds, green coconuts & tree oysters ... forests like Rousseau's, snakes, and dark faces peeping out'. Pierre, his driver, recommended fried scorpions, which tasted like shrimps. He loved the shop signs, 'Sincere Company Limited'; 'Mr Chin-a-Fat, manager'; and an Indian restaurant playing Greek bouzouki music and advertising Paella Valenciana.

For ten days he travelled through Caribbean paradises, not yet familiar to tourists – Barbados, Antigua, Martinique, Guadeloupe. He had a fever at the Blairgowrie Hotel at Montego Bay, occupying a luxurious bungalow in a tropical garden above a bay full of mangrove islands 'like salads floating on the water'. The birds made noises like sewing machines or clock springs running down. Gaunt buzzards wheeled overhead. 'The people are most elegant walkers, and the country folk with dark smokey faces remind me of Aunt Kathleen. They have long thin arms and large expressive hands.' He wrote his piece, loaded with evocative imagery, on his verandah at sundown, with a glass of rum and a penny Jamaican cigar.

Yasmin, still shy, introverted and unsocialised, was thrown in at the deep end of Laurie's London social life, as he sometimes took her to parties. He also took his niece Anthea, now fifteen, to whom he had been a good uncle ever since his brother Tony's death; she put up her hair for the farewell to John Hay Whitney, the US ambassador. Laurie's diary was full of gatherings that spring: a jeans & sweater ball; a dinner in Hamilton Terrace ('Told to be casual: everyone in dinner jackets'), and soirées where he met L. P. Hartley, Sir Herbert Read, Eugene Ionesco, Henry Green. He sat on a Brains Trust panel with Monica Dickens and John Braine. At Ronald Searle and Kaye Webb's he met Michael Redgrave ('Laurie! how are you?

We last met sixteen years ago with Beatrix Lehmann') and James Mason, who was playing Humbert Humbert in *Lolita*: 'a large, solid friendly man, collects Victorian bun pennies'. Robert Graves's entire family were at Diana Cooper's: 'Four huge pies and a bit of singing – John Julius interminable; Iris Tree with Aztec face, metal white hair in splinters over forehead; Graves sang a lot – a curious self-absorption which mars him.'

In March Laurie took Kathy and Anthea to Boulogne for a weekend at the Hôtel Bayel. (He promised to show Anthea a real French restaurant, having already taken her to the ballet, to Madame Tussaud's, and a recording of *Juke Box Jury*.) Three weeks later, he took Yasmin on a similar trip, to Calais and Boulogne. On the way back they ran into Yehudi Menuhin and his wife Diana, who approached Laurie on Calais Station. 'Clever darling,' said the maestro. 'She always recognises people.' They lunched together on the train: 'Yehudi eating raw carrots. Mild, generous, wise, yellow slanting eyes. She garrulous, talking of him as "the Fiddler".' Nigel Tangye was on board too, with two girls – which reminded Laurie of 1948, when Tangye had spotted him crossing the channel with Jennifer Gault and her friend Cynthia, who had also been visiting a lover in Paris. At Dover, the official looked at Laurie's passport, snapped it shut, returned it briskly. 'Thank you Mr Lee. And thank you for *Cider with Rosie*.'

Laurie, always fascinated by the moon and the sun, was naturally excited about Yuri Gagarin, the first man in space. So in May, when Laurie and Kathy were sailing back from America on the *Queen Mary*, Laurie was especially pleased that during the Captain's cocktail party the telephone rang. The Captain took the call, turned to his guests and announced: 'The Americans have put their man in space & got him back safely.' There were cheers all round.

Laurie found he was already a name in the United States: a school textbook on 'Advanced Composition' included an extract from *Cider* about his schooldays, with questions such as 'What were the specific deficiencies of the village school and its program? What advantages, if any, did this schooling provide for Laurie Lee?' The textbook was subtitled: 'Shakespeare, Queen Victoria, Laurie Lee, Samuel Johnson'. 'What would my old mother think?' remarked Laurie to Tom Matthews.

Home from America, Kathy took on the search for the perfect cottage in Slad, and found it: the seventeenth-century Rose Cottage, oak-beamed and built of stone. 'It is in the heart of the village,' Laurie told Tom, 'six stumbling paces from the pub, door to door.' It was just behind the Woolpack, faced west across the valley, and had the only flat garden in the village. Bus stop, telephone box, post office and church were all a few yards up the bank. But it was under offer to the manager of the Bon Marché in Gloucester. Kathy met him at Bulls Cross in the rain and pleaded tearfully with him. Four days later, he wrote to say they could have Rose Cottage, adding, 'I liked that picture of you in the *Tatler*.' The photograph, of Kathy in her glamorous black velvet gown, was taken on the *Queen Mary*, and this clearly impressed him.

Rose Cottage had been lived in by the Fern family since 1860. The previous owner was Mabel Fern, who married the postman Harry Vick. She was a lay preacher, and when she went away to end her days at the seaside, she left behind the Fern family bible, and texts such as 'The Lord Will Provide'.

'I've bought my cottage at last,' Laurie told all his friends. He felt euphoric. He planted morning glory in his London window-boxes. He held a drinks party for brother Jack. He took Yasmin to the Test Match, 'best summer day so far', and to an Apollo Society poetry reading (with Julian Bream and Peggy Ashcroft) where he was surrounded by his harem of womenfolk: Kathy, Yasmin, Antonia and Anthea. (Antonia remarked, quite unwittingly, on the resemblance between the cousins Anthea and Yasmin.) When filmed in the Queen's Elm leaning on the bar, glass in hand, for a television programme called *To Stay Alive*, he twinkled merrily: 'I'm concerned in the celebration of living. I'm not concerned about the consolation prize of the hereafter. I like this world. I haven't yet heard of a better.'

Life was good. Every weekend they were off to Doddington with the Jarvises, or Culham Court in Henley with the Behrenses, or Amersham with the Canfields: playing croquet, watching cricket, lunching with Lord and Lady Hambleden and Lady Diana Cooper. 'Large picture of London river. I thought Canaletto. Said to Lady Diana, "Is that Canaletto?" She said, "No, the Tower Bridge of course".' That summer, they had five invitations to go abroad, to stay at four villas and a schloss.

But was he writing? 'Can't be very busy,' he wrote in his diary that October, 'just seen spider's web stretched from window to pencil on desk.' When he allowed a journalist, Allen Andrews of *Harper's*, to see inside his London flat, Andrews described Laurie's workroom as 'more a temple of ritual evasion'. 'I do all sorts of things in the morning rather than write,' Laurie told him.

> I note down the temperature and the barometer reading. I count the buds and record the blooms on the geraniums. I count all the money in my pocket and examine the dates. I separate bun pennies into one pile, Jubilee Victorian into another, Edwards into another. I put all my sixpences into a beer mug and at intervals buy travellers' cheques.
>
> And then I stare at the wall on which I have fixed a chart of the daily temperatures over the past three years. It is partly a mechanism but it is, too, a confirmation of order. There, spread out on the wall, I see the year grow unsteadily to a peak from January and then come down again. A seismograph of the year. It keeps me in touch with the force of the sun and the cycle of time.

He did read 500 poems for the Cheltenham Poetry Prize, reeling from 'so much bad Eliot'. When the *TLS* in July ran poems from twenty-one living poets (Larkin, MacNeice, Ted Hughes etc.) Laurie submitted one poem, 'Bird in a Square', and an editorial singled it out as 'the least gimmicky and pretentious'. He made a record of his poetry with Christopher Logue on the flipside (and wrote a verse addressed 'To the Man on the Other Side'): the reviews unanimously praised Laurie's warm voice and beautiful poems, while poor Logue's work had 'a crosspatch whimsicality, effectively emphasised by his rather needling tones'.

To Elizabeth Jane Howard's question in *Queen* magazine, what did he expect to achieve in the sixties? Laurie said he 'would be content with one book and four or five poems'. His royalties enabled him to turn down work he didn't want to do. He didn't want a car and he always kept his fiddle 'hanging on the wall like a sword of Zorro, knowing that I can take it out, go out into the street and earn myself a slice of bread'. His next book – 'half noise, half silence, half light, half darkness' – would take him another seven years.

That summer of 1961, Laurie and Kathy joined the Behrenses at St Jean Cap Ferrat, the Hepples at Lake Garda, and Peggy Ashcroft and Jeremy Hutchinson at the Villa Abati, Malcesine. They were driven by the Hesses' chauffeur through the Tyrolean passes to the fantastic ninth-century Schloss Tarasp Graubundenwild, built by the Hapsburgs on top of a rock in romantic mountain country. Laurie wrote to tell Yasmin all about it.

> We eat in the armoury, where the stairs are cut out of the walls
> & my bedroom hangs over the cliff & if I throw a cigarette out
> of the window it falls 2,000 feet. The head of the bed where my
> pillow is has only a board between me & oblivion ... there is an
> eagle's nest clearly visible across the valley.

From Tarasp they were chauffeured to St Moritz and took buses and trains to Lake Maggiore, to stay with the Harrises at the Villa Capanna. They got back 'brown as Bisto' and on 13 September they moved in to Rose Cottage, with nine bags, guitar and violin. Laurie bought a new notebook. 'Heavy dank smell of mothballs, matting rotting on floor,' he wrote on day one, 'but place full of domestic treasures.' They went through cupboards and drawers, finding linen and lace, nine bibles, and a cross-stitch sampler embroidered with the words 'God First'.

(Kathy embroidered another sampler for Laurie saying 'Me Next'.) His study overlooked Swift's Hill and Fletcher's farm where he went hay-making as a boy. Laurie felt he had 'dropped anchor' at last.

Of his first night in the old lady's black iron bedstead with brass knobs and heavy flock mattress, Laurie noted: 'Roll into hollow, sleep well.' From his bed he could watch the moon going down into the trees. The front of the cottage had small mullioned windows and one ancient climber that had 'withered to a cat-like claw'. The walled garden was virgin territory, profuse and disordered, a wilderness of weeds: 'self-seeded spinach like elephant grass, onions tall as street lamps, monstrous cabbages apparently shot through with shrapnel, all knotted into a Bolivian hell' but the unpruned roses were blooming. He bought billhook, pruning knife, gloves, whetstone, oil, rust-remover, paintstripper, woodworm-killer. 'Built bonfires, burnt canes, weeds, old lady's bonnets, gaiters, rags, old lino and mats. Neighbours brought broad beans, carrots etc. and peered over wall: "Doin' a bit of diggin' then?"' Kathy did more than her share of the digging. They dug the whole thing over except for a box hedge. Up came 'bushels of broken clay pipes, china dolls' legs, teapots, knucklebones, coins and cutlery, pots and pans, silver shoebuckles'. They had no running water, no telephone, no gas.

They planted clambering Albertine roses, white clematis, honey-suckle and wisteria, trailing willow, white lilac, cherry and peach trees against the wall, sunflowers and hollyhocks – ritually pouring wine over the roots with each planting. They raised the borders and terraced them with dry stone walls, and screened the rhubarb patch with a larch trellis of Sander's White roses. Laurie was photographed, pipe in mouth, drawing water from his spring which old Mr Tuck, the stonemason from Elcombe, said had never dried up in the last hundred years.

In the Woolpack for a Saturday night singsong, Charlie Foxwell from Painswick brought them 'a boiling of black kidneys'. 'Black kidneys are local potatoes, dark purple skin, rare and sacred, grown from handed-down seed, kept for special eating Christmas Day & Boxing Day. No seed sold. I remember them as a child.'

Outside Stroud Town Hall there was now a push-button map with a single arrow pointing out of town 'To Slad Valley'. 'No other villages shown.' They put his picture up in the pub. Soon he was noting the arrival of the first tourists with books to sign. Laurie was gazing down the slope to Annie's old cottage one day when Mr Nipper, the Slad odd-job man, sidled up. 'I could a bought that place for £600 a few years back. If I'd known you were going to cover yourself with glory I'd a bought it & put in a tea-garden.' He had opened a floodgate of reminiscence in the village and wherever he went people stopped him. Harry Bartlett cornered him in the Star and told him about the eight mills there had once been in the Slad Valley. He was given an old leaflet from 1883 advertising 'auction of 4 Slad cottages'. One was the cottage of George Brown, known as 'Topper', which went for £30 then. This was the derelict site bought by Laurie with the Matthew Smith money. The fourth was Rose Cottage. 'Says "pleasant dwelling house with good walled garden, brewhouse & piggery (opposite school)". Harry B says brewhouse meant wash-house with copper. "Brewhuss we still calls 'em."' Someone else told him that labourers used to wear yarks (yorks) tied round legs, to keep trousers from rubbing against knees. 'Labourers in yarks,' wrote Laurie, 'leaning on their farks.'

Laurie was truly happy to be home, enjoying 'fine warm still days of absolute peace'. He watched the full harvest moon rise over Swift's Hill at 8.50 p.m. on 28 September. He went to see Painswick Clipping on a brilliant clear day, when village children circled the church, hand in hand, singing a medieval hymn. 'Little girls with chaplets of flowers in their hair, some carrying baskets embroidered with flowers. Moving ceremony, older than Christian. Bishop of Gloucester gives address, children file through church & are each given a bun. I add a sixpence to each.'

He finished levelling the ground for his lawn and scattered 6lb of grass seed. 'The following dawn,' he reported to Yasmin, 'the birds were all out there tucking in.' He rigged up a washing line, zigzagging across the lawn with table napkins attached, with the line through his bedroom window so he could pull on it and frighten the birds without leaving his bed. By 12 October the grass was two inches high.

Peggy Ashcroft, who was in Zeffirelli's *Othello* and rehearsing *The Cherry Orchard*, motored over from Stratford. Wilma wrote to say that her autobiography, doomed from the outset by its title *Reluctant Feet*, to which she had devoted 'the best of my brain & most of my health', had been turned down by a literary agent. Laurie soothed her and said if she sent it to Chatto or André Deutsch he would write a letter to accompany it.

He and Kathy went up to London when invited to dine with Princess Alexandra at John Julius Norwich's. The Princess ('plumpish, rather shy, beautiful hazy eyes') sat by Laurie and told him she was

> hungry for the natural life, for spaces like Islay, genuinely disliking London. Said she'd really like to marry a farmer & keep chickens ... Talked of Julian Bream & his wonderful face. Asked about Spain. Said in 5 years, when she was free of her duties (Princess Anne then taking over), could we all go to Spain together, over the old tracks. (Had read both my books & knew of my 'dying' in Granada.)

Because he was up in London again for the W. H. Smith award to Nadine Gordimer, he managed to miss Yasmin when she called at Slad twice, on an urgent mission. She had come to tell him she had fallen in love with a handsome young psychologist called Julian David. Laurie was quite taken aback. 'Darling, I'm terribly pleased at what you tell me, yes I'm sure I am,' he wrote, unconvincingly. He added:

> I knew that when it happened, you would be taken completely by it, & that you would be shaken to your marrow. I don't care who he is if you can feel this for him, and I pray that it will prove to be true ... I'm jealous, but I want you to be in love & I don't really think I shall lose you.

Two weeks later she told him they were getting married. Laurie wrote a careful letter, saying what 'utter contentment' he felt.

> What a year it has been for you, November to November; two new men in your life ... but then what a year it's been for all of us ... I'm proud & glad. I thought I'd be jealous, even physically jealous, and I'm that too, I'm glad to say. But at least it shows who I love.

In November Kathy went to Italy to see her mother, and Laurie resumed his metropolitan winter life where, at a Foyle's literary luncheon for Bertrand Russell, among a leftish *galère* including Lord Attlee and Michael Foot, he was 'the tweedy poet' (*Londoner's Diary*). Yasmin stayed at his flat, buying things for her December wedding. He took part in a BBC *Perspectives* programme on solitude. Chad Varah, founder of the Samaritans, spoke on loneliness; Laurie spoke of his yearning for solitude – 'the right atmosphere for work'. In fact, Laurie had plenty of solitude, but was not writing, and not at ease about his life. The ecstasy brought on by the reunion with Yasmin had been short-lived. He was having 'terrible nightmares (no, not so terrible, but nightmares)' involving strange men, floating shadows; a man 'making up to Cathy & I seize beer bottle to strike him. Sees the expression on my face & runs in panic. He doesn't know I haven't strength to lift the bottle let alone hit him.'

On the way to their honeymoon, the newlyweds Yasmin and Julian called at Slad, bringing champagne. And on 17 December 1961, with Kathy away and Yasmin gone, Laurie met Antonia in Paris for a weekend. They went to the Grand Guignol, returning at midnight to the Hôtel Cardinale to find a police barrier across the Rue L'Echaude, and the fire brigade in attendance. A plastic bomb had exploded in the club opposite, blowing in the front door and windows of their hotel. They had missed it by half an hour. And Antonia had of course not told her mother where she was. It was a narrow squeak. The year of 1961, having started with a fire, had ended with a bomb.

20

Laurie the Magician
1962–1963

CIDER WITH ROSIE elevated Laurie Lee to household-name status, but relegated him within his peer-group from poet to best-selling author. 'I sold too much, and I wasn't asked to their literary parties any more … It changed the orbit of my friendships. You don't sell five million unless you're suspect as a writer, I'm afraid. I should have been more inscrutable, dear boy. I couldn't be inscrutable.'[110]

Not so long before, in *Faber Modern Poets* in 1960, Laurie had been alongside Eliot, Graves and Dylan Thomas in the fraternity of Forties poets. Now, he might be seated with Spender at a luncheon, but he felt he was at a remove. When he went with Elizabeth Jane Howard to a Mansion House banquet in June 1962, he found himself the only one in a dinner jacket among 'other white-tied plump decorated poets C Day L, Spender, Auden. I suddenly ashamed,' he confided to his diary.

In the new year of 1962, Kathy was called back to Italy where her dear old stepfather Sarfi was dying at eighty-four. She was away for two months. Laurie was sorry for himself: he had bronchitis. A Fortnum's hamper of delicacies arrived from Princess Peg: 'Chicken breasts & Pâté; tinned Wild Boar & Pheasant – a regular Hesse of Pottage.'

He noted privately: 'Chaos in my workroom. Floor stained with tobacco. Knocked oil-stove over. Floor covered in paraffin. Like living in army tank. Electric fire spits, dead bar comes on, glows red, spits & goes out again. Work with dressing gown over cold thighs.' But 'girl comes every afternoon, preparing tasty teas'.

He asked himself why he was so fortunate. He had been driven to

Stroud Station by his next-door neighbour ('quiet devoted woman')
with a packed luncheon of chicken, ham, peach, pear, grapes.

> Arrived Paddington to be met by beautiful girl [Antonia] who
> gives me a glass of Guinness & drives me home. Also out in
> evening with handsome woman [Elizabeth Jane Howard]
> & return to find girl, cool as a stick of chicory, curled in bed,
> waiting. And I nearly 50. Shall I one day think of this luxury
> with tears of age & longing? Yes.

From her honeymoon at her brother Michael's house in the south
of France, Yasmin wrote to her father and Laurie sent love to the
couple, 'but as far as Julian is concerned, mixed with the right
amount of jealousy'. The following month he wrote to Yasmin on
her twenty-third birthday. 'Twenty-three years since I heard your
first cry on the telephone. (The same age as I was when I met your
mother.)'

He had been reading some old dreams he had had about Yasmin,
in a 1952 diary. 'Haunting they are, but very final – as though you
were the ghost of some departed. They were very sad, but it's a
pleasure to read them now.' In one of the dreams, in his 1952 Dreams
notebook, he is sitting

> with the golden child … 'When shall I see you again,' she said
> earnestly. 'Or does seeing me make you unhappy?' I held her
> hand. I was too full of emotion to speak. But what I was saying
> inside me was 'No, there is nothing in the world more than to
> see you. And nothing that gives me greater joy.'

In another dream,

> the young daughter is kicked by a horse and dies. Terrible inex-
> orable remorse, now there is no one. To the mother, despair,
> then wild hope: she cannot just die & disappear like this. There

must be something else left of her, in the garden? Yes says the
mother. At the bottom of the garden I see two young bushes
growing: they are her.

He was still feverish in March – Dr Martinez puffed up the stairs, played
Laurie's guitar and prescribed penicillin and lime juice – when Kathy
came home with 'barmaid-bright blonde hair', and they returned to
Slad for the summer: seven degrees of frost. Frank Entwisle came
down from the *Evening Standard*, for a series on 'Heartwarmers' and
described Laurie as 'a well-fed Michael Foot' (annotated by Laurie:
'Just a well-fed Michael Foot-warmer'). Over dinner, Entwisle told
Laurie that he thought *Cider with Rosie* would still be read 100
years hence. They talked of the Spanish Civil War, and Laurie was
almost honest about his homecoming: 'He fought in the International
Brigade,' wrote Entwisle, 'but was shipped out after a bout of the
recurrent pneumonia that has trailed him from his Cotswold childhood.' Pneumonia was a socially acceptable cover for epilepsy.

Every few weeks he was performing in one of the highly successful
evenings of poetry and jazz organised by the young poet/publisher
Jeremy Robson. The first was held at Hampstead Town Hall, where
hundreds were turned away, and was followed by a packed concert
at the Royal Festival Hall, where Laurie made his debut. Many then
followed in town halls, festivals, theatres, schools and student unions,
in places as far flung as Cardiff, Coventry, Exeter, Cheltenham and
– on the night Kennedy was assassinated – in Aberystwyth. Poetry
readings, until then regarded as snoringly boring, became the height
of early 1960s cool, drawing large audiences. *The Times* ran a leader
on the resurgence of the spoken word via these poetry readings, San
Francisco style. The core team for the Poetry and Jazz in Concert
events was Laurie, Dannie Abse, Vernon Scannell, Christopher
Logue, Adrian Mitchell and Robson himself. Stevie Smith and Ted
Hughes also participated and – occasionally, drawing the crowds –
Spike Milligan the clown-poet: 'Jumpy, light, funny,' noted Laurie,
'yet offstage green-eyed & deadly serious.' Spike won over every

audience: 'I was going to begin by reading one of Shakespeare's sonnets,' he would say, 'but then I thought, why should I? He never reads any of mine.' He used an epitaph which he would rewrite to suit any locality:

Here lies the grave of Mary Charlotte
Who was born a virgin and died a harlot.
She remained a virgin till her 17th year
A remarkable thing in Gloucestershire.

Discarding pages like confetti, Spike would end with a sad poem he had written during the war: 'Young are our dead, like babies they lie...' Logue and Mitchell, in jeans, injected tough contemporary realities. 'This is Hanratty week,' Logue began, in the week James Hanratty was hanged. Then Laurie 'in an elderly brown suit with bandy trousers' came on with his pastoral brogue, his unassuming manner. 'I'm a bit drunk,' he told the cheering undergraduates packed into Oxford Town Hall. 'I got on the wrong train and arrived too early. I've been sitting in the public library drinking gin out of an inkwell.' Everywhere, queues formed. Laurie would tell the same stories. One was about a small boy coming up to him and asking him if he was Mr Lee. '"Did you write 'Apples?'"' "Yes." (Pause.) "My teacher made me learn it." (Longer pause.) We spent a moment of scowling intimacy together.' Then Laurie would say, 'I don't think I'll read "Apples",' and would tear up a sheet of paper, scattering it on the stage. 'I'll read instead a poem called "Day of These Days".' And he would tell how he wrote that on the top of a London bus.

Audiences were charmed by Laurie, as much for his engaging personality as for the poems themselves. At the end he brandished his 48-page *Pocket Poets* volume: 'My life's work,' he would say. 'You can have it for two-and-six.' Spike Milligan found Laurie 'the most open-hearted man I knew'. 'Laurie was always fun to be with,' Dannie Abse recalled, 'though on one occasion while on tour he somehow secretly deposited some girl's navy knickers in my luggage – almost causing me trouble when I returned home to my wife.'[111]

Vernon Scannell and Jeremy Robson once appeared with Laurie on Harlech Television in Bristol. They were met by a young producer whose first words were, 'Let's go along to wardrobe straight away.' 'Wardrobe?' Laurie said. The young man replied, 'Well, let's face it, you don't *look* like poets, do you?' 'What have you in mind? Bardic robes?' asked Scannell. The young man said he thought leather jackets and jeans. 'Laurie, who was wearing a baggy tweed suit and, with his long undisciplined hair, looked decidedly poetic but in a style of a bygone time, said firmly, "I've looked like a yard and a half of old knitting for many years now, and I've no intention of changing."' They went on as they were.

Country life was his refuge. 'I'm a minute landowner now in my old Glos village,' he told Val ffrench Blake proudly. Nine bean rows could he build there. He rolled the new lawn each night with a beer barrel and fought back the rioting rhubarb. The garden was his 'pillared temple'. It had 'a kind of beauty that is sometimes difficult to share – like showing the neighbours one's holiday snaps'. The real pleasure of gardening was a solitary one: 'going out before breakfast to examine each plant for minute advances; the flattery of bees visiting one's sown flower; the bird nesting in one's planted tree; and the hours bent down, working over the garden's face, close up'. A mistle-thrush had nested in a roof gutter; she sat anxiously while builders began noisily replacing the gutter. But they lifted the old section with nest, and put it carefully back again. 'Country people do this,' noted Laurie. 'Bill Washburn, farmer, hasn't been able to use his tractor for a week: bird nesting in axle.'

A cottage garden needs seven years, he knew, but already that summer Rose Cottage was 'half-embowered in tangled creepers', wisteria and passion-flower. Snowdrops, violets, crocuses and tulips were followed by rampant colonies of pansies, petunias, violas, snapdragons, sweet williams. Nasturtiums erupted in every crevice. He preferred 'vigorous and native anarchy' to setting things in rows at graduated heights, and he wanted no hot-house exotics.

> Such a simple obsession may be the refuge of one's years, the desire to keep a finger in time, to play a minor god, or even to come to terms with death. I only know that small as my garden is I again have a living root, that even for me something can come to perfection; that I still have a place on earth.[112]

He had a formula letter for friends. 'Ours is a rumplestiltskin cottage with roses like crumpled Kleenex.' He would describe himself as 'very deep in my valley, lost in a pleasant green-seeded haze'. 'Whatever the weather turns out to be, there always seems to be a kind of amnesty in the morning when the sunlight is so radiant on the fields you feel you could eat them.' When Elizabeth Jane Howard came she thought Laurie looked fifteen years younger, so the life clearly suited him. When Nicolette Devas came over with the sculptor Lynn Chadwick, Laurie killed an adder with a stone. 'An hour later we saw him, head crushed, tail still waving.' In June he took Alan Ross, cricket correspondent of *The Observer* as well as editor of the *London Magazine*, to a match at Sheepscombe, the steepest cricket pitch in the land, where the bowler has to run uphill and is invisible to the batsman until he crests the rise.

He had bought an old hand-carved stone urn, on Pen Dugdale's advice, for £5. Filled with geraniums it was 'a Lucifer of the morning, catching the early sun'. Pen invited him to open her summer fete at Bushton, and he did it beautifully. Pen had not yet found out about Laurie's affair with her daughter; when she did, she felt bitterly betrayed and refused to see Laurie for many years, even though Kathy herself wrote to Pen telling her nobody was being hurt, and she and Antonia would remain good friends. Kathy said no one had the right to own someone entirely. 'I'm lucky,' she wrote, 'that I have so much love in me I find it easy to forgive, and as a result we have all had moments of sunshine and mutual concern one for the other.'

Whenever Laurie succumbed to another fever, a microphone in the trees relayed birdsong to his sickbed. Summer brought 'hot gingerbread days; hay-making on hills opposite: Fletcher's, Webb's, Teakle's, leaving hay standing in gaunt megalithic blocks instead of the voluptuous breasted haycock ... Oh the golden fields. Aztec pheasants walking royally & unafraid thro' stubble near Whiteway.'

While the builders were in, he took a room during the day over a pub in Stroud, with 'a view of the brewery and a nice whiff of hops', let to him on the understanding that he drink two bottles of beer a day ('I'm well ahead with my rent,' he told Val ffrench Blake). Every day he caught the nine o'clock bus into Stroud, and the 4.30 bus back up the valley 'to tea & garden sunshine'. In the Woolpack (which had a new sign, described by Laurie as 'a brown depressed carthorse carrying what looks like bulging armchair cushions'), Laurie steeped himself in bucolic life, his ear ever cocked for the local patterns of speech. Each snatch of dialogue told a story, funny or sad.

Frank Green came in. Paddy said: 'Did you hear your father had passed on Frank?' 'No. No bugger told I.' He picked up drink. 'Well – cheers.' But he looked thoughtful for a bit. 'Marvellous old man though,' we said. '85, 86, still gardening, to the end.' 'Well, he never did a bloody stroke for I.'

Ernie Cook ranting on about giving up drink: 'I'm giving up the bloody stuff you. Ain't touchin' it no more. It drives I round the bend. No good to yer 'ealth or yer pocket. I've got to the bottom of this drinkin' racket. All these bloody brewers make millions but they ain't goin' to make any more out of I.'

Met Ernie Vick in the lane. Was postman for 20 years. Got to know nature by getting up at four in the morning, having the world to himself. Used to sit on wall listening to nightingale before dawn on way to work ... They buried Charlie Green this morning. Said to be the best poacher in Gloucestershire. Sat with dog in Star every night ... Long talk with Norman Vick who showed me photo of Slad cricket team 1925. Sunny faced boys, some only 15 or 16. Memory enlarges the men remembered, hence myths of giants ... Lewis Eyers in his gaiters and cap: last of the true Slad line. His kind never seen again.

Wally Bishop ('"ere, I want to tell 'e summat') found dead this morning in his Elcombe kitchen, his head in a bucket of water. Two years ago remembered his gaiety in the Star, enjoying late release (nearly seventy) from farming. Brother found drowned in water trough on farm. Wally sold everything, went on merry spree ... Became quiet and sad. Was seen yesterday walking past Woolpack, head down, with dog.

That summer, Elizabeth Jane Howard was artistic director of the Cheltenham Festival. She flung her energy into it (being paid £300 for eight months' work), inviting Kingsley Amis to discuss 'Sex and censorship in literature' with Carson McCullers, Romain Gary and Joseph Heller. She put Laurie on a panel to discuss autobiography.[113] The panel argued about how truthful an autobiographer could be. Not very, said Elspeth Huxley: most people cheated wildly, they had to protect the living, and memory was never reliable. Laurie thought the discussion pointless. He had written *Cider with Rosie* because his publishers had given him a sum of money and told him to get on with it.

The Festival ended with an auction (Laurie sold the manuscript of 'April Rise' for £8, 'Apples' for £9; Day-Lewis sold one of his detective novels for £80) and a cabaret. Laurie sat on the edge of the stage, played his guitar and sang Spanish songs and was 'entrancing', said Judy Campbell, who performed 'A Nightingale Sang in Berkeley Square', the song written for her in 1940. As a finale Jane had spent £100 on fireworks: some members of the Committee harrumphed that they had 'had enough of that sort of thing in 1940, *personally*,' but Laurie thought it was one of the best displays he had seen, in an exquisite setting, lighting up the great park trees. 'There hasn't been a more imaginative lit fest ever,' he said. 'You are a bit of a treasure in my life.' One day in London, Laurie told Jane, he had noticed a girl in the street, 'a baked-bread girl I thought I'd love to know, and looked harder and it was Nicola' – Jane's daughter, aged eighteen, who had begun to resemble her mother. Jane had something to tell Laurie: 'I think I've got to change my life rather a lot.' She was about to bolt again, leaving her second husband Jim, and eloping to Spain with Kingsley Amis.

That summer, Kathy had gone to Lake Garda for two months as her widowed mother, almost blind, needed a companion to read to her, and someone to help young Walter with his school work. Aunt Kathleen Epstein was there too, and the orphaned little Roland Joffé. Kathy wrote to Laurie: 'Six o'clock in the morning, bells are ringing across the wind. I'm just longing to have you safe and sound again in our gentle cottage. Always your adoring Mrs Lee.'

But while she was away, Laurie would find the London flat 'lightly touched by willing hand' – Antonia's. He also went to Nice for two weeks at Cap Ferrat, and was driven from there to Andalucia, where in September he met Monica Sims to make a film for her BBC television series *Let's Imagine*, which took writers back to their favourite places. Laurie was to retrace his 1935 steps, to the strains of a plangent guitar. 'I walked knee-deep in the heat,' he recalled, in his commentary, 'alone in that space of dusty skies and horizons…' They filmed in Vejer de la Frontera, a village he'd once walked through, hungry and blistered, on the way to Cádiz. They filmed Moorish villages, the white bulls of the savannah, the donkeys and muleteers and swineherds and *vaqueros*. They filmed in Tarifa where Atlantic and Mediterranean meet, and in the market, the quayside and the narrow streets of Algeciras.

Monica found Laurie a delightful working companion: patient, generous and inspiring, especially to small children, whose faces would light up when he talked to them. Their cameramen, known as Don Quixote and Sancho Panza, were unaccustomed to random outside broadcasts and to Spanish heat, and they expected hot three-course meals every day. 'Laurie managed to rustle up plates of sardines on dusty roads, and knew exactly where to get the best sherry in Jerez. The whole expedition ran on brandy and sherry, starting at breakfast.'

When they flew home Kathy met them at Gloucester Road. In Slad, they found the neglected garden choked with weeds, the cottage damp, the village at its wettest, the house shaken by gales. Laurie's friend Frank Mansell had been arrested on his birthday for driving when drunk. A local spinster, 'Miss Godsell's companion', had drowned herself in the Avon.

Kathy's warm exuberance, despite Laurie's independent life, was remarkable. She wrote to Tom Matthews full of girlish enthusiasm for his new book of poems. 'You wouldn't believe it but I'm quite a good judge.' She told Celia Goodman that Laurie's life was too hectic, with the Cheltenham festival and BBC television work, for them to get away; and 'he keeps rushing back and forth to London'. (Once, he was spotted by a neighbour: 'Col Brooking turned head surprised to see girl run into my arms on Paddington Station.' Antonia again.)

Kathy, now aged thirty-one, spent a lot of time that year, as Laurie records, 'just gazing at the ground or out across the valley. Someone who felt locked out: a wistful fugitive wondering where and to whom she most truly belonged.'[114] But when visited by journalists, Laurie and Kathy presented an idyllic image in Rose Cottage. 'Down the slope, beyond a grey stone pub, I saw a little cottage,' a typical interview that year began. 'The hillside opened out behind me ... The tiny windows were shiny, dark and secret ... But from the interior of the cottage I now heard the sound of a violin playing...'

Inside, Laurie was in corduroys, khaki army surplus shirt and baggy tweed coat. 'His light blue eyes in his bronzed gentle face looked out at me ... While Laurie works at his poetry, Kathy makes wine from nettles and elderseed and other country recipes...'[115]

It was a pretty, rustic picture. Kathy did indeed make wine: elderflower, beetroot, carrot and damson. Laurie was writing not poetry but one of his best-known essays – on 'Autobiography' – commissioned by the *New York Times Book Review*, in which he said, 'The urge to write may also be the fear of death – particularly with autobiography – the need to leave messages for those who come after, saying, "I was here; I saw it too."' He was also bedridden in October

1962, 'waiting for inflammable flash-up of world' as President Kennedy declared his blockade of Cuba.

A visit to Celia Goodman at The Cedars was restorative for both. Celia's music room, in the Queen Anne part of her house, over-looking the garden, made the music they played sound 'richer and shinier. In London it sounds damp & displeased.' Kathy sang and helped with the children and enjoyed 'coming out of the quietness and silence of one's own company,' Kathy wrote.

After New Year's Eve at the opera (Sam Wanamaker's production of *La Forza del Destino*), Laurie felt 'cold and low'. The long hard winter of 1963 brought the worst blizzards since 1881. Sheep were buried in snowdrifts, easy prey for foxes. Kathy departed for Italy in a winter gale. Laurie took to his bed with 'flu, and thoughts of death. Not long before, the irrepressible Geraldine Lawrence had died of cancer. Laurie had visited her a few days before her death. 'She was a shrunken corpse, skin of dried pink paper, but she had ordered champagne for us. She said "Do you know I feel better today?" It was goodbye.'

He was in bed with a fever, alone for 36 hours until Jack visited, and Antonia came to take over. It was Bunny Keene's funeral that day. His old friend, with whom he had been to Cyprus and India, had died of a coronary.

> Kind old Bunny, ex-Marlborough, gentle, talented, frightened, handsome: His wife Jane, beautiful, sad, in her late 30s died 2 months ago. I feel bad about being so unfriendly the last years. Should have gone to his funeral Chiswick today, but for this fever. This is how we'll all go. A pause between mouthfuls.

Norah Smallwood of the Hogarth Press tentatively asked whether he might tell them how 'Opus II' was coming along. It was not coming along at all. But despite the snow, he turned out to Poetry and Jazz evenings in freezing theatres. Then he escaped to the sun, to Mexico for *Mademoiselle*, producing a prototypical but vivid 'Mexico, land of contrasts' essay – 'sky-scrapers of glass and mudbaked hovels, colonial churches and Hilton hotels, Parisian boulevards and open-drain back streets, blond Americans and obsidian Aztecs'. His Edwardian hotel had brass cuspidors, potted palm-trees and bell-boys. He had been warned to watch out for altitude sickness and beware the spiced food, but he had never felt better. 'I walked on my toes, the altitude cleared my head, food was various and delicious, and after three quick tequilas I felt I possessed the secrets of the world…' He recovered his old knack of finding quirky behaviour ('a man in a doorway eating fried eggs from his hat') and was excited by Diego Rivera's *History of Mexico* murals on the palace of Cortés. A driver took him on a 600-mile round trip through Guadalajara, to the temple of Tula, the holy city of the Toltecs; and to Queretaro where he watched a boy digging opals out of lumps of quartz and throwing them into a bucket of water where they sprang alive like instant fire. In the market a group of Indians 'appeared to be eating the heads of wolves'. He was enraptured by the colonial architecture, its colour and grace and Gothic detail; and by young men in tasselled hats, donkeys in embroidered harnesses; girls with waist-long hair in red skirts and black stockings.

At noon one day he came upon San Juan de los Lagos, where 60,000 pilgrims assembled for the feast of the Virgin:

> like a mass gathering of Biblical tribes. A thousand white tents, flapping in the hot, dry wind, covered the hillside round the little town, filling the woods and canyons. A roar of life rose above the encampments, a mixture of music, laughter and cries; smoke from a thousand fires filled the sunny air; magnificent horsemen rode among the tent poles … I sat in the square and hired a wandering orchestra to play for me. For about 3s 6d I got a heart-rending song accompanied by four fiddles, three guitars and a trumpet.

Back from Mexico he spent twelve manic days at his desk, writing the article from 10 a.m. to 11.30 p.m. 'Y pregnant,' his diary noted, 'but fearing she might lose it. She lost one last autumn.' Innately superstitious, and inspired by the possibility that he might be a grandfather before he and Kathy produced their own child, he had brought back a corn-doll fertility aid from Mexico.

'On the first night of my return,' he wrote in *Two Women*, 'when Cathy was asleep, I slipped a box of Mexican corn-dolls under her bed. I reckoned we needed the help of any gods we could gather.'

While away, Laurie had missed the drama of brother Jack finally leaving his wife Nora for Isabel Kidman. The last film Jack had made in Britain was *Circle of Deception* (1960), since when his career had been in the doldrums. A newspaper had referred to him, at forty-eight, as 'the veteran film director' and he felt it was time to go. He left Nora at their house in Chalfont St Giles. 'I deserted her and my sons in the middle of the night,' he said, 'and drove to London through snowdrifts.' So Jack went to make a new life in Australia. When Laurie got home, he received Nora's letter ('One turned to Laurie,' she told me, 'feeling that he was wise, and that he knew the human heart'). He told her he was 'entirely behind you and the boys' and that 'you will always have my love'.

That February Laurie was interviewed in the Queen's Elm by Sally Vincent, an unusually keen-eyed journalist, for the *Daily Mail*. She was too perceptive to buy the usual flannel. This must be the only interview with Laurie which did not even mention Slad, *Cider* or Spain. Laurie was determined not to give much away, but the result was an insightful portrait.

He looked, she said, like a lugubrious goblin, with his 'lanky, folded face and long pointed ears'.

> When he puts his glasses on you miss half the folds, his face broadens and he looks like a jolly nice chap. Around the rims of the lenses are traces of ink. He tells me they are plain lenses, and that sometimes he inks them over. The fact that when he does this – if he does it at all, for he is seven-eighths fantasy – he cannot see at all seems not to have occurred to him. This is the depth of

Laurie Lee's self-protection. He leaves himself as defenceless as a
child who goes wide-eyed and pink when it tells stories.

She listed other mysterious secrets:

If you ask him how old he is he says his mother doesn't know
which year it was. Then there's his home. You can't go there. His
best kept secret of all is his wife. All the newspapers describe her
as Laurie Lee's beautiful wife. He describes her as an enormous
woman with enormous blue eyes and enormous sandy hair.

Clearly it was best just to go along with him.

She asked him what he did all day, and he told her about taking
the temperature and counting the buds on his geraniums. 'Laurie
Lee and his wife have no children,' Sally wrote.

He says he doesn't want to see pocket editions of himself running
about all over the place. 'Horrible that would be,' he says. 'They
repeat your own weaknesses and you take it out on them because
you're too idle to take it out on yourself. Nothing's more irritating
than your own faults and they're the ones you always complain
about in other people. You never see people so hot and bothered
as when they've got somebody else's sins to take their minds off
their own … when they're discussing capital punishment or how
to persecute someone. Those Tory floggers … Inversion and
evasion gone mad, that's what they are.'

His glance rests on somebody's rather idiotic-looking dog.
'Having pet animals is evasion,' he declares. 'People who love
animals are only making substitutes for the more difficult business of loving people. I don't like dogs. They seem to take
on the worst aspects of human beings. The drooping tail, the
self-consciousness, the guilt … I like wild dogs though. I like
animals when they're left alone. I like foxes and stoats and squir-
rels. I respect birds.'

He told Sally he hadn't had a job for fifteen years, and reiterated the pitfalls of too many possessions. 'I'm free,' he said. 'But anyone can be free, you know; anyone can live alone and not be told what to do.' 'Sometimes you have to take Laurie Lee with salt,' Sally Vincent concluded. 'Only don't get it on his tail.'

Ironically, in view of Laurie's stated thoughts on having children, Kathy was already pregnant.

He describes in *Two Women* what a puzzle it was that ripe, golden Kathy, 'boxed up in sterile London', was inexplicably childless after twelve years of marriage. He tells how he brought her back to Slad and, by some magic, one morning found her perched on the kitchen window-sill. 'She looked at me transfigured, her eyes full of confusion and triumph. "Oh, Lol!" she said. "Would you believe it? ... I'm pregnant."'

That day, 5 March 1963, the *Daily Express* had published a poem commissioned from Laurie about 'Spring'. Laurie's mood was hardly spring-like: he was beset by dramatic nightmares of guilt and retribution. Still, the poem called 'Spring' duly appeared. On a copy of the *Evening Standard* he had scribbled tentative lines. Tucked into the drafts of this poem are these pencilled lines: '"One day, when you're a grandfather" they used to say, and laugh.

'Now that I am a grandfather, they laugh again, and push my wheelchair with cool-gloved hand.' He had just heard that Yasmin's pregnancy too was confirmed: he was to be a grandfather in September.

They went down to grey and stormy Slad. Kathy had lost some blood and Dr Brayshaw came through gales from Painswick to tell her it was a warning. She was not to do heavy work, and they were to prepare for the worst. Laurie himself was in Upper Wimpole Street seeing an ear, nose and throat specialist, but had to rouse himself to make an ITV film called *Boy Meets Girl*, about rural courtship. They filmed in Sheepscombe and he was interviewed by Dan Farson ('square, pink, soft face, remote bored eyes') at Forester's Inn. The cameramen shot Anthea and a boyfriend running down Swift's Hill in cold afternoon sun, and there were long convivial evenings with the film crew.

Commiserating with Tom Matthews about the end of his ten-year marriage to Martha Gellhorn, Laurie told him about Kathy's pregnancy, to Kathy's annoyance: 'We had been keeping it quiet just out of superstition, I wanted to feel safe & sure first,' she wrote to Matthews. 'It is a little miracle, isn't it. I still can't believe it though at last I'm beginning to change shape.' She had been making gallons of home made wine, of which Laurie drank quantities with no after-effects.

Everyone joined in the astonishment about the 'Blooming Burgeoning Floribunda Lees', as Jeremy Hutchinson put it. 'It is so wonderful I can hardly write about it,' wrote Peggy Ashcroft. Impending fatherhood galvanised Laurie. Dozens of anthologies were reprinting 'April Rise', or 'Christmas Landscape', and the royalties (a guinea here, four guineas there) mounted up. For *Mademoiselle* he went twice to Holland: 'like no other place on earth, a gift from the sea'.

On 20 April he and Kathy heard the first cuckoo, and he was writing to Yasmin that night at 11 p.m. when Kathy called out, 'Ah, he's moved.' 'Baby first moved,' Laurie noted in his diary. Outside in the drainpipe, five mistle-thrush chicks sat 'like 5 fat dowagers trapped in a rubber dinghy'. Laurie took a series of loving photographs of Kathy with a pigeon that roosted under the kitchen table; she wept when it left. Then a jackdaw took over; quite tame, following her everywhere, seemingly guarding her. (The photographs Laurie took of pregnant Kathy and her feathered friends are among the most touching in *Two Women*.)

In September Yasmin stayed in P. J. Kavanagh's flat off Sloane Square, waiting for her baby; Lorna went up to see her, and so did Laurie, so the two met again at last, the first time for at least thirteen years. 'Suddenly all was normal between them,' Yasmin says, 'as their daughter was having her first baby.'

On 19 September Laurie wrote to Yasmin, sympathising with her waiting days. At one end of Avenue Road, St John's Wood, was the nursing home where his grandchild would be born, and at the other, 400 yards away, the Hampstead Theatre which was showing James Roose-Evans's stage version of *Cider with Rosie*. 'But your production won't suffer any comparisons,' Laurie wrote to Yasmin, 'being first-hand flesh & blood. Anyway I'm glad of the continuity, because there hasn't been much of it in the past.'

Eleven days later, on 30 September, Laurie was in bed with a fever when he heard Kathy groaning. 'Three weeks early. I thought of country girls who complain of colic then find a baby lying in straw at their feet ... Lay by her & noticed that the bed was wet. Went to the Atwoods' 7 15 a.m.' Joan Atwood, their neighbour, drove Kathy to hospital with her little blue bag and book. During the morning, Mrs Atwood shouted to Laurie: he was wanted on the telephone. 'It's about your daughter.' You mean my wife? 'No,' they said, 'your daughter.' It was Lorna, ringing from Yasmin's room in London, to tell him that Yasmin had just had a daughter, 7lb 2oz. 'A daughter, a grand daughter,' wrote Laurie in his notebook. 'I could hear it crying. So Cathy's was bound to be a son.'

For a few hours more he tried to work, then rang Kathy's hospital at 4 p.m. 'Nurse says there's a message – tell your sister in law not to come to tea tomorrow.' Then Marion, Laurie's cousin, the hospital matron, came on the phone: 'She said, "You got a daughter." Silence. "You dropped dead or something? I said you got a daughter. 7lb 2oz."'

In his diary he wrote: 'Monday Sept 30, 1963, two girls, daughter & granddaughter.'

Yasmin concluded that this amazing coincidence – two babies, twins in birthdate, identical in weight – was the work of Laurie the great magician.

He spent the evening at the hospital. They had champagne and the baby was brought in. 'She curled back her lips to wail & I saw Cathy's mouth.' Marion handed her, howling, to Laurie. 'I kissed her forehead & she lay still. The first flattery.' Kathy, awash with flowers and telegrams, wrote forty-eight letters. Kathy wrote to Laurie,

I saw the most remarkable sunset I had ever seen, the trees dripping pink and gold and the extraordinary blue of the sky. I brought three young mums-to-be to have a look, to have a

nice effect on their babies. The girls in the main ward are a
real bunch of gasworks toughies, but they are funny, and fun
to visit.

A photograph appeared in the *Stroud News*, showing Kathy with
hair in plaits and sleeping baby. As Laurie walked about the town
everyone smiled and stopped to talk; a policeman made rocking
gestures with his arms. 'A famous baby. All say she looks like me.'
The Registrar of Births had just read *Cider with Rosie*. The baby
was registered as Jesse Frances. Among the old photographs in
Rose Cottage was one of Jesse Frederick Fern, a handsome young
man who had been killed in the First World War and commemorated in Slad church. So Kathy decided that the baby, male or female,
would be Jesse. (Later, Laurie decided that he preferred 'Jessy'.)
When mother and daughter came home, Laurie had removed the
gate, made a cane archway with nasturtiums and sunflowers, hung
kites and flags and nailed Jessy's birth certificate on the door. The
birth was announced on *Woman's Hour*, where Laurie was interviewed. He went to see *Cider with Rosie* at Hampstead, but could
not visit Yasmin and her baby Esther down the road, because Wish
was there. He went next day: Yasmin looked 'beautiful'.

Laurie wrote petitioning the six godparents: Elizabeth Jane
Howard ('I have always felt that if it was a girl she should have you. It
would enrich her so much and you could teach her all your womanly
magic'); Tom Matthews, whose lifelong grumble had been his
burden of sons; Michael Behrens; Peggy Ashcroft; Laurie's cousin
Frances; and Antonia Dugdale.

For Jessy, being born in his childhood village was an inextric-
able link with her father, and she became an integral element in the
Laurie Lee legend. As he wrote twenty years later,

> I'd been away from this valley for twenty years when suddenly
> she appeared and was born here, as I was. My return here was a
> mysterious act of fate. The special magic, the mystery which still

haunts me, is that having come back – whether it was the angle of the light, the slope of the fields, something – but suddenly there was Jessy … a late miracle born to my roots. It was almost as though my return to Slad was not only to revisit my childhood, but also to find Jessy.[116]

He would wrap her in a blanket and take her into the garden under a full moon, holding her aloft to be bathed in moonlight. He would feed her to the sound of the slow movement of Schubert's Trio in the hope that she would always associate music with pleasure. Kathy reported to Celia Goodman,

Laurie is so sweet with her I always thought he would be much more detached. He feeds her with music when she cries – lovely trios, duets, quartets, I do hope she'll be musical.

Oh Celia I keep thinking I'm dreaming it all, like those dreams one has which seem more of reality than of dream quality … I do hope I don't wake up out of this one. I never realised one could feel so satisfied and happy – I think the joy is enhanced by Laurie's own joy. I think finally he is going to be able to recapture joy again even if it's only for a short while.

They exuded this joy to everyone. Peggy Ashcroft wrote that her day at Rose Cottage with the threesome was

one of the most golden I ever remember – every minute of it – from entering under triumphal arch, the first sight of the pram, the first glimpse of Jesse, every glorious minute of the tale of labour, the croquet match & the picking of the blackberries and through it all Cathy shining like all the mother goddesses that have ever been.

Congratulations and blessings flowed in, from Monica Dickens, from Lady Diana Cooper, from the poet Elizabeth Jennings who said, 'I'm so glad that my priest in Rome's prayers helped to bring you a child.' Jessy was baptised on All Souls' Day and lay in Laurie's arms in Aunt Alice's christening robe while he recited his 'Poem for Jessy's Christening' which started:

> Sweet Jessy, late, but no less wanted,
> Here in my arms now lie undaunted;
> Much of my life has gone before you,
> But what I've left of love is for you.

Their first Christmas with the baby was different from any they had known. Kathy's mother came from Italy to see her granddaughter. 'I haven't seen my mother-in-law for 15 years,' Laurie told Celia Goodman. 'We don't quarrel, but just observe a policy of withdrawal.' His withdrawal was so total that Kathy sent him away altogether. 'TERRIBLE CHRISTMAS ON MY OWN,' says his diary.

'The birth of my child,' Laurie later wrote, 'meant a farewell to the child bride who bore her.'

21

Jessy
1964–1966

SEASONAL AFFECTIVE DISORDER, or SAD, might have been invented to describe Laurie's wintry malaise. 'Monotonous now, these winters,' he groaned, in bed with another fever in January 1964. 'Comes so quickly & then I can do nothing … Winter is becoming a write-off. I can't go out or see anyone – have to cancel dinners – people doubt the reason. But worst of all, the depressions and helplessness.'

That winter, Jessy was a consolation. At four months, she would gaze at him entranced as he sang to her, 'eyes round with fascination, mouth moves as I speak, trying to follow sounds'.

Every chuckle, each wriggling attempt at crawling, was logged in Laurie's notebook, day by day. When he first played his guitar for hre, she splayed her fingers like a pianist. He was besotted, transfixed. Like many middle-aged fathers, Laurie was in danger of being a baby bore: 'How they ensnare one at this age, the silken nets they loop around you.' Jessy's first word was 'Dadda' he told friends, 'what else?'

He compared notes with Yasmin, signing himself 'Grand L', about the weight, first teeth and sleeping habits of his Jessy and her Essie (Esther). He pinned photos of Yasmin as a baby on his study wall 'and can't tell whether it's Y, E or J'. Jessy 'has a delightful old man's face – tiny white button nose like Cyril Connolly, & small twinkling eyes'. At Easter, the two six-month-olds met. Laurie compared Essie's bright-blue shining eyes ('fixed, intelligent, but of an unvarying light, like an electric bulb') with the livelier light in Jessy's which 'flickers around smiles and emotions like a live flame in a wind'.

Jessy was indeed a charming child, with a 'fat-lipped' smile, a Beethoven brow and a mop of golden curls, recorded by Laurie's adoring camera. She woke her parents each night and demanded entertainment. To Yasmin Laurie confessed that he wished she could stay like that for ever: 'I don't want J ever to crawl or talk, but just to look up from the floor & smile when I come in, like she does now, & lie kicking to be picked up & carried round the garden.'

They got back to Slad 'just in time for the winter' at the end of March, to a cottage 'damp and cold as the grave'. There were blizzards, frost, hail. Jessy was handed around the pub to cries of acclaim. When summer arrived, village children brought trinkets and posies, made coronets of daisies, and covered Laurie with parsley-blossom as he lay in the garden 'till I looked like a snowdrift'. They danced on the lawn, made biscuits cut into hearts and stars, crayoned a large picture captioned 'A House of Love to the Three Who Live in Rose Cottage'. 'They are too good to be true,' said Laurie. On Mayday morning as the cuckoo called, he took Jessy out to pick cowslips and gillyflowers. It was 'a celestial' May.

He even wrote a new poem, 'Night Speech', having at first resisted the Arts Council's £30 commission for the Stratford festival. The poem had to incorporate lines from Shakespeare: Laurie chose 'The bright day is done,/And we are for the dark...' from *Antony and Cleopatra*. He joined in a Society of Authors discussion (chairman: Roy Fuller) about how to sell poetry books. Laurie, of course, was always unabashed about selling his wares at readings. At Lewisham library he 'slightly shocked the librarian' by producing a briefcase full of books for sale. 'Sold all of them.' That July the Revd Simon Phipps (later Bishop of Lincoln) read 'Day of These Days' in Coventry Cathedral to the accompaniment of Bach, and told him 'the effect was magical and immensely touching'. Several composers began setting Laurie's poems to music: Samuel Barber and Sir

Lennox Berkeley both chose his 'Twelfth Night'. Sir Lennox, a Gloucestershire man, was commissioned by the Stroud Festival, and his *Signs in the Dark* was performed by the Hirsch Chamber Players and the Stroud Festival Choir in October 1967.

But most of Laurie's work now was radio talks and magazine commissions. Though he always found writing laborious he proved a proficient hack who could turn out nostalgic sentiment about anything: the magic of water, for instance.

> I discovered water at the age of four, at the mouth of our cottage pump ... A magic plaything with a brilliant life of its own ... like liquid sky ... Fire is masculine, blundering, crude; water is feminine and far more subtle ... Water is all things to me, and most of them good.

For an *Evening Standard* series, he wrote about 'The Street Where I Live', describing Elm Park Gardens as 'a kind of buffer-state between Chelsea and Fulham, a layer cake, a Chinese box'. He wrote a poetic tribute to Churchill's funeral ('A cold east wind blows over the roof of Westminster...'). For *Mademoiselle* he went to Ireland. Being away, he missed Jessy's first tottering steps: 'hardly recognized the blonde curly sun-burnt heavyweight standing in play-pen on lawn' when he came home. 'I never want to leave her.'

The summer of 1964 was a time of high contentment, when Laurie one day wrote the heading 'A Happy Day' in his diary. For weeks on end, the sky was cloudless, the garden still. They would breakfast al fresco before Laurie went off to Stroud. Kathy and Jessy would meet him from the bus home, and they would walk with a flask of tea to the long high grass of Bulls Cross or Swift's Hill, or take a bus to Dursley. 'C & J waiting at bus stop with kite, picnic...' 'J in papoose... happy in her bag on shoulder drumming my head.'

For once, summer in the south of France held no allure: but he did go, without Kathy, and told his diary 'only wanting home & the garden & the bright faces & the children'. The fascination with

Jessy was total. 'J found way up stairs, puffing, groaning "oh dear", using her knees like a mountaineer' ... 'J fell down stairs, but without real hurt, falling like a fat plump pillow slowly from stair to stair' ... 'Tonight very gay, in my arms, dancing round & turning her head like a ballroom beauty as we turn & spin – would not let me stop – looking with mad gaiety out of the corner of her eyes to see that mum was watching.'

He did have moments of sudden panic in all this pleasure, to think of death. But the fruit of this paternal bliss was to be that apogee of sentiment, *The Firstborn*, which he wrote first for the *Evening Standard*. This meant that by the time she was being photographed blowing out her first birthday candle, Jessy was famous. Laurie was much interviewed about fatherhood: 'When A Poet Becomes a Father at 50' ('A late only child is specially vulnerable to indulgence'), and 'What I Would Like to Give My Child'. The picture, in dozens of interviews, was roseate. 'Sunshine slanted through the leaves bringing a golden glow to the little white-washed cottage in the heart of the Cotswolds...Laurie Lee unhooks a Spanish guitar from the wall to sing flamenco to his small daughter, Jessy.' He told reporters: 'I said I'd never have children till I could see them being bathed in a tin bath in front of a Cotswold cottage fire just the way I was.' He was photographed walking out, pipe in mouth, Jessy strapped to his back. The journalistic impression was of three lives, still without telephone, television or refrigerator, locked in serene rural simplicity.

Three days before Laurie's fiftieth birthday, Princess Peg sent a note headed 'BAD NEWS': Celia Goodman's husband Arthur had been found shot dead that morning, his dog Guy beside him. 'Celia calm but broken utterly.' The safety catch on Goodman's gun was faulty; perhaps, the coroner concluded, he had sat down to smoke a cigarette, propping his gun against a tree, and the dog had jumped up suddenly, releasing the trigger. Arthur was not yet fifty, their children only seven and eight. Celia had been on her way home from Aldeburgh on the fateful day. For the fourth time in eight years,

Laurie wrote a 'good' letter to a young widow after a sudden, 'utterly wasteful and tragic' death.

This year, instead of enjoying their usual Guy Fawkes night in the square of Elm Park Gardens, Laurie lit the bonfire at Sheepscombe's village firework display, with Jessy on his back, rockets whizzing over the valley. But in mid-November they went back to London and Kathy took Jessy to Italy, returning 'looking beautiful as a queen in her furs', in time for the launch of *The Firstborn*.

Illustrated with Laurie's own photographs of mother and baby, this charming little book ('She was born in the autumn and was a late fall in my life...') was received with rapture. 'A proud-dad confection I'm afraid,' he apologised. But even the hardest heart melts at the idea of the newborn. One letter typically told Laurie: 'I wouldn't have believed that even you could have done it. Anything new about anything so old; anything beautiful, even, about anything so private.'

But when he wrote, 'I have got a daughter, whose life is already separate from mine, whose will already follows its own directions, and who has quickly corrected my woolly preconceptions of her by being something remorselessly different,' he surely wrote with hindsight, having watched, twenty years before, Yasmin's transformation into a self-willed toddler.

The question is, did Laurie not hesitate to call his book so blatantly *The Firstborn*? Yasmin, her primogeniture thus denied, was understanding. Laurie had sent her the book with a note inside, saying he had her in mind too when he was writing it. Yasmin said:

> If you have a baby at twenty-five, and it's stolen by fairies in the night, and you think you'll never have another, and then you do have one at fifty, it must seem like a gift from the gods. I had been kidnapped, and now at last he had his own baby who would not be taken away.
>
> I might have felt differently if my mother had lived with Laurie and I'd known him on a personal basis as Jessy did. I think Laurie had an extremely conventional idea of honour and

31. *top left* Annie Lee at the christening of Jack's son Johnny, 1949 (*Nora Lee*)
32. *middle left* Kathy in Martigues with an old fisherman friend of her father's, 1951
33. *middle right* Kathy and Laurie on the road near Martigues, 1951
34. *bottom left* Kathy, photographed by Laurie, late 1950s

35. Laurie on guitar, Kathy practicing her flamenco in the bungalow in the Vatch, 1959

36. Laurie, Curator of Eccentrics for the Festival of Britain, 1951 (*Larry Burrows/Life Magazine –Time Inc./Katz Pictures*)

37. T. S. (Tom) Matthews with Kathy in Spain

38. Major Nigel Dugdale with his wife, Pen, and five-year-old daughter Antonia at Bushton Manor (*Antonia Young*)

39. Virginia Cunard and her sister Pen Dugdale, with Smokie (*Antonia Young*)

40. Elizabeth Jane Howard and Kathy at Lake Maggiore

41. *top* The best-seller: Laurie with *Evening Standard* placards for *Cider with Rosie*, 1960 (©*Mark Gerson*)
42. *bottom* Antonia Dugdale, photographed by Laurie, Paris, 1961 (*Antonia Young*)
43. *opposite top left* The yokel of Slad: Laurie with old yoke and pails, 1961 (*Topix Collection/Scotspan Publications Ltd*)
44. *opposite top right* Yasmin aged twenty-two, photographed by Laurie on the wall of Rose Cottage, 1961

45. Kathy and Laurie at Rose Cottage with Jessy, the Firstborn, 1964

46. Laurie with his daughter and granddaughter, 1964. Left to right: Julian David, baby Esther, Yasmin, Kathy with Jessy on her lap, and Laurie, father and grandfather

47. *top left* Laurie with Jessy and guitar, outside Rose Cottage (*John Summers*)

48. *top right* Laurie, Kathy and Jessy, Christmas 1964 (© *Express Newspapers*)

49. *middle left* Troubadours: Laurie with Jeremy Robson, Vernon Scannell and Dannie Abse, at a 1960s Poetry & Jazz evening (*Jeremy Robson Collection*)

50. *middle right* Georgina Hammick (*Georgina Hammick*)

51. *bottom left* The Queen's Elm, on the corner of the Fulham Road and Old Church Street

52. *bottom right* The Queen's Elm denizens, 1976: (left to right) Lord Valentine Thynne, Jak the cartoonist, Peter Owen, Laurie, Kerry Hamilton, Marshall Pugh, Jan Kenny (Mrs Sean Treacy), Sean Treacy, Elisabeth Frink, Babs Craig, Bill Travers, Virginia McKenna, Dr Geoffrey Dove and the artist Bill Thomson

53. *top left* Julian Bream (and guitar) listening as Laurie recites at Bream's local church in Dorset, late 1970s

54. *top right* Laurie (watched by Kathy and the landlady, Nolie Covington) signs a book for a fan in the Woolpack: 'There aren't many pubs where you can sell your books' (*The Citizen*, Gloucester)

55. *bottom left* Jessy aged seventeen, 'the one compelling interest in my life', photographed by Laurie, 1980 – from *Two Women*

56. *bottom right* Jessy ('I rely on Dad being around a lot') with Laurie in Santander, 1996

57. *top left* Laurie with fellow poet Frank Mansell and friend in front of the Slad churchyard, 1970s

58. *top right* Laurie, saviour of the Sheepscombe Cricket Club, aged eighty

59. *middle* Wine, women and song: Laurie in the garden of the Chelsea Arts Club, 1977 (© *Bryan Wharton*)

60. *bottom left* The churchyard at Slad, Laurie's final resting place

propriety. He was married now, and this was *their* firstborn. His
relationship with my mother was something quite other. Also,
he was incorrigibly a dark horse, a man of privacy and intrigue,
who loved having a secret.

When they returned to Slad for the summer (the cottage damp
again, and also smelling of dog, a relic of their winter tenants), Laurie
discovered, as he had with Yasmin, that a mobile toddler was a different
proposition from a cradle-bound infant: 'Jessy aged 18 months
trampled on the crocuses.' 'Tough, aggressive, independent, restless,
domineering now ... J very belligerent, strong, rebellious.' But then,
on May Day, he heard the first cuckoo with her. And she knew sixty
words; he listed them all, from Daddy to Baccy. Like Ted Hughes's
small daughter Frieda[117] she was moon-crazed: 'Woke her night of
full moon, and she leapt in my arms, wouldn't sleep again for hours.
Morning ran into garden: "Moon gone."' She seemed to have 'a natural
whimsy' but also compassion ('Poor cows in the mist'). She loved
polysyllables like *'fantastic hippopotamus'*. Her voice was distinctively
husky, sometimes raucous: in church one day the kneeling congregation were praying in silence when Jessy yelled, 'Wake up, Jesus!'

She was to go to Laurie's old village school, now reduced to
only nine pupils and threatened with closure. Laurie wrote to local
papers pointing out that the village without a school would become
'nothing but a bus stop in children's lives'. In June he went to see
Anthony Crosland, then Education Secretary, about it, to no avail.

He went again for a fortnight to the Behrenses' villa at Cap
d'Antibes without the family and returned at the end of June on an
evening of 'buttery sunlight' to find Kathy and Jessy both in pink,
the child with a rose in her hair, waiting at the edge of the beech-
wood as his bus arrived. Jessy ran at him like a golden bull with 'fat
wet orchid kisses'. Rose Cottage's garden was 'full to the brim with
roses'. He had trained wild briars among the climbers 'like a revolt
among the peasants'. Madame Albertine had clambered right over
the roof; the foxgloves were seven feet high.

Yasmin was now pregnant with her second child; Laurie hoped she would have a boy, and when on 8 July 1965 Yasmin's son Gabriel was born, he was atavistically delighted.

The royalties from *Cider* cushioned him from real need, and he was in demand to make nostalgic little television films about 'my village', but otherwise he was getting only two-guinea reprint fees for anthologies or five guineas for a poetry reading. Tom Matthews tried to fix a creative writing fellowship at an American university for him, but Laurie baulked at this: 'Part of my nature is a phobia of being turned down – which is why I seldom ring up even close friends to suggest myself.' And he just did not want to go away. 'I would have loved this once, but I think it is too late now. What with my commitment here, life with Jessy etc. and a growing middle-aged fondness for home, I can't really envisage going off for a prolonged sojourn abroad.'

Laurie said 1965 was the quietest summer he could remember. Kathy's half-brother Walter Sarfatti and Roland Joffé came to stay. One night they went up to Painswick Beacon at 9 p.m. to see the chain of torches lit across the land launching Operation Neptune, the project to save Britain's coastline. 'Line of dark figures on ridge at dusk. Jonathan Blow, lord of the manor, with eighteen-month-old son on shoulder, lit beacon. Another glowed on Robinswood Hill. Soon could count eight...' Jessy rode in a pony and trap with Laurie when he opened a church fete at Sudgrove House, the home of the show-jumper Pat Smythe, at Miserden. They went down to Yasmin's farm in Devon, where Laurie lay on bales of hay while daughter and granddaughter played the old game of removing his glasses.

When Yasmin had a solo show of paintings in Worthing that summer, Laurie bought one 'which I would have wanted whoever had painted it – the honeysuckle & rose, which is you, me, my mother, and summer, full of light and perfectly delineated ... a window into the summer world'. While there, he saw Lorna, to whom he now referred always as 'Mum'. 'I had a lovely day with Mum,' he told Yasmin. They had driven about Sussex talking non-stop and ended up in Bognor having fish and chips for old times' sake. 'Our first day together for perhaps ten years, thanks to you.' The once infatuated passion had been resolved and normalised by time. Laurie still made jokes about the power she had over him; but the jokes were a way of exorcising it.

Kathy struck a blow for freedom that summer by taking secret driving lessons whenever Laurie was away, and passing her test in September. He bought a little Morris Traveller, plus a new red notebook in which to log every mile, noting the time of departure from Slad and arrival in London, the stops at filling stations and the mileage on the clock.

Elizabeth Jane Howard, now Mrs Kingsley Amis, gave them dinner in the jungly conservatory of their dilapidated Maida Vale house. Jane said she would never have done so if she had known about Amis's *Spectator* review ten years before, 'but Laurie's kind of writing would never appeal to Kingsley'. In Jane's new novel, *After Julius*, Laurie recognised a character with several attributes of his younger self: an impecunious poet with a rustic accent, a long white scar on his chest and a predilection for well-bred girls, party tricks and fireworks. But Jane had never told Amis about herself and Laurie. 'He wasn't very interested in my past. Just as well: let it lie, really.' The two men later met often in the Garrick Club bar. But Laurie said he always made sure his stuff was in front of Amis's on the book-stall at Paddington.[118]

The new year of 1966 found him at home in bed with a seasonal chill and Tom's annual gift crate of Perequita wine. He always let the flat while in Slad (Nell Dunn was one tenant) but now they often had lodgers: Rebecca John, granddaughter of Augustus, lived with them while preparing her art portfolio for the Central School. Her father, the First Sea Lord, Caspar John, had a Cotswold cottage at Needlehole, where Laurie had once enthralled Rebecca during a walk, explaining every stone and hedgerow. In awe of Laurie, she had 'lapped up all the jewels on offer'. Kathy, who had once danced flamenco in a circular skirt at her parents' house, seemed to her a goddess. In Elm Park Gardens, however, Rebecca would observe Kathy forever running upstairs from the kitchen with trays, waiting on Laurie in his study. Kathy believed this was her unquestioned destiny. But Rebecca was made uneasy by it. Laurie seemed distant, Kathy lonely. 'I had never seen anything like it. My mother never danced round my father.'

Josceline Dimbleby too remembered a summer weekend at the Astors' house, Bruern, when Laurie played his recorder and Josceline, who had just left the Guildhall School of Music, sang Scarlatti arias. Laurie was 'instantly friendly and extremely flirtatious. I was very embarrassed that his wife was there with the baby, and kept wondering what she must think.'

In the pub, Antonia observed, Laurie was incorrigible: 'He'd see a pretty girl, gaze into her eyes and say, "You do know, don't you, that your eyes are enough to make any man kill himself for love?" and the girl would melt before such flattery.' The public Laurie was always easy-going and full of mischief. He seemed to slot neatly into an artistic peer-group, one whose signature appeared with those of Hockney, E. M. Forster, Elisabeth Lutyens and others, on a letter to *The Times* that April: 'We 54 voted Labour and do not support US policies in Vietnam nor British endorsement of these.'

Privately, however, he was often depressed. '4 April 1966: A week in bed, most of it alone. Terrible vacant timeless time. Sleeping shivering, watching television. Bitterly cold weather too.' Wintry SAD had taken hold again, complicated by his double life, about which he had pangs of guilt, reflected in dreams such as the nightmare he had about Pen Dugdale finding out about his relationship with Antonia. He was also convinced that his old friends were disappearing. He felt chilled and joyless.

Laurie returned to Slad that spring, the cottage a 'damp death-trap' to play the celebrity, judging bonnets at the Stroud Licensed Victuallers' dance. The cheerless reality was that he felt 'weak & depressed, cold and feeble, despite threadbare moments of amusement with Jessy and visiting children'. Lewis Eyers told him 'there'll be a white one tomorrow' and there was: snow in April. 'Fierce blizzard. Went to Stroud to buy rug. All shops closed at 9.15. Everyone ill in Slad. And me. Sick bouts of fever; very low, all doors closing; drink, music, love, friends – hope I will not grow too cold to love Jessy.'

Within a week, spring arrived and Laurie was out taping bird-song, taking Jessy into the garden before breakfast to look for spider-houses in the dewy grass. The temperature rose, flowers erupted, they went for picnics in the Colne Valley and at Arlington Horseshoe and on the 'most perfect May Day I can remember' they were having Bloody Marys and lunch in the garden at Combe with Tom Matthews and his new wife Pamela. 'The sun & the village are working their usual consolations,' he told Celia. 'I have been busy building stone walls and have lost several pounds and gained some patience and played a tape of the Mozart which I had not for months.'

He had just bought Beech Cottage, down the lane, to renovate and rent out furnished, and Kathy drove about buying secondhand furniture for it. They took Jessy to the Behrenses on the Cote d'Azur, where there was nothing to do except eat, drink and wallow in the warm Mediterranean, and Jessy turned a pale toast colour.

He was thinking of going abroad for the whole of the next winter, but instead of escaping to the sun he was suddenly taken into St Stephen's Hospital, with gallstones and a hernia: a very impatient patient, 'imagining the worst & watching the great black wall roll up around me'. He was there all through Christmas of 1966, which was, he told Roy Fuller, 'a bit of a blur'.

22

'A wave through a dark window'
1967–1969

IT SEEMS EXTRAORDINARY that ten years elapsed between
Laurie's first and second volumes of autobiography. He was a slow
and painstaking writer, but his persons from Porlock were magazine
commissions, depressions, and that old obstacle, the pram in the
hall. Jessy, although 'winning & voluptuously loving', cramped
Laurie's former social style. He explained to Tom Matthews that he
and Kathy were 'so domestically disorganised' that seeing friends
for dinner was impossible. Weekends too were out, Kathy told
Celia, because of Jessy's 'terrible energy' in the early mornings:
'Once we were staying away and she woke at 3.15 and never went
to sleep again. She was perfectly all right the next day – but I wasn't.'

Laurie's travelogues provided an escape, but in July 1967 he
was commissioned to write a piece of reportage. The American
magazine *Redbook* sent him to Aberfan, the Welsh village where
116 children had been buried under a toppling tip of coal-waste
one year before. The families of Aberfan took to Laurie, said John
Summers, who was there for the *Telegraph* magazine – 'and they
were ready to tear the skin off most journalists who hung round
there'. It was Summers who found him an old Leica camera for £17
10s, and who introduced Laurie to the blue Japanese Pentel pens
with which he wrote letters for the rest of his life.

The Aberfan piece could hardly fail to be moving, but Laurie
brought to it his instinctive sympathy with small village lives, in
'a huddle of anonymous terraced houses of uniform ugliness

unrelieved except for chapel and pub'. There was no need to inflate his prose. His quotations from the parents who had lost their children, some of whom he met in the graveyard, told all. The children who survived, he noted, were lavished with expensive toys and treats. 'The presence of the children who were spared adds to the tragic problem. Aberfan, it is said, suffered from two disasters – first the landslide, then an avalanche of money.'

Rosamond Lehmann suddenly resurfaced that year, writing *The Swan in the Evening*, her book about her dead daughter. In it she mentioned that Laurie shared her belief that a fragrance of flowers, 'an unearthly aromatic sweetness', filled her flat when (she was convinced) her daughter's spirit was present. But as Laurie privately said, 'Of course I didn't witness anything – but I couldn't hurt her feelings, poor woman.' In fact he was appalled by Rosamond's self-delusion.

> She took me into the flat one day and said, 'There: Sally's been again. She knows those are my favourite flowers. You can smell it, can't you?' It was self-deception on such a moving scale. She was getting love messages and flowers every day from a medium, and was convinced that they were genuine. Anyone who had a touch of awareness would know that Sally didn't write like that, didn't think like that.

When Laurie congratulated Cecil Day-Lewis on succeeding John Masefield to the Poet Laureateship in January 1968 he was preoccupied with finishing *As I Walked Out One Midsummer Morning*. At last.

For the tale of his Spanish adventure he drew heavily on his precious diaries: how else could he have recreated so vividly, in his mid-fifties, the feeling of being carefree and twenty, 'fat with time', without responsibilities and with the world on his side? 'I haven't a good memory,' he said. 'Without the diaries I couldn't have written the book. With them, the physical sensations all return. Wham! It's like playing a tape.' And he was also free to excise totally the presence of Wilma from his story, since she had died in 1963.

To refresh his memory of *tiempos perdidos* he took Kathy and Jessy back to Gibraltar, Algeciras, Ceuta and Almuñécar in March 1968. He had been longing to take Jessy to Spain. Kathy was greeted with rough cries by old friends, and Jessy with kisses from policemen at whom she would shout 'Here! You! stop it!' She flung her chubby arms quite indiscriminately, his notebook records, round 'an old gypsy witch, an elderly waiter, an Arab woman and a bus driver'.

Laurie went back again to Spain the following month, via ferry to Santander, this time with Antonia who drove him about in a hired car, and by the end of April he had finished the book and felt 'wonderfully relaxed now that it is done'.

Laurie told Celia he had been reading about the Hesse family, filled with admiration for Peg and Lu who had always maintained their high spirits and generosity despite the way 'life has insulted them with more than their share of tragedy'. But within weeks, Prince Ludwig was dead, at fifty-nine. On the day of the funeral, despite 'utter utter misery', Princess Peg was writing to Laurie about 'the fun we four had together, the adventures, the laughs, the red wine (or white for that matter!); burning castles; songs and Easter eggs. I suppose I will carry on somehow ... but the centre of my heart is empty & will always remain so.'

Laurie went to Wolfsgarten for the memorial service, but collapsed on his return, and for two weeks had to keep to his room with drawn blinds, under sedation. He was in a trough, and would hear Jess calling him from the summer garden and be unable to join her. Reading, writing and even music were denied to him.

One consolation was the new book. His publisher was to be André Deutsch: not, after all, Chatto & Windus, who had been waiting for this book ('Opus II') for nearly ten years. Deutsch explained that he was driving Laurie home after a W. H. Smith prizegiving at the Savoy, and Laurie suddenly offered him the manuscript of his Spanish book, if he wanted it. 'Are you kidding?' said the incredulous Deutsch. It turned out that Laurie had been irritated, at the party, to be asked by Ian Parsons of Chatto, 'How's life in Slough?' An unforgivable error. So Deutsch got the prize, and he told *Smith's Trade News* that the new book was 'simply a masterpiece'. Norah Smallwood was extremely distressed, but Laurie assured Deutsch that he had 'cleared' his move with Chatto. The title, it had to be explained, was a traditional opening to old ballads, a way of saying 'once upon a time', but it was constantly mangled (the Day-Lewises called it '*As I Walked Out One Somerset Maugham*').

Jessy had started at Slad school, 'going off down the lane with a bow-legged swagger'. When the school was closed, Laurie arranged for her to attend Painswick Primary in summer, and a school in Park Walk, Chelsea, in the winter. ('Which didn't do much for my education,' Jessy said.) These constant migrations were soon complicated by a hamster, a goldfish and a bright blue budgerigar named Cherry, a present from Peggy Ashcroft on Jessy's fourth birthday. As Jessy described it:

> The three of us had this different life, travelling up and down to London. And as far as Laurie could see, there was no need for me to acknowledge the local relations he had around Slad. So I grew up thinking I had no family, when in fact, counting both sides, I had eighty-seven cousins.

Jessy's godfather Tom Matthews and his vivacious third wife Pamela, the Anglo-Irish, horse-loving widow of Colonel V. Poliakoff ('Popski'),[119] had now bought the beautiful Palladian Cavendish Hall, Suffolk, Pam's childhood home. 'Cavendish sounds rather eighteenth-century pastoral,' commented Laurie. It was indeed: another sumptuous country refuge for the Lees, with horses for Jessy to ride.

By September 1968, despite having overcome the hurdle of finishing the book, Laurie was in a mysterious state of nervous depression, and in November he spent a week in the National

Hospital for Neurology and Neurosurgery in Queen Square, Bloomsbury. His diary records that he was injected with Valium.

Princess Peg, after her first Christmas without Lu, was concerned to hear that he was ill. She was staying in Drottningholm with her friend the King of Sweden, aged eighty-six, in his old palace, 'a living cosy museum, vast but warm ... The king and I walk through snow-covered parks and watch the full moon come up at 15.30 hrs.' Peg thought it would be good for Laurie (and her) to be reminded of people who bore up well in the face of real tragedy.

> The king has lost two much loved wives & his eldest son was killed in an air crash so he knows. And can give tips on how to carry on – not become a sad bore – or egocentric, & how true it is 'laugh & the world laughs with you' etc.

But as Laurie wrote to Celia: 'Winter seems always to be a time of heavy groans for me, and I don't spare my friends the sound of it, which by now is something I should have learnt to do.' He was finding it difficult to write even letters. 'I've no doubt that this is a phase, but it loses more time than is tolerable & wastes more friends than I can afford. This is not so much a letter as a wave through a dark window.'

One reason for his latest gloom was that for some years Laurie had been encouraging Antonia to find a husband, and she'd met someone she wanted to marry. So the convenient arrangement of being looked after in London by her, and chauffeured on foreign trips, would come to an end. Antonia's wedding to Nicholas Young was to be in September, on the publication day of *As I Walked Out One Midsummer Morning*.

Laurie did manage, in the spring of 1969, to write a spirited foreword to a new edition of Roy Campbell's memoirs, *Light on a Dark Horse*. Campbell had died twelve years before, in 1957. His wife Mary was at the wheel on a lonely road south of Lisbon when a tyre burst; Campbell was killed and she was badly injured. Laurie's foreword was a warm tribute to 'a romantic idealist'. Roy Campbell was, he wrote, 'perhaps one of our last pre-technocratic, big action poets who, like D'Annunzio and Byron, were not only the writers of exquisite lyrics but whose poetry was part of a physical engagement with life.' There was something fantastic about Campbell's stories of derring-do, Laurie said, but 'Personally, I much preferred his style to the English passion for understatement, which is only boasting stood on its head.' The publisher said he had hit just the right note, and sent 50 guineas. Laurie also wrote an extravagant foreword to a book of poems by his Slad Valley friend Frank Mansell: 'The poet's voice reverberates with the resonance of the Cotswold Highlands, with all the smooth-wrapped hardness of moss-dressed stone…'

The spring migration to Slad in 1969 once more coincided with snow, sleet, hail and gales. But he had one more excursion to the sun. He flew to Gibraltar and was driven to Ronda, where he produced a poem called 'Gitano y Gitanas',[120] datelined 'Ronda, Spring 1969'. Laurie's diary is blank for the rest of that summer. But he did his usual poetry readings, and judged the Young Writer of the Year for the *Telegraph*. And in July Matthews arrived in his Jensen to take Laurie on a week's laddish jaunt up to Hereford, Ludlow and into Wales, calling on Emma Smith in her Welsh cottage.

The prospects for Laurie's new book were certainly propitious. Four extracts in the *New Yorker* would pay \$20,000. For this he had to endure the editor William Shawn's queries over the punctuation which spattered each galley-sheet: 'Every comma is questioned. They cut out all my jokes (perhaps rightly) and also each and every one of the few references to sex … You feel as if Nanny were giving you a wash and brush up so you'd be ready to go down to the drawing-room.' André Deutsch, after a sales conference at which Laurie played his violin for the reps, printed an initial run of 50,000 copies.

Meanwhile *Cider with Rosie* sales were boosted by its becoming that summer a set text for O-level English Literature, so pupils were asked questions such as: What did Laurie Lee mean by saying 'Nothing happened at all except summer'? What did they understand by 'the grass *scaffolding* the sky'? Had Laurie succeeded in recapturing the presence of his mother? The first coaches full of teenagers began to arrive in Slad, as teachers took their pupils to see Laurie's old family cottage – just as Laurie was trying to assume a new public image in order to relive, at fifty-five, his wandering minstrel youth. He told Sally Beauman (now a novelist, but then a *Telegraph* feature-writer of twenty-three) that he was sick of being written about as a country bumpkin.

What Sally saw instead was a metropolitan figure in his Chelsea eyrie 'in his Alabama planter's suit and Bermuda tan' – although the photograph showed him setting out for a picnic on Swift's Hill with Jessy, and Kathy in her Jackie Kennedy shades and headscarf, carrying a hamper.

'No one ever comes in here,' Laurie told Sally, allowing her a glimpse of his study overflowing with yellowing papers, letters, books and manuscripts piled on shelves, spilling from cupboards, covering table and floor. 'I used to mock my mother,' Laurie said, 'because she never threw anything away. "Ooh our mother, she's terrible." Now I find I'm just like her.' But Sally found the living room 'a beautiful jumble: jugs of flowers, sheets of music, a guitar, photographs, books, plump sofa and chairs, a screen hung with brass rubbings and on the walls, paintings of blue girls by Laurie Lee'. He told her: 'I always wanted to be a painter. Best of all after music I liked to draw. But I also like to feel wanted, and nobody ever said to me, we'd like some more of your paintings.'

They lunched at the Chelsea Arts Club, which she found 'reminiscent of a small Cambridge college'. In the garden with its fountain and benches in little arbours, Laurie ordered barley wine and told Sally she must not over-emphasise 'the Gloucestershire angle'. (But he never completely sloughed off the hayseed image; and he was perfectly prepared, later, to be visited by journalists in Slad.)

He no longer had a companion for Spanish travels, but the BBC took him there in August to make a film to promote his book. This brought about 'the Spanish disaster'. In Segovia the BBC car was broken into, and his priceless 1935–37 diaries were stolen. It was the bitterest of ironies that this should happen just when he was publishing a passionately pro-Spain book which has inspired countless readers to travel there ever since. 'A nightmare,' he said later. 'Nothing could be worse for a writer.' Not only had he lost his record of his Spanish Civil War days – on which his promised third volume would so depend – but he had lost his faith in the Spanish people. 'The one thing I thought I knew about Spain was how honest it was – you could leave anything anywhere.' He was driven from Segovia by Michael Astor's son Jamie and his then girlfriend, the writer Marina Warner, who were travelling around Avila and Seville on a working holiday. He got back to torrential thunderstorms in Madrid.

Tom Matthews, to whom Laurie had dedicated the new book, suspected that the theft must have been General Franco's secret police at work. For Laurie it was 'the end of a 30-year love affair': the unhappy result of travelling in cars stuffed with expensive cameras, he added. He had lost some irreplaceable things, including a photograph of Kathy on the roof of Santa Eulalia 'which I always carried in my diary'. He had kept those diaries safely since 1938. 'I was in despair,' he remembered, twenty years later, when struggling to write his Spanish Civil War book from memory.

As I Walked Out One Midsummer Morning was bound to be a Christmas bestseller. But on publication day Laurie was 'shaky', taking his knockout pills. He was also buying Littlecourt, the house next door to Rose Cottage, having borrowed money from Deutsch on the strength of expected sales. About these he was mulishly determined to be disappointed. But Cecil Day-Lewis, absent from the launch at the Chelsea Arts Club – 'I avoid publishers' parties like the Black Death. Also, I am recovering from a coronary' – told him the new volume was every bit as effective as *Cider*. 'The early days of the Spanish war you do marvellously.' Edward Blishen called it a gem. S. J. Perelman sent 'a deep comradely bow'. The *TLS* said it was 'a work of art, the finer for appearing artless'. All reviewers were tantalised by the last paragraph, about the rich lady who had abandoned her husband and children for him. His final sentence, 'I was back in Spain, with a winter of war before me,' left them 'clamouring for more'.

E. S. Turner unwittingly pinpointed Laurie's dependence on diaries in his review in the *Listener*.

> How did he have time to notice, and how could he remember, that the dog which savagely bit him had 'eyes like yellow gas'? How could [he] … remember all the phantasmagoria of heat-stroke? How could any writer in search of copy be so fortunate as to find his inn shared by four circus dwarfs sleeping in one bed? These are things I am content to let others worry about.

And of course all this rich and telling detail came straight from the diaries.

'What is it like to be famous again?' asked Michael Astor, adding that he was counting on Laurie to come for Christmas among old friends. Laurie was indeed famous again, but he felt quite raw, he told Celia, with 'that inevitable sense of emptiness one gets when one launches something'. Having been briefly revived by a weekend at the Hampshire house of the enterprising Farnham bookseller and former Grenadier Guards officer Charles Hammick, he wrote Hammick a gloomy letter, doubting that the book would sell. Hammick assured him his fears were groundless. The book was doing well in Farnham. Forget the critics and sales figures, he said. 'Then the opinion of those whom you respect will come to roost, and this, other than your own conviction, is the only test that counts.'

'Life at half-cock,' says Laurie's notebook, 'slowly stifled by an implacable & relentless stupidity … Friendship offered, not rejected so much as left to decay through inertia. At home, have nothing to offer my friends but flustered chaos.'

Once again it was to Celia that he confided the details of his malaise.

> My trouble is mostly concerned with the *physical* act of writing, and it is obviously one of those dotty things that one

can't explain but that one hopes will pass eventually... I am compelled to lose one or two days every week or two to a deep drug treatment which lays me out completely. It has been going on now for about 18 months. The loss of time is the worst thing – and of opportunity to write to one's friends, or to explain why one couldn't.

23

Dear Mr Lee...
1970–1974

AS I WALKED Out One Midsummer Morning was at the top of the bestseller list, with Elizabeth Longford's *Wellington* and Kenneth Clark's *Civilisation*. But a lingering despondency hung over Laurie at the start of the new decade. Like any Peter Pan, Laurie disliked ageing: he woke every day feeling young, quick and full of hope, but by evening he was a tottering old man. How could he write another book? Anything over 500 words laid him low. Several days a week he was under sedation.

From his slough of despond, Laurie had managed to write a light-hearted introduction to *A Flook's Eye View of the Sixties*, celebrating the twenty-first anniversary of the cartoon character created by Wally Fawkes and George Melly. Laurie joined their Foyle's lunch in the Dorchester with 'assembled cartoonists, comedians and Diana Dors'.[121] He could still cheer others. Elizabeth Jennings ('sick in mind and body') thanked him for a letter of 'intuitive poetic understanding'.

He also began writing skittish letters to Georgina Hammick, wife of Charles the Farnham bookseller. She was thirty, the mother of two small children, and a published poet before turning to short stories and novels. Like Nicolette Devas she saw that there were two Lauries. 'In public he was all bonhomie. In private he could be sharp, and often a hugely gloomy, Eeyore person with an innate disbelief in the possibility of promised pleasure. He expected disappointment.' She and Laurie liked the same jokes, knew the same poems, and could finish one another's lines, catching instantly a reference to William Blake or to the obscure seventeenth-century poet and satirist George Wither. So began an intimate penfriendship based on a punning literary one-upmanship that neither could enjoy at home. Even when 'the very act of writing scrambles the brains', Laurie could always sparkle for Georgie.

'What a fun-pun person you are,' he wrote. 'Sharp's the word – so sharp indeed you put me on my metal and I'll cut you in the street one of these days...'

He called her jokey names: 'Dear Miss Understanding' or 'Gorgeous Georgie Goolagong' (he was very keen on the tennis player Evonne). Laurie ended that letter with 'Too Goolagong hangs the light in this valley lamenting' (playing on a line from his poem, 'Summer Rain'). Georgina tried to discuss contemporary poetry with him and gave him Ted Hughes's *Crow* but he was instinctively wary of the younger poet: to Siriol Hugh-Jones in 1960, he had said of Hughes, 'I was an expert on badgers when he was still mewling and puking in a buzzard's nest.' 'As for Dylan T,' he wrote to Georgina, 'I can understand but don't want to know. Even more than most writers I demand single-minded devotion or nothing. If my works her neck don't crick, what care I whence comes her kick?' – a reference to George Wither's

> If she be not so to me
> What care I how kind she be?[122]

Their in-jokey correspondence could only properly be understood by the two participants. He felt free to tease Georgina. 'But as for teasing Cathy, she doesn't always get it, so we will indulge in that at our yellow Pekin peril...' 'What would you like for your birthday Georgie dear; a casket of your favourite ambiguities, evasions, riddles, recoils, retreats, & tiny beautifully-executed sideways leaps – or a tiger lily burning bright, claws safely sheathed and out of sight?'

Although Laurie was funny and good with small children, he had, Georgina discovered, a cruel and unforgiving side where women were concerned. 'He liked bright women, but he still demanded mothering, and womb-like embracing, at home.' Georgina's feminist stance was anathema to him. She challenged him: why did he always keep his womenfolk at home? Weren't women more than slaves in kitchen and playthings in bed? He wrote back to 'Darling Georgie Simone' (as in de Beauvoir):

> Listen to me ... it is possible to have an equal relationship with a girl, one whose mind is a delight, with whom one plays intellectual tennis with pleasure (and no sulks), and to see her in the kitchen, cooking one's dinner; AND, at times, to see her as an object apart, thank God, to be dressed up, undressed, adored, caressed, and put to bed like a doll. End of message.

To Georgina he confided about sexual fantasies:

> They can be kinky, quirky, pre-Raphaelite, Genghis Khan-can, sadistic, masochistic, set in ivory towers or cellars, but one should never be ashamed of them any more than of one's sleeping dreams. It's true that few lovers ever get the chance to act out their fantasies together and I think it's probably better that way, because fantasies are generally too fragile to take the weight of our physical presences in them.

But he had, he added, once 'magically' had such a chance. We may guess with whom.

He hinted at his reluctance to declare love.

> Haven't you ever said in an idle silence, 'Say you love me,' and not wished for a word more than just that? Love's deepest satisfaction, security, comes from that whispered 'Tell me, tell me again...' But what do you tell? Symbolic, secretive, endearing,

incendiary phrases … But NEVER all your heart – or from me
she doth depart.[123]

How I know this to be true, don't you? and how one wishes
it not to be true. The bliss of not needing to hold back anything.
In the hooded cowled whispers of the dark close night one
should be … able to receive & gather in all love's echoes &
messages. Without hindrance or doubt.

This intense correspondence continued for two years, but he and
Georgina were 'bound to fall out', she knew. 'When he called me
"thickness" or "Dead loss" it was for not reading between the lines.
It was difficult to please him for any length of time. He was always
suspicious, trying to set traps for you. You walked a tightrope.'

She also made the error of questioning the second line of one of
his most anthologised poems, 'Apples':

Behold the apples' rounded worlds:
juice-green of July rain…

'You have to say JOO-lye,' I told him. 'Why didn't you go for
August? That would sound better, and it's more true of August
anyway, and you wouldn't have that ugly emphasis on the wrong
syllable.' He shook his head in sorrow and disappointment, that
I had the temerity. He considered it a huge impertinence, which
I daresay it was. I had crossed some invisible line.

Their intimate sparring was a verbal flirtation. He sometimes ticked
her off like a father, but assured her she was 'loved, cherished in mind
& matter, looked forward to, relished deeply in recollection'. But
it made her nervous. 'His tricks and games were tests, you weren't
meant to win. He would catch you out for not reading his last letter
properly. "Oh you don't read my letters I can tell."'

Once, Laurie arrived unexpectedly at Georgina's house, and
became ill. It was awkward. She had to attend her son's sports day. She

put him in the spare room, which was unsatisfactory – 'the mattress was not feather-filled' – and there wasn't time to cook the kind of stew he liked. He broke out in such a terrifying cold sweat she thought he might die. She rang Kathy, who said that if Laurie took his pill and went to bed for the rest of the day, it would be safe to leave him. In the evening she drove him back to Slad. During the two-hour journey he told her that nobody had ever got over seeing him ill, citing Rosamond Lehmann as one who hadn't. Reassurances made no difference: he would not be comforted. But what remained in Georgina's mind of this 'frightening' visit was the homecoming at Rose Cottage: 'all the lights blazing, a delicious supper ready, the table laid, jugs of roses and lilies everywhere, Cathy calmly in charge. And Laurie's undisguised pleasure and relief at being home and safe.'

When Georgina's much admired first book of short stories, *People for Lunch*, came out, Laurie said: 'I gather you've written a rather good book,' but did not read it.

Every year followed a pattern now: a long chill and fevered winter, 'a see-saw of doctors, drugs, dumps & doubts' followed by a spring 'the cruellest since the birth of Prufrock' redeemed by sunshine in May, 'a temporary balance of serenity after the sticks & thorns of April'.

He was now in need of a new companion/driver for his foreign trips. In July, Laurie asked Elizabeth Jane Howard to come with him to Spain to help him research for a book. 'There was something in the papers about my wanting an assistant/companion, and feminine, and intelligent, and I have had over 50 replies, but how could they compare with you? ... please write and say yes. Love Laurie.' 'Strictly business,' he added, 'strictly pleasure.'

One of the young women who came to see him at the Queen's Elm about the job was the future writer Miranda Seymour, aged twenty-one, who decided instantly that it was a job she did not after all want. Laurie was 'older than I expected; and I was slightly unnerved by the kind of companionship he might require'.

Jane could not go. But Laurie was 'profoundly nourished' by her affectionate reply, 'because I need such words from you and no doubt always will'. He had been crazy to think she might drop everything and accompany him. He'd had a reasonably good time, he told her, 'but my companion was young, attractive, dull, witless, and at first inclined to be aggressive, and had to be slapped down hard, good and early, after which she drove me round quite well'.

'I would like to see you very much,' he added, 'almost more than anyone else, as I need what you have for me and it don't grow on trees ... I love you. L.'

Her god-daughter Jessy, he said, was now 'a husky, loving, strapping Cathy type ... She is a good reader but a poor writer which is OK by me as we could do with some readers in this family.' With Kathy and Jessy he had spent part of the summer with Lis Frink (one of whose *Horse and Rider* sculptures he had just bought for £50) at her farmhouse in the Cevennes. In the autumn he took his two girls to New York, staying at the Chelsea Hotel. A pun-filled letter arrived from Georgina, calling herself Queen Bee, announcing the birth of her daughter Rose. 'Dear Glory Bee [Laurie Lee] Will your honey suckle Rose? We are giving her that name in the hope that she might be A Rose for Winter (she's undoubtedly the Last Rose of Summer).'

They stayed with Tom Matthews's son Paul (whose new baby Joshua Lee Matthews became another of Laurie's godsons) and Laurie had Algonquin lunches with the *New Yorker*, *Playboy* and Frances Koltun from *Mademoiselle*, who told him their talk was 'among the best hours of my life'. But on the return flight he caught a virus which became pneumonia: an opportunity for more punstering postcards from 'Wun Lung Lee' to Georgina: 'It was Old Monia who drove me to the new-curled World, where I picked up NEW Monia, who sent my temperature blushing up into the chill-turned hundreds. But then I like a change of girl from time to time. I suppose it's the nympho-monia in me.' They were with the Astors for a snowy Christmas at Bruern again, where Laurie came down with another chest infection.

But in January 1971 he was soothed by being the castaway on Roy Plomley's ineffably bland *Desert Island Discs*. Music, Laurie told Plomley, gave him the deepest sense of enchantment. His eight chosen records were: Duke Ellington's 'Stevedore Stomp' – 'the first jazz record I ever bought'; 'Seguidillas', a pre-Spanish Civil War recording of guitar with La Nina de los Peines ('the true Spanish voice'); the Spanish carol 'Belen', sung by Victoria de los Angeles; Julian Bream playing Dowland's 'Lachrimae Antiquae'; a Chopin Nocturne played by Artur Rubinstein; George Harrison's 'Isn't It a Pity'; the slow movement of Beethoven's String Quartet Op. 132 ('this would be almost as important as food to me'); and finally Menuhin playing a Bach Chaconne. His chosen luxury was 'an inexhaustible supply of yeast and sugar in order to make wine or beer'. Plomley was the least probing of interrogators. 'Your Spanish War experiences presumably will be Volume Three?' Laurie: 'Yes.'

To the question of how he would face loneliness, Laurie replied: 'Pretty well I think. Even in the crowded world of today I've often chosen it. It isn't that I don't like people, I'm very gregarious, but I like to be able to withdraw from people … I only seem to operate for myself best when I'm entirely alone.' That year Tom Matthews insisted on putting up Laurie's name for Garrick Club membership. Laurie echoed Groucho Marx: 'What kind of club can it be that wants me in it?' But Matthews assured him his page had so many signatures he'd be a shoo-in.

Just as Laurie was planning to play down his countryman image, the village was invaded by cameras for the BBC's film *Cider with Rosie*. Luckily Slad still looked much as it had half a century ago, once they disguised telegraph poles as trees, and removed bollards and aerials, and the new porch from Laurie's childhood cottage. The designer Eileen Diss recreated the school in the now disused building. Hundreds piled into Stroud Subscription Rooms to become extras at £5 a day, and a search began for the perfect Rosie. Annie was played by Rosemary Leach who, having grown up as the schoolmaster's daughter in Diddlebury, Shropshire, found Slad 'just like coming home'. They re-enacted the Treaty of Versailles holiday of 1919, with a six-year-old Whiteway boy playing little Laurie in John Bull outfit; Chalford Silver Band led the procession through the village to Steanbridge House.[124]

Laurie sat in Rose Cottage garden 'out of the way like a hedgehog' fearing that Claude Whatham, the director, might over-romanticise with lyrical camera-work, 'floating through cornfields with Vaseline smeared across the lenses'. To interviewers he stressed that Slad wasn't unique, and that 'what I was writing about was not myself but a way of life, in which poverty, epidemics, filth, malnutrition, and early death were as important a part as beauty and days filled with sun'.[125] At fifty-seven, he was quietly metamorphosing into the crusty veteran who tells the world it is not what it was.

> We have lost the sense of wondering and discovery. Life is impoverished now and TV imprisons one. It steals your time and diminishes your imagination. Every night you have a ration of horror. Pakistan and Vietnam, massacres, famine and children weeping. But the viewers' compassion is no longer engaged.

As for Spain, 'What people go for is not to discover the world and foreign ways but to be guaranteed familiar food and sunshine...' The paperback of *As I Walked Out One Midsummer Morning* was just out, and Georgina told him the jacket was terrible. Laurie angrily agreed:

> Authors are not shown their book jackets for some extraordinary reason. I was appalled. Didn't I tell you – or didn't you listen? Shoals of protest letters from me to Deutsch and Penguins. 'What's this middle-aged Skid Row alcoholic doing crumpled up in the ditch of a phoney Harrods plastic Englishe hedgerow?' I ask them. 'The book is about youth, adventure, discovery and 80 per cent about Spain.' Too late, they'd already printed 90,000 copies. They promise a new jacket for the next edition

and an artist, thirtyish, very professional, is sent to Slad to talk about it.

I suggest a young man, preferably uncrumpled and light-footed, walking through a vast empty and torrid Spanish landscape. I got the result last week: it shows an old man, wearing Chinese hat and crumpled Maoist peasant jacket and trousers, tottering shoulders-drooping down an anonymous road. The artist wrote, saying, 'I know you didn't wear a hat, but ... it would save me the trouble of drawing the back of your head.'

Laurie concealed from the world his illnesses and the 'modern wonder drugs' he took 'which fortify the resistance of the body by lowering that of the spirit'. He would never write about his miseries, he told Georgina: 'I can write poems about love, about wanting, almost never about loss. A bad limitation perhaps, where my poetry is concerned.' He was 'a melancholic man who likes to be thought merry'.

In a washout summer, 'our spreading Jess-nut tree', now almost eight, had completed her first literary commission, a piece about her parents for *Vogue*:

My mummy is clever and makes lots and lots of wine and drinks it and she also digs hard in the garden. My daddy is more clever than mummy. He doesn't dig in the garden. He writes books and looks after us all. My mummy has long fair hair, blue eyes, pink cheeks and drives the car. I love her. Daddy has a light brown face, silver hair. Today he doesn't go under the sea any more, but he drinks wisky and plays the violin and guitar. He's often ill or lazy. I wouldn't choose any other mummy or daddy. They shout a lot and mummy's got a very loud voice and dad's got a very soft voice and they shout at me and each other...

That winter the *Telegraph* magazine sent him to fly on Concorde. Laurie, who kept a vigilant record of every air crash, noting flight details and numbers of dead, had always been both fascinated and awed by flight, ever since his first flight in 1933 when he was piloted by Sir Alan Cobham in 'an old Imperial Airways liner' round Gloucester. Now he would fly in the cockpit of Concorde from the Cotswold test-base near Fairford to the north of Spain and back, in just 105 minutes – a journey that had taken 'two years of foot-slogging and scheming in my youth'. He concluded: 'True, for the first time I had travelled faster than sound. I had even reached Mach 2.07 without pain. But emotionally, in fact, I'd been nowhere, seen nothing. We might as well have been circling over cloud above Cheltenham.'[126]

While Kathy and Jessy stayed with Helen in Italy that winter, Laurie had 'a peaceful solitary Christmas' when words of praise were showered on the televised *Cider with Rosie*. It was found to be enchanting, lyrical, evocative, authentic, masterly. Some found it too reticent about poverty and bleak winters and Annie's feckless improvidence; Mary Holland pointed out that Laurie had been wryly aware of writing from middle age, so that even hunger was sentimentally remembered. 'Take away this saving self-knowledge and he can come very close to Patience Strong.' But as a final moving touch Laurie himself was filmed in the lane, turning his head to watch the child he had once been walk by. And the playwright Hugh Whitemore got the Writers' Guild award for his script.

Laurie now wrote only on commission. A travel piece about Copenhagen; Berkeley Castle's history for the *Telegraph*; Hong Kong ('full of Lees', he reported); and in May 1972 to Beirut – still a prosperous, cosmopolitan pleasure-ground – maintaining in print at least his exuberance and lively curiosity. In London, he was at every literary gathering. 'There was Laurie Lee,' wrote Jilly Cooper (a neighbour in Bisley) after the Royal Academy summer exhibition party, 'looking gloomy, as if he didn't want to drink cider with anyone.' He protested, and Jilly sent a mollifying note: 'Dear Laurie, I only said you looked gloomy because in real life you look so lovely. We must have lunch...' He was constantly asked to judge things: poems by the young for the *Daily Mail*, poems by inmates of H. M. prisons for the Arthur Koestler award; the Whitbread award with Elizabeth Jane Howard and James Pope-Hennessy. He read an Anglo-Saxon poem at a Queen Elizabeth Hall concert of electronic synthesiser music. At the Stratford poetry festival in July, he gave his 'familiar and warmly captivating busking act as poet-entertainer'.

While he was away in Beirut, Cecil Day-Lewis died at Lemmons, the Hertfordshire home of Kingsley Amis and Elizabeth Jane Howard, and was buried at Stinsford in Dorset a few feet from Hardy's grave. Laurie wrote to Rosamond Lehmann thanking her for a moving letter.

> I am garrulous about everything except the loves which touch me closely (as you well know) & this one I will discuss with no one. I have not been quite persona grata for many years in that direction – except for his vague but distant goodwill. You are right about the awful mask, but I don't think it covered a 'degeneracy of spirit' but rather guilt & unhappiness, which of course he would never admit to anyone … He kept up a good front, but he was always aware of the destruction he had caused to himself & others; & I think secretly he was always haunted by the Smiler & the Knife – the Smiler was for his friends, but the Knife was self-inflicted & he carried it deeply.

At Day-Lewis's memorial service on 25 October 1972 at St Martin-in-the-Fields, he sat in a side pew. 'Widow in white. Air of theatrical first night – last entrance K. A. & Dark Lady of the sonnets [Amis and Elizabeth Jane Howard] – large black hat, black coat, black glasses. Fauré's Requiem.' As Jill Balcon received mourners on the steps, Laurie left by a side door. Later, when Sean Day-Lewis approached Laurie for help with his father's biography, Laurie told him he couldn't talk about Cecil, even to Sean. 'What remains is either vague or too difficult, although he was the man I liked most among my friends, and was the kindest to me.'

Laurie had made a decision that summer of 1972: 'I haven't said much about it but I don't mean to live in Slad any more,' he told

P. J. Kavanagh, 'except perhaps for a brief summer visit.' Perversely, in the same letter Laurie tried to persuade Kavanagh and his new wife Kate, who lived nearby, to buy Snows Farm in Slad. He advertised Rose Cottage for rent at £10 a week in the *Sunday Times*, and had a deluge of responses. Not long before, he had bought (for £400) the Sheepscombe village cricket ground, where his uncles, grandfather and great-grandfather had all played, to preserve it in perpetuity. Sheepscombe was his ancestral village, and the cricket ground had one of the best views in Gloucestershire.

But he had decided that creative artists can only work in cities. Gloucestershire had never produced an artist of great stature because life there was too satisfying. He also felt he was drowning in *Cider*: following the television film, the play was now being performed in every local rep, college and school. A horse called *Cider with Rosie* won at Newmarket at 100–6. Richard Covington, landlord of the Woolpack, had concocted a '*Cider with Rosie*' cocktail for trippers.

Back in London that autumn he grew a beard, and appeared at an anti-Franco deputation to protest against Spain joining the Common Market, organised by Rosamond's former husband Wogan Philipps (Lord Milford), who told him he looked 'very imposing & handsome, magnificent in the fur coat, the envy of all in the deputation'. Inside he was feeling far from enviable. Princess Peg wrote from Tarasp, urging Laurie to join her and Benjamin Britten in the peace and snow: 'good & bad days shared'. Celia had reported to Peg that Kathy was 'at the end of her tether' with Laurie's illnesses, 'a slow and relentless doom'.

> So it is knockout drugs, depression from having taken them, drink to kill the depression, and then back to square A again. Cathy wants to get out and do something to use her mind and get away from household chores, for she has no help with them ... Oh what an awful life for both of them, and it has been going on for so long.

Kathy's letter to Celia about the Laurie problem was indeed despairing:

> We really are at a loss as to what to do for him... It's so diffi-
> cult to explain to either doctor or friends how this clever
> lucid & witty man is privately plunged in a war against
> despair – loss of hope & frustration. I think they would try
> to help more if he was reduced to a gibbering idiot – when
> it's too late of course. It's such a shame that no one in the
> medical profession cares enough to take that extra trouble
> over a man like Laurie.
>
> They don't seem to realise that perhaps he does know
> his own situation better than they do, that by listening to
> him they could be learning more about a disease that people
> know very little about. Epilepsy allied to a simple ordinary
> mind is difficult enough but in conjunction with such a
> sharpness of focus as L's has, is more difficult.

She dealt with it by being a bit vague about everything, she said,
and keeping cheerful, especially when she heard him playing music
in his room, often a tape of himself playing his violin with Celia's
accompaniment, which was 'balm'. He had just written a poem, the
first in years, 'another moment of sudden happiness'. The poem
Laurie had written was a moving sixtieth birthday tribute to Princess
Peg, when all her friends, including the Prince of Wales, clubbed
together to buy her a new Steinway grand. It ended with a heartfelt
lament for her loss of Prince Ludwig.

Laurie affected to be wryly amused in 1973 when Philip Larkin's
Oxford Book of Twentieth-Century English Verse, 'criticised in the
press for having too many poets from the 1940s onwards in it',
excluded him completely. Yet Laurie was a guest of honour at the
Foyle's luncheon, sitting a few feet from Larkin. After the speeches
the actress Margaret Rawlings stood up and declared, 'I would like
to applaud a poet not in the anthology – Laurie Lee'; and Ralph

Richardson declaimed 'Hear, hear.' John Lehmann wrote next day
to say that if Miss Rawlings had not mentioned it, he might have
done so himself: 'A scandal.' But the damage was done; Laurie never
forgave Larkin.

'There's no fun in my face now,' Laurie told Tom. The notebook he wrote during a two-month trip to Tangier and Marrakesh
for *Mademoiselle*, vividly reflects the depressed state of mind. He
walked in cold rain on cobbled streets, noting poverty, 'smell of
boiling seafood', people with small eyes. He was losing his sense of
taste: 'most expensive meal I've ever had & couldn't taste a thing'. In
the market they sold gaudy plastic toys and fretwork plates; a tribes-
woman looking like a Murillo in a candlelit tent stall sold rock salt or
sandalwood: 'Everything else sham.'

He was tired and sick, 'legs aching & shaking', kept awake at
night by storms and quarrels in the streets. 'Used to land in Tangier
straight off boat into town. Now half mile walk along quay. All new
& hideous concrete. Nothing gets easier or cosier. Rough crossing
– most people sick – Algeciras unrecognisable. A kind of Detroit
of skyscrapers.'

Tangier's sandy beach was somehow obscene: 'No girls, only
solitary furtive figures, elderly Anglo Saxons, or leathercoated
pimps, or djellabahed louts trying to sell wallets & themselves.
Robed figure (brown) lying on sand like Henry Moore. Some Arab
boys startlingly dressed by elder Ang Sax boyfriends I suspect'
including one 'about 13 striding long-legged in crushed raspberry
from head to toe'.

He had a 'crisis' on the beach, and had to run back to his room and
draw the shutters. But in any case, foreign ways no longer charmed
him. Why did men stand about or sit in cafés all day, talking and
whistling, while women scurried about, loaded, anxious, carrying
food, 'keeping things going'? How come, when he tried to summon
the barman, 'suddenly eleven inert men ordered whiskies'? 'At bar
you can pay & go at will, joke with barman,' he grumbled. 'At table
you are trapped in a ritual, brought unrecognisable & cold food,

wine one hasn't ordered, then waiter disappears; when after 2 hours boredom you wish to get the bill it is like a savage sentence which you must pay to achieve liberty.' He felt

> pitiless even to cripples – how bitter I am become by my old age. Losing my temper when men in small shops don't understand one of 3 languages but only frown; I shout. In bar near hotel, nodded & smiled to Arab with fez – he tipped it on front of his head – was this insult? smell of cats. Whores yawning in café at 8 p.m. All's fair in love & whore.

On his last day he went shopping ('Bracelet – too much'; 'Bargained for birdcage – didn't buy it') and panicked when he thought he had missed his ferry ('was I stuck for another week?') On the homeward voyage 'drank whiskies all afternoon with Capt Renshaw – he bachelor with 2 room flat in Hove, furniture covered with plastic wrappings, seldom there – "very lonely".'

When Tom Matthews introduced him to the Garrick Club as a new member, he had to apologise for departing abruptly. 'I suddenly felt ill and didn't want to be burdensome (probably too much good drink).' After the memorial service for his old friend Ralph Jarvis in March 1973, he and Celia repaired to Fortnum's for tea, where Laurie, still with greying beard, seemed dejected. Jessy was always dashing off to play with friends, he said, or rushing at him in high spirits when he felt awful. Celia told him this was normal at the age of ten. 'He feels that Jess is his "last love" and he can't help setting too much store by her, so he is sure to be hurt, for how can a child realise that? It would be asking it to be grown up, a contradiction in terms.' Laurie wrote afterwards to apologise for burdening Celia with such things.

Yet that same month, Iain Morley, head of English at a Brent comprehensive, took two coachloads of fifth-formers, studying *Cider with Rosie* for O-level, to Slad, and when they went into the Woolpack they were amazed to find themselves talking to a friendly and receptive Laurie Lee. 'He even wrote a special letter to a girl called Jacky who had been ill and missed the trip. We were all very struck by his affability and kindness.' The trip from Brent was repeated every summer for the next four years. And when Iain Morley took early retirement in late 1988, disgusted with attitudes to education in Brent, then in the grip of the 'loony Left', he won £4 in a *Spectator* competition for the following clerihew:

> The world of '*Cider with Rosie*'
> Is traditional, touching, even cosy –
> (Thus causing discontent
> To educationalists in Brent.)

When schoolchildren first 'swarmed' through Slad, in 1969, Laurie said he wished they would not: they could never see the village as he had known it as a boy. 'I sat playing in the middle of the road. These children come and see cars whizzing through at 60 m.p.h. They expect a remote little village full of eccentrics, bullies and daffies. They read about me as a scabby little boy. They find a grey old man.' But a girl wrote to say she had visited Slad that June before her English exam, and had seen 'a stage-set worthy of a play. For us the outing acted as a sort of tranquilliser. I will never forget it because you have passed on the magic through your book.' The Gloucestershire poet U. A. Fanthorpe, former English mistress at Cheltenham Ladies' College, wrote her poem 'Dear Mr Lee'[127] which probably expresses best the fond feelings children everywhere began to have for the author of *Cider with Rosie*.

Laurie was, as the Irish say, 'a street angel, home devil' – sweet to outsiders and children, but sometimes monstrously irritable with his own family. The indifferent way he treated Kathy was observed with dismay by friends. He criticised her cooking, and seemed to berate her for not being a different kind of person. (Once he told her, in front of guests, to go and change her dress.) If anyone clattered plates, he would lash out. Much contrition was called for, after splendid country weekends. Laurie was not visibly drunk; but he did drink without regard to the seven pills he was taking daily, including 5mg of Valium thrice a day. From 1973 Laurie's doctor in Painswick was Jim Hoyland, who himself became epileptic in his sixties, possibly (like Laurie) as a result of a blow on the head in youth. He told me Laurie was 'a law unto himself' medically, with his 'battery of idiosyncratic drugs'. What Dr Hoyland enjoyed about Laurie's visits was talking about poetry.

'All epileptics are shy about epilepsy,' said Dr Hoyland, 'There is a stigma: people are afraid that you might pass out and start frothing at the mouth.' It explains a great deal about Laurie's secretiveness, that he was constantly aware of the possibility of, and often trying to ward off, a blackout. To Philip Oakes, on a train journey down to Slad, he confided his constant terror about being suddenly afflicted by an attack. He was 'pursued by caravanserais of demons'.

The televising of *Cider* had brought a letter from brother Jack (who had once bought a film option on *Cider* himself for £100) in Sydney, urging Laurie to come out and visit him, suggesting that he approach BOAC to pay his fare – 'after all you're pretty famous now'.

It was Jack and Laurie's first reunion for ten years. But something came between them afterwards. They met only once again, in Slad a year later, but after that Laurie did not speak to Jack for the rest of his life. Jack bitterly regretted the rift. What happened? Their boyhood companionship had first been damaged by their separation at school. Annie would chide Laurie for scorning Jack ('he did all he could for you when you were lost in Spain & afterwards, & I never hear you speak a good word for him and it hurts me Laurie it does'). But they had outgrown childhood grievances. Both had done well in different fields. And they had some good times in Sydney.

Julian Bream, who had got to know Jack on his Australian tours, thought Jack and Laurie were in fact so alike they were bound to irritate one another. Kathy believed there was a rift over pictures. When Laurie started collecting art, he gave Jack and Nora his Paul Klee, Leonard Rosoman and Henry Moore paintings for safe-keeping. Later these all went to Rose Cottage. When Laurie told Jack he needed cash and was selling the Henry Moore, Jack bought it from him for £100. Nora eventually sold it, with Jack's approval, when their son Howard was going to Cambridge. This may have rankled with Laurie. Nobody was certain what made Laurie suddenly cut Jack out of his life. The Australian trip that year had ended amicably enough, when Jack drove Laurie 850 miles to Adelaide.

There, Laurie was a great hit with Jack's sister-in-law Anne Kidman and her family, entertaining them on the violin, recorder and kazoo. Anne drove Laurie round the pubs and he gave Anne's son Will, aged ten, a tiny silver gun which could shoot a bullet through a pile of newspapers. An interview in the *Australian* that Christmas was perceptive about Laurie. 'Despite his wit, his tendency to self-parody and to bouts of teddy-bear humour,' Elizabeth Riddell wrote, 'he says he is, and I believe him, a melancholy and solitary man.'

In January 1974 the two brothers, along with Humphrey Fisher, son of the Archbishop of Canterbury, went to the Test match against New Zealand. Instead of watching from the members' pavilion they stood on 'the Hill', which Laurie had wanted to see ever since bicycling to see Gloucestershire playing the Australians as a lad. Most spectators were stripped to the waist, pot-bellied, and each had an ice-box of beer. New Zealand were batting when the trouble began. Laurie and Jack were caught in crossfire between cheering New Zealand fans below, and jeering Australians above, hurling cans and bottles at one another. Laurie was struck on the head by a bottle and large drops of blood fell on his Somerset Maugham tropical suiting. Next day he made the front pages of both the Sydney and Melbourne *Heralds*. 'I bled like a slaughtered calf,' he told them, but 'I fell into the soft arms of some young student nurses, who held my wound closed with their long scented fingers until the bandages arrived.'

A bronzed Laurie arrived home to Kathy and went straight to bed: 'Fever, stomach, cold. Woozy all day. Big pill evening.' Two weeks later he was 'still coughing and seismatic sneezing' followed by 'Drinking. Drunk. Hangover.' His trilogy in a gift set had been among the top five Christmas sellers, as André Deutsch told him over lunch at the Gay Hussar. Laurie bought himself a youthful denim suit at Austin Reed, but in many respects the year of his sixtieth birthday looked like being one he might prefer to forget. Or so the diary evidence indicates.

'24 Feb. Drinking heavily. Fell down at station. Broke glasses.' Next day: 'Bed stomach cold fever.' 3 March: 'DC 10 Turkish airline crash in Paris all 347 killed, over 200 Brit, worst ever. CAUGHT CHILL.' By 31 March, a sunny day, his alcohol tally was a neat '6 beers 6 whiskies 6 sherries'. Neither of his daughters could please him. Jessy in a restaurant was bad-mannered. Even the adored Yasmin was now 'scatty'.

But he still inserted the occasional joke: 'I say I say. Lord Elgin's lost his marbles. Oh how a museum.' And

> I'm dancing with wool in my eyes
> For the girl in my arms is a ewe.

Tom Matthews, who had just published his book on T. S. Eliot, took Laurie to dine at the Garrick. 'A cloud of benign unknowing seemed to settle on me during the latter part of the evening,' Laurie later apologised; had they really ended up dancing down Piccadilly at 1 a.m? Matthews nobly took charge of Laurie's sixtieth birthday celebration, inviting Laurie and Kathy to the Commem Ball at his Alma Mater, New College Oxford, on 25 June – 'a glimpse of golden youth in my green old age,' wrote Laurie afterwards.

Through the rest of that year, a jagged line could be drawn, with whisky rescuing him from 'subdued panic'. Days in bed, days of recovery, days when he 'kept going on drink all day', nights in 'the Elms' followed by 'hangover'. A hit-and-run driver knocked down the Rose Cottage garage wall. Life was full of such tribulations, and rain came in through the roof. Douglas Chisholm, the Chelsea barber who since 1972 had been cutting Laurie's luxuriant 'artistic' hair (about which he was rather vain), tried to warn him that he'd be an alcoholic if he carried on like this. He drank too much at the Spanish Embassy on election night in October 1974 – it was also the 'anniversary of Spain's discovery of America' – when Labour scraped in with a majority of three.

Towards the year's end, however, he managed to carry off a sobering social occasion that might daunt anyone. One Saturday that November, they were staying in Sussex with Jim Rose, old friend and music-lover, who was now chairman of Penguin Books, and his wife Pam. The Roses' neighbours, Lord and Lady Rupert Nevill, invited them all to dinner, saying 'Rupert's boss and his wife are coming' – i.e. the Queen and Prince Philip. Laurie was seated by the Queen. Pam Rose recalled:

> A lady called Lulu de Waldner had brought some pate de foie gras 'for la reine d'Angleterre' which was handed round. When Laurie said, 'Oh I thought it was kipper paste from Tunbridge Wells,' Her Majesty was very amused and put on a Gloucestershire accent to talk to him.

After dinner Laurie, Kathy and Prince Philip sat on a sofa together, with much laughter. Prince Philip complimented Kathy on her blue eyes, and later he and Laurie exchanged books. Laurie sent his trio of bestsellers. In return, Prince Philip's volume of *Selected Speeches* arrived, inscribed 'for Laurie Lee: some of my embarrassingly large old stock. Philip'.

24

I Can't Stay Long
1975–1979

AFTER FIVE FALLOW years, André Deutsch suggested publishing a collection of Laurie's travel pieces and essays. Recycling journalism – or as Laurie put it, clearing the 'barnacled chaos' of his room – is a refuge or diversion for unproductive authors. Re-reading his essays on 'Charm', 'Love' etc., he was struck by the 'confident enthusiasm and unabashed celebration of the obvious'. And most places he had written about with such exuberance were now ineradicably changed by war, prosperity and tourism. But *I Can't Stay Long* was an illuminating repository of Laurie's observations over three decades. He bet André Deutsch £25 that it would never sell 5,000. Deutsch knew better. Eventually, a brown envelope arrived at Deutsch's house in Fulham containing five £5 notes.

Laurie's mid-1970s pocket diaries are much possessed by money, drink and death. As inflation took hold, he noted the soaring price of everything from cassettes to train fares. His Chelsea rent increased to £560 a year. He owed £4,500 to Deutsch, soon repaid. Jessy started at Queen's Gate School at £275 a term, and Laurie reckoned he was left with £78 a week to live on. Quotidian irritants such as tax returns, residents' parking fees, a rail strike, a rates revaluation jostled with grim entries about deaths, whether he knew the deceased or not. Two of his half-sisters, Dorothy and Phyllis, died in 1975. Jim Donleavy, the Queen's Elm barman, 'died (heart)'. So did Aristotle Onassis, Lord Montgomery, Sir Carol Reed. Benjamin Britten died (heart) at sixty-three. The Behrenses' son lost his wife in a riding accident.

Claude Whatham, director of *Cider with Rosie*, lost his son ('motorbike'). Often, such deaths were the only entries in the diary.

He still recorded each blooming daffodil, the weather, the state of the moon, his own weight. But he was also making a daily tally of what he drank. 'Champagne wine 2 large whiskies.' 'Champ. 4 beers, red & white wine.' On 5 April 1975 he got 'v. drunk' when Frank Mansell won on the Grand National. Retiring to bed with hangovers and fevers was a continual refrain. He felt he was losing all sense of taste. He marked with an 'X' days when he took his knockout pill. 'Pill 8.30/4.0 Out evening pub. Mistake.' And so on. Interviewers still found him 'relaxed, courteous and good-humoured'. *The Guardian* man who went down to Slad in 1977 had a good day out: they shot at beer bottles with a .22 rifle in the garden (Laurie now had a gun licence) and Laurie played his violin, took him to the Woolpack and down to the pond where, he said, he'd once brought 'a debby girl' and photographed her in the nude. And those who met Laurie in pubs in the 1970s saw the bar-room charmer who gathered around him an adoring coterie. He lunched at the Garrick with Tom Matthews, Hugh Casson, John Betjeman. But he was drinking recklessly. After one Dublin spree with Matthews, Laurie thanked Tom for 'leading me out into the paths of light & Kildare Street. You were in splendid form; it was I who cracked in the end.' Two weeks later he told Matthews that 'the travellers' cheques I lost in Dublin were found in a Nighttown Bar near the Liffey and handed in to the authorities intact. God bless Ireland.'

In the snowy spring of 1975 they were in 'damp, cold' Rose Cottage during the building work on Littlecourt, the much bigger house next door. Littlecourt is not traditionally pretty, but it is a secret house, wood-clad, backing on to the lane behind the Woolpack, with a broad, steep south-facing garden and terrace overlooking the panorama of Swift's Hill. Laurie installed a big picture window to capture the whole valley, knowing this to be a vulgar excrescence on a period house, but masking it with climbing

'Albertine' roses and clematis. The view made the house, and was 'one of my great refreshments' for the rest of his life. He knew exactly where the sun came up over the trees in the morning, and the moon over the hill at night. He could leave the Woolpack at sundown, and be home (eighteen paces) before shadows fell.

In the heatwave of June 1975, dairymaid dresses in ruffled cheesecloth were in style, and words from *Cider with Rosie* were used as fashion captions in *Vogue*. Courage off-licences offered *Cider with Rosie* paperbacks with three packs of beer. Daimler used the *Cider with Rosie* passage about the Squire's Daimler in its ads. Laurie simmered in Slad as the temperature climbed to 90, with occasional forays to 'Weston-super-Nightmare' and local horse shows with Jessy. It was their silver wedding that May. Laurie was commandeered by the local press ('Laurie Lee in Fight to Save Valley') to lead a petition against a Bovis Homes development of 700 houses in the Slad valley: the first of many such campaigns. Visitors came (including brother Jack and his wife, for the last time), but Laurie was either bedevilled by whisky or saved by it: 'Crisis morning averted by whisky.'

Alan Ross found his old friend Laurie was now 'happiest in the pub, surrounded by cronies, people sitting at his feet, listening to the sage talking'. The *Telegraph* magazine suggested a piece about his favourite pub, the Queen's Elm. 'The Elms', as he called it, was more like a club than a pub, a byword for camaraderie, centred on the ebullient Irish landlord Sean Treacy who kept his clientele 'in a perpetual state of good spirits'. Moreover, Treacy would protect Laurie when he wanted to be alone; and like the Woolpack landlord, was willing to sell Laurie's books behind the bar.

'It's not the comfort, it's not the service, it's the people,' Laurie's 'Elms' notes began.

Oliver Reed, Michael Craig, Bill Travers, Ronald Fraser, Sean Connery, Eric Sykes, John Tavener, Lucian Freud, Bobby Birch, Reg Bosanquet. Cartoonists Gerald Scarfe, Frank Dickens,

Jak. Artists Bill Thomson, Lis Frink, Nicola Bayley. Peeresses,
Olympic swimmers, diminutive Corsican crooks, Turkish
pearl divers, Jet Harris Cliff Richard's guitarist, Ava Gardner,
bare-midriff models, students, Irish, Russians, Basques.
Photographers. Cops. Robbers. Lone drinkers. Writers. Poets.
Golfers. Psychiatrists. Barristers. Judges. Drifters. Dentists &
doctors. Bank managers. The Vicar of Chelsea. 6 o'clock empty.
7 o'clock accountants & solitary boozers, & a warm wave of
erotic air...

What Laurie loved about 'the Elms' was its honest squalor.
Behind its handsome Victorian art nouveau doors, it was 'a stage
set surrounded by bottles. Scene of love affairs, suicides, changing of partners, where tears & blood might flow...' On the walls
were Treacy's collection of pipes (later sold at Christie's) and
framed cartoons by the *Evening Standard* cartoonist Jak, himself a
legendary drinker, a Judo black belt and high-spending ladies' man.
Treacy published his own bar-room anecdotes in *A Smell of Broken
Glass* – in which Laurie features as busker, billiards champion and
darts-player who aimed his darts through a two-foot blow-pipe.
Once, Laurie had burst through the door of the pub in a djellabah,
brandishing an Arab flintlock rifle which he pointed at Sliwo Isaac,
the Babylonian Christian barman from Baghdad, and cried, 'I've
come to take you back.'

The barmaid was Mavis Cheek (not yet a well-known novelist),
a remarkable blue-eyed black-haired beauty. Treacy would place
the most popular drinks on the bottom shelves so that Mavis in her
mini had to do a lot of bending over. Having just left her husband,
Mavis found Laurie a sympathetic listener on his stool at the bar. But
he was never alone for long. Girls flocked. He and Bryan Wharton,
the nattily dressed *Sunday Times* photographer, were usually
surrounded by pretty girls, and each thought the other was the lure.
They talked of doing a book together, about seaports: what larks they
could have in Marseilles, Algeciras, Famagusta ... Laurie accused

Wharton of dressing too flamboyantly to be a photographer, and bet him a bottle of whisky he couldn't take his picture without Laurie realising it; he lost the bet, since Laurie was distracted by Wharton's then girlfriend, a beautiful Yugoslav, while Wharton snapped away.

Laurie's charm in action was something to witness. Jill Balcon saw him at a BBC luncheon, holding a table of women producers spellbound. Mavis Nicholson wore a fetching lavender frock 'to look *Cider with Rosie*ish' when she interviewed Laurie in 1975 for her Thames television programme *Good Afternoon*, and Laurie, in white safari jacket ('my Ernest Hemingway look'), gave her a lot of flirtatious sidelong eye contact and made teasing claims such as 'I'm not a women's libber by any means; I like chasing women up trees and tying them to the topmost branches.' Mavis took to Laurie and brought her teenage son Steve to meet him. 'Laurie said to Steve; "Do you like books?" and Steve said "No." Laurie said, "Ah well, it's up to you. Here's £1 and you don't have to spend it on a book".'

On the programme he told Mavis: 'I know what you're going to say – I haven't written much, have I?' He said it took him half a day to write a letter to the gas company. Writing was 'sheer agony'. But he always needed his old diaries. 'They bring back an avalanche of feeling and emotion that would have been lost and forgotten if I hadn't written it down.'

When *I Can't Stay Long* was launched, Laurie spoke at an *Evening Standard* luncheon with Dame Margot Fonteyn, but was certain the book was 'dying the death'. J. B. Priestley admired the essay on 'Charm'. 'It seems a long time since we drank rum together in our room in that old hotel in Mexico City,' Priestley wrote. 'I am now old and grumpy and try to keep away from London.'

Melvyn Bragg invited Laurie on his television programme, *Read All About It.* 'He took some persuading,' Bragg recalled. They spent a long evening in the Queen's Elm, during which Bragg told Laurie he had grown up helping out in his dad's pub in Wigton. Laurie told Bragg he would appear on his programme if Bragg passed a test: to take, and remember, an order from everyone in the Queen's Elm. 'We had drunk an immense amount, and I had to concentrate like mad, and all these hardened drinkers tried to put me off my stroke,' Bragg said. But he managed it, and Laurie duly came to the studio to record the programme, still grumbling that he didn't want to, didn't like this sort of thing, and was 'unpredictable'. And so he was. After the rehearsal, Laurie locked himself in his dressing room (with bottle of whisky) and would not come out. They recorded the programme with a panel of three instead of the usual four.

Laurie had dedicated his book 'to Pen and Virginia with love'. He wrote to ask if they would mind, and they said they'd be delighted. So the falling-out with Pen Dugdale – which had lasted since she had discovered the liaison with Antonia in 1962 – was now ended. Pen herself had remarried, and with Antonia now a mother, the rift was healed. 'Pen and Virginia,' he told Elizabeth Jane Howard, as she had inquired, 'are venerable sisters I've known for ages, long before I met you, and who were good to me in my golden days, and I wanted to offer them something, though I hadn't seen them for years.' He told Jane he would dedicate a book to 'Isabel' too, 'before I die. It is overdue and most certainly one of my life's imperatives. Gerona,' he added, 'is always with me. I have never ever talked about it, let alone tried to write it, yet the most vivid impressions remain ... Dearest Isabel, I have been out of touch with almost everything. I have missed you.' She sent him 'unaltered love'.

He took Kathy and Jessy to Tangier one Christmas, to New York for another: 'madness really', he told Tom Matthews, who suggested that they stay at the Royalton: 'It's old-fashioned and there's nothing fancy about it.' (Today it is the height of minimalist glitz.) The criticism of *I Can't Stay Long* in the US was mild, apart from that of Eve Auchincloss in the *Washington Post*, who accused Laurie of 'slack and wanton verbiage': 'His language is swollen, hectic, off-target (briars bleed, skies ache).' But even she had to admire the gritty, self-mocking journalism of 'A Wake in Warsaw',

'Ibiza High Fifties', the Cannes film festival piece, and the down-to-earth reportage of Aberfan.

Thanks to beer, whisky, Cinzano, wine and fevers lasting for days, Laurie was having a 'difficult and chaotic time', he told the *Telegraph*, putting off delivery of his Queen's Elm piece. He had also agreed to write a piece for *Vogue* on 'My Day'. In his notebook, 'Whose day?' he asked himself. 'How many left – with age, tumbling faster down a slope into a dark slot marked "Don't Remember." "Lost."'

In the account of his days alone in the flat (where he now spent most of his time), he described being brutally torn from dreams each morning by a 6 a.m. jet-plane landing at Heathrow, 'just for two dozen Dutch businessmen with briefcases'. At 7 a.m. he switched on Radio 3, 'the most civilised way to wake', hoping for Telemann or Scarlatti. He slept in a room 'walled-in by books, unframed pictures, packets of other people's poems, antique glasses, oil-lamps, crucifixes of straw and wood, spools of recording tape, bits of sculpture and jars full of swizzle sticks'. His clothes were scattered. His workroom was even more disorganised and squalid, with 'a leaking roof, four kinds of peeling wallpaper, a sagging bookcase, cardboard boxes full of wine and papers, first editions signed by friends long dead … defeated poems, old manuscripts … the rusty medallions of once bright lecheries and loves'. Cupboard drawers 'fluttered with letters exhaling the heated breath of girls whom marriage has now chastely cooled or plumped into Titian matrons. Little in this loaded room is ever thrown away. There are no visitors. I am its lone curator.' He reflected: 'I remember the days when I could carry all I owned in my two hands. I decide I really must get this stuff sorted out. I know I never will.' (And he never did.)

In the shaving mirror he now saw the shade of his father. He had lunch with a TV researcher, a beautiful young girl, but she spoilt things by asking, 'Has anyone ever told you you look like Angus Wilson?' (His notebook said: 'Danny Kaye yes, even Alec Guinness – but never Dame Angus, whom God preserve.')

He recorded drinking for five hours at a stretch at the Garrick with Pat Kernon, Willis Hall and Jeff Hoare. His weight went up to fourteen stone. He wrote with some fellow-feeling when he reviewed Dylan Thomas's biography by Paul Ferris. Laurie felt close enough to Dylan not to be dazzled, or to judge him, he said. In childhood, only the Severn had divided them. Both published their first poems in the same *Sunday Referee* column, both came to London in the 1930s, and Laurie had lodged across the street from Dylan in the house of his wife Caitlin's sister (Nicolette) in Chelsea. 'Has too much been made of him? Perhaps it has,' said Laurie. 'Most of his best work was written by the time he was 30' and 'although he was a star poet and performer on both sides of the Atlantic ... yet for much of his later years he was also vulnerable, sick, self-disgusted, lonely, unhappy and mortally frightened'.[128]

Despite the woes and muddles of Laurie's life, Jessy recalled their country weekends – at Cavendish, Biddesden, Culham, Bruern, among families with children and horses and rows of gumboots – as the best years of her childhood. At Biddesden, where a grey Arab stallion called Zebedee would canter over to greet visitors, and hot Ribena was served in the mornings, she was 'the happiest child'. Bryan Guinness, Lord Moyne, looked forward to the Lees' visits with 'rejoicing' and organised country tasks like chopping logs and pulling up nettles.

The summer of 1976 was again memorably hot: a summer of parched lawns and Mediterranean evenings. The cows were motionless, the garden full of butterflies, and at Slad Laurie sat out at midnight under the stars ('Moonlight like honey'). He loved such extremes of weather, 'the smell of sun-burned leaves and the droning sound of insects' wings'. When the rain finally came, it leaked into his bedroom. He went to a dinner for the twenty-fifth anniversary of the Festival of Britain, and several poetry readings, when he was 'a proper old ham', said Ted Walker, his fellow poet, 'with his alarm clock'. This Laurie would place ostentatiously on the table, in case the readers overran their allotted time.

Ted Walker – whose bond with Laurie was chiefly Spain, where

Ted emigrated – found Laurie in the street during the Stroud Festival on 9 October 1976.

> Laurie was trailing along miserably through a lightly falling drizzle, holding a cut-glass tankard with a wan drop of beer in it. 'I'm a favourite son of Stroud,' he said. '*Un hijo preferido.* They've given me this thing today. Got my name on it, look. I hate cut glass. But I don't know what to do with it, there's nowhere I can put it down. Someone'll find it and seek me out.'

He took Walker to 'a roughish bar'. 'After a few pints Laurie said, "We'll be expected at dear old Christopher Fry's reading, won't we? Half past seven kick-off."' (A week earlier all three had performed at Chichester.)

Laurie led the way, still clutching his tankard, to the packed Subscription Rooms. Walker and Laurie stood at the back, where Fry saw them and gave a half wave. While Fry was reading from *A Phoenix Too Frequent*, Laurie whispered, 'Follow me.' They negotiated an imposing staircase with red plush carpet, a landing, another corridor with coconut matting, then another with old worn boards.

> At the end we reached a door behind which one knew there would be mops and canisters of Vim and galvanised buckets, and a chipped sink and tea-making equipment for ladies in floral wrap-around housecoats. In we went. 'This,' said Laurie, 'is where I wrote a good deal of *As I Walked Out One Midsummer Morning.*'

There was 'a state of confusion on the domestic front', Laurie told Tom Matthews, who was a lifeline, 'a rock in the ocean', still offering weekends, theatre visits, dinner at New College, a trip to Dublin. But Laurie was constantly writing apologetic letters after aborted weekends. When Tom invited Laurie and Kathy to a dinner at Brooks's for Hugh Cudlipp in January 1977, he received this letter: 'Dear Tom, It may sound unbelievable to organised people but Cathy & I have not been out to dinner together for a long time. I am not particularly proud of this but then we are a most disorganised & rather out-of-touch family.' (But Laurie did get to the Cudlipp dinner, a memorable evening. 'My Lord Cudlipp in his cups grew positively cuddly.')

This was the Queen's Jubilee Year, and Laurie found himself alongside Kingsley Amis on the *Daily Mail*'s judging panel to find a jubilee poem better than Betjeman's. Over bottles of Glenlivet on the floor of Amis's house off Flask Walk, Hampstead, they sorted through the entries. Laurie was struck by 'the drowsy evensong drone of the church harmonium' in many poems, and the way the amateur poets saw the Queen as a vulnerable wife and mother who had suffered. 'She has sometimes a look of pain on her face and yet she always carries on with the job. I think people have responded to that,' Laurie said. Kingsley Amis wasn't having any of it. 'Nobody said about George V or VI how tedious it must be to launch a battle-ship,' he snorted.

Penguin celebrated *Cider with Rosie*'s continuing success – by May 1977 the hardback was in its thirteenth impression, and it had sold a million in paperback – in some style, giving him a gold foun-tain pen and a miniature Lis Frink eagle, and a party at the Chelsea Arts Club on a glorious summer day. The Hogarth Press reissued *The Firstborn* in paperback. There was a Decca triple album of Laurie's readings. *I Can't Stay Long* was a paperback bestseller and when Laurie read extracts on *A Book at Bedtime*, in January 1979, Jill Balcon wrote thanking him for 'spellbinding evocations'. Her son Daniel Day-Lewis (now twenty-one and at drama school, 'very like Cecil – gloriously funny & handsome') had 'practically wept, as I did … I felt you were talking to me. You are so deeply associated with Cecil in my mind & heart & therefore with the most central part of my life & its happiest days.'

Poetry had left Laurie for ever. 'You need the passion,' he said. 'You have to write for someone.' Instead, he would turn out a nostalgic piece for *Reader's Digest* on 'A Village Christmas',[129] or a personal reminiscence about love – a subject on which he was considered an

expert. In a St Valentine's Day piece in 1979[130] Laurie came closest
to describing the two distinctly different female types he had long
regarded as his ideal. One was the Rosie type – gold-haired, with
petalled curls: 'The recurrence of this healthy, romping, innocently
carnal little blonde has been with me like perpetual summer.' The other
was the type he had first discerned as a boy in the publican's daughter:

> something sinuous, slant-eyed, oriental or celtic, with hair
> black as slate or the oils of Oman. You did not play lightly with
> this smoked night-figure. The involvement was graver, more
> deeply entangled, and her reincarnation over the years has
> ever in some ways been witchlike, announced by a pricking of
> the thumbs, a fatal chill of excitement.

From what crevice of the mind, he wondered, did 'the dark one
rise, that she should so incessantly command my senses?' He had
met the dark one since,

> in flashing glimpses or in longer possessions, under different
> names and in different places, in India, Spain, Cornwall,
> London. Looking back, I see this recurring image as one of the
> preservatives of love, a succession of occupations by a spirit
> unique to herself and to which all one's passions belong.
>   I don't say that this way happiness lies (believing mere
> happiness to be one of life's shallower experiences). This
> hovering visitation need not always be a physical presence. It
> can be a quality of mind, a way of regarding the world. But for
> me ... the stronger and most compelling has always been the
> dark one, her panther tread, voice full of musky secrets, her
> limbs uncoiling on beds of moonlight.

This is the closest Laurie came, in print, to confessing to the hold
Lorna – or the spirit and essence of Lorna, or Lorna's physical
and spiritual type – had over him. And the mention of 'Cornwall'

is the only public reference to the place where she first cast her seductive enchantment.

In the same year Laurie firmly turned down the *Telegraph* magazine's invitation to write a serious analysis of how post-Franco political changes had affected Spanish life, arts, mores and religion. But he would go to Venice for them, to write about Harry's Bar. Forty years earlier he had arrived there, 'a melancholy city cloaked in November mists, with signs at canal corners saying *Andante* and *Grave*'. This time he spent the best part of a day searching for Harry's Bar, which 'looked like a small country bank'. On the bar were plump white sandwiches 'moist and cool as the breast of nuns'. After a few dry Martinis, 'keen and crisp as arctic crevices', he sampled Bellinis, Tiepolos and Giorgiones. He got on famously with Arrigo Cipriani, whose father Giuseppe had founded Harry's Bar. Cipriani gave him some short stories and said he had always wanted to be a writer himself.

Jessy was now entering her teenage years. This bolshy stage is a commonplace pain for all parents and Laurie was not good at facing it. His diary records exasperated scenes about Jessy's rudeness, ill-temper and the usual war between mother and daughter over hairstyles, make-up, and Jessy dancing alone in her room. But then, a father who was in the pub or lying in a darkened room for much of the time was hardly helpful to mother or daughter. And Laurie's epilepsy, he insisted, had to be kept from Jessy at all costs. 'Carefully planned to conceal illness from J,' says his diary on 22 March 1976. 'Took pill after she left for school – forced self to get up, shave & dress before her return.'

Keeping Jessy happy, keeping her protected, and keeping her at home became a major preoccupation. When she was born, he had (rashly) written: 'I don't want to educate my daughter at a level above her parents, so that she'll be … an uneasy aristocrat fed by parent serfs. I want to try to keep her classless. Her childhood is too precious to hand her over to the boarding school factories…'

But in 1977 they moved her out of her London school, Queen's

Gate, to board at the highly academic Cheltenham Ladies' College. Laurie thought he was protecting her from London temptations. Kathy said it was 'to separate her from these two adults going on all around her'. Jessy was furious: 'I'd been closeted in the triangle of the family. And now my parents had sent me away.' Her father wanted to keep her from the influence of friends 'but he would also ask me, why aren't you making any friends?'

When Jessy's blue budgerigar, now aged ten, fell off his perch while sitting next to Laurie in the big window, he was put in the deep freeze, occasionally brought out to show guests, whereupon Laurie would say, 'That's where I'll end up one day.' In the same year, 1977, Laurie bought Jessy a new pet: a horse called the Red Baron, known as Red. Jessy was an unconventional and intrepid bareback rider.

But Jessy was 'not at all what I had planned', Laurie wrote, in May 1978, in an update on *The Firstborn* for the *Daily Mail*. In the photograph she was a sultry milkmaid with long curls in an embroidered dress, surrounded by flowers. 'She is fourteen now and as tall as I am...' (She was five foot ten and as shapely as her mother had been at that age.)

The 'tiny bruised plum' he had eulogised in babyhood had become 'a rich round peach centred with an immoveable diamond stone'. Almost nothing that he had wished or expected had happened between them – but then, he had foolishly wished her to grow up into 'a wisp of Colette-style sensitivity'. This was, he now admitted, 'a doddering dad's vulgar fantasy'. Absurdly, he claimed he had pictured her 'inquiring grave-eyed and listening to my god-like illuminations, seeking my presence above all others, comforting me in the evening with chords of Chopin and perhaps waking me in the morning with a light kiss or a flower.

'She has taught me to know better. As she has grown up, I too have had to grow up, and learn to bury away my wistful images of her.'

In retrospect, his words in *The Firstborn* had been prophetic.

'A late, only child is particularly vulnerable,' he had written, 'liable to be cast into roles that have little to do with her nature in order to cut out some paternal fantasy.'

And what, meanwhile, had become of the next book, the book Laurie 'cared about most', about 'the real Spain of the Civil War' which he had promised would be out in time for the fortieth anniversary of the war in 1976? (In 1977 he was 'halfway through'; in 1978, he was saying it would be 'ready next year, with luck'.) In fact he was to carry the unfinished manuscript around in his battered briefcase for nearly fifteen years. One day in 1977 Philip Oakes, old friend and sometime poet from Yates's wine bar days in the 1950s, interviewed him about it. 'His problem is that he has no notes on the period,' said Oakes, relating the story of the theft of Laurie's diaries, and his resulting despair. Laurie felt 'imprisoned in the need to complete the trilogy. I've got to write the book before I'm free to write anything else.'

'It's a winter story, a lonely story, a story of muddle and brutality and heroism,' he said. 'I was thrown into jail several times.' He told Oakes he had been

> in it for real. I mean that I carried a gun, not a stretcher. I felt that an atrocious crime was being committed against my friends and it was being ignored by France and Britain and America. I still believe that Franco was one of the great monsters of the twentieth century, a man who turned his country over to the fascists for bayonet practice. But at the time, I didn't fit my feelings into any dialectic. Nor do I now.

He didn't know, or even know about, any of the other English writers who were over there: not Orwell, not Spender, not John Cornford. 'They were intellectuals and I'd only just come from a Gloucestershire village. I was barely hatched.'

Considering the eventual reaction of Spanish Civil War veterans to *A Moment of War*, it is interesting that in this same month Laurie wrote to Bill Alexander, veteran Commander of the British Battalion of the International Brigade at Teruel, to ask him for names of survivors from the winter of 1937/8. Alexander replied with the names and addresses of twelve survivors: including Frank West, who had been at Tarazona and was taken prisoner in Aragon; Miles Tomalin the writer (and father of Nicholas), who had been in Barcelona; Patience Edney, a nurse in a front-line casualty station; Bob Doyle, the Irish seaman, and Bob Walker, Scots Guards engineer, from the British Battalion; and of course Alexander himself. 'They would all be pleased to answer any questions or talk over their experiences.'

In Laurie's notebook that year, too, is a list of historical facts and queries about the Spanish Civil War, with page references to Hugh Thomas's massive and definitive history of the war.[131] Laurie was, at sixty-three, plainly trying to sort out the historical facts from his own increasingly vague and muddled memories.

He told Oakes it was an agonising process.

> I have vivid mental pictures of places, weather, faces, fear and other sensations. But they're all without reference and in no special order. Trying to assemble them in a book is like attempting to piece together a love letter which has been scattered by a cyclone. Going about it I feel I am scraping at my sinews with a rusty knife. I can't let it go though. I have to finish the book. It was a long ride to the graveyard for so many of my generation. It's their story, as well as my own, that I have to tell. It's a debt I owe to dead men, to dead friends.

He also told Oakes about the five scented one-pound notes, sent to him by 'a girlfriend' as a Christmas present in December 1937 (which was of course quite true and typically Lorna).

> The government men sniffed the envelope and said they'd look after it for me. Months later when I left Spain I asked what about my cash? and the officer in charge looked me in the eye and

said 'Comrade, you are going home. Do you really need the money?' And I stared at the floor in shame and said, 'Of course not,' and the notes still heady with Chanel No. 5 went back into the drawer.

25

Two Women
1980–1983

> You come through an anonymous black door, and there is this
> bar, a restaurant and beautiful gardens. I can come here and eat
> or take a nap and no one will bother me. I am behind walls that
> only a few people can enter, and most of the time, I am alone.

THE CHELSEA ARTS Club in Old Church Street was Laurie's
home from home, equidistant from his flat and from the Queen's
Elm pub. It was founded in 1890, when hundreds of artists had their
ateliers and workshops in that quarter: a gathering place which, by
agreement, was to be 'bohemian in character'. In 1901 it moved from
the King's Road into two old cottages at 143 and 145 Old Church
Street, between the King's and Fulham Roads. Its shabby country
house interior suited Laurie, more so than the Garrick, and it was
only 180 paces ('I am a great counter') from his flat. He had joined
in 1949, along with Edward Ardizzone, Rodrigo Moynihan, John
Minton, Henry Lamb, Henry Moore, Ronald Searle, Ruskin Spear,
John Ward and Carel Weight. Laurie became a fixture, among writers
and painters all looking like minor figures in literary memoirs,
hovering around the snooker table where Laurie had once played
with Sir Alexander Fleming. On one wall is Paul Wyeth's 1960
painting *Concert at the Chelsea Arts Club*, with Laurie playing his
recorder. The small ladies' bar was later renamed the Laurie Lee bar,
a quiet donnish study with red walls covered with drawings, Indian
rugs, red velvet curtains, piano, smoky fire and a bust of Laurie by

Lynn Bamber. People would enter here like disciples and kneel at his feet to talk.

In 1980 Laurie moved across the square to the top-floor flat at 40 Elm Park Gardens, which he bought the following year. This became his den: a small sitting room with green velvet armchair, television, videos, hundreds of books and a Lis Frink sculpture. On the walls were his violin, crucifixes, a corn dolly, a Victorian pub mirror emblazoned 'Fine beers and famous lagers', paintings by friends and by Yasmin. In the corridor, a desk piled with papers. On the kitchen wall, Laurie pencilled (in 1987) the point where the last of the evening sunlight came through the window in winter: Nov 21, 3.35 p.m.; Nov 30, 3.30 p.m.; Dec 15: 3 p.m. etc.

There was an old-fashioned bathroom, and in the bedroom an imperial bedstead left by a previous occupant and a mahogany cheval mirror. The small back bedroom was where Laurie wrote. Rarely, a visiting journalist would be allowed a peep at 'a room of unspeakable chaos'.

He told people his flat was 'full of locked rooms containing rejected manuscripts and other men's mad wives'. It was his fortress against the outside world. 'I have no housekeeper, no cleaning woman, no mistress, no visitors,' he would say. He claimed never to answer the telephone (though his number was in *Who's Who*) and that his doorbell did not work: 'Bells of any nature fill me with the greatest alarm. It is either bad news or someone saying, "You don't know me but…"' His passion for privacy struck journalists as wilfully obdurate. 'He makes arrangements about arrangements about arrangements,' said Angela Levin of the *Mail on Sunday*.

The public Laurie, as he approached seventy, could have lived out the rest of his life on his past glory. He became a Freeman of the City of London in 1982. He was constantly anthologised. He was always at Foyle's lunches (e.g. for Angus Wilson, when he sat between Baroness Falkender and Cate Haste, Mrs Melvyn Bragg; or for Sir Roy Strong, who sent him a postcard of himself, thanking him for having encouraged him to write). Artists would follow his footsteps across Spain (by car) and exhibit their paintings. At any given moment, half a dozen theatres would be performing *Cider with Rosie*, in either the James Roose-Evans or the later Nick Darke adaptations. Amateur players would descend on Slad to visit Laurie's old home, where Wally and Ruby Marwood got used to being invaded, and on the Woolpack, where Laurie was happy to be photographed with his arm around the girl playing Rosie, gallantly telling her she was just like the real Rosie only prettier. One January, when Tom Matthews sent his annual crate of Perequita wine ('Glug', said Laurie gratefully), he invited Laurie to come and see *Cider with Rosie* at Colchester. 'I've seen it three times,' replied Laurie, '& there must be better ways to meet.'

Poetry readings sometimes felt like 'a dry run for my memorial service', as he told P. J. Kavanagh, fellow poet-performer. But audiences were never disappointed by Laurie. ('In his voice you hear poetry, the dryness of rustling leaves, his tones belong to the earth,' wrote Michael Watkins in *The Times*.) The charm could manipulate and seduce anyone. When he met Princess Michael at a party, she too was captivated and invited him to lunch at nearby Nether Lypiatt.

His predilection for whisky was forgiven; it added to the air of mischief. When Mavis Cheek, chairman of the Writers' Circle, asked Laurie to judge their short story competition in October 1981, he refused to do the adjudication in public, but agreed to be filmed at his flat, discussing the stories, halting the filming every so often to slip out to the kitchen for a swig of whisky. 'By the time we finished he was pretty pie-eyed,' Mavis said. 'But his judgement was good, and he gave a sober adjudication.' (Afterwards, driving down the Fulham Road, Mavis and her crew were stopped by police, who searched the boot. 'But when we said, "We've been filming Laurie Lee," the miracle was, the police had heard of Laurie and let us go.')

A few months later, Laurie was among the publishers' choice of the '20 Best of British' writers. A group of them, including V. S. Pritchett, Anthony Burgess and Rosamond Lehmann, assembled for a photograph at Lord Snowdon's studio. Reporting the shoot for the *Sunday Times* magazine, Ian Jack noted that John Betjeman was 'tirelessly congenial' even after 90 minutes, while Laurie Lee 'was helped to even greater congeniality by the whisky concealed in his briefcase (which Beryl Bainbridge was pleased to share)'.

This was all very well, but what about that dog-eared manuscript still entitled *A Winter of War?* Jock Gallagher, his BBC friend, was allowed glimpses of it and so was André Deutsch, but Laurie would not let it go. Then one day Gallagher happened to see some of Laurie's romantic photographs of Kathy and Jessy posing in leafy places – and suggested he publish them in book form. In August 1981, Laurie signed the contract with Deutsch (a £12,000 advance) for a book called *Two Women* – 'the two women who have occupied most of my late adult life, enclosing it in a double embrace, like bookends' – without mentioning a word about this to either his wife or his daughter.

The state of his relationship with his two women requires scrutiny here. In May 1980 *The Sun*, which had just run a series, 'The Tortured Teens', asked Laurie to write about Jessy, now going on seventeen. He produced another lyrical essay on a girl in adolescence, a 'billowing extrovert' who swept through their lives 'as though the windows had just blown in'. A headstrong, ebullient beauty, with corn-gold hair and a complexion as rare as her mother's. 'She has all the vitality of a sunburst, huge passions, a voice of Viking command,' he wrote, 'and bubbling South Sea enthusiasms.'

He said Jessy regarded books as 'chiefly for throwing', and conversation for interruption and argument. 'I don't think I've ever sat down with her in a state of quietness, just knowing her to be there. Even when she's asleep the experience fills her room with a nautical flapping of sheets in a storm, with tossings and heavings.' She liked Hammer horror films, the Beatles, the Osmonds, *Starsky and Hutch*, Mike Oldfield, David Bowie, and 'the honest to God animalism of Police'. (He originally wrote, but excised: 'Love is the tonsils & torso of the many-splendoured Sting.')

> She hates to be alone, yet has a paradoxical independence. She
> treats her horse and her friends with the same rough-handed
> affection ... She is very funny, thank God, and as quick as
> anyone could wish. But for all her gaiety she can plunge into
> blank despair, and withdraw to some close-shuttered cell...

'My daughter, I must confess, is a self-indulgence,' he added, waxing
introspective, 'and the one compelling interest in my life ... I believe
her forces have kept me alive.' He admitted to having spoilt her, and
burdened her with expectations, both 'natural blunders'. 'But she
has taught me more about women than I have ever learnt in a lifetime
of devoted interest in the subject.'

Watching her dancing alone, he felt 'all the sad enchantment of
seeing something about to take wing ... she would be risen and
away and gone from me at last, leaving the dropped dolls, the circling goldfish, the empty hamster cage and the horse in the field with
its turned, raised head'.

His love for her, he declared, was something that

> neither moods, exasperation nor even occasional flashes of
> dislike can alter. It is a love of pride and compassion, an urge to
> protect and guide, something for which I must suffer, forgive,
> stand waiting in the rain, ask no questions, or even kill. (This
> feeling I know will last out my life.)

In fact, Laurie's exasperation with his womenfolk had begun to create
a sense of dread at home. It was a relief when he left for London. At
the same time he ensured that they felt totally dependent on him, and
made a point of mentioning to journalists his pride 'that with my little
pencil I can feed and clothe these two great glowing engines of health'.
Kathy, his child bride, was now forty-nine but he could still make her feel
foolish and incompetent, correcting her like a disobedient child; hence
the scatty air she sometimes displayed. Her habitual demeanour became
one of apology as she tried to smooth things over. Jessy remembered:

All the waiting at his command meant she couldn't act for herself, and everything she did was wrong. I would talk to Dad about this, and he would attempt to kiss her in front of me, but it wasn't convincing. And yet I know he loved her, and there was no other woman on the planet who would have given her entire self to him as she did.

People remarked that Kathy and Jessy were like teenage sisters; both referred to Laurie as 'Daddy' and sometimes Kathy felt like the younger sister. 'He had these two children, my mother and me,' Jessy said, 'hence our dependence. And he was a great father to us both. His moods weren't reliable, but his love was never questioned.' One night in 1977, in front of visitors including the publicity director of Penguin, Jacqui Graham, Laurie threw his dinner on the floor and walked out into the garden – and Kathy found herself relieved 'that at last he'd shown other people the intensity of his rages'. A neighbour, meeting Kathy for the first time, found her 'unbelievably self-effacing'. 'I was born to be an artist's wife,' she told him, 'or at least bred to be.'

Jessy felt she had grown too big for him, and too noisy. 'He was always saying how beautiful I was, and taking photographs of me, but I felt instinctively that I wasn't his type.' She was very aware of his having imagined 'a dreamy waif, a delicate flower' of a daughter, and of his astonishment as she blossomed into 'a rousing and awakening reality'. 'Nobody could have fulfilled the expectation of *The Firstborn*,' she said. 'What a thing to live up to! And I was the sole focus of attention, and the solace of both sides in the parental battle.'

Yasmin – who, so far as Jessy knew, was just a cousin of her mother's who sent thoughtful birthday presents – observed from a distance how hard it was for her half-sister growing up. By now mother of three teenagers, and married to a psychologist, Yasmin could see that Jessy was suffocated by parental neuroses. And Kathy too was, in Yasmin's view, subjected to Laurie's idea of wifeliness.

'He wanted her to sit in the country making wine and picking flowers, to give him a sense of domestic stability: but what about Kathy? She was really a Trilby to his Svengali.'

So here was Laurie, planning to publish his exquisite photographs – he had an artist's touch with the camera as with the pencil – of these two lovely creatures about whom he felt so ambivalent, and keeping it all a secret. When André Deutsch went with Diana Athill to Laurie's flat to see the transparencies, they were amazed. The photographs were beautifully composed, romantic, mostly set in country gardens. The most striking was of Kathy lying back magnificently naked in the grass. 'Are you sure Kathy wants this published?' Deutsch asked. Laurie replied that not only did she want it, she 'would be upset if he left it out'.

But Kathy knew nothing about any of this. And before Laurie submitted his text, two unforeseen upheavals took place that rocked the foundations of the domestic triangle dominated by Laurie. First, Kathy fell in love, in her fiftieth year, with a young film-maker who came to the village to see Laurie. And he fell in love with her. After years of Laurie's prolonged absences, patriarchal putdowns and humiliations, Kathy enjoyed the novel experience of being truly adored and cherished. Laurie saw what was happening. The lovers even took a holiday in France, and Laurie knew all about it. Kathy glowed, and seemed rejuvenated; it was a passionate affair.

But it was a short-lived interlude. Kathy was adamant that she would never leave Laurie; and within months the problem was resolved, in the unhappiest possible way: her lover took his own life. Kathy's grief was agonizing and she says she could not have coped at that time without Laurie's support. He was all kindness and tender sympathy. 'The three of us were so enmeshed,' she said, 'that whatever tragedy happened to any of us, the other two understood.' But Laurie never spoke of Kathy's affair to anyone (though Georgina Hammick, in whom Kathy had confided, wrote offering help and solace). He fell into a silent, melancholy state, 'living in a sealed capsule, seeing no one', he told P. J. Kavanagh.

Kathy's therapy was to fling herself into church matters by becoming intensely involved in the Churches' National Nuclear Freeze campaign. She wrote endless letters to clergymen and bishops asking how they felt about the fallacy of the nuclear deterrent, and the government's betrayal of the teachings of Christ in allowing the manufacture of destructive weapons in the name of peace. A year after her lover's death, she went to the East Anglian coast (where he had lived) with Tom and Pam Matthews, to walk along the seashore. But by then she was reconciled to her loss, and whole-heartedly consumed by her anti-nuclear campaigning.

Meanwhile Jessy, who had left Cheltenham Ladies' College one year into her A-level course, was determined to leave home. Laurie rented her a rather grim bedsit in Cheltenham. She was singing with a rock band called Beat About the Bush – she has a remarkable singing voice – and the rock scene led inevitably to experiments with drugs. In London, when she was at her London school and friends were taking uppers and downers, she had managed not to be tempted. In more sedate Cheltenham she succumbed. In October 1982 she 'just flipped'.

> I stopped sleeping, stopped eating, became hypermanic, close to the edge. I was questioning God and the devil and Mary and Jesus. Dad couldn't face it. And when the psychiatrist told him, 'This is a lot more to do with you than it's to do with drugs,' Daddy was furious and walked out of the room. My parents tried to blame drugs and my friends. Both were in deep denial when the psychiatrist told them they had to take some responsibility.

She came home from Cheltenham, and Kathy had to cope, because Laurie stayed in London, writing the words for his *Two Women* book. In it, he related how he had fallen for the schoolgirl Kathy; he recycled *The Firstborn* and his later essays about Jessy. He was pondering on death, too, and wrote to the Society of Authors for advice about his Will. His accountant Pat Kernon, assessing Laurie's capital worth to be £125,000, advised him and Kathy to leave in their wills a trust for Jessy's benefit in property and other assets, exempt from gift tax. He stayed in London during Christmas of 1982. On 16 February 1983 he delivered his secret book to his agent, Pat Kavanagh. She thought it 'beautifully written and very affecting'. 'I suspected that it was an almost impossible task fraught with booby-traps, but you have avoided all the dangers so completely ... It is just wonderful.'

By May, Laurie's *Selected Poems* came out, dedicated to Jessy. In a brief foreword he explained that most of the fifty-two poems spanned a single decade, i.e. 1940–50. 'They were written by someone I once was and is so distant to me now I can scarcely recognise him any more. They speak for a time and a feeling which of course has gone from me, but for which I still have close affection and kinship.' He gave a copy to Kathy, signed 'with unselected love from the old man'.

And in October 1983 'that difficult book' (as André Deutsch called it) was published. *Two Women* was warmly reviewed, for its lyrical text and its pictures. But Kathy was shocked and angry, with Laurie and with Deutsch. Newspapers reprinted photographs, including the one of her naked in the grass. What would the milkman think, and the man at the garage? Everyone assured her she looked beautiful – and even she had to admit, her body was beautiful – but she made Laurie promise that any later editions would not carry that photograph.

In interviews, Laurie admitted that he was 'uncertain' about how his two women would feel. He said he had never, in thirty years of marriage, said 'I love you' or 'Darling' to his wife. 'Darling is the phoniest word,' was his view.[132] *Two Women* was an odd work for one so notoriously secretive, wrote Henry Porter of the *Sunday Times*, in an interview that was almost aborted. They met one Monday morning at the Great Western Hotel on Paddington Station, planning to take the train to Stroud together. Instead, they fell into the bar and into an intimate conversation – about women, love and lust – that lasted until six in the evening. Porter fell completely for Laurie's charm (and later made Laurie godfather to one of his daughters, reporting to Laurie that at four she was 'bossy, flirtatious, imaginative and very bad. God knows what she is going to be like at seventeen'). At the end of that day Porter's notebook was blank. So Laurie suggested they meet again the next day in the Queen's Elm.

The resulting interview began with an account of how Laurie spotted a pretty girl in the bar as they were leaving, and pretended to get his foot caught in her boyfriend's chair. The young man rose to free the trapped foot; Laurie ignored him and gazed at the girl, apologising for disturbing them.

> She smiled beautifully, and he departed through the door murmuring 'pale ... slim ... wild creature'. Later Laurie explained: 'At my age you become invisible. One is no longer in the market and young girls simply look through you ... So you see, I've had to develop one or two techniques for being noticed.'

To prove his invisibility he and the tall, handsome Porter walked together up the Fulham Road to Brompton Cross, and sure enough, the girls looked at Henry and ignored Laurie.

But Angela Levin found him 'still handsome' at sixty-nine, 'with thick white hair and blue eyes flecked with yellow like glass marbles'. He wore a hearing aid, which he claimed to have dropped into the wash basin that morning. 'So,' he said with a sly grin, 'I'll only be able to hear you if you sit very close to me.'

He was 'lovable' but somewhat exasperating, 'a professional eccentric' in his Chelsea garret. He told Angela he had always been a devoted family man, but was also a loner. 'I cannot write unless I am alone. I am like a fisherman. My family often don't hear from me for a few days, but they know I will be back again on the next high tide.' He also said that if Kathy 'made trouble' about the nude photo, he had an answer ready: 'Her aunt was married to the sculptor Jacob Epstein and *she* is nude in public areas all over London.'[133]

In publication month, October, Laurie had arranged that he and

Kathy were safely away, flying to Malaysia to write for the *Telegraph* magazine's series on 'Dream Holidays', for a fee of £600. Kathy, exhausted by the emotional crises of the past year, badly needed a dream holiday. They were to have three nights at Raffles Hotel in Singapore, then depart by car (Kathy driving) for Malacca, spend a night in Kuala Lumpur and three days in Penang 'generally relaxing by the sea'. In the event it was not very relaxing.

On 22 October 1983 – one year to the day since her first crisis – Jessy 'flipped' for the second time, and was having paranoid hallucinations. Kathy and Laurie had just arrived at the Hilton, Kuala Lumpur. Their neighbour Margaret Pollock, who had been asked by an anxious Kathy to watch out for Jessy, went to the rescue. Margaret was one of those dependable women to whom anyone would entrust a wayward daughter. Laurie had met Peter and Margaret Pollock when they first arrived at Knapp House in Slad, having moved from Manhattan with their children and horses, in 1978. The Pollocks had become like family. Peter was a jovial Viennese refugee, vice-president of an American engineering corporation in Cheltenham. Margaret, an electrical engineer, sang and played the piano. She took Jessy into her home, until her psychiatrist moved her to a nursing home outside Gloucester, where she was given hypnosis ('when all my childhood stuff came out'). She was to stay in the home for two months.

When he got back, Laurie went to see Jessy and they walked in the garden of the nursing home, having long confessional conversations, during which Laurie found a ring that Jessy had lost, placed it on her finger and told her: 'We're wedded forever.' It was after she came home that her relationship with her father found a new footing, based on a shared 'paganism' and affinity with the natural world.

That autumn, with Jessy still in hospital, Laurie went round dutifully signing copies of *Two Women* in bookshops but he told his closest friends that he had written the book because he felt that the edifice of his family was crumbling. 'It took me two years to plan it, and to keep the secret,' he told Tom Matthews. 'But all the time I was preparing and writing what I thought was a tribute to "the Two" I realised it was also a farewell. I am more convinced now that this was so, as I see most of it breaking up before my eyes.'

And six years later, talking again to Mavis Nicholson on television in 1989, when Mavis expressed surprise that he could ever write such a book secretly, Laurie again explained that it was meant as a gift of love. 'But writing it was a major masculine blunder. On the other hand, I was feeling old and I thought it might be the last message. The last pages of that book were a secret farewell to them. ("A love lives by slowly moving towards its end and is sharpened by the snakebite of farewell in it.")

'I'd never really told them how much I loved them,' he told Mavis.

Never tell a woman just how much you love her. Blake wrote a poem, 'Never seek to tell thy love', about this –

I told my love, I told my love,
I told her all my heart,
Trembling, cold, in ghastly fears.
Ah! she did depart!

And I realised that, love as deeply and as fondly as you may … it's as well if you're canny, not to declare yourself too much.

26

'An old poet rambling on'
1984–1986

THE ANNUAL ROYAL Academy dinner is a grand occasion, held in glittering surroundings, attended by 350 of the great and good. It was Sir Hugh Casson's idea to invite Laurie to give the address on behalf of the guests at the dinner on 18 May 1984. Laurie did not care for formal speeches. But he had always been fascinated by artists, and often said he had really wanted to be a painter. So he agreed.

After-dinner speaking is a cruel test of endurance, obliging the speaker to choose between spending the dinner in nervous sobriety or reckless conviviality. Laurie veered towards the latter, and this was a particularly daunting occasion. He was seated next to HRH Princess Diana and was captivated by her. The first speakers were the Prince of Wales and the Rt Hon. William Waldegrave. Then Sir Hugh Casson introduced Laurie, 'a friend of many of us here tonight' whom he had first met in his Festival of Britain office, 'when he was busy with a machine for grinding smoke, and playing Bach on a violin made of spent matchsticks'. Despite Laurie's distaste for public speaking, Sir Hugh said, he had been persuaded to propose a toast to the Royal Academy.

Members then rose to drink to the guests. Laurie too rose, and was told, 'No, Laurie, we're drinking to *you*.' So he then stood up with a nervous 'Can I get up now?'

He began well, with some good jokes. He said what a 'disloca-tion' from his normal life this was, as if he had been sailing in a little coracle on an immense ocean, only to be hauled aboard an ocean liner, and bidden to sing at the captain's table.

Could they have got the wrong Laurie Lee? He knew of at least four. 'One is a racehorse. One is a professor of stained glass, one runs a boutique in Lambeth, and the other is a Battersea bricklayer who spends his weekends doing a drag queen act in Campden Hill pubs.' He had been asked to speak for seven minutes, in rhyming couplets if he wished. 'Do you know what seven minutes of rhyming couplets cost these days? Only Clive James would do it at the price.' He then searched for his famous clock, with a great rustling, so the sound of loud ticking accompanied the rest of the speech – which went on a great deal longer than seven minutes: more like twenty-seven. His friend Hugh, he said, had told him 'I will see you get all the drinks you want in the world...'

His speech was, at its heart, an apposite one, its theme being the difference between the solitary writer's life and the more gregarious painter's. He pointed out that writers never put on great binges for themselves like this one. Writers are hermits, but painters are brotherhoods. At least that's what he meant to say. But he got them the wrong way round – at which point his concentration left him completely.

'I've been rehearsing this for several days,' he said, several times.

> Where was I? Oh yes. When I first came to London I wished to be a painter. I thought how marvellous to be a writer. Imagine the painter with a studio the size of Leighton House, surrounded by nude, long-legged models, drinking iced hock at ten o'clock in the morning, ripping off a brilliant canvas, to be sold for 2,000 guineas to a cringing dealer and off they go to the Café Royal in champagne and slippers for the rest of the day.
>
> Imagine the writer – hunched in his little attic, a glass of flat beer at his elbow. They don't give him half-clad beauties lying on the rug to sort out his verbal confusion. No, this is one of the perks of the painter. 'Where are you going, Fiona?' 'I'm posing for Sir Ruffan Tumble RA.' 'Starkers again?' 'Yes mummy.' 'Oh,

super.' No writer or novelist would get away with it! So imagine the writer in his attic. Two years of writing his novel, two years of slow compassionate isolation ... then you send it off to a publisher, and he sends you a post-dated cheque, rather small, and says he doesn't think it's as good as your last one ...

This is a problem. Where was I? I've been rehearsing this for four weeks. Where was I? Was I talking about Hugh? You must forgive me. I was not...

By this time there were murmurs in the hall. Laurie gamely carried on, with much riffling through papers as he tried to find his place. 'I'm not asking for sympathy but I think the difference is one of arrested movement and restless ... somewhere along. Can I go home now? Where was I?' A few rambling minutes later (about writers having to clamber through acres of boredom before lighting on a moment of truth, whereas painters can create a moment of truth in an instant) there followed a good half-minute of total silence during which Prince Charles rose from his seat to assist him, because Laurie swayed and appeared to be about to fall over.

Could I go home now?

I've got to read it. Do you know I thought I could get away with it but I can't. Where am I? Painters are brotherhoods and ... never lay on binges like this. When I first came to London I wanted to be a painter. And I used to cling to the edges of painters' lives because I thought they had a better time of it. Imagine painters ... they have a studio the size of Leighton House ... Have I said this before?

(Silence, then murmurs, then a 'Yes you did!')

Yes I did. Now come on. Right. The fundamental difference is ... God I wish I hadn't done this. It's him that did this. I've never made a speech before ...

Seurat. The bathers are held in a unique stillness of light.

I'll never be asked again. Now stop that! They're trapped. No I've forgotten. I'll not waste my ... They're caught in a moment of thrall and they're there for ever. Now will you listen to me because this is important. Keats. I'm talking about the differences of painters and writers. One has the quality of holding the moment and a writer can't hold the moment because he has to move ...

Keats seemed to sense this when he was looking at the frieze on the Grecian urn. 'Thou still unravish'd bride of quietness, Thou foster child of silence and slow time ... Bold lover, never canst thou kiss ... yet do not grieve; Forever wilt thou love, and she be fair...' This time of stillness is something I envy. I envy the artist his physical freedom, his gregarious friendship, his appetite and love of life. I have never met a dyspectic ... dyspectic? dyspeptic artist in my life. They stand up and attack canvases. Picasso, Miro, Braque, Augustus John, Henry Moore, most of them seem to live to a ripe old age ...

I had a little Hockney, nothing would it bear, But 192 per cent increase in value every year...

There was prolonged and relieved applause.

But up spake Laurie again. 'I was sitting outside my village pub the other day...' and he proceeded to tell his stock story about the two schoolgirls asking him where Laurie Lee is buried. He ended with a toast to the Royal Academy, and a hope that no politician would ever try to crop its extravagant glories ... 'as I stumble towards the end of my ... this is a mess, a real mess'. (More applause.)

Lord Hailsham, the Lord Chancellor, immediately proffered the use of his chauffeured limousine to get Laurie home, and poor Laurie, whose misery can only be imagined (since there are no diaries for these years), sent him a book in gratitude. Afterwards, some diners were more sympathetic and good-natured than others. 'Well, William, we were there!' remarked Melvyn Bragg to

Lord Rees-Mogg. In Anthony Powell's heartless account in his published *Journals*, he described Laurie's speech as 'an absolute fiasco, appalling meaningless ramblings'. The much kindlier John Ward said: 'Public speaking was not really Laurie's thing. Especially not at the RA, one of the more exacting audiences.' And kindliest of all, Prince Charles wrote the next day from Highgrove a letter of warmest praise and sympathy. He had surmised that Laurie would far rather have been somewhere else altogether, but assured him that he had 'made my wife & I laugh a great deal & I loved the way you created some memorable phrases and apposite alliterations! *Please, please* can you send me a copy of your speech, as I would *love* to read it in a quiet moment.'

The writer Angela Lambert told me that in the late 1980s she was at a dinner giving the after-dinner speech. Laurie was seated next to her. He put a hand over her glass and said: 'If you are going to speak you *must not drink*.'

A few weeks later, Laurie celebrated his seventieth birthday. There was a jolly lunch at the Garrick with his two women and a dozen good friends including Jill Balcon, Sean Treacy, André Deutsch and Jock Gallagher.

Gallagher and Deutsch had now waited fifteen years for volume three. Gallagher believed Laurie was genuinely rewriting about a paragraph a day, alone in his garret, rearranging each word and 'caressing them' as he put it. Gallagher offered a word processor, and gave him a tape recorder; but all Laurie recorded was the sound of birdsong, and nocturnal wildlife rustling in the undergrowth. Also, in Gallagher's view, Laurie liked being the centre of attention, and while everyone was waiting for the next book he was at his happiest. 'Once he'd handed it over there would be nothing more to write.'

In February of 1984 there had arrived a welcome diversion from the book, in the big, handsome, bear-like person of John King, who directed films for the BBC. King had been 'banjaxed' by reading *As I Walked Out One Midsummer Morning*. 'I realised I was listening in my head and dreaming the dream. It's not travel writing: it's poetry.'

Now he was determined to film it, with no screenplay, no stars, no wardrobe, no dressers, no props, no on-site catering ('Why feed people as well as pay them?') and a skeletal crew. All he would need was a young man to play Laurie, and all Spain for the location. Alan Yentob of BBC 2 gave him £45,000, with which to make two fifty-minute programmes. First, King persuaded Laurie to come with him to Spain and revisit the route he had walked. By car of course. In April 1984 they flew to Santiago, drove to Vigo, and began the recce, driving hundreds of miles to Madrid and then Andalucía. Laurie always carried a ginger beer bottle of 'medicine', i.e. whisky. 'I saw at once that nobody could have walked his walk, and done all he said he did, in the time allotted,' King said. 'But so what.'

They would use Laurie's own voice reading his story, and Julian Bream's guitar music. King found John Wild, an actor who looked reasonably like the young Laurie; all the other dramatis personae would be Spaniards picked up en route. Finding locations was easy: much of Spain was unaltered, once you left the tourist areas, and all the bars were full of old men talking and directing as they had fifty years before. 'Poverty precludes change,' said King, 'and in the process preserves beauty.' In any case, what Laurie's book had evoked was atmosphere. 'He remembered the girl whose skin smelled of olives. And we found a girl just like that. So it all came to life.'

Laurie was jaundiced about the whole shoestring expedition. 'There I was – no agent, no publisher, no family, no assistant, no girlfriend – carrying my bag alone through the rain to get to the Underground to Heathrow, and I thought why am I doing this at my age? I must be crazy. Never again, say I.'

In November it was a quarter of a century since *Cider with Rosie*. In a celebration on Radio 4 called *Vintage Cider*, Kathy told Marjorie Lofthouse: 'We've lived for ever on this one book really. And this is a cottage in his village, and I run around it in a chaotic way, just like his mother, so it mirrors his own childhood cottage in a way.' Laurie, though he did a hilarious imitation of the Finnish trans-lation of *Cider with Rosie*, had 'an air of anxiety about him, despite his success', said Miss Lofthouse. He told her: 'I don't think writers should ever do too well out of one book. They should always be lashed by hunger. Sometimes I'm a bit ashamed, I must admit.'

Still, the evergreen popularity of *Cider with Rosie* ensured an unflagging interest in Laurie himself, and he was often in a corner of his pub or his club, telling again the story about the schoolgirls coming up to him outside the Woolpack and asking where Laurie Lee is buried. (He had two versions of his reply. The polite one was, 'Laurie Lee is usually buried with his nose in a pint of beer, if you'd care to join me in the public bar,' and the saucy one was 'Oo arr, come up the wood, girls, and I'll show you where Laurie Lee wants to be buried.') He told every interviewer that he saw his wife and daughter no more than once a week. After Sunday lunch he would catch his train back to Paddington. 'Up the valley towards Sapperton tunnel I get that feeling, I'm back alone now! I love being with my loved ones, but what bliss it is to be alone.' And so back to the Queen's Elm, and home, to settle down 'with my books and the quietness'.

He told Mary Blume of the *Herald Tribune* in 1985 that he was 'gregarious, but with a pronounced defensive attachment' which meant he could be 'shy and extremely devious, with spurts of self-advertisement'. He wore the 'secret contented smile of a man who all his life has been cosseted and adored by women' and summed up his life as 'enduring, and trying not to be knocked down by cars'. He now usually wore a pale suit and a cravat or his Garrick tie, confounding people's expectations of a bumpkin – 'straw in hair, cidrous in speech, inane grin on face. I should be living in a hollow tree curing rabbit skins.' Back in Slad, Jim Fern, who had been at the village school, was now offering *Cider with Rosie* days out, guided walks around the valley with a lunch stop at the Woolpack. Laurie was perfectly happy for 'Little Jim' (six feet tall, of soldierly bearing and extremely fit into his eighties) to entertain the tourists. And when the *Daily Mail* revealed that the real Rosie had been found, now aged seventy and living in a semi in the Cheltenham suburbs, Laurie made no demur. Rosie Green was the fairy at Laurie's elbow in the John Bull photograph of 1919:

dressed by sister Marjorie in an angel's outfit with cardboard wings. Rosie Green was actually Laurie's cousin, and had married the village policeman, Tom Buckland. When she was an extra in the televised version of the book, Laurie had signed her copy 'To you know who, with long ago love from you know who.'

But as Laurie explained dozens of times, 'Rosie' was just a composite.

> There were six or seven girls in the village school she could have been – Doreen, Bertha, Betty, Clarice, Edna, Maureen, Poppy, and Rosie. When it came to a title for the book I had to make a choice. Cider with Edna? Cider with Doreen? It could have been any of those girls, but Rosie sounded right.

Women would come up to him in Woolworths and say 'I was Rosie, wasn't I Laurie.' They were all Rosie. And it might not even have been Laurie who rolled under the haywagon with her. 'I was a watcher,' he often said. 'Observing everything. I sprawled in the long grass and saw what was going on.' The title was 'a bit of a cheat. It intrigued people, although there was very little cider, and come to think of it, not much Rosie.'

By now Kathy was working almost full-time for the Nuclear Freeze Campaign, 'busy bullying bishops', as Laurie called it. In 1985 she garnered the support of the new vicar in Slad for a Hiroshima Vigil (forty years on) and was dashing round the diocese with posters, and meeting mitred bishops at Gloucester Cathedral. She told Tom Matthews, 'I see at last Gorbachev has agreed with me – three years ago I said that we should have an International Law preventing the using of nuclear power for war or weapons. I go a bit further than him.' 'My wife has left me for a Synod,' wrote Laurie to Matthews. 'Her ambition now reaches the Heavens.'

He was proud that his wife was now a churchwarden. 'She winds the clock, she lights the fires in the mornings, she puts out the hymnbooks, she tells the vicar what to say in his sermon.' He himself seldom ventured inside the church 'because it's too cold and though I want to be buried in its graveyard I don't want to expose myself to an early death'.

In March 1985 Sean Treacy, one of the cornerstones of his London routine, died. 'He was an orchestrator of people,' Laurie said in his funeral address. 'I went in there last night and the lights had gone out. There is no replacement for Sean.' Val Hennessy, a good friend of Laurie's from the Chelsea Arts, interviewed 'the old rascal' for *The Times* when John King's film was televised, in 1986. Laurie had been on the Terry Wogan chat show, he told her, and had taken his recorder along, to surprise Wogan with an Irish air, whereupon 'the twinkle in Wogan's eye turned to ice'.

So what was Laurie writing these days, asked Val. 'Cheques,' he replied, gazing evasively out of the window.

> Gas bills, VAT returns. I spend a lot of time answering letters from people wanting their poems published ('So, Susan, you have left me/Then') and from students doing dissertations on *Cider with Rosie*. My serious objection to being on the syllabus is the daft exam questions they set. But I won't say more on that topic in case they take me off the syllabus and my royalties dry up and I'll be poverty-stricken.

She tried again, about work in progress. 'That's the question I always shy away from,' he replied, topping up their glasses. But there was a book coming:

> It's a book of defeat, pain and disaster. About a winter when the anti-Franco side were in retreat, Franco was winning and our side had no arms. I'm also writing my Deathbed Confessions, but that's all I'm prepared to say. No one wants to hear an old poet rambling on about his next book.

27

Sans Everything
1986–1990

'SANS TEETH, SANS eyes, sans taste, sans everything.' Laurie often quoted this line, from Shakespeare's *As You Like It*, as his eyesight, hearing, appetite, sense of smell and taste faded. His writing was almost entirely founded on sensual experiences and he lamented their loss. Cataracts and an eye condition called split iris made it hard even to read. Words would break up and stagger out of line, and his elegant handwriting deteriorated.

Of course, he claimed, there were certain sights he could still appreciate: landscapes, and glimpses of girls' thighs in the Chelsea Arts. But he was generally constrained, needing a driver even to get to Stroud. Parties were no longer fun, even at Jilly and Leo Cooper's nearby: he could not hear or be heard, and would apologise for leaving early: 'I talk too much, & hear myself doing it, and the more I talk the sillier I become.'

Others saw him differently. 'He soothed people, stroked them with words, his voice marinaded in cider,' Henry Porter said. 'But he also listened very attentively.' Brian Patten noted in his diary: 'Sometimes in ordinary conversation Laurie's language would take flight. He could paint vivid portraits with words and recall incidents in rich detail, speaking with the same lyric intensity as he wrote.' When Patten mentioned that he'd been to Deyá, Robert Graves's village in Majorca, Laurie closed his eyes and recited from memory Graves's poem 'Lost Love'. (Laurie recited this poem at a commemoration of Graves at the Imperial War Museum in April 1988.) 'In the richness of Graves's early lyric I see his own intense lyricism,' Patten wrote.

He also had do-not-disturb days. People would stop to talk to him as he sat writing outside the Rose (another Fulham Road pub) and he wouldn't even look up. Cornered in the Woolpack by fans who had come from Canada or Australia, he could be charm itself. But friends in the village knew he might evade their eye, or suddenly end a conversation with 'I'm off.'

At seventy-three he looked, to Brian Patten, ill and doddery and 'rather forlorn'. He kept his hearing aid in his pocket, and would show it to people as if it were a small mysterious toy he'd found. But he was furious to be referred to in a paper as '80-year-old Laurie Lee', and wrote to the editor in protest: 'Kindly print an apology or send me four bottles of best malt whisky in lieu' and he was amused to receive four bottles, including one separately wrapped with the brand-name 'Old Grandad'.

Nobody imagined that Laurie had another ten years to live.

In the late 1980s Jessy took a job managing an adventure playground for children with special needs at Seven Springs, near Cheltenham. Being Laurie Lee's daughter, she sometimes felt, was something of a special need in itself. In January 1986 a two-page spread had appeared in the *Daily Mail* about 'the tortured life of a girl placed on a public pedestal by her father', describing Jessy's wayward youth on the Cheltenham pop scene, her wild parties and drug-taking ('I have nearly been round the bend from taking naughty things. But it's all because I was brought up in a cocoon by Mummy and Daddy. Although I adore them, I had to escape.') Laurie was 'devastated' by this article, and rang André Deutsch, who put him in touch with the heavyweight libel lawyer Lord Goodman; an out-of-court settlement was reached. Within months, Laurie and Jessy were engaged in a damage-limitation exercise, being photographed by the *Sunday Times* magazine in a loving father-and-daughter pose for a 'Relative Values' interview (in which two members of a family give separate interviews about their relationship). Laurie again spoke of Jessy's 'punitive charm' and their shared rituals and intuitions. Sometimes they had the same dream on the same night. Jessy would dream that she was a child again in Slad.

> I'm on a string, flying like a kite, with Dad holding on to the string. He's totally in control, but he's not going to let me go and fly off into oblivion. It's a wonderful experience. And he has the same dream. That's how close we are … It's a total love affair, my relationship with Dad.

Of course, Laurie admitted, there had been troubles. Jessy had been exposed like other teenagers in these cruel times to the drug-pusher at the school gate. And he mentioned her emotional breakdown three years before: 'more a crisis of identity than anything else – from which she's made a valiant recovery'. He admitted reacting 'in the age-old atavistic way of a father when suitors come for his daughter's hand – I'm jealous'. (He was always reluctant to let Jessy meet boyfriends in the Woolpack, until she had to remind him, 'Dad, I'm twenty-three.') He was conscious of not being like her friends' squash-playing young dads, of putting pressure on her to be what she was not, and, like King Lear, demanding the expression of love 'which is perhaps unreasonable'.

Jessy said she never thought of him as old; he had provided the right mix of freedom and security.

> Once, he caught me smoking in a pub in London. He walked up and said, 'Oh, Jess' – he doesn't smoke – 'can I have a drag on your cigarette, please?' I gave it to him and he just walked away with it. He then bought us a round of drinks…

That year, he confessed to Jessy about Yasmin being her half-sister. She had supposed Yasmin to be just an unusually kind and generous second cousin 'who always sent me birthday cards, and some lovely earrings in opal, my birthstone'. Laurie had been agonising for years over how to tell her: she found among his papers, when he died, several drafts of the letters he'd tried to write, one of them tucked inside his Will. But eventually he asked her to come out to supper as there was something he had to tell her. 'I thought at first he was going to say I wasn't his daughter ... He was so upset. I think he couldn't bear it any longer. It was like watching a small child in such pain I could hardly bear it.'

Jessy took it very well.

> I said I just wished I'd known earlier, because I would love to have had a sister. I wouldn't have felt so lonely. Dad forbade Yasmin to have much to do with us really. Well, forbade is a rather strong word, but I think it was the case – from absolute terror that I might not forgive him. But it was misplaced, that fear. I was sad for him, that he had to live with it for so long, when it would all have been all right.

Afterward the revelation Jessy went off with a girlfriend and 'I got very drunk and became very upset. But I didn't let him see that.' It may be significant that Ernest Wishart had lately died, and that Yasmin had gone away with her family to live in South Africa, where she remained until 1994.

But Jessy was still unaware of his epilepsy, the taboo word masked by 'withdrawals into a darkened room', to which he admitted, 'hiding away like an animal in the long grass'. She did not find out until she noticed that the drugs taken by epileptic children in her care were the same as her father's pills. 'He didn't want to show weakness of any kind,' as Kathy perceived. But he did say, in print, that illness 'does make you turn your attention to the reality of having to leave this world one day and if I ask myself if I'm reconciled, the answer is, I'm not. I love this world and all its trivialities, the little domestic details, the postbox on the corner, the wet gutters, the leaves, the buses, the sunset.'

Laurie was increasingly called upon to preserve things. He was enlisted in the campaign to save Stroud's bus station, to plant a new hedgerow, and to protest against Gloucestershire County Council's plans for 1,000 new homes. He released masses of coloured balloons, declaring: 'May they land with a soft caress on the heads of the blessed and with great lumps of bird-dirt on the heads of the developers.'

A letter addressed merely to 'Laurie Lee, Slad' would reach him. He had a compliments slip printed, regretting that he could not reply adequately 'owing to illness'. But he was conscientious about responding to hundreds of letters he got, from people thanking him for inspiring them to write, or for giving them words (from *The Firstborn*) to speak at a child's christening, or funeral. Others sent poems, paintings, memoirs. They asked him to address literary societies, or to make a film about the modernisation of Spain. Teachers requested a visit to their school or items for auctions. He diligently answered a long questionnaire from a schoolchild:

'Do you believe in God?' 'Not in God, but in gods.'

'Do you think you've been corrupt [*sic*] by the consuming society?' 'No. I have very few possessions, and I live in austere surroundings. Material riches deaden the appreciation of life. I was never so alive as when I was poor.'

Laurie appeared accessible, unlike many reclusive authors. People confided to him their love affairs, their long-ago schooldays, their aspirations. They went off to Spain, travelling his route. A lady of forty-three ('I have a lively personality and smile a lot') wanted to work for him, in return for accommodation. A 'mature student of humanities and social sciences' and a young poet sent sub-literate questions and to his credit Laurie replied politely. A Canadian whose grandfather kept the Fountain Inn on the Slad road said Laurie's books had given him 'a fulcrum upon which to face adversity in my own life'. Others wrote boldly in advance that they would be in the pub, carrying his book: 'Do hope to see you,' said one who added: 'I'm big and "bonny" and brunette.' And he kept all these letters, in boxes. Val Hennessy said he would send her stamps and plead for a letter: 'He was a lonely old sod really.'

Laurie hardly needed to write that promised last book. Like J. D. Salinger and *The Catcher in the Rye*, he had written a 'modern classic' a quarter of a century ago which had entered the canon and conferred immortality;[134] he could survive on just being Laurie Lee. He might, if commissioned, turn out a couplet, as he did on St Valentine's Day for *The Times* in 1987 –

> In you, today, I hear the first note of spring,
> Feel the earth's turning towards the sun

– but anthologists constantly reprinted his old poems, or chapters from *Cider with Rosie*, when they wanted country childhood nostalgia. New devotees discovered him. In 1986 David Blunkett, then leader of Sheffield City Council, wrote to say that a friend had read *Cider with Rosie* on tape for him. As a blind person he had found Laurie's word-picture of childhood and Slad life 'unequalled'. 'I was able to feel and experience the things you described in a way which brought them alive.' If Laurie was not overtroubled with visitors, might he come and call? He did call, had a glass of cider with Laurie in the Woolpack, and five years later recorded a *Down Your Way* radio programme featuring Slad. As he said at Laurie's memorial service – by which time Blunkett had become Education Secretary in Tony Blair's Cabinet – Laurie's description of his schooldays was 'not exactly New Labour' but his village school had 'hammered home the golden rules'. Blunkett particularly responded to the story of Joseph and Hannah Brown, their sad ending in the workhouse, 'and the kind, killing authority that arranged it'.

Though never in Salinger's league in his quest for privacy, Laurie was always choosy about whom he wanted to see. He complained when an estate agent advertised Rose Cottage as being 'next to Laurie Lee', and when his new tenants arrived there in 1987, it was a relief to discover that they were a congenial couple, the film-maker John Clive and his actress wife Michelle Newell. Clive was not remotely awed by being next door to Laurie Lee, not having read his books – 'which is probably why we got it. After the fifth glass of whisky at the Arts Club Laurie seemed to think we'd be all right.' The Clives also had a curly-haired toddler, Florence, reminding the Lees of Jessy as a child. (Also, by coincidence, the Clives lived in the St John's Wood house, formerly Ben Frankel's, where Laurie stayed when he first came to London.) They became such friends, it was Clive who insisted on increasing the rent after six years.

As I Walked Out One Midsummer Morning, the John King film, was shown on BBC 2 in 1987, and was acclaimed for being authentic, true to Laurie's own words, helped by Laurie's voice on the soundtrack. It was ravishingly photographed by John Williams, 'excluding anything that might shatter the illusion that the Spain we see is exactly what Lee saw as he made his long walk 50 years ago'.[135] In the *Radio Times*, Laurie said the south of Spain was now 'a concrete cliff of filing cabinets for tourists'. Nothing worse could have happened to Spain except a nuclear war, he wrote. But in the film, only the timeless, unchanging side of Spain was shown: El Greco's house in Toledo, the *posadas* and *bodegas*, the olive groves and the endless dusty roads. In Segovia cathedral John Wild (playing Laurie) was bathed in the glow of its stained-glass windows.

An English artist named Michael Still, who with his sculptor wife Helga ran an artists' retreat in an old *castillo* high up a crumbling trackway in the hills behind Almuñécar, realised that the *castillo* of the film must be Almuñécar, and got in touch with John King. Why not follow up his film with another, of *A Rose for Winter*? So began Laurie's renewed association with the little town he had lived in with Wilma in 1936. King made a second evocative film. He found Cordelia Roche, an actress so uncannily like the young Kathy that when Kathy watched the film, she shed tears. As before, King took a minimal crew, and although the Hotel Mediterráneo had been demolished in 1981, they found suitable locations, and local Spaniards to play the maid Paca or the fey waiter Manolo (actually a young goat-herd). Once they were filming in a bar, when in through the door came a man pushing a trolley of gas canisters, whistling. He made a perfect barman. 'He could slice ham. He could shout orders to the real owner, who cowered in the kitchen. Acted as though he owned the place,' said King.

When *A Rose for Winter was* shown on BBC 2, it was as highly praised as its predecessor.

Before long the mayor of Almuñécar put up a monument to Laurie, '*el gran escritor*' a small phallic obelisk in the style of the traditional Spanish dovecote, thrusting skyward on the seafront by a *supermercado* and an apartment block.[136] Its plaque reads:

El pueblo de Almuñécar *en reconocimiento al gran escritor Laurie Lee que vivió en nuestra ciudad en los anos 1935–36 y 1951–52 y la inmortalizó bajo al seudónimo de 'Castillo' en sus obras Cuando Partí Una Mañana de Verano y Una Rosa para el Invierno*

Almuñécar *a 21 abril 1988*

In the ensuing five years, Laurie and Kathy stayed at the Stills' *castillo* several times. The first time Still drove them up the winding mountainous tracks, Laurie became very excited because although only a mile inland from the town of Almuñécar, there was no electricity or gas up there, or water supplies except springs, just as it had been in 1935. Laurie even did local radio and television interviews, in proficient Spanish.

In 1988 the Gloucestershire musician and singer Johnny Coppin set some of Laurie's poems to music, and asked Laurie to read others, standing at the window of his cottage, for a CD called *Edge of Day: A Seasonal Anthology in Words and Music.* Interviewed for Radio 4 by Christopher Cook, Laurie said he liked the 'radiant simplicity' of Coppin's settings and that he was pleased to have his almost forgotten poems revived. With Cook, Laurie reminisced about playing his violin with Celia Goodman, and said he had not played since his E-string broke during the great storm of October 1987. He told Cook about his twice-yearly trysts with the setting sun on Haresfield Beacon, an Iron Age fort on a 1,000-foot-high Cotswold ridge with a dramatic view of the Severn plain and a sheer drop practically all round.

> I go up there to see the sunset on the longest day, the 21st of June, and on the shortest day, the 21st of December. I'm fascinated by the movement of the sun in relation to our valleys. It sinks behind May Hill on the longest day, and then it moves slowly back to behind Berkeley nuclear power station, out of sheer shame I think. You can just see the edges of Bristol and the great curving horseshoe bend of the Severn, and the Malvern Hills which are like something from India or Malaya.

On the shortest day he would be there by two o'clock, with a celebratory basket of chicken and wine, and on the longest day at about quarter to eleven at night. 'It's a magical experience, but of course it's mixed with melancholy because that is your longest day. From then on, we're for the dark.'

In April 1989, Jessy drove her parents across Spain to Almuñécar, via Toledo and Jaen. Soon after they got back, Jessy re-encountered Damian James, a young man she had previously met at a ball (when he was dressed as Rudolph Valentino), and they decided to get married. He worked for an oil company, and was presentable, gentle and strong. But neither Laurie nor Kathy was convinced that the engagement was a good idea. As she drove to Slad to see her parents Jessy recalls feeling an extraordinary sensation, 'like grief'. 'In my head I could hear Dad's voice saying NO! But he said: "I will support your decision."'

In June 1989, Mavis Nicholson invited Laurie back for one of her *Mavis Catches Up With…* series (revisiting former interviewees) on a hot summer day in the garden of the Chelsea Arts Club. Laurie, in white linen suit, greeted Mavis with outstretched arms, and they walked arm-in-arm across the grass.

As the camera rolled Mavis pointed out that since their last meeting in 1975 Laurie had published only one book, *Two Women*, his 'secret farewell' to Kathy and Jessy. She asked whether he dwelt on the imminence of death. Laurie replied: 'Prospero says, "Every third thought shall be my grave" and round about a certain age, you become very conscious of the ending of a splendid life, in which I've been blessed by all kinds of luck and devotion.' But the interview then took a determined and penetrating tack.

'You have not been a prolific writer, Laurie,' said Mavis. 'I'm a very slow writer,' he said. 'I could have gone on writing *Cider with Rosie* 2, and 3, but I didn't want to write ten books on the same subject like that vet, that James Herriot.'

'It made you a lot of money...'

'It came in one hand, and went out the other ... taxes...'

'And you were a club man and a hearty drinker.'

'When I published that book, beer was a shilling a pint. When it won the W. H. Smith prize I went down to the Star, our local pub, and said, "Drinks on me for the next 20 minutes," and all my chums came in and it cost me about fifteen shillings. So all my money didn't go on drink. It couldn't. I know you're upbraiding me but I'm not a drunkard. I am a heavy drinker, which is a very different thing.'

'But heavy drinkers isolate themselves from people,' Mavis said.

'I do live an isolated life,' said Laurie. 'Although I do depend immensely on my friends and couldn't exist without them, I like to know that I can withdraw to a private cave if necessary.'

He became mildly defensive in the face of Mavis's persistent inquiries. He never drank after nine in the evening, he said.

> And I don't go round beating up people. It doesn't affect me that way. I don't go round roistering and shouting and quarrelling. I fall over the furniture and then go off to sleep. I'm a

pacific drinker really. But I won't deny the accusation that I am a heavy drinker. I suppose I drink till I drop, but not every night.

Drinking to me is a defence against panic and fear ... a visitation I've had most of my life. A fear of not being able to control the next day. A lot of people depend on me, and to be a writer you've got to depend on a clarity of mind. If any of those dependencies are in jeopardy, my defence is a few Scotches.

Might not the panic be brought on by the Scotch, Mavis suggested. 'Doesn't that make you drink more, rather than alleviate it? I mean, it's addictive, we know that ...'

Yes, it is addictive, but it's also in place of prayer. I'm not so convinced of the power of prayer now, as I am convinced of the power of malt whisky. I find that one answers more directly and more positively than the other. The answer to a prayer seems to get held up in the post sometimes, but if I have a bottle of malt in my pocket, I know that the answer will be immediate.

'Does it cause trouble in your life? It can.'

I don't think so, to be honest. 'To be honest' – that's a politician's phrase. My daughter says, you can get more out of him when he's drunk than when he's sober. So I think she's a realist ... My wife's accepted it, apart from breaking the furniture. Not that I break up the furniture, but I fall over the charming side-tables occasionally.

Did he drink to oblivion? Mavis asked. 'People who drink to oblivion say they do it so they don't have to think, they don't have to lie awake dreading the next day.'

'I'm very aware of that oblivion. I'm not seeking it, I'm just seeking reassurance. And pacification of the state I might be in.' After this intensive grilling, having responded with gentle courtesy throughout, Laurie wrote aggrievedly to the producer John Tagholm. So Mavis rang to apologise, and spoke to Kathy, who said, 'What a wonderful interview you did. At last he's admitted something he's never admitted before.'

In May 1990, forty years after her parents' wedding, on a glorious day, Jessy was married to Damian in the church at Slad, thus acquiring (temporarily) the legal name of Jesse James. Canon Brassell of Gloucester Cathedral officiated and Kathy, as sacristan, prepared the vessels for communion. The honeymoon, arranged by Laurie through Michael Still, was in the hills above Almuñécar.

By the following year, Laurie was 'reduced to a state of almost total blindness', as he told Kate Figes of *Cosmopolitan*, who had asked him to review for her. 'But I'd quite fancy being comforted by the voices of Edna O'Brien, Jilly Cooper or Elizabeth Jane Howard reading one of their latest novels, to me personally of course if possible.' That summer Jock Gallagher, organizing a literary festival near his home at Bewdley, arranged a recording of *With Great Pleasure*, the Radio 4 programme, in a local church. Laurie would choose his favourite poetry and prose; Jill Balcon and Martin Jarvis (Laurie's chosen voices) were to read. But at the last minute the actors were told that Laurie was not coming; he was ill. (Laurie's initial excuse, Gallagher said, was that, like the vagrant in Pinter's play *The Caretaker*, he had no decent shoes.)

Gallagher appealed to Stephen Fry to step in, and Fry's choice of poems and prose arrived by fax from his parents' home in Norfolk. 'And there was much too much,' Jill Balcon recalled, 'and no time to do the kind of preparation I like to do, no time to rehearse, and the tickets had been sold out on Laurie's name.' Then on the day of the performance, Gallagher heard that Laurie was coming after all. Jill came downstairs in the pub where they were staying – 'the sort of pub that stank of beer' – and heard the familiar voice, and there was Laurie in the bar.

The recording went ahead, with Stephen Fry introducing his chosen poems. Jarvis and Jill Balcon's readings required several retakes. 'Martin Jarvis was wonderful,' Jill recalled. 'He could do things on the hoof. He said, "I quite like living with danger," but I thought to myself, I don't. I stand or fall by my professionalism, and that night I fell.' Meanwhile Gallagher went searching for Laurie, found him in a pub, and told him he jolly well had to make an appearance. 'No,' said Laurie, 'people don't want to see me at this time of night. You had a good evening with your friend Stephen.' Gallagher said: 'Laurie, these people have been waiting for three hours to see Y O U. You're going on stage now. I'm going to tell them you're here.' So it was that at about 11 p.m. Laurie appeared at the back of the church hall, doddered up the aisle amid cheers, and 'charmed his way out of it by praising us to the audience', Jill said. He put his arms round both actors, proceeded to do some readings from *Cider with Rosie*, which Gallagher had in his pocket, and received thunderous applause.

Few people now had any confidence in Laurie's ever producing that final book. It was a race against time; he was almost too blind to write, and never took to dictating. But in the summer of 1990 the *Sunday Times* announced that Laurie had completed his final volume after eight years' toil [actually more like twenty years' procrastination]. Any publisher could have it, said Laurie, for a six-figure sum: 'It's not going for a couple of crates of malt whisky.'

28

The Last Book
1991

To the writers and poets of England, Scotland, Ireland and Wales:

The equivocal attitude, the Ivory Tower, the paradoxical, the ironic detachment, will no longer do.

Are you for, or against, the legal government and the people of Republican Spain? Are you for or against Franco and Fascism? For it is impossible any longer to take no side. Writers and poets ... we wish the world to know what you, who are amongst the most sensitive instruments of a nation, feel.

THAT WAS THE loaded challenge of the *Left Review* symposium, 'Authors Take Sides on the Spanish Civil War', published in 1937. The signatories included Auden, Spender, Pablo Neruda, Tristan Tzara and Louis Aragon. Most were unequivocally on the side of the Republic. Sixteen were neutral and only five against, including Evelyn Waugh who said if he'd been a Spaniard he'd be fighting for Franco. Eliot sat on the fence, as did Pound, Wells, and Vita Sackville-West. Orwell said the whole exercise was 'bloody rot' but he almost lost his life fighting in Spain. Sean O'Faolain responded with contempt: 'Don't be a lot of saps. If X and Y want to cut each other's throats, why on earth must people "have to choose between them"? If you want to know, I do think Fascism is lousy. So is your Communism, only more so ... But there are other ideas in the world besides either of them, thank God.'

Few conflicts in the century after the Great War so seized the artistic or romantic conscience as did the Spanish Civil War. Poets 'exploded like bombs' about it, as Auden said in his poem 'Spain'. Even those who did not go out to Spain felt impelled to write about it: C. Day-Lewis, card-carrying Communist, wrote 'The Volunteer':

> Tell them in England, if they ask
> What brought us to these wars,
> To this plateau beneath the night's
> Grave manifold of stars —
> It was not fraud or foolishness,
> Glory, revenge, or pay:
> We came because our open eyes
> Could see no other way.

By 1990 Laurie was possibly the only writer who had been to Spain during the war but had never told the tale, although he had started it in *As I Walked Out One Midsummer Morning*. He had read (and dismissed) Hemingway; he possessed books by Orwell and by Koestler, who had been held in solitary confinement for three months in Seville. The words 'long-awaited' had long been fixed to the words 'third volume in Laurie Lee's autobiographical trilogy'. His story was now a matter of very distant recall, as he said. But he claimed he felt he had to tell it, out of guilt. 'I shall never be free. The only way I could have paid the debt which I felt so strongly to those people was to have given my life, and I didn't. Afterwards I always felt guilty. Guilty to have survived.' So he 'scoured the attics of [his] mind' to uncover the events of fifty years before.

Penguin's publishing director, Tony Lacey, had discovered that lunching with Laurie meant a bibulous afternoon at the Chelsea Arts Club. Champagne, wine with lunch, Armagnac afterwards, 'and if you asked for a pint of bitter he would generously bring you a whisky chaser as well'. Though the paperback *Cider with Rosie* had never been out of print for nearly thirty years, Laurie constantly sought reassurance: 'I suppose you'll be letting it go then,' he would say glumly, as if Penguin would drop one of their perennial sellers. And he dithered about whether he would write another book, at all. Lacey began to suspect it might all be a tease.

Then came the night in late 1990 when, as they parted outside the club, Laurie said: 'Do you want to publish this book or not?' Lacey replied: 'Of course.' Laurie asked, 'How much is it worth?' (A difficult question, sight unseen.) As Lacey recalled, 'I said, "Well, let's say £50,000." He said, "OK, you're on." We shook hands in the middle of Old Church Street, and a car came along and hooted. Laurie tapped the car with his stick and said, "I'm a ratepayer here, I've lived here for years"...'

Lacey woke up the next morning and thought, 'God, what have I done?' But he consoled himself that any book by Laurie Lee was bound to be worth £50,000.

A week later the aged manuscript arrived, entitled *A Winter of War*, with a note from Laurie's agent: 'I gather you and Laurie have already done a deal ...' Lacey read it over the weekend with 'intense relief'. 'It was brilliant, spare, harsh, a masterpiece.' But Laurie insisted that he had to show it to his 'literary advisers' and took it away. Literary advisers? He had asked P. J. Kavanagh to recommend someone at *The Spectator* who might give an opinion. Kavanagh suggested Christopher Howse, jovial and bearded Catholic intellectual who knew a thing or two about history, and about Spain. Howse met Laurie at the 'French Pub', the York Minster in Soho, where neither could hear the other speak, so when Laurie mentioned a payment for his task (Howse would have read the book for nothing) he said 'What?' several times, as if forcing up the price. Laurie led him outside with an air of embarrassed conspiracy, and offered £150.

Howse was asked to say whether Laurie's book ought to be published. He said yes it should, and corrected a few literals. He was not asked whether it rang true: 'It seemed to me about as true as *As I Walked Out...*' he said. 'The most striking incident was his sleeping on the altar when billeted in a church, an act to which he gave inauspicious significance.' ('I threw down my bags, stretched

myself along the altar and lit a cigarette. With this idiot impulse of
brash bravado, I believe I stained the rest of my life.') After Howse
had written his report, Laurie sent him another £50 – in gratitude, or
from a wish not to appear mean. They never met again, although in
1996 Howse tried in vain to get Laurie together with the writer Peter
Kemp, who as a young Cambridge graduate had fought on Franco's
side at the battle of Teruel.

Laurie's editor on the book was Mary Omond, who was struck
by his old-world graciousness, his air of vulnerability. Their editing
sessions took place in June 1991 upstairs in the Chelsea Arts Club,
Laurie bringing his Ruddles. 'For Mary, who put me in order,' he
dedicated her copy of the book. Despite his near-blindness he was
extremely concerned about accuracy, so she wrote out her queries in
huge black infant-school print. 'I sat at the table drowsing through
my girl's extravagant letters and inhaling their heady unforgivable
magic.' Might he mean 'unforgettable'? 'NO. Unforgivable magic,'
replied Laurie emphatically. 'How could she rouse me to such intensity when I was so far away?'

Here is Laurie's tale as it unfolds in the short 190-page book. He
crossed the Pyrenees ill-shod and alone in December 1937. Far from
being welcomed, he met suspicion, was accused of being a spy, and
imprisoned in a freezing, pitch-dark hole in the ground for a fortnight. His fellow prisoner 'Dino', a Spanish deserter, was eventually
taken out and, in Laurie's hearing, shot dead, leaving Laurie holding
his cap. He was then taken to a camp for newly arrived volunteers
at Figueras barracks, among Cockney, Scots and Welsh volunteers.
In the town he was seduced by a sensuous Andalucían girl of fifteen
or sixteen named Eulalia. Transferred ten days later to Brigade HQ
at Albacete, seeing an air raid over Valencia en route, he was once
again interrogated as a spy and only narrowly escaped the firing
squad, a young boy being provided to 'comfort' him on the eve of his
execution. Moved to Tarazona de la Mancha for training, Laurie was
reunited with Eulalia (whom he now knew to be a murderer) and
posted to 'special duties' with a sinister Stalinist hit-squad whose job

was to track down and liquidate traitors to the cause. He was then summoned to Madrid to make a propaganda broadcast to America from the besieged city, playing his fiddle into the microphone in the midst of a fascist artillery barrage. Eventually he got caught up on the fringes of the dreadful battle of Teruel in January 1938. Five miles from the front, with a gaggle of Spaniards, he was under bombardment and shellfire; in a confused confrontation he killed a man ('I remember his shocked, angry eyes') and was appalled that he had come here 'to smudge out the life of an unknown young man in a blur of panic which in no way could affect victory or defeat'.) He 'began to have hallucinations and breaks in the brain'. He was found and driven back to Tarazona, received orders for his reluctant repatriation, and was handed back his girlfriend's letters, but not the Chanel-scented pound notes. On his way home he was arrested in Barcelona as a deserter and spy and again imprisoned in a cell for three weeks, until the war correspondent Bill Rust, later editor of the *Daily Worker*, persuaded the authorities to release him. Finally Laurie was sent home, to be met at Victoria Station by his girl with 'her blue steady gaze ... her deep mouth, and love without honour. Without honour, but at least with salvation.'

A Winter of War was a great title. But shortly before publication, Laurie asked if he could change it. 'It's too grand a claim,' he told Lacey. 'I wasn't there all that long.' So it became *A Moment of War*.

Nobody ever knew exactly how short Laurie's 'moment' in war-ravaged Spain had been. In fact it was nine weeks. In the book it is made to seem like four or five months. Wilma (the only person who knew what actually happened to Laurie in those months, though she was never mentioned in the book) was long dead. More than half a century had lapsed between the events of the winter of 1937–38 and the book's publication in October 1991. Laurie's first piece of prose about Spain, written for John Lehmann in 1941, when he still had his diaries and it was all fresh in his memory, was about pre-war Spain. The earliest published references to Laurie's war had appeared when *Cider with Rosie* came out and press stories revealed that Laurie had been 'a strolling troubadour' for thirteen months in Spain, and a year later 'went back to fight with the International Brigade and was arrested as a spy. Then he was invalided to Britain.'

In 1969 came the catastrophic theft of his Spanish diaries. It was then that he began drinking more than ever before, which is not recommended as an aid to memory. We know he had written to the former battalion commander Bill Alexander for a list of Civil War survivors, and took notes from Hugh Thomas's *The Spanish Civil War*. So he had done some research. But the sense of expectation about that next book must have been inhibiting for Laurie, though the creative impasse, or writer's block, was masked by his habitual secrecy. Over the decades, he had sometimes mentioned being arrested or even shot at, sometimes referred to having led a young man to his death, sometimes confessed that he'd killed someone, sometimes said he'd been shipped home with pneumonia. He never mentioned a girl named Eulalia. He recalled only a time of winter, hunger, defeat; and he always mentioned guilt. Jock Gallagher said Laurie claimed only that he was 'with the International Brigade', as in 'travelling with'. 'He never communicated any heroic feelings about his time there.' In 1986 when the Imperial War Museum asked Laurie to take part with Stephen Spender in a sixth-form conference on the Spanish Civil War, he declined.

Laurie's publishers gave a lunch at the Ivy, with much to celebrate. Every newspaper featured the blown-up mug-shot of Laurie's innocent, dreamy-eyed young face, legibly stamped 'Commissariat', on his identity card. The book was serialised in *The Observer*, met a chorus of rapturous praise, and went straight into the bestseller lists. Across the Atlantic critics were equally impressed. The seventy-seven-year-old author had written a more profound, more intense, darker and less sentimental work than his previous books, they agreed. The Oxford don Valentine Cunningham gave it the kind of credence, in the *Times Literary Supplement*, that would vouchsafe its respectability. In a review headed 'On the Road to Teruel', he said Laurie's account was 'momentous, extraordinary, compelling, stunning, mesmerizing'.

Laurie's sense of smell predominated, hence the 'fabulously scented inductions to be invoked in that magically wide-eyed, synaesthetic prose'. And of all the testimonies to that icy war in the high sierras, 'nobody has, I think, succeeded so well as Laurie Lee in dramatizing the wintry horrors – personal, political, military, geographical – when Spain's potential for sourness, sickness and rot took over completely'. What impressed Cunningham above all was Laurie's truthfulness: 'What Spain did for Laurie Lee was to bring home the importance of, and to enable, truthful words, truthful art, in the face of the liars, rhetoricians, and propagandists.' John Sweeney in the *Literary Review* also found it 'an honest book' and a 'great, heart-stopping narrative'. Edward Blishen in *The Guardian* called it 'a story that aches with unforgotten cold and trembles with unforgotten terror'.

The Times reviewer was more moderate: it was really 'a series of postcard observations from the periphery of the war' with 'a rough chronology', and its coincidences 'strained credulity'. But the writing was full of rich cameos, poetic cadences, potent images, lyric intensity. In the *London Magazine*, Jeremy Lewis was sceptical about Laurie's 'phenomenal memory' that could recall whole conversations fifty years on, and said some would find his story 'verging on the fantastic'. Laurie's old friend Val Hennessy, who reviewed it lovingly in the *Mail*, was also 'extremely suspicious about the luscious sixteen-year-old Eulalia (tight black dress and long Spanish-Indian eyes) whose slim body almost bare to the waist is eagerly meeting the young Lee's "with the quick twist of a snake" on page 36. She strikes me as the seductive fantasy of a canny old rogue, particularly when she miraculously crops up again 400 miles away running her mouth across his chest and emitting an unforgettable fragrance of "fresh mushrooms and trampled thyme, woodsmoke and burning orange".'

The *Morning Star* reviewer concentrated on the rescue of Laurie from the Barcelona death cell by its editor Bill Rust (who had died in 1948), who had vouched for Laurie and arranged his release. But the reviewer laconically speculated what Rust would have made of 'of these confessions of a disappointed idealist'.

A Moment of War is a marvellously rich piece of prose. The early paragraph about crossing the border into Spain gives a foretaste: 'At my back was the tang of Gauloises and slumberous sauces, scented fish and opulent farmlands; before me, still ghostly, was all I remembered — the whiff of rags and woodsmoke, the salt of dried fish, sour wine and sickness, stone and thorn, old horses and rotting leather.'

'Few of us yet knew that we had come to a war of antique muskets and jamming machine-guns,' he wrote, 'to be led by brave but bewildered amateurs...'

And many key moments in the narrative have the convincing ring of truth. Recalling the 'almost wolf-like hunger' felt by the volunteers, fed on acorn coffee and thin donkey soup, Laurie remembered his childhood hunger, when he felt 'so in love with bread and butter and the cloudy meat of a new-boiled egg that I could hardly wait to go to sleep at night so that morning breakfast could come again.'

Dawn awakenings brought the sound of a bugle, 'a sound pure and cold, slender as an icicle, coming from the winter dark outside ... the crystal range of the notes stroking the dawn's silence and raising one up like a spirit'. Gifts from home – a twopenny bar of Cadbury's Milk Chocolate, a shilling packet of Players – brought 'an almost erotic excitement', affecting him 'as much by the piercing familiarity of their flavours as by the homely reassurance of their wrappings'.

Madrid in 1938 was now a besieged city of emptiness and silence, and his old landlord, huddled in the kitchen over a smouldering brazier of oily rags, was no longer 'the towering man I'd known ... who once, when I was playing the violin in the courtyard, struck a chiming clock with a brandy bottle for daring to interrupt'.

Under bombardment, he discovered the 'queer satisfaction' bestowed by his 'detachment and lack of fear'.

Laurie had dedicated his book 'To the defeated.' This factor possibly protected him, at that time, from discovering the doubts expressed by veterans of the International Brigade. In November 1991 Bill Alexander, the commander at Teruel, circulated among his old comrades a detailed critique of *A Moment of War*, and so did another veteran, John Dunlop, who had been in the front line during some of the heaviest fighting.[137]

Alexander appreciated Laurie's support for the Republican cause, and his 'defeated' dedication. But as autobiography this book was 'a fantasy', he claimed. He could confirm that Bill Rust had got Laurie released from prison, because Rust had told him so; Rust had arranged a medical examination, and Laurie 'was found to have epilepsy', said Alexander, 'and sent back to Britain. He never joined the British Battalion and the I. B.'

Laurie's movements and the dates in December 1937 'do not add up', wrote Alexander: 'Two imprisonments, then a ten-day stay in Figueras, then Albacete, then Tarazona when "a few days after his arrival" he went to a meeting where Harry Pollitt spoke. This was Christmas Eve, 24 December 1937.' Laurie's description of life in Tarazona was unlike others'. 'The Commander was Major Alan Johnson (ex West Point, USA) a stickler for organization and discipline …' Laurie's stories of amorous encounters with Eulalia, claimed Alexander, were uncannily like a story told by Arthur Landis in his 1967 history *The Abraham Lincoln Brigade*.

Also, he asked 'Why should Laurie Lee, unknown, inexperienced and untrained, have been selected for the mysterious, unexplained special duties?' Both Alexander and Dunlop were certain that only Communist Party members of proven character, courage and dependability were recruited to the SIM (Servicio de Investigación Militar). 'Much of LL's story,' Alexander concluded, 'must be classified as fiction and fantasy and not a true picture of his own real experience.'

He allowed that in contrast to the 'muck and fantasy' of the bitter anti-Republican writings of Orwell and Jason Gurney, Laurie's book did contain 'some positive points'.

But the veterans wondered why Laurie had waited so long to publish his book – until the possibility of verification had faded? – and why he had never associated with other International Brigaders, 'avoiding contact and discussion' when others had kept up the comradeship forged in Spain. He cited Wogan Philipps and his wife Tamara, the former Mrs Bill Rust, with whom Laurie had been 'reluctant to talk about Spain'.

And, of course, both took exception to Laurie's descriptions of British Brigaders as 'ex-convicts, alcoholics, wizened miners, dockers, noisy politicians, dreaming undergraduates, motivated by failure, poverty, debt, the law, betrayal by wives or lovers'. Slanders, said Alexander. 'He does not attempt to explain how these men, deprived of weapons by the Tory government, were able to stop the professional armies of three dictators for nearly three years.'

The diehard old International Brigaders never liked anyone alleging that they were disorganized, or anything but splendid and dedicated fellows. It was a war of chaos and confusions, deceptions and delusions. And Laurie, presumably, knew nothing of these behind-the-scenes rumblings among the veterans. He did ask Mary Omond to make changes before his paperback came out. He had muddled the names of Largo Caballero, the Prime Minister, and Azaña, the President, he said; and he had referred prematurely to the Ebro, which 'must have been a mistake when transcribing notes,' he told Mary. 'I do so apologize for the mess.' No doubts about the facts were raised, publicly, in Laurie's lifetime.

But he seemed subdued when the writer Cal McCrystal arrived at the Chelsea Arts Club to interview him for the *Independent on Sunday*. They met in the Laurie Lee bar, Laurie wearing his Garrick tie, a cream linen jacket and mushroom waistcoat. 'Laurie Lee cannot see well enough to read *A Moment of War*, the final book in his trilogy,' McCrystal's piece began. On the table, alongside books, flickering candles and empty bottles, lay a magnifying glass. Laurie was sipping hot whisky; his eyes were 'rheumy and benevolent behind thick bi-focals'.

McCrystal found the book a remarkable feat of memory. Reading it made him feel as if he were there, 'with the young blond Briton from the Cotswolds: the "reek of burnt dust" as the bombs fell, the taste of bean soup, the snowy silence "broken by a goat-bell or the chirp of a bird"'. But Laurie kept lapsing into silences, saying his mind was elsewhere. In Spain, perhaps, asked McCrystal. No, said Laurie, he was distracted by anxiety over one of the club barmaids. McCrystal detected in his book 'a degree of nonchalance, if not fatalism'. 'You are absolutely right,' said Laurie.

Bryan Wharton came along, bringing photographs. Laurie peered at 'a former female acquaintance with very long legs'. 'He is silent again,' wrote McCrystal, 'and I wonder what he is thinking about ... And when I beg him to inscribe my copy, there are several moments of uncertainty before he uncaps his felt-tip and, his face almost against the page, writes: "For Cal in memory of a warm though speechless encounter."'

Yet six months later, when the paperback was published, Laurie aged seventy-eight was positively bushy-tailed with renewed success.

At the Penguin party at the Arts Club in Dover Street, a reporter asked him would he be writing any more? Laurie hesitated before replying. 'I could of course write about love ... Failed love, rejected love, all sorts of love.' (He twiddled with his hearing aid which he said was tuned to the sports coverage on the radio. 'I keep hearing this voice saying "Extra time",' he said. 'It's very encouraging.') And in another radio interview, Laurie again hinted that he might yet write a book covering the last fifty-five years, 'because I think to break off my life aged twenty-three is a bit peremptory don't you think?' Perhaps he meant premature.

'Since I came back from Spain I've lived and loved, gained love and lost love, and married a most beautiful lady and have a most beautiful daughter, and I've been blessed with their companionship, and with the good fortune of being back in my valley, and knowing that I am where I belong, in this close embrace.'

29

The Old Man of the Woolpack
1992–1997

> The longer I live here, the more devoted I am to this place but
> the less I hear from old friends. It is like floating up-river in a
> boat which used to be crammed with the noise of children, but
> one by one they disappear and eventually you are left alone
> sitting at the front of the boat slowly going out to sea.

IN HIS LAST years, Laurie could always be relied on for a well-
honed sentiment, wistful or nostalgic. Journalists portrayed him
as the Old Man outside the Woolpack, 'watching the shades and
shadows and the seasons change', in the valley which had become
as synonymous with Laurie Lee as Haworth is with the Brontës.
He was a local monument and tourist magnet, ready to reminisce
about the days when the carrier's cart would take you into Stroud for
twopence. In fact, there was a great deal more life in the old dog yet.

Energised by his burst of success with the completed trilogy, he
was back at literary events in London such as the *Sunday Express*
book prize luncheon. Among the judges was Clare Francis, the
yachtswoman turned novelist, who found herself seated opposite
'this benign white-haired figure', smiling at her. When told it was
Laurie Lee she had almost fallen off her chair.

> I grew up on his books. I went to sit beside him and found
> him totally un-English, in the sense that not only did he love

conversation and people, but he liked women and set up an
immediate easy intimacy which is very rare. He made you feel
like a co-conspirator.

Clement Freud offered to cook dinner for Clare and Laurie. 'I'd
love this beyond the dreams of gluttony,' Laurie wrote to Clare, 'but
my jaw remains clamped against such temptations. I am forced to
survive on low tides of whisky and plankton.' (He had a growth
inside his mouth, which proved benign.) 'One day we may at last
join Clement for foie gras and trumpets.'

Mavis Cheek, the blue-eyed barmaid from the Queen's Elm, was
now a successful novelist, and she too would gravitate to the side
of Laurie's armchair at the Chelsea Arts, for a joint moan about
publishers. She too loved Laurie because he listened. 'He wasn't
a chap for blokey talk. He adored women in an old-fashioned and
wholesome way. He would wax lyrical about my eyes. He played at
being flirtatious, slightly laughing at himself.'

His Chelsea Arts Club friends saw to it that he never walked home
alone. Sometimes his neighbour, the tall and glamorous Jill, Duchess
of Hamilton, would accompany him; but usually it was his hairdresser
Doug Chisholm, or the painter Don Grant, who had painted the
Princess of Wales and the Duchess of York naked under their Ascot
hats. Don recalled Laurie stopping on the pavement to turn round three
times and make a bow when he saw the new moon, 'even when he could
barely stand up'. Vera the barmaid invented a 'Laurie Special' – baked
potato with tuna or chicken. He adored the club's pretty manageress
Katie Paltenghi, who regarded him as 'a second dad', a soulmate,
someone to confide in, especially when she found, at thirty-three, that
she had breast cancer (from which she recovered). He was reluctant to
see people anywhere else except the Club. His accountant had to tell
him firmly: 'The Chelsea Arts Club is absolutely delightful, but it is not
easy to explain the niceties of bond investment there.'

Down in Slad he was equally a fixture. The landlord of the
Woolpack allowed Laurie to sit outside with his Waterstone's bag

containing his pewter mug. He could give two rings on his mobile phone when he wanted another light ale. This impressed interviewers, usually young and pretty, who came down to listen to his wisdom. Mary Killen arrived from the *Telegraph* to talk about his obsession with light, the sun and the moon. 'I often go and sit in the garden wrapped up in blankets and say – "The moon will rise over *there* tonight, behind that tree or hillock, at the appointed time,"' he told her. It restored his feeling of affinity with the 'slow revolving almanac of the year'.

> A kind of primeval reverence surrounds the orbit of the moon. Before a full moon rises, there is a quietness in the valley, almost an anticipation. When it slowly lifts its light above the horizon's edge, all the farm dogs begin to bark. It may sound rather precious, but the motions of sun and moon are a constant reassurance of my place in the valley...

Laurie's reassurance of his place on the school syllabus came in January 1993. The Schools Examination and Assessment Council published an anthology of texts which all children aged fourteen should study. This one included Laurie alongside Shakespeare, Chaucer, Dr Johnson, Wordsworth, Keats, John Clare, Browning, Dylan Thomas, Dickens's *David Copperfield*, Wilde's *The Importance of Being Earnest*, and poems by Derek Walcott and A. S. J. Tessimond. Doris Lessing was included, but not Jane Austen or George Eliot. Inevitably there was a fuss: no two people can ever agree on such a selection. The novelist A. N. Wilson said the Education Secretary should publicly burn 'this rag-bag of mutilated texts' chosen by the Cambridge don Dr John Marenbon, SEAC's English committee chairman.[138] A *Times Educational Supplement* columnist discerned a political motive, to give children a dishonest vision of a simpler, safer world.

> Just as all recent educational policy has looked back to some mythical golden age – basic skills, the security of learned facts –

so this anthology represents a simplistic pick-and-mix approach to literature ... Thus *David Copperfield* and *Cider with Rosie* are the two texts which every pupil in the country can now be guaranteed to read, whatever their background.

But Daniel Johnson in *The Times* perceived that Dr Marenbon's anthology had a common theme: the relationship between youth and age, children and parents. And these texts were 'teachable'. He was right. Teachers of all levels and types of pupil – from primary schools to prisons – have always found that *Cider with Rosie* elicits an affectionate response of recognition and familiarity, no matter how distant from Laurie's their background might be.

Though one of the few living authors selected, Laurie took no part in these arguments. He was putting on cap and gown to receive his only honorary degree – along with Dr Sheila Cassidy, who was tortured in Chile – from the Cheltenham and Gloucester College of Higher Education. Two days later Laurie wrote with Pooterish courtesy to the *Stroud News* thanking them for mentioning his honour, but regretting that the photograph captioned 'Laurie Lee' was in fact the former Bishop of Gloucester.

In June 1994, Laurie was eighty. His mother might have muddled the exact date of his birthday; all she'd said was that 'I know it was Thursday because it was early closing.' Celebrations were planned. On the hot sunny Saturday of 18 June, Penguin held a buffet lunch in the Chelsea Arts Club garden, presenting Laurie with a new stereo and a violin-shaped birthday cake. Among the guests were Elizabeth Jane Howard, Julian Bream, André Deutsch, the Cunard sisters Virginia and Pen, Antonia Young, Jim and Pam Rose, Sir Hugh Casson and the Eshers (the honeymoon couple from the Hotel Mediterráneo in 1935). Celia Goodman gave him a Schubert CD, Georgina Hammick a pen. Laurie made a mischievously barbed speech. John Martyn the singer, who happened to be staying in the club, played an impromptu 'Johnny B. Goode'. For many club members it was the first sighting of Kathy and Jessy: Laurie did not usually allow them to venture inside.

The Slad party was held in the garden of Down Court, home of Mrs Anne Mills, once used for the interior shots of Laurie's childhood home in the BBC's *Cider with Rosie*. The Woolpack cricket team took on Sheepscombe, and Laurie handed over the keys to the new pavilion for which he had paid, and gave the entire village a glass of beer. A ploughman's supper was served. There were fireworks, and music from madrigal singers, and Laurie was toasted by Brian Jones, also eighty, nephew of the Squire Jones of his childhood. Laurie raised his white stick aloft and invited everyone to his ninetieth.

He was actually rather ill that summer – though he looked hale and durable in his panama hat in the elegiac television film David Parker made of Laurie in his haunts in the valley. After a spell in hospital, he was told he absolutely should not fly, so he at once booked a flight to Málaga. With Kathy and Jessy he went back to the Stills' *castillo* at Almuñécar. He returned bronzed and invigorated, and dictated a letter to Kay Dunbar agreeing to speak at a 'Ways with Words' literary luncheon in Bath the following spring: 'I'm ghastly old and to your fellow revellers would appear like Banquo's ghost.' But since 'the immortal Frances Partridge' would be there, he would 'hide behind her extra years and spirit'. There was a handwritten postscript: 'I used to play violin duets with Frances Partridge. She was more tuneful than I.' His talk was a triumph: everyone was moved by his warmth and humour. Laurie told his audience he still had a couple of books in him, if he could get hold of a magnifying typewriter: 'The trilogy stopped when I was twenty-three. I have such areas of life to cover: confessions, celebrations, marriage, infidelity, children.' Children? He had never publicly acknowledged 'children' before. Or infidelity.

He still sometimes played a Bach sonata on his violin, but no longer attempted Paganini's 'Devil's Trill'. He preferred to listen to chamber music ('I don't want lots of hullabaloo'). Operatic voices gave him a sense of anxiety ('I don't like raised voices: they suggest domestic discord') and he never listened to what he called 'great gusts of roast-beef music – Elgar – blaring me out of the room'. He remained devoted to Schubert: 'a rare genius whose innocent yearning for affection was expressed in music as pure as spring water'. When Classic FM asked for his choice of records in 1994, this was the list he requested:

> Mozart's 'Serenade' (tea shop trio); Suppe's 'Poet & Peasant Overture' (light orchestra); Elgar's Violin Concerto (original Menuhin recording); Chaliapin (frag. *Boris Godunov*), Schubert's Trio No. 1 in B flat, D898 (slow movt) by Casals, Thibaud & Cortot; Bach's Double Violin Concerto (last mvt) Oistrakh father & son if poss; Mozart's String Quartet in D minor; 'Recuerdos de la Alhambra' played by Julian Bream; and Mozart's Violin & Piano sonata frag. Allegro played by Laurie Lee with the pianist Denis Matthews.

(Laurie had played duets with the late Denis Matthews at the home of Jim and Pam Rose.)

On Radio 4, Kenneth Branagh was to be heard reading *As I Walked Out One Midsummer Morning* in a woefully inadequate voice – 'too high and dry for such a lustrous text', said Gillian Reynolds in the *Telegraph*. Later that year Isis, the Oxford audiotape company which had recorded Laurie's incomparable voice reading the first two books in his trilogy, re-released them and Laurie signed 2,000 covers for the boxed sets.

As an octogenarian he was more than ever the favourite son of his valley. He opened a supermarket in Stroud on the site of the Ritz cinema of his boyhood, spurning a bouquet of flowers ('too Jilly Cooperish') in favour of a bottle of Jack Daniel's. He joined Jilly and Joanna Trollope in campaigning to save Stroud Library, his 'university'. He cut the ribbon at Hoyland House, a new NHS surgery at Painswick, as one of Dr Hoyland's most indestructible patients: 'I think I first went to him when my voice broke. He's kept me going ever since.' He opened Painswick's annual Victorian street fair, where villagers wore period costume, arriving in a horse-drawn carriage. Having an aversion to the *New English Bible* (he was enraged that 'Arise, and take up thy bed and walk' should become 'Get up! pick up your mat and go home'), he was enlisted in the Tyndale quincentenary celebrations in Wotton-under-Edge. 'I stole many good things from Tyndale,' said Laurie.

He received a rapturous reception in the packed Stroud Subscription Rooms on a cold, wet Monday night in March 1995, speaking against plans to build ninety houses in the valley, now an Area of Outstanding Natural Beauty. Wrapped in a tartan blanket and stifling a hacking cough, with a temperature of 100 degrees, he apologised for speaking first but 'I am the oldest man here.'

The Slad valley, he said, was 'the green lung' of Stroud.

> If we permit this to go ahead without resistance, it will be a self-inflicted wound that not even time will heal. The word 'development' is just a euphemism for ravagement and exploit-ation ... The valley, with its landscape of tangled woods and sprawling fields, should be left to rabbits, badgers and old codgers like me.

The *Daily Mail* asked him to write a piece about his campaign, and Val Hennessy agreed to write it for him, producing a credible parody of Laurie ('It was in these meadows where I breathed the first faint musks of sex and where Rosie Burdock shared her cider with me during hay-making, on a motionless day of summer...') and when it appeared, by-lined Laurie Lee, he told her they were paying him twice what she'd have got, 'and a number of my old chums and my publisher have phoned to say, "You're writing better than ever, Laurie."'

One day in April 1995 Laurie sat – shining white hair, bow tie, cherubic pink face – in the window of the crowded drawing room of Lord and Lady Monson's Kensington house on their fortieth wedding anniversary. Emma Devas, Lady Monson, had asked

him to say a few words; Laurie demurred, and she had been told
he might not be up to it. So she turned to Leighton Thomson, the
gentle and scholarly vicar of Chelsea Old Church, who had married
the Monsons, and asked if he would kindly propose a toast. Five
minutes later the vicar rose to speak – and so did Laurie. Laurie
reminisced fondly about Emma's childhood roller-skating round
Markham Square, and selling her paintings for sixpence from the
doorstep. The Monsons sat engulfed in laughter, as Thomson stood
speaking on one side of them, and Laurie held forth on the other.
'And nobody could get either of them to stop.'

Two months later Laurie's wizardry seemed to be at work again.
On 26 June 1995, his eighty-first birthday, Yasmin's daughter Esther
gave birth to his first grandson, William. Laurie sent William a gold
watch. And a hotel in Cheltenham named its honeymoon suite 'the
Cider with Rosie suite': 'Perhaps the bridal mattress could be stuffed
with the finest hay,' Laurie suggested, 'with a jar of sweet cider by
the bedside.' He presented them with a watercolour, 'Laurie Lee's
Cottage', to hang on the wall.

Christopher Fry, another literary monument (approaching
ninety), wrote a poem for Laurie's eighty-first birthday at the West
Country Writers' Association lunch in Torquay. His artful verses
included the rhyme 'gowp at' & 'cowpat'. 'Dear friend,' wrote the
admiring Laurie, 'you have been kinder to me than I can find thanks
for, or the merit to deserve it.'

Being a grand-old-man literary survivor meant joining fellow
writers at Penguin Books' sixtieth birthday party in March 1995,
presenting the Society of Authors prizes in the great hall of King's
College London, and attending another Foyle's luncheon where
Laurie sat in the absent Spike Milligan's chair next to Claire Rayner.
'She thinks I'm Spike Milligan,' he told the *Times* diarist, 'and has
been laughing at my jokes very encouragingly.' At the Cheltenham
Festival, the Nobel laureate Seamus Heaney recalled that at his
first Cheltenham thirty years ago, he was runner-up in its poetry
competition. 'I sat next to Laurie Lee, and that was a big high for

me at the time.' Laurie shared the Cheltenham stage with Andrew Motion, future Poet Laureate, and there was no mistaking which of them was the star turn.

At the May 1995 Hay-on-Wye Literary Festival, he made a slow shuffling entry on the stage, hand held aloft in a salute of thanks for the tumultuous welcome. Bulmer's Cider, the sponsors, had been 'a great consolation to writers over the years,' he said in his countryman tones. As one reporter remarked, 'he has the gift of old-fashioned eloquence, schooled as he was on the Prayer Book and the King James Bible'. To the stock tale of the schoolgirls in Slad he had now added another, of how he used his white stick to get beautiful young women to help him across the road. 'I grip them,' he said, 'holding on with great craftiness ... It is ... elbows and things that I cling to. And then, when we are safely over, I say: Thank you very much, young man, you've been most helpful.' After his performance, the queue for his book signing was the longest in the Hay festival.

Jessy, who was now working with homeless families in Cromwell Street, Gloucester (later infamous as the scene of the Fred and Rose West murders), came back to live at home, as her marriage had ended. All three mourned when her horse the Red Baron died on Twelfth Night 1996. And Laurie had outlived many older friends. In 1995 Pen Dugdale (now Loveday) died; Tom Matthews had died just before his ninetieth birthday. Laurie wrote a tribute for the New College magazine, declaring that Tom had brought to England a rare piece of America: civilised urbanity and humour and a love of the power of words. 'We remember Tom as a handsome paternal figure, generous, hospitable, catholic in his curiosities, who when sitting among his guests at dinner, would be as likely to break into a Mississippi Ragtime as to quote freely from Plutarch or Pound.' Laurie and Kathy went to Oxford for the opening of the McGregor/ Matthews library at New College.[139]

'Laurie Lee is a literary legend,' declared the *Gloucestershire Echo*, in January 1996. Having made the landscape of his childhood come alive, and for 'continuing to fight to this very day to preserve some vestige of a bygone age that he so richly celebrated' he deserved a knighthood as a just reward. Henry Porter took up the cause in the *Telegraph*: 'He has given at least as much pleasure as Sir Kingsley Amis or Sir Victor Pritchett.'

Honoured or not, Laurie had, by his final year, achieved all the immortality an author could desire. His name was invoked whenever Spain was mentioned, or rural life, or childhood. 'A Laurie Lee childhood' was shorthand, however erroneously, for a carefree idyll. In March 1996 there was an evening of Laurie's poetry and prose at Cheltenham Ladies' College. Brian Patten sent a poem, imagining a granddaughter of Rosie having to study Laurie's work at school. It began

> She's sitting in the back row of the class
> Warm and lank and dreaming...

and wickedly ended

> English literature demands
> That his verses be stripped bare
> Though I imagine Laurie would
> Rather do the same to her.

Patten said Laurie was delighted. In May he was at the Chelsea Flower Show, in the green latticed tent of Jill, Duchess of Hamilton for her Flora for Fauna project (promoting plants that encourage butterflies). Laurie told her he had added buddleia and mignonette to his garden, and looked forward to 'floating waves of Peacock and Tortoiseshell which, launched by you, may even yet salvage our summer'.

On 28 June 1996 Michael Wishart died of cancer, aged sixty-eight. At his funeral his mother Lorna, now eighty-five, prowled about with her feline stride, stricken at losing her favourite son and soulmate, but still strong and unsentimental. Laurie sent a card, and he and Lorna planned to meet again, but they never did. A month after Michael's funeral, Laurie collapsed (with fluid on the lung) and Kathy took him to the Royal Gloucester Hospital; on the same day, Lorna drove out in her car to go to mass and was hit by another car, breaking her collar-bone. She never fully recovered from that accident, and died in January 2000, a day before her eighty-ninth birthday. Her obituaries celebrated her as the muse of Laurie Lee and Lucian Freud.

Laurie, increasingly blind, had been dictating all his letters to Kathy for some years. ('I am getting an aged aunt to type this for me…' he wrote wickedly to Val Hennessy. 'Yours through a glass darkly, but with the brightest love.') He also got Kathy to note down odd thoughts he wanted to record. These, in her hand, had an increasingly valedictory tone:

'I've had a long bright life but now I feel the dark doors closing.'

'All my best friends are dead, and some are not even my friends.'

'I don't know whether I owe more to women than they to me.'

'I'm still a going concern, but a little concerned about going.'

'Golden wedding conversation: "I'm proud of you." "I'm tired of you too."'

'The thread of light grows greener, the birds' cry sharper, as they prepare for spring.'

'My room still cluttered with starts and endings will at length be sorted, and I hope forgiven.'

In summer 1996, Kathy realised that he might be dying. Laurie issued orders about various pieces of writing left lying around his room. He was frail that autumn, but still just well enough to travel to London – to see Antonia for instance.

Now widowed, and having begun a new career as a sculptor, Antonia had bought a Georgian house on the river alongside other artists at Hammersmith Terrace. She invited Laurie for lunch in the garden. 'I'm passionate about the view of the river,' she said, 'and I wanted him to see it. And I felt he blessed this garden. It was important to me that he'd approved of it.' The grandmother clock that Laurie found for her when she first had a house of her own stands in her hall; and a bust of Laurie, sculpted by Antonia, looks out from a corner of her drawing room towards the river.

In November 1996, the Imperial War Museum held a sixtieth anniversary celebration for veterans of the International Brigades. Laurie went along, mingling with veterans wearing their medals. He re-encountered Martha Gellhorn, who had been a reporter of the Civil War, and had a chat with the Spanish ambassador, proudly showing him his ancient passport with its stamp '*sale sin dinero*' from February 1938. That year, the Spanish parliament granted Spanish citizenship to all those who had fought in the International Brigades. (Juan Negrin, the Republic's prime minister, had promised this in return for their courage, and now that Franco was dead the promise could be fulfilled.) Fewer than 500 veterans were still alive, eighty-two of them in Britain: Bill Alexander welcomed the news on behalf of the Britons who fought in Spain, 'including Laurie Lee, the author'.

Early in 1997 Laurie signed, in a shaky hand, his last contract: a £1,000 advance on the Robson Books edition of *The Firstborn*, which was to be published in May. Laurie signed bookplates, and wrote to Jeremy Robson: 'Mother and daughter doing well and much pleased by being born again.' In March, his agent wrote to say he would soon be receiving his £35,000 tranche of Penguin's five-year renewal licence covering the paperbacks of *Cider with Rosie* and *A Rose for Winter*.

On 16 February 1997 Laurie went back into hospital for various tests. 'The signs upon me do not presage bright news,' he wrote to his doctor, Roddy Jaques. Bowel cancer was diagnosed, and an operation arranged. Laurie began dictating many letters. He wrote to Clare Francis about her applying for membership of the Chelsea Arts Club, explaining that as an honorary member of the Club he was denied a vote. 'But I do hope that when I rise from my bed and return to London, I shall find you there, adorning the bar or the spring flowers in the garden.'

On 12 March Laurie wrote to Antonia, regretting that he would be not be at the exhibition of her sculptures in April. 'I know that your exquisitely fashioned heads will be a great success (even though one is missing).' She finished her head of Laurie after his death.

He even dictated a letter to an actress playing the part of his mother in *Cider with Rosie*:

Dear Mum, I'm so glad to hear that you've agreed to carry the Lee banner to the outside world, and with it all the colour and wild dignity of the original. I send my warmest love to you – and to Rosie lying in the long summer grasses. I will be thinking of you on the night of the opening, and may my loyal spirit accompany all of you always.

In his interview with Mavis Nicholson, eight years before, he had told her that the landscape from his window was even more precious to him now than in his childhood:

a grand kind of extravaganza with no beginning and no end. Everything is ordered, the graveyard beyond me has a quiet sense of expectancy, it's waiting for me, and that will be my second home, and I will be back in my roots. I acknowledge that with a feeling of gratitude because I know where I am, I know where my beginning was, and I know that will be my end, and I am quite ready for it when it happens.

On his way into the Royal Gloucester Hospital for the last operation, he told Kathy and Jessy what he wanted engraved on his tombstone: 'He lies in the valley he loved.'

Kathy and Jessy understood Laurie's insistence on coming home from hospital to die. 'I have a terror of medical authority,' he had said in 1987. 'I think, please don't let me fall into their hands. Let me be born at home, stay at home, die at home.' Jessy assured him he would never go far from her again. They brought him home several weeks before the Labour government was elected on 1 May 1997. He was *compos mentis* enough to be elated about that, and they drank a toast 'to Labour, Love and Laurie'. His bed had been moved downstairs, so that he could see his valley view from the sunny sitting room. During Laurie's last days, Kathy kept a constant vigil, and Jessy was there all day, with Dr Jaques and two district nurses. As Laurie's mind began to falter, Jessy would get him to recite his poems with her. 'I managed to recite "April Rise" by heart. "If ever I saw blessing in the air…" and "Slow moves the acid breath of noon".'

The last days in May passed with the aid of Mr Kipling's baby treacle sponges, and morphine. They made sure Laurie was in no pain. The day before he died, he called out to Kathy to come over. 'Yes, Lol?' 'I've got a secret,' he said. She said, 'Yes?' Jessy was listening. Both waited. But Laurie said nothing more.

Kathy knew beforehand when he was going to die, and held his hands as he drifted into unconsciousness. Jessy recalled:

> Suddenly there was this tiny little moan, it was like a wailing song, It sounded like a tormented soul from purgatory: I had nightmares that he might have been trying to say something. I had a very strange two hours with him before he died. I could feel him going, in my solar plexus. I sent him away on his journey with Schubert's Quintet in C. It was our music, his and mine. I played it three times, and by then I wanted him to die, to go and be free from earthly torment. In so many ways he was tormented, all his life; such a tormented man.

Kathy was pleased that she had preserved 'Laurie's fantasy' of his two women; that he was able to die with his two women around him, 'enclosing him in a double embrace, like bookends'. 'At least he was able to have entirely what he wanted at the very end. He could hear our voices. And we were able to say goodbye. At the moment of death, he looked so young, and sun-tanned, he smelt lovely and he looked lovely.' Kathy went in to spend the last five minutes with him, while Jessy listened from the kitchen. 'I heard Mum say, "It's all right. Go now. We'll be together soon," and she raised her hand above his head and gently drew it along the length of his body – as if to help him on his way.'

It was Tuesday, 13 May 1997, when he died. Jessy recalled the moment.

> Everything went golden, an extraordinary light filled the house. And there were two brilliant rainbows across the valley, so astonishing that many people in the village took photographs – such a strange phenomenon, in black sky. A transcending moment. And it was so quiet that he was instantly gone and away.
>
> I looked at my watch and it was 9.25 and all of a sudden I heard his last breath and I had a feeling of such strength – his strength perhaps. And we went into the garden and danced, and then picked masses of white tea roses, Dad's favourite – and sprinkled their petals on him. We had this extraordinary sensation rushing up through our feet and we just had to dance.

The funeral in Slad on Tuesday, 20 May 1997 was a village and family-only affair. Jessy carried a spray of lily-of-the-valley, as Kathy had on her wedding day. In light summer rain, his coffin was borne up the path opposite the Woolpack to the churchyard. Laurie had insisted that he should not be buried in the new graveyard above the church; he must be in the lower churchyard. He had said:

> I came back here because starting as a scruffy little scab-kneed boy, and going round the world, in many countries, I've never found a place which has such intimate significance for me. The trees, the very slope of the valleys are so intensely special to me. I want to be buried between the pub and the church, so that I can balance the secular and the spiritual, and my long sleep

will be punctuated by rowdy Saturday nights in the Woolpack, and Sunday morning worship in the church. It would give me a feeling of continuity.

His poem 'April Rise' was read in the church:

If ever I saw blessing in the air
I see it now in this still early day
Where lemon-green the vaporous morning drips
Wet sunlight on the powder of my eye.

30

Epilogue
1997–2014

LAURIE'S OBITUARIES IN 1997 eulogised him as a national treasure and a local landmark – a writer rooted in a particular place. When Laurie greeted his readers in Slad, it was 'as if Dickens had shown tourists round his blacking factory'.[140] The obituarists hymned his 'voluptuous, enamelled style', his skilful way of treading 'the slippery path between myth and memoir'.[141] They allowed him to retain his secrets: 'I am a person of concealment. No one has ever managed to get through.'[142] Some pointed out that Laurie's output was slender. But Jane Mack, who had made a literary study of Laurie's work, argued in *The Guardian* that his range and scope were wide: the poetry alone 'ranged from Lorca-inspired surrealism to war poetry in the spirit of Wilfred Owen'. There were three verse plays, several film scripts, and 'even in his MOI report, *Land at War*, his style shines through ... Who but Laurie Lee could make an official document read like prose poetry?'[143]

He was 'A Many-Coated Man', which was the title borrowed for Laurie's memorial service at St James's, Piccadilly, in October 1997. Jock Gallagher gathered a dozen men who had known Laurie in his several coats: as poet, musician, traveller, clubman, countryman. Laurie's army greatcoat cloaked him in secretiveness, Gallagher said: he imagined Laurie 'looking down on us with childlike delight at the difficulty we have in pinning him down'. Fellow poets Christopher Fry, Brian Patten and Roger McGough read their own poems for Laurie. P. J. Kavanagh read Laurie's poem 'The Pollard Beech'.

McGough said that when his own late-born first daughter arrived, in his early fifties, Laurie told him to enjoy it: 'Before you know where you are she'll be asking you for money.'

John Mortimer recalled Laurie sending him off on his bicycle from Pinewood Studios to Watford Junction: the beginning of his writing career. Richard Ryan, then Irish ambassador in Madrid, recounted having told Laurie, in their last conversation, of a recent visit to Segovia, where gypsy women had stolen his wife's handbag. 'Dear boy,' Laurie said, 'don't be boring. Don't tell me about handbags. Tell me about their eyes, their teeth, their hair.' David Blunkett, Education Secretary, recalled his glass of cider with Laurie in the Woolpack. After the service, there was a wake at the packed Chelsea Arts Club. The sculptor Lynn Bamber's head of Laurie was on display for the first time. It toppled over, unharmed, on the billiard table.

But Laurie did not rest in peace. On 31 December 1997, in *The Spectator*, an article by Simon Courtauld ('A Not Very Franco Account') commemorated the battle of Teruel sixty years before. He had spoken to Bill Alexander, who repeated all his old doubts about *A Moment of War*. Courtauld agreed that the dates in Laurie's book did not make sense. Reporters rang Kathy, who was 'angry and upset' that Laurie's account should be questioned now that he was no longer there to answer for himself.

To several journalists – and to me – Bill Alexander again said he wished Laurie had made *A Moment of War* a novel. He admired Laurie's writing and was still grateful that he dedicated his book 'To the defeated.' But he felt he must now put the record straight since a recent book, *Britain and the Spanish Civil War* by Tom Buchanan, citing Laurie's account, might now be read by history students. (In fact, Buchanan's mention of *A Moment of War* was not that misleading. Commending its 'sense of tragedy and futility', he added in his chapter on 'Intellectuals', 'Lee's war did not last long: after taking part in the desperate fighting at Teruel he suffered a temporary breakdown and was sent home.')

The reaction of most writers to the fuss was summed up by the novelist Allan Massie, who declared that it was naïve to expect a poet's version of events to be historically accurate. He cited other authors – Waugh, Ford Madox Ford, Orwell – whose impressionistic, imaginative memoirs contained novelistic episodes. 'Hemingway's *A Moveable Feast* is full of invention or, if you prefer, packed with lies. Yet this book gives a keener sense of what it felt like to be young in Paris than any reconstruction by a scrupulous historian could provide.'[144]

Nor were Laurie's old friends terribly shaken. 'After all, *A Moment of War* does not pretend to be a heroic book,' Jim Rose said. 'It is the story of lamentable failure … an unvaunting book.' Michael Still likened the book to an abstract painting 'which adapts and transmutes, taking artistic licence'. The poet Vernon Scannell, a gallant soldier himself, suspected that for romantic Laurie, conscious of his unheroic Second World War, 'the imagined drama of bloodshed, heroism and sacrifice possessed a powerful fascination'.[145] It didn't matter whether his experiences were factually true. 'I don't care two hoots, myself,' Ted Walker agreed. 'A good tale is a good tale.'[146]

'It comes as no surprise to me,' wrote a *Guardian* reader in Manchester,[147] 'that some old tankie would crawl out of the woodwork to smear an author's name – after he's safely dead, of course.'

But writers' memoirs and letters are often embellished. In 1927 V. S. Pritchett wrote *Marching Spain*, about walking across Spain, sleeping on stone floors with peasant families. Nobody ever accused Pritchett of dishonesty, but as he revealed in 1970, he had been 'purposely silent about knowing Spain already because I wanted to preserve an instantaneous impression'. He had actually been living in Spain for a while as a foreign correspondent.

Meanwhile Dr Barry McLoughlin, an Irish historian, who was doing research in Moscow's Comintern archive, had examined the files of the International Brigades and had seen documents relating to Laurie's early days in war-torn Spain. In these[148] (which I quote in Chapter 7 of this book) Laurie was singled out from the volunteers by Bob Doyle for his excellent conduct despite his illness. (Poor Doyle was soon captured, and spent the rest of the war imprisoned near Burgos – never imagining that what he wrote in 1937 would be exhumed from a Moscow vault sixty years later, to verify Laurie's presence.) In another report by the American officer Constantino Dubac, Laurie was described as 'willing to do his best for the revolution' and recommended for an unstrenuous post at a base camp, as he seemed 'a responsible person and trustworthy'. Here was clear evidence that Laurie had indeed joined the International Brigades in December 1937, before he 'fell with a fever below the Bahía de Rosas', as his poem 'The Return' put it, 'letting the mad snow spit in my eyes'.

McLoughlin paid further visits to the Comintern archives and the documents he copied for me identified Laurie's comrades, and his likely interrogators, including the American 'Sam' (probably Tony de Maio who worked for Servicio de Investigación Militar). Laurie was certainly transferred from Tarazona to the Cultural Commission. But his activities during the British participation in the Teruel conflict, in the first five weeks of 1938, remain unverifiable.

Laurie's eye-witness story of the Spanish Civil War remains vivid (as to atmosphere) and imaginative (as to hard fact) where some of his adventures are chronologically impossible. He bravely crossed the Pyrenees in a blizzard. It is highly probable that Laurie was detained and cross-examined, since his passport revealed that he had been in Morocco in March 1936, at precisely the place and time Franco was mustering his rebel army. It is also credible that he was summoned from the barrack square for interrogation, given Wilma's alerts to the Communist hierarchy about the need to find Laurie and send him home. But there are no archive records of any imprisonment in a death cell.

His book must rest in the no man's land between history and invention. It gave a graphic impression, like that in Ken Loach's 1996 film, *Land and Freedom*, of what it felt like to be under bombardment in Spain in that bloody winter. 'Ill-fed and ill-armed, many of these young men died,' as Laurie wrote. 'The survivors returned home to ignominy. But to me this seems to have been the last time that the young had a cause they could believe in and could fight from the heart.'[149]

I learnt not to dismiss any of Laurie's stories lightly. The girl from Buenos Aires who taught Laurie to ask for a glass of water in Spanish had sounded like a romantic fantasy, until the summer of 1998, when I came across the '*lección en castellano*' letter from Sufi Rogers. Days later, Kathy opened her door to a small moustachioed man who said he was from Buenos Aires. It was Sufi's younger brother Richard, back in Slad for a visit, who confirmed that the unlikely tale was entirely true.

Exactly a year after Laurie's death, the village was taken over by cameras again, for Adrian Bate's new version of *Cider with Rosie* with screenplay by John Mortimer. Juliet Stevenson played Laurie's mother, and cousin Charlie's actor grandson, John Light, also took part. Laurie's voice, recorded in 1988, was used for the narration, which was the film's ace card when it was televised at Christmas in 1998.

Kathy had devoted fifty years to Laurie. Now she became the keeper of his flame: attending tributes and celebrations in Gloucestershire (including *¡No Pasarán!* – a performance of Spanish Civil War songs and poems by Stroud Football Poets). Jessy moved into Rose Cottage, efficiently refashioned it, and deployed her vibrant personality in psychotherapy, since she had found analysis so helpful herself. In recent years she has become instrumental in the continuing struggle to keep the Slad valley safe from encroachments by predators. In the 1960s Laurie had bought the woods on Tranters Hill, opposite his house, but Jessy found it increasingly difficult to protect this wood from thieves and tree-fellers; the local authority and police seemed powerless. So she advised the trustees of the Laurie Lee estate to sell the woods to Gloucestershire Wildlife Trust which already owned the adjacent land, a nature reserve, at Swift's Hill. On 26 June 2013 this precious woodland was renamed The Laurie Lee Woods, protected as a nature reserve for future generations.

At the same time, the arrangement whereby the cricket ground at Sheepscombe, bought by Laurie in the 1970s, was used by the local cricket team free of charge was considered unsustainable by Laurie's estate. Kathy and Jessy urged the trustees not to put the ground on the open market, but to sell it to the Sheepscombe Cricket Club at a price below its potential value. They did buy it, and the English Cricket Board also awarded the club £25,000 to maintain its facilities including the old pavilion.

All this would have pleased Laurie enormously. But nothing would have delighted him more than the celebration of his centenary year in 2014 by the Unicorn Press's publication of The Laurie Lee Folio, containing 90 of his sketches and paintings, introduced with an extended essay by Jessy on her father. Laurie always said he wanted to be a painter first. Jessy had never looked inside the old A2 portfolio in his study until his death: now she organised a month-long exhibition of his art at the Chelsea Arts Club, and another at the Stroud Museum. There were also new publications including a reissue of *The Firstborn*, and poetry readings and events including an exhibition of his wartime memories at the British Library (keepers of the archive since 2003). In Gloucestershire, the current owners of Annie's old cottage in Slad were offering cream teas to tourists. In his centenary year Laurie was not forgotten.

A school-age reader had once written to ask Laurie: 'What frightens you in our modern world?'

'Ignorance, racism, nationalism and intolerance,' he replied. He was not a philosopher, he added. That would suggest an academic and theoretical mind at work. 'I am an observer. My reactions to life are intuitive rather than analytical.'

He had started out in life with no money, small education, absolutely no connections, and parlous health. He had to survive entirely by his wits. But he was remarkably blessed, in his mother, in his artistic talents in his wife, and in his devoted friends. As Yasmin said, Laurie's orbit was an extremely magnetising one. Charm is a gift, as he wrote, 'only given to give away, and the more used the more there is'. Everyone mentions how Laurie charmed and beguiled them, giving all his attentiveness, his listening absorption.

It was impossible not to love Laurie, when working on his life. I loved the fact that he turned his face to the sun, and became mahogany brown every summer. I loved his fine clear handwriting, and the care he took over crafting his prose, in soft pencil on the backs of old radio scripts: 'I couldn't write on clean paper – I'd get inhibited. As it is, I can turn over and it says, "Good morning, Mrs Dale, and how are you today?" and I feel comforted.'

I loved Laurie most for according humour a proper place in his life by making a note of jokes:

– A notice in the grocer's: 'Please do not sit on the counters, as we are getting behind with our orders.'

– Edgar Allan Poe – otherwise known as the Chamber of Horrors.

– 'Can you tell me the way to Rillington Place?' 'Sorry, I'm a strangler here myself.'

– Judging a poetry competition, finding dozens of poems from an old General, about hooves ringing out on frosty roads: 'a slight case of Tallyhosis'.

– Why do they never say 'old', always 'elderly'? Elderly Tyme Dancing. Elderly King Cole was a merry elderly soul. The Elderly Bailey.

– The sound of the hoover: the dentist's drill of marriage.

– A succinct summing up of the life cycle: Sperms, germs, worms.

'I often make such good jokes asleep I wake myself up laughing,' Laurie wrote in his Dreams notebook. 'I like dreams. They give me special powers. I can talk foreign languages and commit crimes. I am possessed with the gift of argument. I have put many a bishop in his place and even corrected the Pope on a point of ritual.'

In his poem 'Night Speech', Laurie extols the powers bestowed by dreams:

This fur-lined hour
Makes princes of each wretch
whose day-bed wasted,
points each lax tongue
to daggered brightness,
says what we could not say.

He invaded my own dreams too: in one, I drove Laurie to his brother Jack's front door in Sydney, telling him: 'We're going to see Jack' – and then woke with a start of disappointment. I suppose I longed to reunite them after their long estrangement. 'All these years gone by,' Jack told me wistfully, '& so many of them wasted. We could have had such a wonderful relationship … & it all came to such a wretched end.' When Jack died in 2005, the funeral service was held in Slad, and his ashes were scattered, according to his wishes, on Swift's Hill.

Living with Laurie's life for two years was addictive, obsessional, and full of chance coincidences. I remember the pleasure of discovering that Laurie had copied into his 1954 diary a Lancashire dialect poem (anonymous) called 'Micky Thumps'. I longed to tell him that I too had copied down 'Micky Thumps', in my 1962 diary. Its last heart-wringing lines are:

Some danced on his grave
Some spat on his grave
But I scraped my eyes out for my old friend Micky Thumps.[150]

In a hotel bar on the tiny Canary island of La Gomera, I was reading Laurie's poems when I looked up to see, at the next table, Brian Patten – whom I had heard reading his poem at Laurie's memorial, not long before. We ended up joining in a wild New Year's Eve dancing party along with Spanish families: grandfathers, señoritas and children, in just the kind of scruffy taberna that Laurie liked.

Much in southern Spain remains as he saw it, despite eighty years having passed. Following in Laurie's footsteps (not on foot but by high-speed AVE train) I saw a cadaverous Cervantes lookalike, playing a guitar in a square in Granada, and a woman dancing down a cobbled street with babe in arms. I saw a circle of old men holding hands in the Plaza Mayor in Madrid; and a raven-haired, blue-eyed gitana named Carmen, of startling grace and beauty, performing in the caves of Sacromonte.

A reader had once asked Laurie how he saw women. He replied: 'Submissives, dominators, predators, inspirers. Women are closer to the earth and to creation than men are. They are guardians of life and chroniclers of social history, and are of course men's supreme motivation for both physical and mental action.' Women were certainly his own inspiration, his muses and mentors. His was a life studded with loves, many unrecorded in print even though his entire opus consisted of fragments of autobiography, 'a celebration of living and an attempt to hoard its sensations'. He said in 1992 that he still had much 'to confess and celebrate'. He was certainly planning to write another book, using his wartime journals,[151] which have many paragraphs marked in red ink, and markers between the pages indicating episodes he intended to relate.

> There is nothing that preserves things so much as writing …
> And nothing obliterates the memory so much as not taking the trouble to make a record of it at the time. You do it in order to arrest time, and fix it in the mind, to perhaps cheat mortality to a point. I think that's as much as my writing aims to do, nothing more.[152]

As I sat in his study, on his leather swivel chair, with its view of Swift's Hill and the slanting shadows, I was grateful that Laurie, like all heart-and-soul writers, had hoarded all those letters 'exhaling the heated breath of girls', and recorded the minutiae of his life so graphically. 'A day unremembered is like a soul unborn, worse than if it had never been,' as he wrote. 'What indeed was that summer if it is not recalled? That journey? That act of love? ... Any bits of warm life preserved by the pen are trophies snatched from the dark...'

Appendix

Dear Mr Lee

Dear Mr Lee (Mr Smart says
it's rude to call you Laurie, but that's
how I think of you, having lived with you
really all year), Dear Mr Lee
(Laurie) I just want you to know
I used to hate English, and Mr Smart
is roughly my least favourite person,
and as for Shakespeare (we're doing him too)
I think he's a national disaster, with all those jokes
that Mr Smart has to explain why they're jokes,
and even then no one thinks they're funny,
And T. Hughes and P. Larkin and that lot
in our anthology, not exactly a laugh a minute,
pretty gloomy really, so that's why
I wanted to say Dear Laurie (sorry) your book's
the one that made up for the others, if you
could see my copy you'd know it's lived
with me, stained with Coke and Kit-kat
and when I had a cold, and I often
take you to bed with me to cheer me up
so Dear Laurie, I want to say sorry,
I didn't want to write a character-sketch
of your mother under headings, it seemed
wrong somehow when you'd made her so lovely,
and I didn't much like those questions

about *social welfare in the rural community*
and *the seasons as perceived by an adolescent*,
I didn't think you'd want your book
read that way, but bits of it I know by heart,
and I wish I had your uncles and your half-sisters
and lived in Slad, though Mr Smart says your view
of the class struggle is naive and the examiners
won't be impressed by me knowing so much by heart,
they'll be looking for terse and cogent answers
to their questions, but I'm not much good at terse and cogent,
I'd just like to be like you, not mind about being poor,
see everything bright and strange, the way you do,
and I've got the next one out of the Public Library,
about Spain, and I asked Mum about learning
to play the fiddle, but Mr Smart says Spain isn't
like that any more, it's all Timeshare villas
and Torremolinos, and how old were you
when you became a poet? (Mr Smart says for anyone
with my punctuation to consider poetry as a career
is enough to make the angels weep.)
Dear Laurie, please don't feel guilty for
me failing the exam, it wasn't your fault,
it was mine, and Shakespeare's, and maybe Mr Smart's, I still
     love *Cider*,
it hasn't made any difference.

U. A. FANTHORPE

Bibliography

WORKS BY LAURIE LEE

Poetry

The Sun My Monument, Hogarth Press, 1944.
The Bloom of Candles, John Lehmann, 1947.
My Many-Coated Man, André Deutsch, 1955.
Pocket Poets, Vista Books, 1960.
15 Poems for William Shakespeare, Trustees and Guardians of Shakespeare's Birthplace, 1964.
Paintings and Drawings of Gypsies of Granada, Athelnay Books, 1969.
Pergamon Poets: Causley and Lee No. 10, Pergamon Press, 1970.
Selected Poems, André Deutsch, 1983.

Plays

Peasants' Priest, H. J. Goulden, Canterbury, 1947.
The Voyage of Magellan, John Lehmann, 1948.
I Call Me Adam (unpublished), 1959.

Prose

Land at War, HMSO, 1945.
(With Ralph Keene) *We Made a Film in Cyprus*, Longmans Green, 1947. *Vassos the Goatherd*, Pilot Press, 1947.
A Rose for Winter, The Hogarth Press, 1955; Penguin, 1971.
Cider with Rosie, The Hogarth Press, 1959; Penguin, 1962.
(With David Lambert) *Man Must Move: The Story of Transport*, Rathbone Books, 1960.

Atlantic Fairway, Cunard Line, 1962.

The Firstborn, The Hogarth Press, 1964.

As I Walked Out One Midsummer Morning, André Deutsch, 1969;
    Penguin, 1971.

The Wonderful World of Transport, Macdonald & Co, 1969.

I Can't Stay Long, André Deutsch, 1975; Penguin, 1977.

Two Women, André Deutsch, 1983.

Laurie Lee: A Selection, ed. Chris Buckton, Longman, 1984.

A Moment of War, Viking, 1991; Penguin, 1992.

Red Sky at Sunrise: omnibus edition of *Cider with Rosie*, *As I Walked
    Out One Midsummer Morning* and *A Moment of War*, Viking,
    1992; Penguin Books, 1993.

To War in Spain, Penguin 60s, 1996.

Films

Malta VC, 1945.

Cyprus is an Island, 1946, Greenpark Productions.

A Tale in a Tea-cup, 1947, Greenpark Productions.

Journey into Spring, 1957, British Transport Films.

BOOKS CONSULTED

Alexander, Bill, *British Volunteers for Liberty*, Lawrence & Wishart,
    1982.

Angus, John, *With the International Brigade in Spain*, Department
    of Economics, Loughborough University, 1983.

Banham, Mary, and Hillier, Bevis (eds.), *A Tonic to the Nation: The
    Festival of Britain 1951*, Thames & Hudson, 1976.

Beevor, Antony, *The Spanish Civil War*, Orbis, 1982.

Brenan, Gerald, *Personal Record, 1920–1972*, Jonathan Cape, 1974.

Buchanan, Tom, *Britain and the Spanish Civil War*, Cambridge
    University Press, 1996.

Campbell, Roy, *Light on a Dark Horse*, Hollis & Carter, 1951;
    reprinted 1969, with a foreword by Laurie Lee.

Carr, Raymond, *Spain 1808–1939*, Oxford University Press, 1966.

Courtauld, Simon, *Spanish Hours*, Libri Mundi, 1996.

Cross, Tom, *Artists & Bohemians: 100 Years with the Chelsea Arts Club*, Quiller Press, 1992.

Cunningham, Valentine (ed.), *The Penguin Book of Spanish Civil War Verse*, Penguin, 1980.

Cunningham, Valentine, *Spanish Front: Writers on the Civil War*, Oxford University Press, 1986.

Day-Lewis, Sean, *C. Day-Lewis, An English Literary Life*, Weidenfeld & Nicolson, 1980.

Devas, Nicolette, *Two Flamboyant Fathers*, Collins, 1966.

Fern, Jim, *Ferns in the Valley*, Millvale Publishing, Evesham, 1995.

Gallagher, Jock (ed.), *Laurie Lee, A Many-coated Man*, Viking, 1998.

Gardiner, Stephen, *Epstein*, Michael Joseph, 1992.

Gardiner, Stephen, *Frink*, HarperCollins, 1998.

Glendinning, Victoria, *Vita*, Weidenfeld & Nicolson, 1983.

Goodman, Celia (ed.), *Living with Koestler: Mamaine Koestler's Letters 1945–51*, Weidenfeld & Nicolson, 1985.

Gowing, Lawrence, *Lucian Freud*, Thames & Hudson, 1982.

Howson, Gerald, *Arms for Spain: The Untold Story of the Spanish Civil War*, John Murray, 1998.

Jacobs, Eric, *Kingsley Amis: A Biography*, Hodder & Stoughton, 1995.

Kavanagh, P. J., *The Perfect Stranger*, Chatto & Windus, 1966.

Lyle, Anna Campbell, *Poetic Justice: A Memoir of My Father, Roy Campbell*, Typographeum, Francestown, New Hampshire, 1986.

MacFarlane, Brian, *An Autobiography of British Cinema*, Methuen, 1997.

Mansell, Frank, *Cotswold Ballads*, with introduction by Laurie Lee, Wittantree Press, Stroud, 1969; reprinted by R. Courtauld, Stroud, 1974.

Marcus, Jane, *The Young Rebecca: Writings of Rebecca West 1911–1917*, Macmillan/Virago, 1982.

Mitchell, David, *The Spanish Civil War*, Granada, 1982.

Mortimer, John, *Clinging to the Wreckage*, Weidenfeld & Nicolson, 1982.

Pritchett, V. S., *Marching Spain*, Ernest Benn, 1928.

Ray, Gordon N., *H. G. Wells and Rebecca West*, Macmillan, 1974.

Rust, William, *Britons in Spain*, Lawrence & Wishart, 1939.

Sebba, Anne, *Battling for News*, Hodder & Stoughton, 1994.

Thacker, Joy, *Whiteway Colony: The Social History of a Tolstoyan Community*, Sutton Publishing, Stroud, Glos., 1993.

Thomas, Hugh, *The Spanish Civil War*, Eyre & Spottiswoode, 1961; reprinted by Hamish Hamilton, 1977.

Tolley, A. T., *The Poetry of the Thirties*, Gollancz, 1975.

Walker, Ted, *In Spain*, Secker & Warburg, 1987.

Walker, Ted, *The Last of England*, Jonathan Cape, 1992.

Wishart, Michael, *High Diver*, Blond & Briggs, 1977.

Wright, Adrian, *John Lehmann, A Pagan Adventure*, Duckworth, 1998.

Endnotes

1   'ordinary poverty': *Cider with Rosie*, 'Mother'.

2   Critchley Bros: now Critchley Electrical Products of Brimscombe.

3   'with rooks in the chimneys': *Cider with Rosie*, 'First Light'.

4   'too honest, too natural': *Cider with Rosie*, 'Mother'.

5   'the Rosie of the title': *Times Literary Supplement*, 20 November 1959.

6   'mother like that': E. B. Mais, *Yorkshire Post*, 13 November 1959.

7   'splendidly and richly mothered': Kate O'Brien, *Irish Times*, 28 December 1959.

8   'and I wish for her own modest sake': letter from L. L. to Wilma Gregory, 14 June 1960.

9   'herbaceous smugness of the English countryside': 'A Drink with a Witch', *Leader Magazine*, reproduced in *I Can't Stay Long*.

10 'ordinary diseases like whooping cough': L. L. interviewed by John Cunningham, *The Guardian*, 23 December 1971.

11 'life was a glass-bottomed boat': *Daily Mail*, 1976.

12 The Bird and Tree essay competition was organised annually by the Royal Society for the Protection of Birds. Seventy years later L. L. confessed that he had never observed the dabchick and had made up the entire essay (*Daily Mail*, 22 January 1994).

13 'a tunnel for my clockwork train': 'True Adventures of the Boy', Reader, *New York Times* book review, reproduced in *I Can't Stay Long*.

14 'question my liberties': L. L. reminiscing in 1989 to Christopher Cook on Radio 3.

15 'gave her a lot of silence': from 'Things I Wish I'd Known at Eighteen', interview with Frank Entwisle, *Sunday Express* magazine, 5 July 1981.

16 'order the earth to bloom': L. L. writing about his garden in *Homes & Gardens*, June 1962.

17 'enveloped by love': 'Things I Wish I'd Known at Eighteen'.

18 'never put it on paper': ibid.

19 'taught me a few words of Spanish': L. L. interviewed by Christopher Eldon Lee, Radio 3, 2 July 1992.

20 'If only I'd known': 'Things I Wish I'd Known at Eighteen'.

21 'Marry, and settle down': *As I Walked Out One Midsummer Morning*, 'London Road'.

22   'a fluid young girl of sixteen': *As I Walked Out One Midsummer Morning*, 'London Road'.

23   Philip O'Connor, surrealist poet: his *Collected Poems 1936–66* were published by Jonathan Cape. He died in 1998.

24   'the life of Reilly': L. L. in an *Evening Standard* article about his teenage years, December 1960.

25   The naval mutiny of Invergordon, Scapa Flow: in 1931 in the Firth of Cromarty, 12,000 ratings stalled fifteen ships for two days over pay rates imposed by the National Government that left them with 15s a week.

26   'brown as an apostle': *As I Walked Out One Midsummer Morning*, 'London'.

27   Eric Coates (1886–1957): composer of many famous signature tunes including 'Knightsbridge', which introduced *In Town Tonight*; 'By the Sleepy Lagoon' (*Desert Island Discs*), 'Calling All Workers' (*Music While You Work*) and later, 'The Dam Busters March'.

28   'He can't be my father': L. L. in conversation with Val Hennessy.

29   'held no memories for me': *As I Walked Out One Midsummer Morning*, 'Into Spain'.

30   'voices that carried from hill to hill': *Daily Mail*, 12 February 1995.

31   John King: BBC film director, who made films of *As I Walked Out* and *A Rose for Winter*.

32   'intimately shared with them': L. L. interviewed by Christopher Eldon Lee, Radio 3, 2 July 1992.

33   'walked tall and talked tall': from L. L.'s foreword to *Light on a Dark Horse*, Roy Campbell's autobiography, first published 1951; repr. Hollis & Carter, 1969.

34   'bizarre children': Michael Wishart in his autobiography, *High Diver*, Blond & Briggs, 1977.

35   'easy to break in': Roy Campbell, *Light on a Dark Horse*.

36   'gentleman with a park': ibid.

37   'Weald Village post office': from *Vita*, the biography of V. Sackville-West by Victoria Glendinning, Weidenfeld & Nicolson, 1983.

38   'like a firefly': *As I Walked Out One Midsummer Morning*, 'Toledo'.

39   'drinking like a madman': Anna Campbell Lyle, in *Poetic Justice*, a memoir of her father, Typographeum, Francestown, New Hampshire, 1986.

40   'one of my favourite names': L. L. to Val Hennessy, in the *Mail on Sunday*, 13 November 1988.

41   The township of Almuñécar has published a memorial journal. 'Almuñécar en la obra de Laurie Lee', an essay published in June 1998, was a collaboration between IES Antigua Sexi, the educational institute's geography and history faculty, and the municipality's department of culture.

42   'possibly with a friend': there were two accounts of L. L.'s trip to Morocco in *A Moment of War*: 'I'd made a quick trip to Morocco with a French student

from Arles … we'd spent most of our time in the rooms of small hotels, behind shutters, smoking hash', and 'my journey to Morocco had been solitary, innocent but damning'.

43   'solid argument': Wilma's thesis was that feminists were mistaken to concentrate on higher education. Instead, women should try to gain a share in the control of industry – though as Rebecca West pointed out, Wilma did not explain how this was to be achieved 'by a sex almost entirely innocent of capital'.

44   'off the menu': letters from H. G. Wells quoted in *The Young Rebecca, Writings of Rebecca West 1911–1917*, selected by Jane Marcus, Macmillan/ Virago, 1982.

45   *Penguin New Writing*: the quarterly review containing examples of recent poetry and prose edited by John Lehmann and published by Penguin.

46   Padworth is still a small village tucked away off the A4, with charming Norman church, St John the Baptist, and ancient yew tree in the graveyard. Padworth House, whose last scion died in 1932, is now a college. Padworth has not been developed, thanks to its proximity to the Atomic Weapons Establishment at Aldermaston. No trace of Rosemary Cottage, the hovel with acreage, remains.

47   'thin, hungry, and gorgeous': from Mavis Nicholson's TV interview 'Mavis Catches Up With…', 1989.

48   'back of boys' motorbikes': Yasmin David in conversation with V. G.

49   'treated me as a doll': Michael Wishart, *High Diver*.

50   'moments of absent-mindedness': William Greaves, *Today*, 3 January 1987.

51   'French dialect': *Two Women*.

52   'like Jean Marais': Kitty Godley in conversation with V. G.

53   Constantino Dubac was a Communist from New York, whose last appointment in the International Brigades was as an operative in Servicio de Investigación Militar (SIM). He died in 1968.

54   'He told Allen Andrews': L. L. interviewed in *Harper's Bazaar*, November 1961.

55   'his Cotswold childhood': L. L. interviewed by Frank Entwisle in the *Evening Standard* series 'Heartwarmers', 6 April 1962.

56   'on the same side': L. L. to Philip Oakes, *Sunday Times*, March 1977.

57   'carried a gun, not a stretcher': ibid.

58   'wounds of her absence': Michael Wishart, *High Diver*.

59   'helped D. H. Lawrence': Frieda, daughter of Baron von Richthofen, left three small children and a husband fourteen years older than herself to elope with D. H. Lawrence. His years of greatest creativity followed.

60   'speechless with dread and misery': Michael Wishart, *High Diver*.

61   In 1922 Vera Pragnall bought eight acres of land in West Sussex to form a bohemian commune, giving parcels of land to anyone who turned up in old

buses, caravans etc. She lived in Sanctuary Cottage, Sanctuary Lane, where there is now a statue of her, and lies buried (with the man she later married, a local property developer) in Washington parish cemetery. The commune disbanded in 1938, and during the Second World War the area was occupied by Canadian servicemen.

62   Jomo Kenyatta: the future president of Kenya had made his first visit to England in 1928, in his mid-thirties, to present a petition to the Colonial Office. He lived in England from 1932 until 1946, by which time he was a controversial figure. He was imprisoned in Kenya for managing the Mau Mau secret society in 1953, and detained until 1961. He was prime minister of Kenya in 1963, became president on its independence and died in 1978.

63   'friend of T. E. Lawrence': T. E. Lawrence had lived nearby at Clouds Hill; when he was killed in 1935 his funeral, attended by Churchill, was at Moreton's churchyard.

64   'heart of a lion': Michael Wishart, *High Diver*.

65   The Marchesa Luisa Casati: she refers to the poet Gabriele D'Annunzio (1863-1938), who won the MC and lived with Eleanora Duse.

66   Tambimuttu: known as Tambi, the pioneer hippie was a much-loved long-haired Sri Lankan literary guru who edited *Poetry London* from 1939 to 1947, publishing Dylan Thomas, Spender, MacNeice. After years in the US he returned to revive the magazine briefly in the 1970s as *Poetry London/ Apple Magazine*. He died in London in 1983.

67   'an operatic goddess of a woman': Nicolette Devas's description of Rosamond Lehmann in her memoirs, *Two Flamboyant Fathers*, Collins, 1966.

68   Rosamond Lehmann was the granddaughter of Robert Chambers, the *Chambers Dictionary* man, whose wife kept a Victorian literary salon, and the daughter of Rudolph Lehmann, classical scholar, fencer, oarsman, founder of *Granta*, Liberal MP, *Punch* editor.

69   'as two complicated men can be': from Sean Day-Lewis's biography of his father, *C. Day-Lewis, An English Literary Life*, Weidenfeld & Nicolson, 1980.

70   'really caught up with': Lucian Freud, quoted in Lawrence Gowing, *Lucian Freud,* Thames & Hudson, 1982. [NB for VG: this seems to be in the wrong place, as the quote appears in the next paragraph]

71   Laurie had recently stood godfather to the baby son of Sebastian and Elizabeth Leigh-Browne, whom he had met in Sussex.

72   Laurie still had Mavis's address in Australia in his address book in the 1960s.

73   'Sat-Down-And-Wept': Elizabeth Smart's most famous work was her novel, *By Grand Central Station I Sat Down and Wept,* published in 1945 by Editions Poetry London.

74   'had collected in their student days': Michael Wishart, *High Diver.*

75   The Hon. Wynne Alexander Hugh Godley (b. 1926), younger son of Lord
      Kilbracken, was professor of Applied Economics at Cambridge 1980–93.

76   Odette Massigli: according to John Lehmann's biographer Adrian Wright,
      Madame Massigli, wife of the French ambassador, later became Lehmann's
      only female lover.

77   'which was threepence': L. L. interviewed by Christopher Cook, Radio 3,
      1989

78   'ambiguous protector': *Two Women.*

79   'intimations of mischief': Sean Day-Lewis, *C. Day-Lewis.*

80   'isolation even more': *Two Women.*

81   'to betray both': L. L. in conversation with Selina Hastings, 1996.

82   'twice the size': *Two Women* (a story cited by the *Evening Standard* journal-
      ist Anne Sharpley years later as the only known instance of anyone actually
      being weighed on the scales at Victoria Station).

83   'bright and bragging and English': from Mary Banham and Bevis Hillier
      (eds.), *A Tonic to the Nation: The Festival of Britain 1951*, Thames &
      Hudson, 1976.

84   'had ever seen': Misha Black in *A Tonic to the Nation.*

85   Walham Green Empire: *Two Women.*

86   'Beer was flowing, of course': G. S. Whittet in *A Tonic to the Nation.*

87   'Festival English': 'A Few Words on Festival English' by Desmond Fitzgerald,
      in the *World Review, June* 1951.

88   'fantastic cast of mind': Roy Fuller in *A Tonic to the Nation.*

89   'Telemann concerto': Charles Plouviez in *A Tonic to the Nation.*

90   The contributors of exhibits were: Mr A. C. Wood, Commander J. D.
      Richard, RN, Mr L. A. V. Davoren, Mr Hugh Allen, Mrs A. A. Johnson,
      Mr Jack Hall and Mr P. Henniker-Heaton, Founder of the British Snail-
      Watching Society.

91   'endless parties': Stephen Gardiner, *Frink*, HarperCollins, 1998.

92   Colquhoun and MacBryde: Robert Colquhoun (1914–62) and Robert
      MacBryde (1913–66), known as 'the Roberts', met at Glasgow School of Art
      and were inseparable companions. Their London studio became a writers'
      and artists' salon 1941–47.

93   'bloodiest as the latter undeniably is': from Kingsley Amis's correspondence
      with Robert Conquest, quoted in Eric Jacobs, *Kingsley Amis, a Biography*,
      Hodder & Stoughton, 1995.

94   Lady Mary Walker's house, and the home of the Brinton-Lee family, near La
      Línea, both remain much as they were in the 1950s.

95   Lewis Eyers: the Slad carrier.

96   Epstein's *Ecce Homo* was in Battersea Park in 1960, later removed to
      Coventry Cathedral.

97   'weeping over long-lost friends': L. L. did not reveal to Sally that the long-lost friend was her mother, Rosamond Lehmann, who had fallen out with Enid Starkie over Enid's championing of Cecil Day-Lewis for the Oxford Poetry professorship, a job Day-Lewis had told Rosamond he could do only with her at his side. Rosamond sent L. L. Starkie's letters about this.

98   'shaved him forthwith': from L. L.'s *Encounter* article, 'Ibiza High Fifties', reproduced in *I Can't Stay Long*.

99   Winifred Bryher's father was Sir John Reeves Ellerman, newspaper tycoon and shipping magnate. Bryher often wrote her novels in the person of a young man, and although in her twenties she formed an association with Hilda Doolittle which lasted until H. D.'s death in 1961, she also married, twice, to acquire the freedom of a married woman.

100   'no less a person than Laurie Lee': *Stroud News,* 5 August 1959.

101   'spread the gospel of the country to the world': *Bristol Evening Post*, September 1959.

102   Ann Elwell (née Glass) was a 'beautiful spy' recruited by MI5 at the age of eighteen. Matthew Smith left all his paintings and drawings to Mary Keene (including a Van Gogh and an Epstein sculpture) and the residue of his £173,948 to her in trust for life.

103   'a chill wind blew from the west': L. L. in *Evening Standard,* December 1960.

104   That year, Kathy's head was sculpted by Loris Rey and drawn by Edward Ardizzone.

105   Prince Ludwig of Hesse: as Ludwig Landgraf, Prince Ludwig published poems and translated texts and librettos for Benjamin Britten.

106   Gerald Brenan (1894–1986): poet, scholar, traveller, military man (winner of the M C and the Croix de Guerre) famous for *The Face of Spain* and *South from Granada.* His association with Spain began in 1919 when he settled in an Andalucían village. He married the American writer Elizabeth Gamel Woolsey, and when he returned to Spain for good in 1953, he became an object of literary pilgrimage.

107   The Stewarts of Gibraltar: John D. Stewart was a Northern Irish civil engineer employed by the Gibraltar government, who published a book called *Gibraltar the Keystone.* He died in 1996.

108   The Searles: John Searle was for thirty years editor of the *Gibraltar Chronicle.*

109   Dame Veronica Wedgwood, speaking about *Cider with Rosie* in 'Vintage Cider' on Radio 4 in November 1984.

110   'inscrutable, dear boy': L. L. to Christopher Cook in Radio 3 interview, 1989.

111   'when I returned home to my wife': Dannie Abse in his autobiography, *A Poet in the Family,* Hutchinson, 1974.

112   'have a place on earth': L. L. in an article on his garden, *Homes & Gardens,* June 1962.

113   Cheltenham Festival panel to discuss autobiography: with L. L. were Elspeth Huxley, Alec Waugh and Danny Blanchflower.

114   'a wistful fugitive': *Two Women*.

115   'country recipes': Jeremy Sandford reporting for *Radio Times* on his 1962 interview with L. L. in Slad.

116   'to find Jessy': 'Relative Values', *Sunday Times* magazine, March 1986.

117   Ted Hughes wrote 'Full Moon and Little Frieda' about his daughter's first word: "Moon!" you cried suddenly. "Moon! Moon!"'

118   'bookstall at Paddington': from Ian Jack's account of Lord Snowdon's picture session in the *Sunday Times* magazine, 14 February 1982.

119   'Popski', Col. V. Poliakoff, was a distinguished Polish-born army officer who made his name in the Second World War leading 'Popski's Private Army' in jeeps in the North African desert. Their courageous exploits led them to be regarded as the precursors of the SAS.

120   'Gitano y Gitanas': published in *Paintings and Drawings of Gypsies of Granada,* Athelnay Books, 1969.

121   The Flook luncheon, 8 May 1970: other guests included Frank Norman, Kenneth Allsop, Edna O'Brien, Joan Bakewell, Spike Milligan, the cartoonists Emmwood, Leslie Illingworth, Jon, Wally Fawkes, and George and Diana Melly.

122   'What care I how kind she be?': George Wither (1588–1667), poet and satirist, imprisoned for his verses. No complete edition of his work has been published, but the poem referred to is in *Palgrave's Golden Treasury*.

123   A reference to Blake's 'Never seek to tell thy love'.

124   Steanbridge House had by this time been restored to its former glory by Mr and Mrs David Naylor.

125   'days filled with sun': interview with Gordon Burn, *Radio Times,* 16–23 December 1971.

126   'circling over cloud above Cheltenham': 'Concorde 002', *Telegraph* magazine, 4 February 1972, reproduced in *I Can't Stay Long*.

127   'Dear Mr Lee': the poet Ursula Fanthorpe had been head of English at Cheltenham Ladies' College. 'Dear Mr Lee' is in her collection *A Watching Brief* (Peterloo Poets), and is reproduced here on page 479.

128   'mortally frightened': 'Books' page, *Daily Mail,* 21 April 1977.

129   'A Village Christmas': *Reader's Digest,* December 1976.

130   *The Sun,* 14 February 1979.

131   Hugh Thomas, *The Spanish Civil War*, Eyre & Spottiswoode, 1961, repr. Hamish Hamilton, 1977.

132   'was his view': interview with L. L., *Wilts & Glos Standard,* October 1983.

133   'all over London': Angela Levin, *Mail on Sunday,* October 1983.

134   'conferred immortality': in July 1977, Bevis Hillier's Generation Show for the Jubilee at the Corn Exchange, Brighton, included a list of books which had 'changed attitudes or epitomized them' since 1953, starting with Dr

Spock's *Baby and Child Care*, Salinger's *The Catcher in the Rye*, Hoggart's
The Uses of Literacy and Berne's *Games People Play*. Hillier appealed to
Sunday Times readers for their own suggestions. As a result the year of 1959
included Burroughs's *Naked Lunch*, Delaney's *A Taste of Honey*, Gombrich's
Art and Illusion, Sillitoe's *The Loneliness of the Long Distance Runner*,
Waterhouse's *Billy Liar*, Thomas's *The Establishment*, and *Cider with Rosie*.

135   '50 years ago': Peter Davalle in *The Times,* December 1987.

136   'an apartment block': Val Hennessy, *Mail on Sunday,* 13 November 1988.

137   Quotations from Bill Alexander and John Dunlop's critiques of *A Moment of
War* come from the Spanish Civil War archives in the Imperial War Museum
and the Marx Memorial Library.

138   'rag-bag of mutilated texts': A. N. Wilson in the *Evening Standard,* January
1993.

139   The McGregor/Matthews room at New College is one of the most beautiful
rooms in Oxford, on the top floor of the front quadrangle. Formerly known
as the Wyatt library, it had been lined with deteriorating leather books
which obscured the fine seventeenth-century windows overlooking the
garden quad. The then Warden, Harvey McGregor QC, and Tom's widow
Pam Matthews jointly paid the substantial cost of removing the books and
restoring the room, now used for college meetings and concerts.

140   'blacking factory': Philip Oakes in conversation with V. G.

141   'between myth and memoir': *The Times* obituary, 15 May 1997.

142   'a person of concealment': *Daily Telegraph* obituary, 15 May 1997.

143   'read like prose poetry': Jane Mack, letter to *The Guardian,* 17 May 1997.

144   'a scrupulous historian could provide': Allan Massie in the *Daily Telegraph,*
1 January 1998.

145   'a powerful fascination': Vernon Scannell in *The Guardian,* 1 January 1998.

146   'a good tale': Ted Walker in a letter to V. G., February 1998.

147   'safely dead, of course': Paul Burroughs, letter to *The Guardian,* 2 January 1998.

148   In February 1996, Dr McLoughlin had actually written to Penguin to
tell them he had these documents pertaining to Laurie's arrival at the
International Brigades HQ, which he would be glad to show to Laurie. But
he received no reply.

149   'fight from the heart': L. L. in *Evening Standard* article on his teenage years,
December 1960.

150   'Micky Thumps': the anonymous Lancashire ballad was included by C.
Day-Lewis in *Poetry for You*, a book for schoolchildren on the enjoyment of
poetry, published by Blackwell in 1944.

151   'using his wartime journals': Clare Alexander of Penguin discussed another
book with L. L. in 1995.

152   'nothing more': L. L. to Mavis Nicholson in her television interview, *Mavis
Catches Up With...* 1989.

Index